Save OVER 50% off t

Shojo Beat

MANGA from the HEART

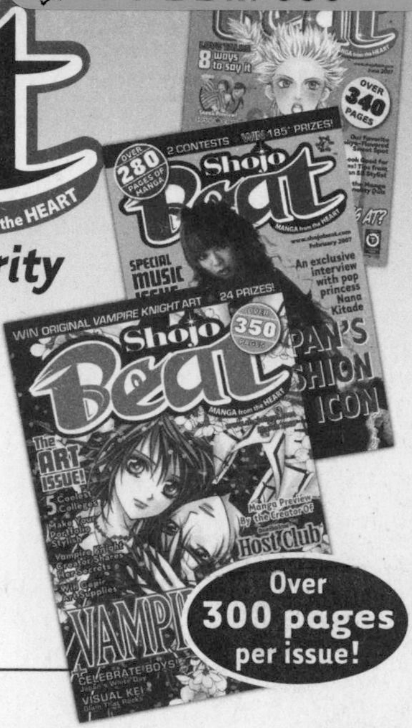
Over
300 pages
per issue!

The Shojo Manga Authority

This monthly magazine is injected with the most **ADDICTIVE** shojo manga stories from Japan. PLUS, unique editorial coverage on the arts, music, culture, fashion, and much more!

☑ **YES!** Please enter my one-year subscription (12 GIANT issues) to ***Shojo Beat*** at the LOW SUBSCRIPTION RATE of **$34.99!**

NAME

ADDRESS

CITY **STATE** **ZIP**

E-MAIL ADDRESS

☐ **MY CHECK IS ENCLOSED (PAYABLE TO *Shojo Beat*)** ☐ **BILL ME LATER**

CREDIT CARD: ☐ **VISA** ☐ **MASTERCARD**

ACCOUNT # **EXP. DATE**

SIGNATURE

P7GNC1

CLIP AND MAIL TO

SHOJO BEAT
Subscriptions Service Dept.
P.O. Box 438
Mount Morris, IL 61054-0438

Canada price for 12 issues: $46.99 USD, including GST, HST and QST. US/CAN orders only. Allow 6-8 weeks for delivery. Must be 16 or older to redeem offer. By redeeming this offer I represent that I am 16 or older.

RATED T+ FOR OLDER TEEN
ratings.viz.com

Shojo Beat™

MANGA from the HEART

The Shojo Manga Authority

The most **ADDICTIVE** shojo manga stories from Japan **PLUS** unique editorial coverage on the arts, music, culture, fashion, and much more!

12 GIANT issues for ONLY $34.99*

That's 51% OFF the cover price!

Subscribe NOW and become a member of the 🅢 Sub Club!

- **SAVE** 51% OFF the cover price
- **ALWAYS** get every issue
- **ACCESS** exclusive areas of www.shojobeat.com
- **FREE** members-only gifts several times a year

Strictly VIP!

3 EASY WAYS TO SUBSCRIBE!

1) Send in the subscription order form from this book O
2) Log on to: www.shojobeat.com OR
3) Call 1-800-541-7876

Shojo Beat

SKIP·BEAT!

Vol. 16

The Shojo Beat Manga Edition

STORY AND ART BY YOSHIKI NAKAMURA

English Translation & Adaptation/Tomo Kimura
Touch-up Art & Lettering/Sabrina Heep
Design/Izumi Evers
Editor/Pancha Diaz

Editor in Chief, Books/Alvin Lu
Editor in Chief, Magazines/Marc Weidenbaum
VP, Publishing Licensing/Rika Inouye
VP, Sales & Product Marketing/Gonzalo Ferreyra
VP, Creative/Linda Espinosa
Publisher/Hyoe Narita

Printed in Canada

Published by VIZ Media, LLC.
P.O. Box 77010
San Francisco, CA 94107

Shojo Beat Manga Edition
10 9 8 7 6 5 4 3 2 1
First printing, January 2009

VIZ MEDIA

store.viz.com

RATED T FOR TEEN

PARENTAL ADVISORY
SKIP·BEAT! is rated T for Teen and is recommended for ages 13 and up. This volume contains a grudge.

ratings.viz.com

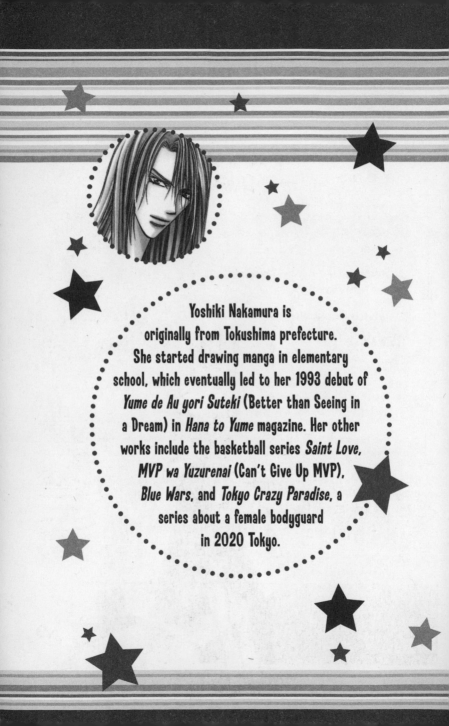

Yoshiki Nakamura is
originally from Tokushima prefecture.
She started drawing manga in elementary
school, which eventually led to her 1993 debut of
Yume de Au yori Suteki (Better than Seeing in
a Dream) in *Hana to Yume* magazine. Her other
works include the basketball series *Saint Love,*
MVP wa Yuzurenai (Can't Give Up MVP),
Blue Wars, and *Tokyo Crazy Paradise*, a
series about a female bodyguard
in 2020 Tokyo.

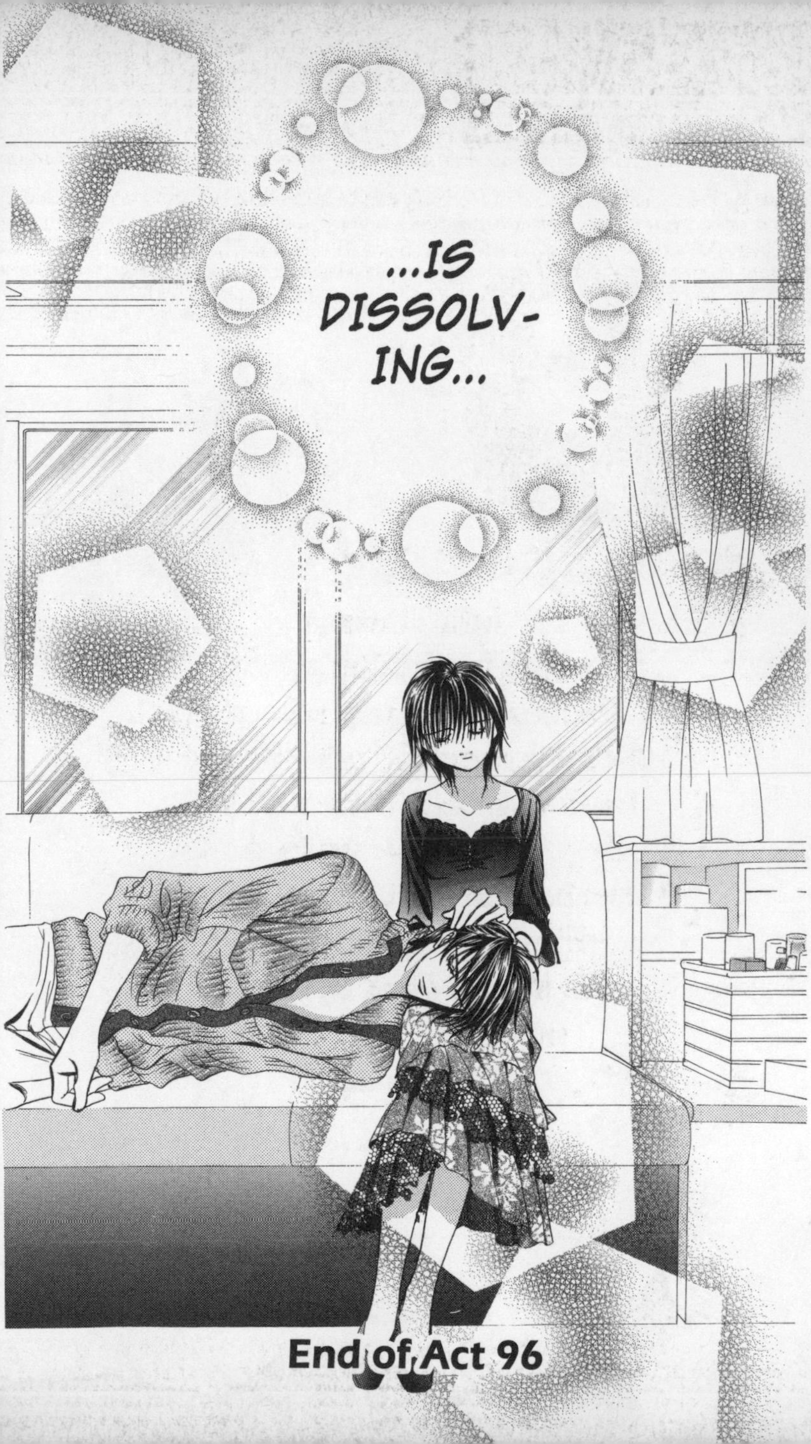
...IS DISSOLV-ING...
End of Act 96

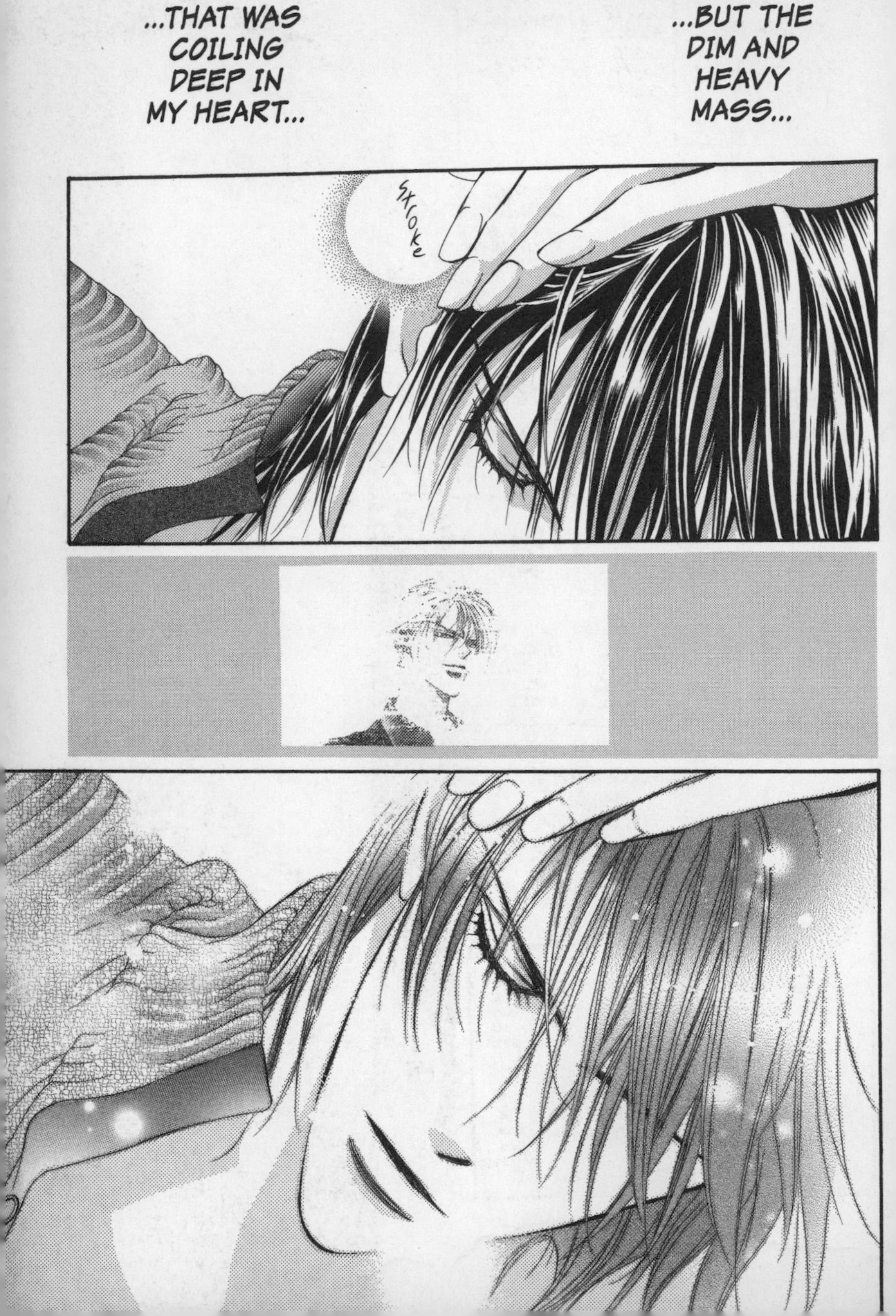
...BUT THE DIM AND HEAVY MASS...
...THAT WAS COILING DEEP IN MY HEART...
stroke

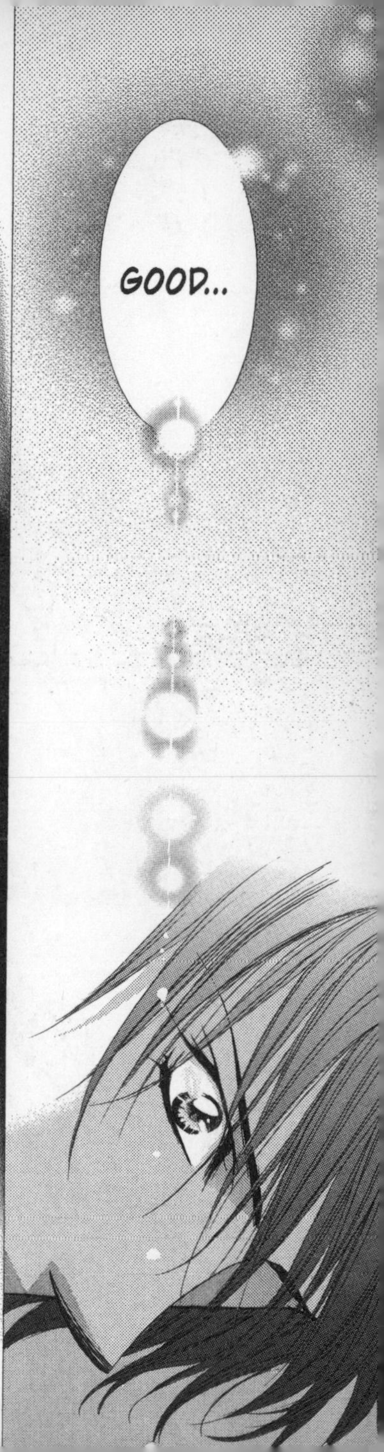
GOOD...
MR...

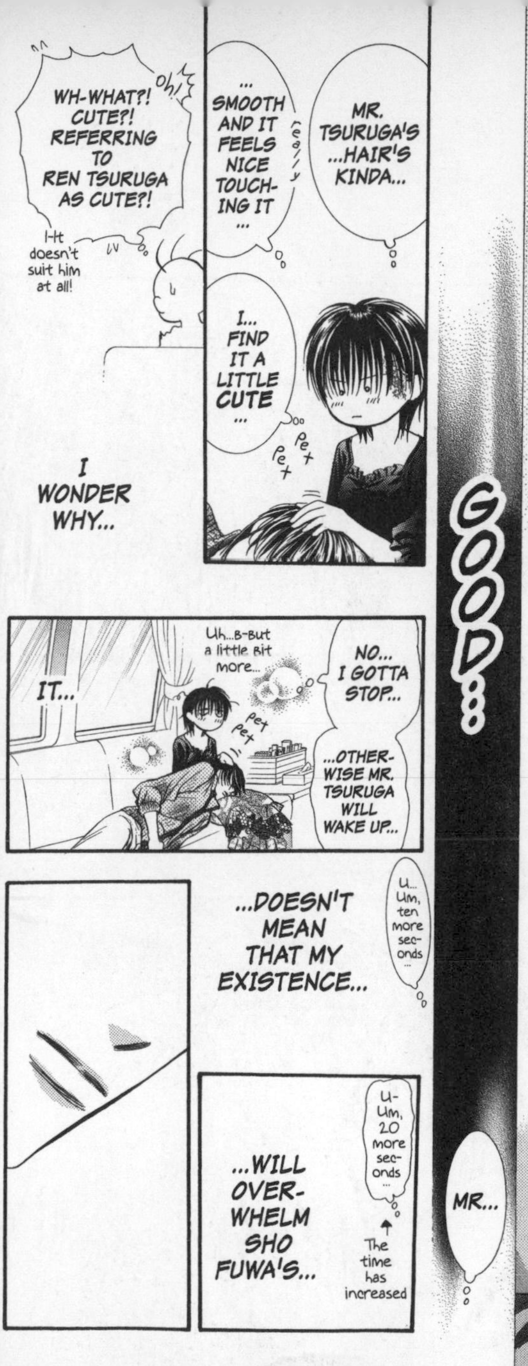
MR. TSURUGA'S ...HAIR'S KINDA...
... SMOOTH AND IT FEELS NICE TOUCHING IT ...
really
I... FIND IT A LITTLE CUTE ...
Pet Pet
Oh!
WH-WHAT?! CUTE?! REFERRING TO REN TSURUGA AS CUTE?!
I-It doesn't suit him at all!
I WONDER WHY...
GOOD...
NO... I GOTTA STOP...
...OTHERWISE MR. TSURUGA WILL WAKE UP...
Uh...B-But a little bit more...
Pet Pet
IT...
U... Um, ten more sec-onds ...
...DOESN'T MEAN THAT MY EXISTENCE...
U-Um, 20 more sec-onds ...
The time has increased
...WILL OVER-WHELM SHO FUWA'S...

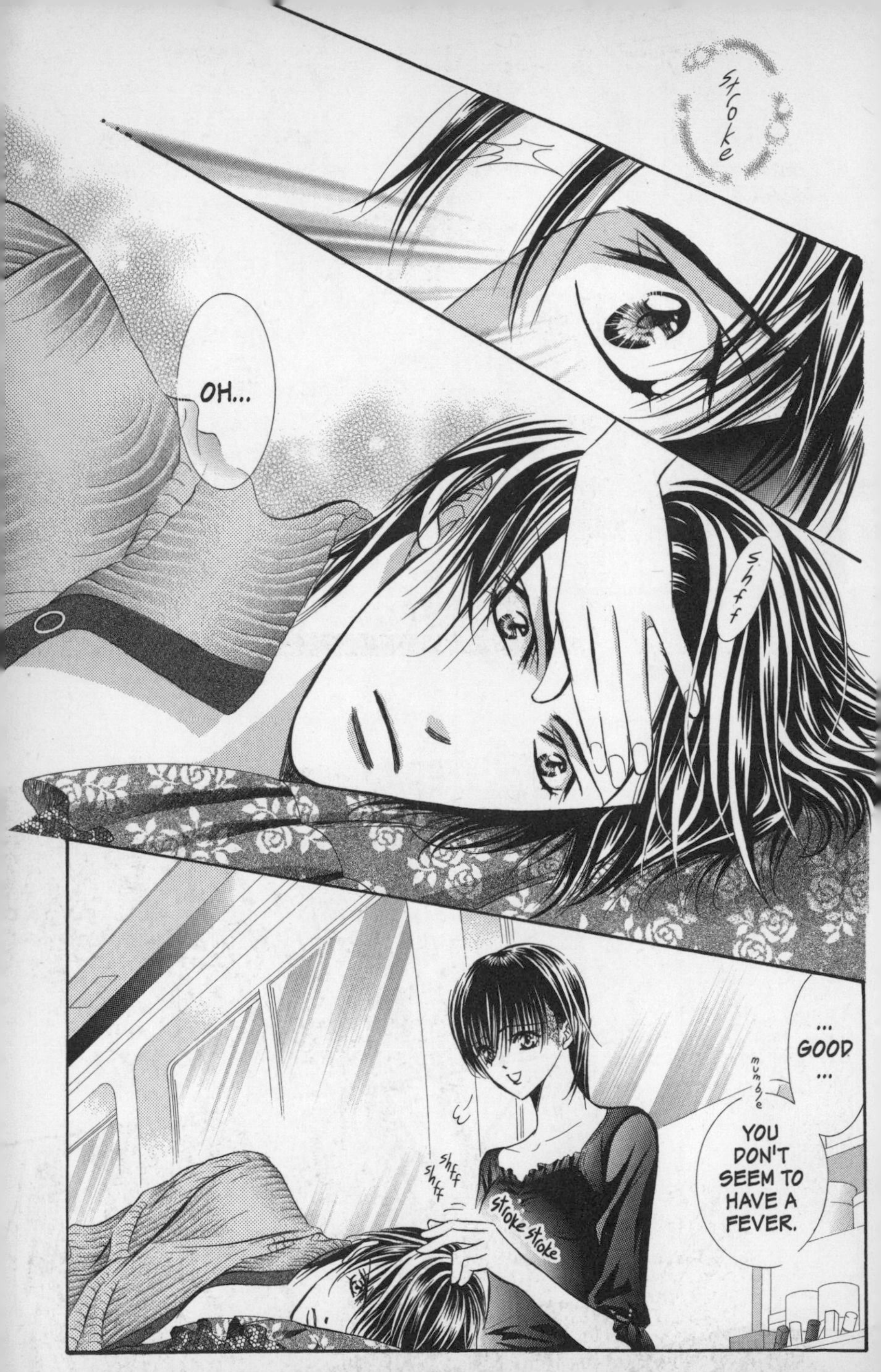
stroke
OH...
shfff
... GOOD ...
mumble
YOU DON'T SEEM TO HAVE A FEVER.
shff shff
stroke stroke

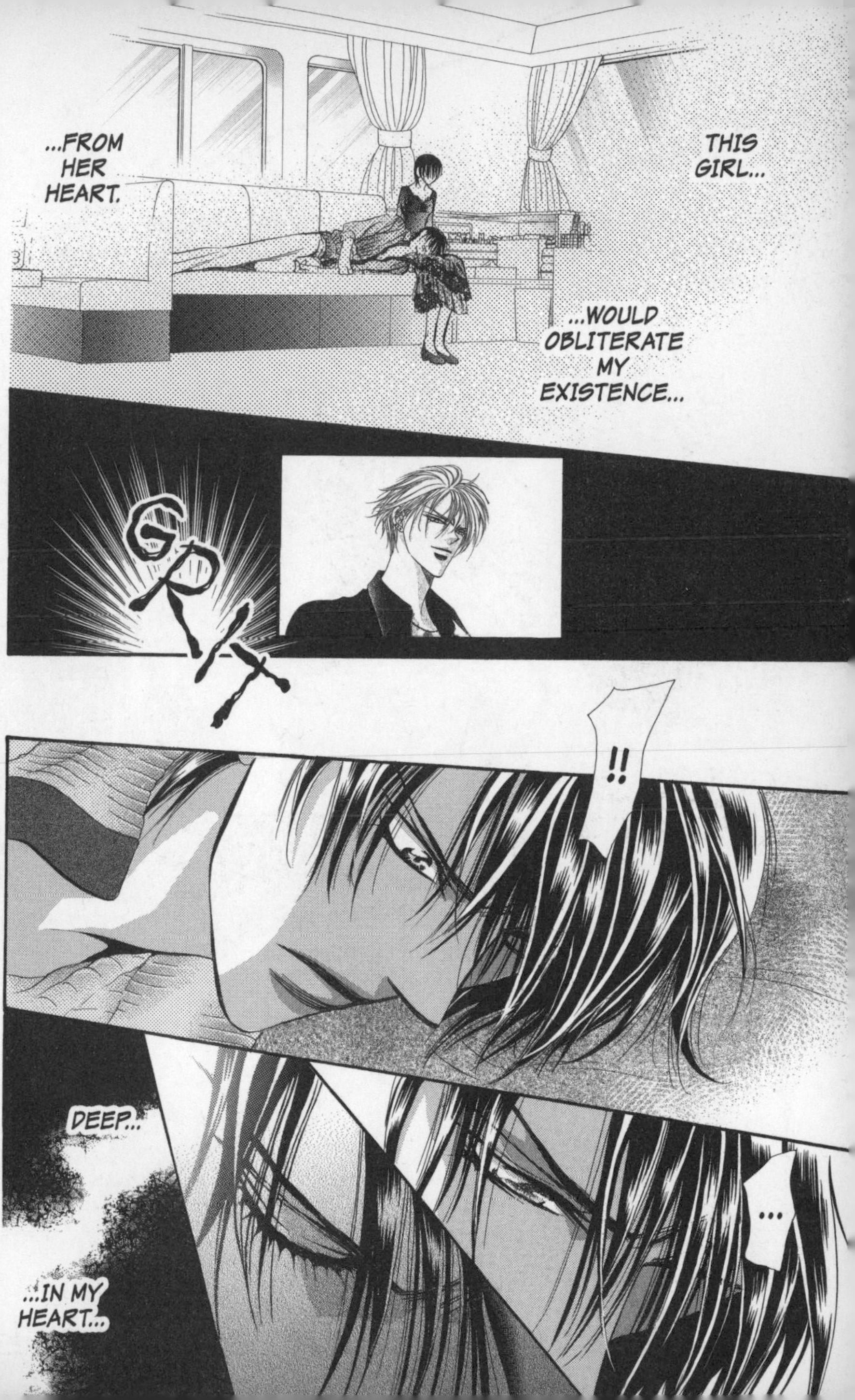
THIS GIRL...
...WOULD OBLITERATE MY EXISTENCE...
...FROM HER HEART.
GRIP
!!
...
DEEP...
...IN MY HEART...

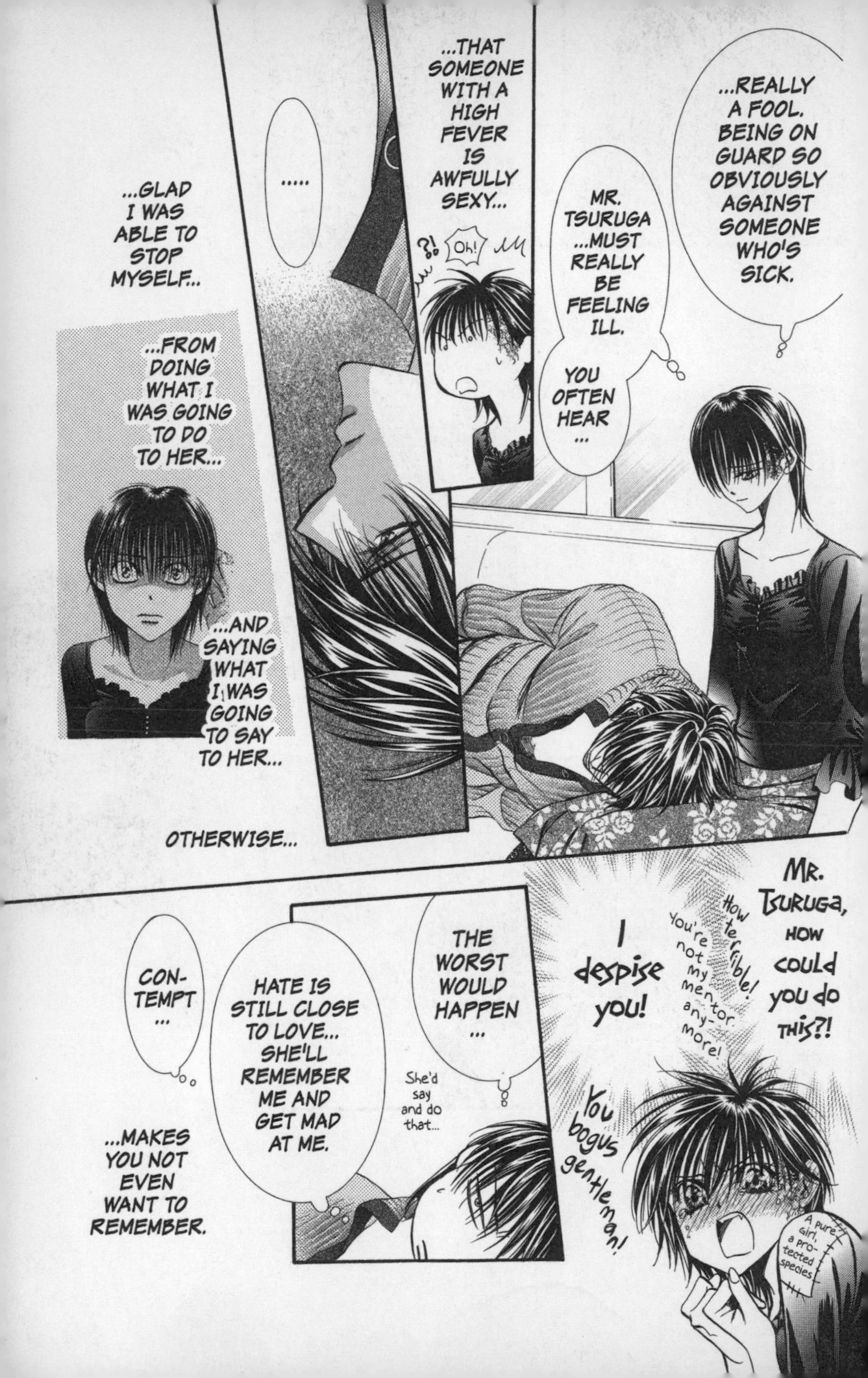

...REALLY A FOOL. BEING ON GUARD SO OBVIOUSLY AGAINST SOMEONE WHO'S SICK.
MR. TSURUGA ...MUST REALLY BE FEELING ILL.
YOU OFTEN HEAR ...
...THAT SOMEONE WITH A HIGH FEVER IS AWFULLY SEXY...
?!
Oh!
.....
...GLAD I WAS ABLE TO STOP MYSELF...
...FROM DOING WHAT I WAS GOING TO DO TO HER...
...AND SAYING WHAT I WAS GOING TO SAY TO HER...
OTHERWISE...
Mr. Tsuruga, how could you do this?!
How terrible!
You're not my mentor anymore!
I despise you!
You bogus gentleman!
A pure girl, a protected species
THE WORST WOULD HAPPEN ...
She'd say and do that...
HATE IS STILL CLOSE TO LOVE... SHE'LL REMEMBER ME AND GET MAD AT ME.
CONTEMPT ...
...MAKES YOU NOT EVEN WANT TO REMEMBER.

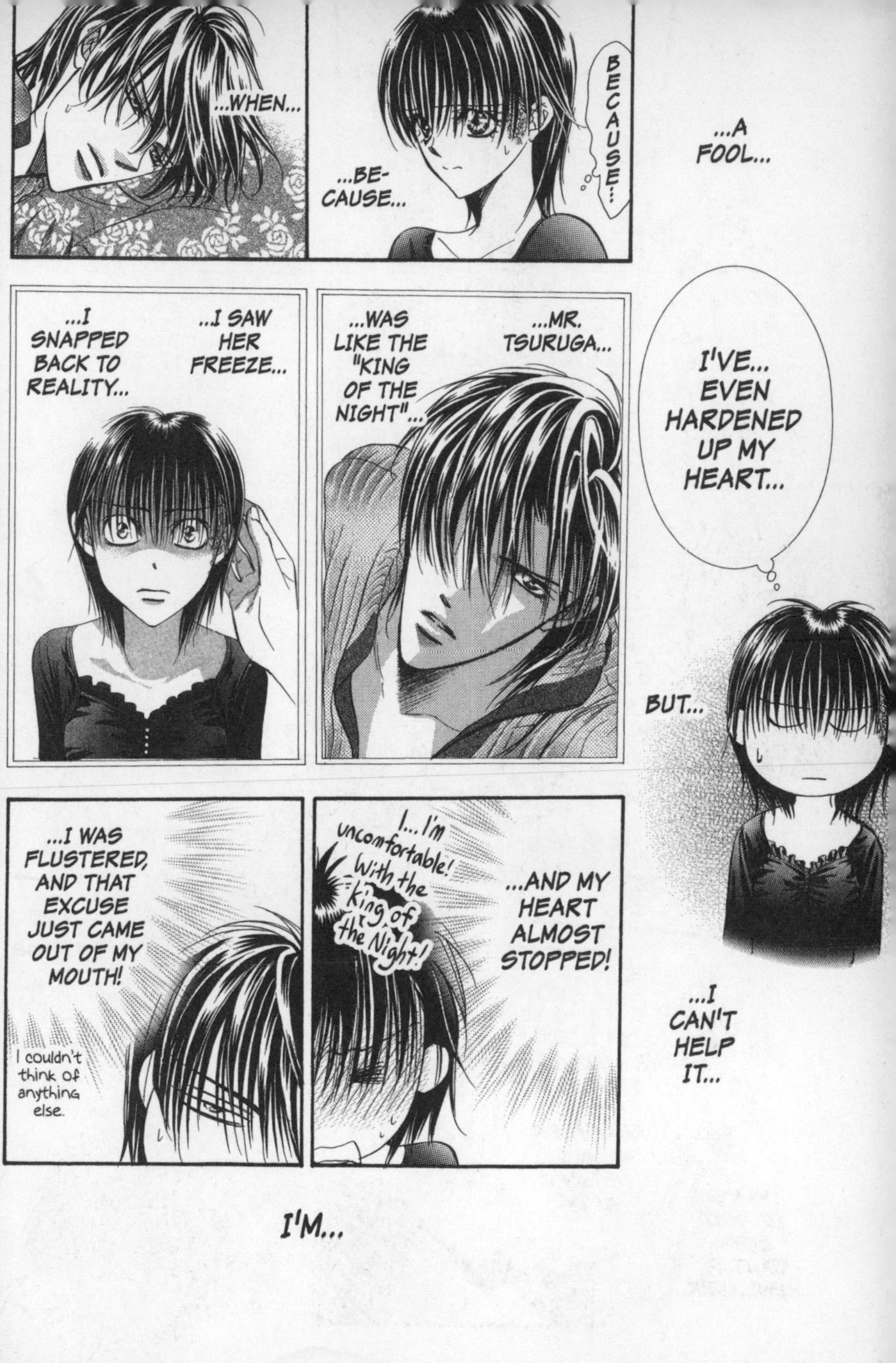
...A FOOL...
I'VE... EVEN HARDENED UP MY HEART...
BUT...
...I CAN'T HELP IT...
BECAUSE...
...BE-CAUSE...
...WHEN...
...MR. TSURUGA...
...WAS LIKE THE "KING OF THE NIGHT"...
...I SAW HER FREEZE...
...I SNAPPED BACK TO REALITY...
...AND MY HEART ALMOST STOPPED!
I... I'm uncomfortable! With the King of the Night!
...I WAS FLUSTERED, AND THAT EXCUSE JUST CAME OUT OF MY MOUTH!
I couldn't think of anything else.
I'M...

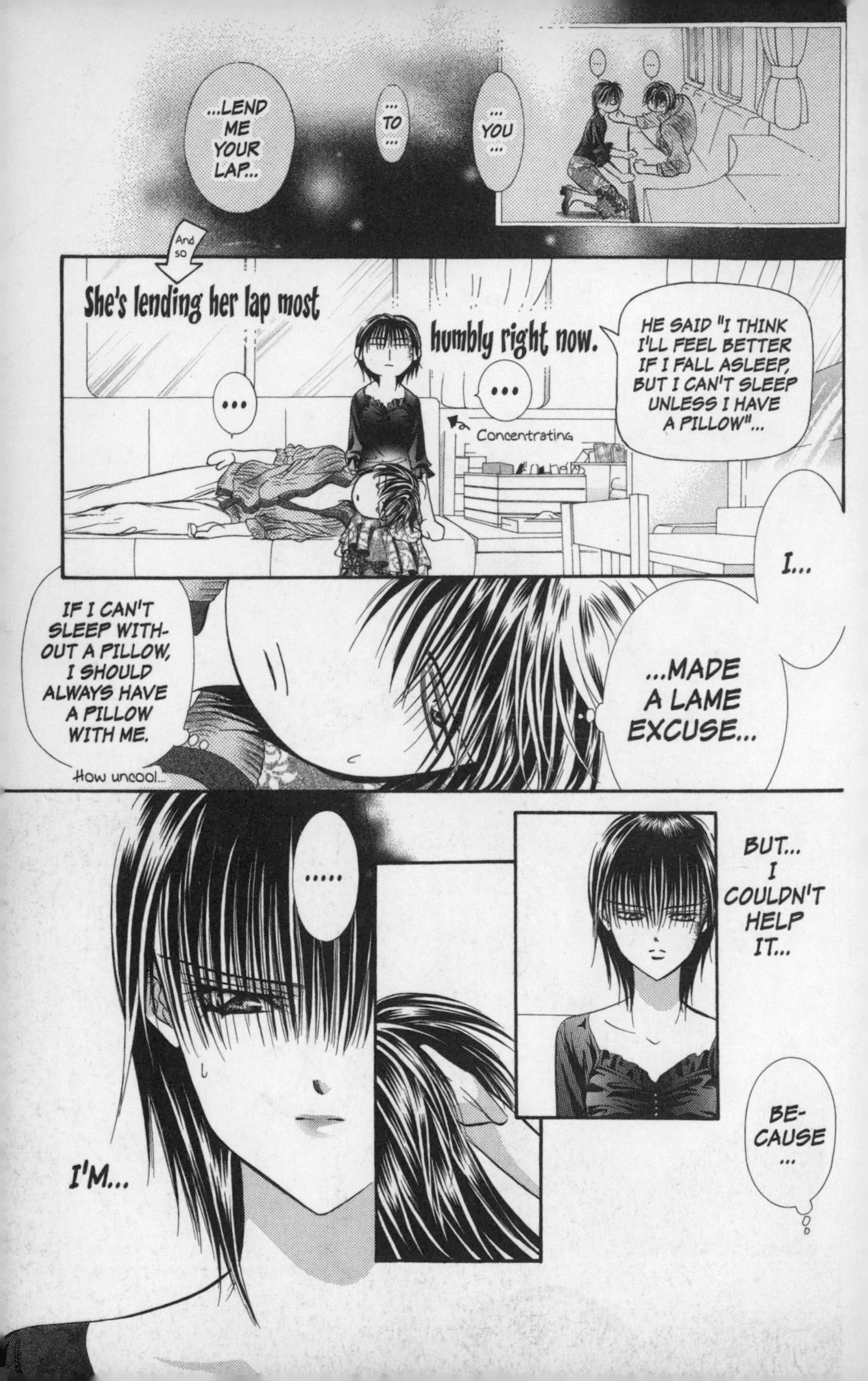
...
...
...YOU...
...TO...
...LEND ME YOUR LAP...
And so
HE SAID "I THINK I'LL FEEL BETTER IF I FALL ASLEEP, BUT I CAN'T SLEEP UNLESS I HAVE A PILLOW"...
She's lending her lap most humbly right now.
...
Concentrating
...
I...
...MADE A LAME EXCUSE...
IF I CAN'T SLEEP WITH-OUT A PILLOW, I SHOULD ALWAYS HAVE A PILLOW WITH ME.
How uncool...
BUT... I COULDN'T HELP IT...
BE-CAUSE...
......
I'M...

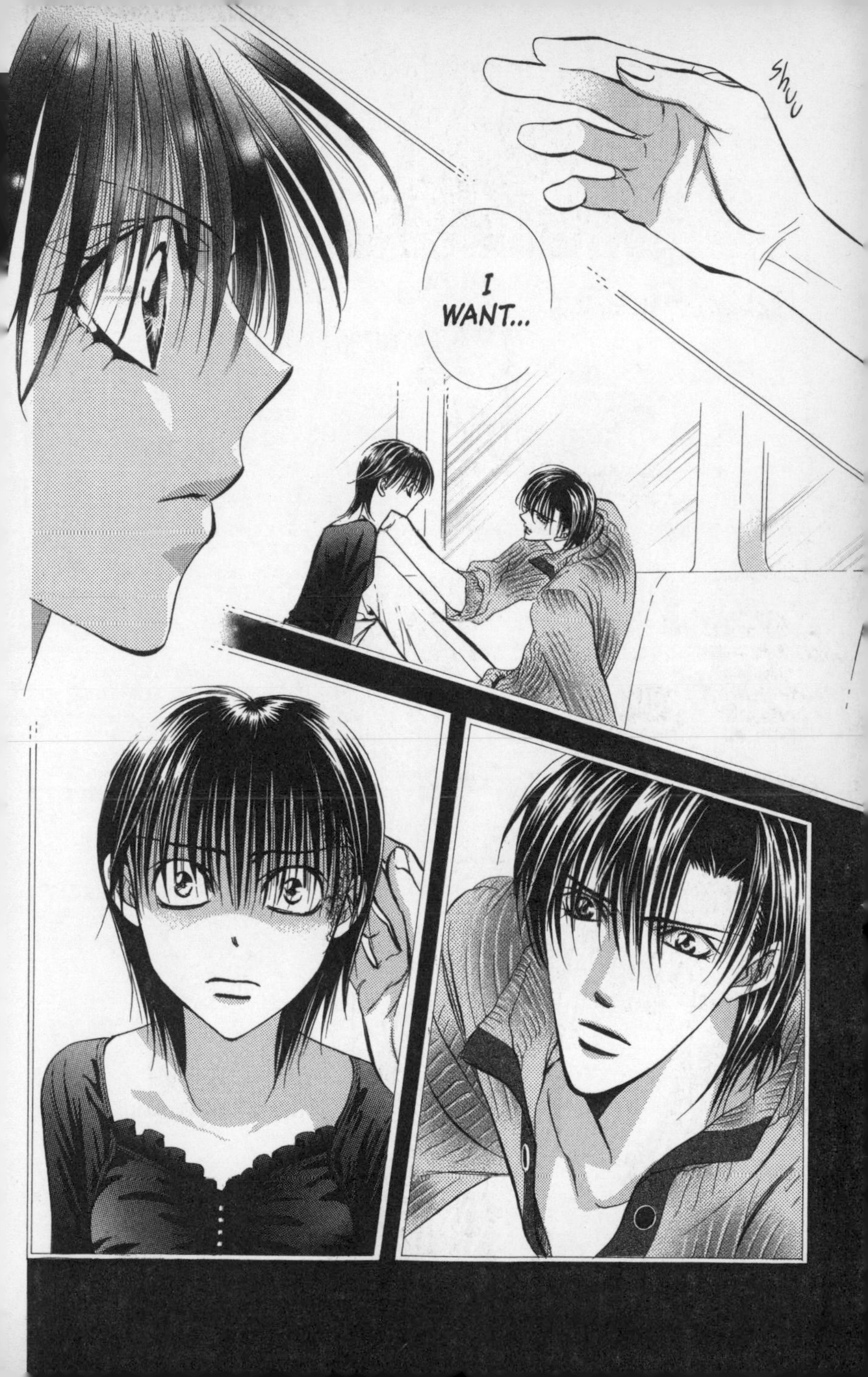
SHUU
I WANT...

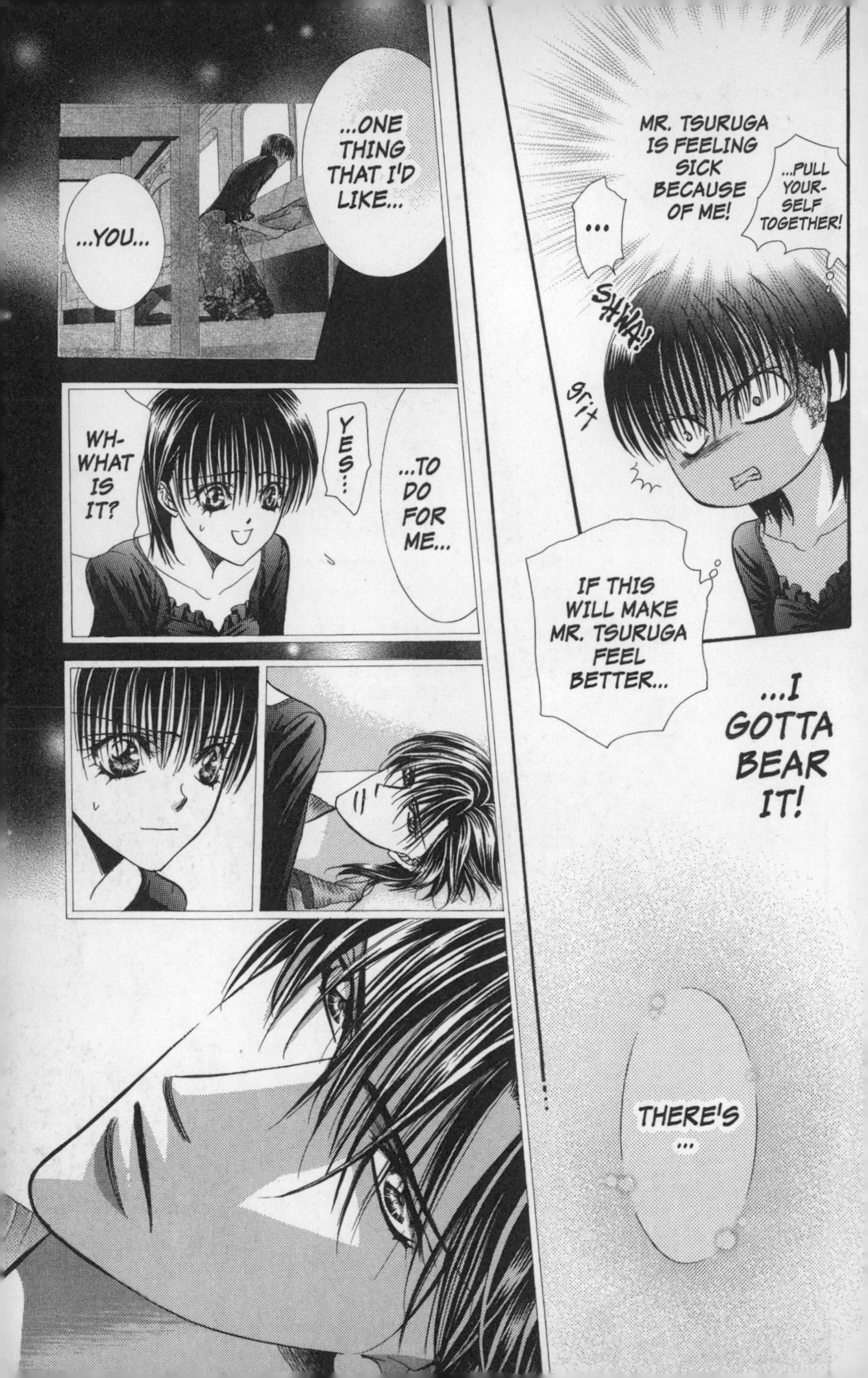
MR. TSURUGA IS FEELING SICK BECAUSE OF ME!
...PULL YOUR-SELF TOGETHER!
...
SHWA!
grit
IF THIS WILL MAKE MR. TSURUGA FEEL BETTER...
...I GOTTA BEAR IT!
THERE'S ...
...ONE THING THAT I'D LIKE...
...YOU...
...TO DO FOR ME...
YES...
WH-WHAT IS IT?

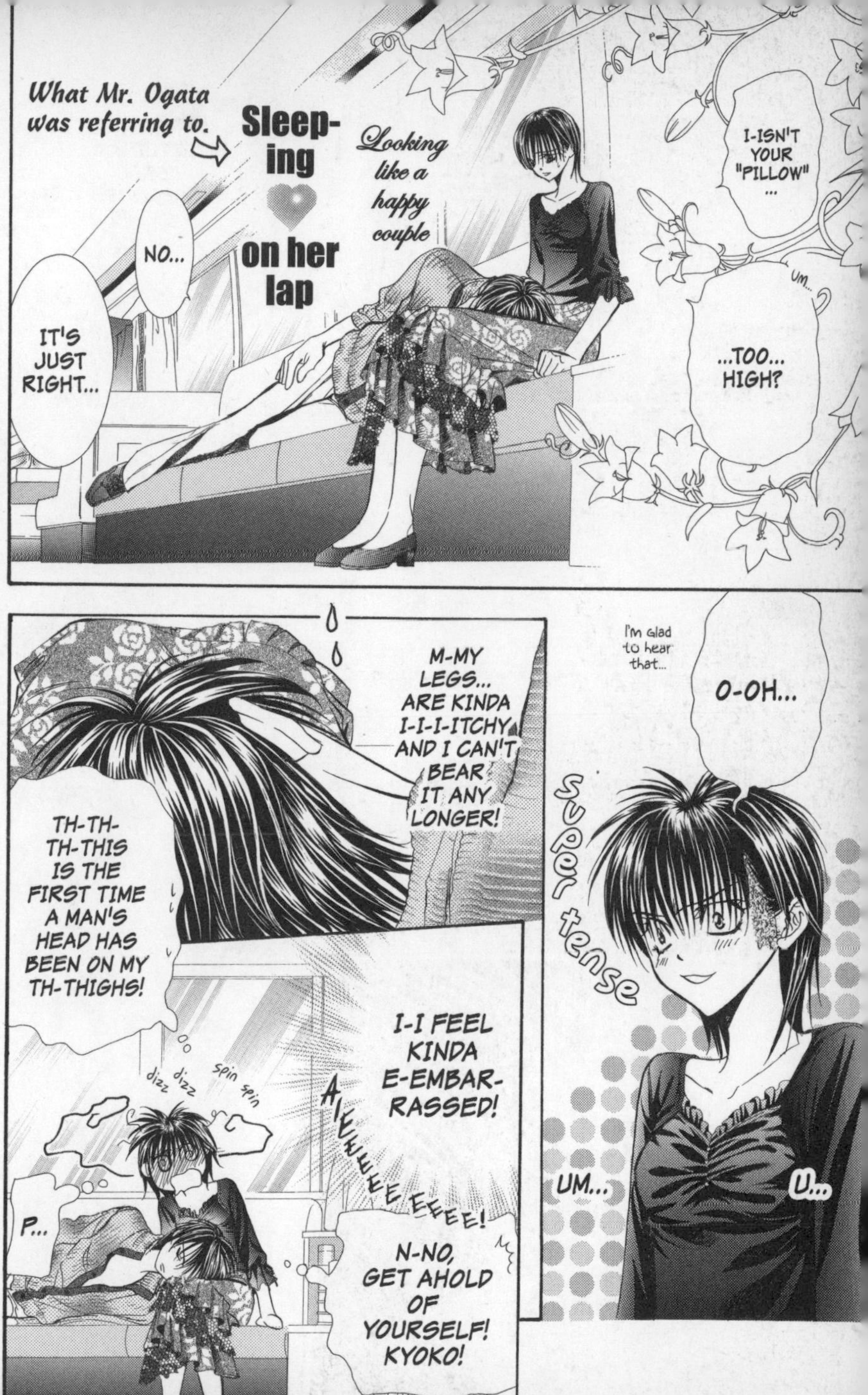
I-ISN'T YOUR "PILLOW" ...
UM...
...TOO... HIGH?
Looking like a happy couple
Sleeping ♥ on her lap
What Mr. Ogata was referring to.
NO...
IT'S JUST RIGHT...
I'm glad to hear that...
O-OH...
Super tense
U...
UM...
M-MY LEGS... ARE KINDA I-I-I-ITCHY AND I CAN'T BEAR IT ANY LONGER!
TH-TH-TH-THIS IS THE FIRST TIME A MAN'S HEAD HAS BEEN ON MY TH-THIGHS!
I-I FEEL KINDA E-EMBAR-RASSED!
AIEEEEEE EEEEE!
N-NO, GET AHOLD OF YOURSELF! KYOKO!
spin spin
dizz dizz
P...

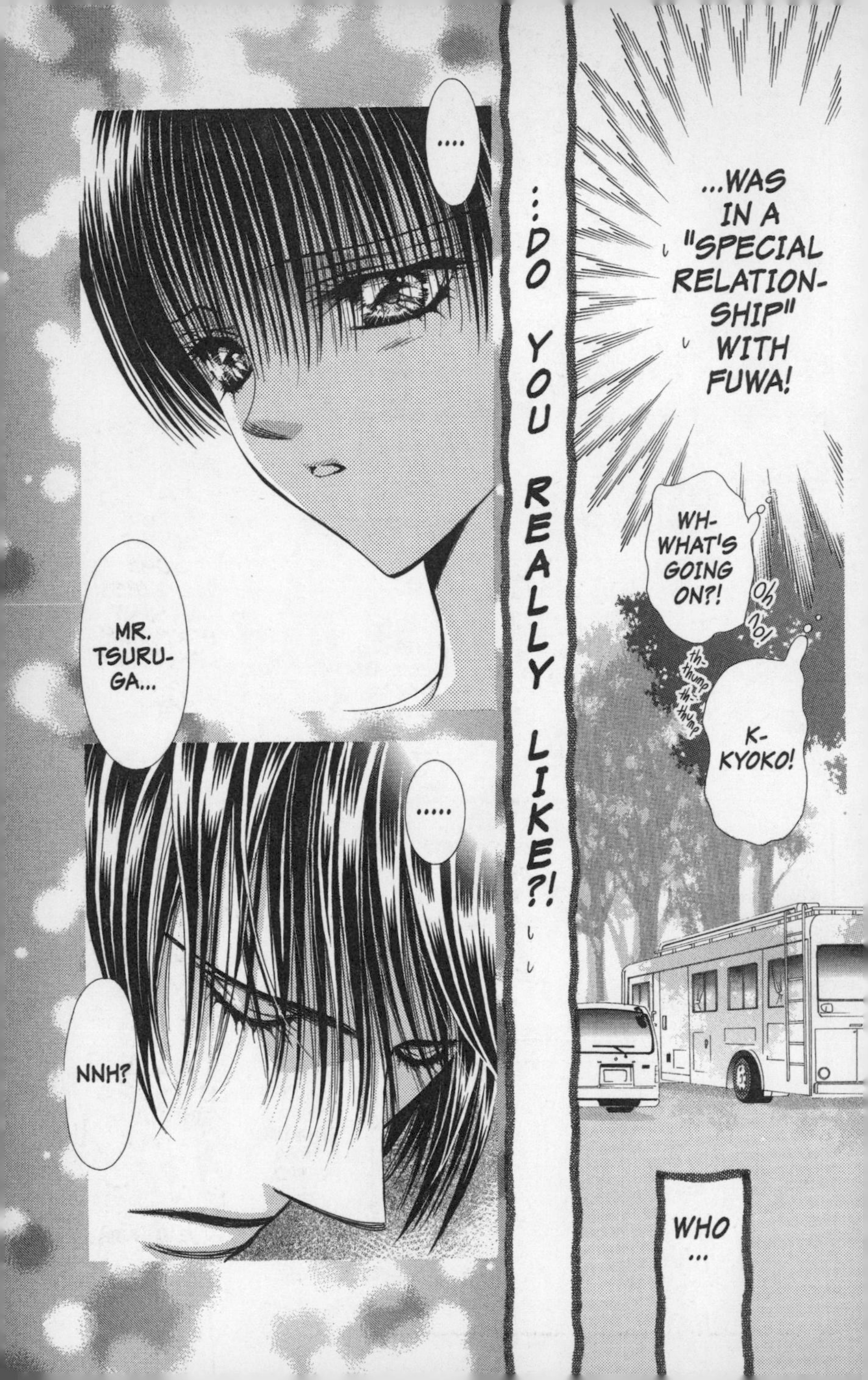
...WAS IN A "SPECIAL RELATION-SHIP" WITH FUWA!
WH-WHAT'S GOING ON?!
Oh no!
th-thump th-thump
K-KYOKO!
WHO ...
...DO YOU REALLY LIKE?!
....
MR. TSURUGA...
.....
NNH?

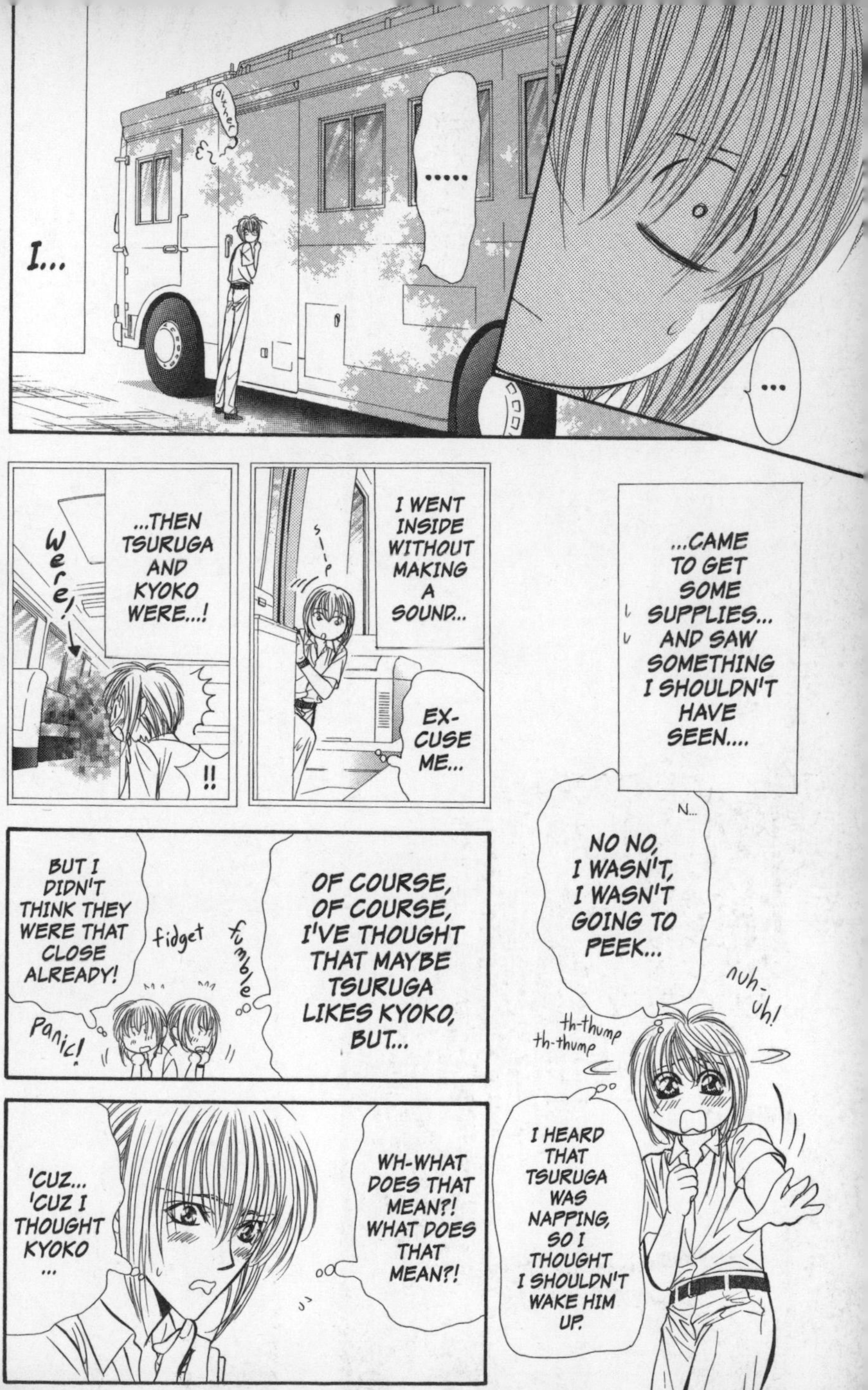
...
......
dinner
I...
...CAME TO GET SOME SUPPLIES... AND SAW SOMETHING I SHOULDN'T HAVE SEEN....
N...
NO NO, I WASN'T, I WASN'T GOING TO PEEK...
nuh-uh!
th-thump th-thump
I HEARD THAT TSURUGA WAS NAPPING, SO I THOUGHT I SHOULDN'T WAKE HIM UP.
I WENT INSIDE WITHOUT MAKING A SOUND...
slip
EX-CUSE ME...
...THEN TSURUGA AND KYOKO WERE...!
Were!
!!
OF COURSE, OF COURSE, I'VE THOUGHT THAT MAYBE TSURUGA LIKES KYOKO, BUT...
fumble
fidget
BUT I DIDN'T THINK THEY WERE THAT CLOSE ALREADY!
Panic!
WH-WHAT DOES THAT MEAN?! WHAT DOES THAT MEAN?!
'CUZ... 'CUZ I THOUGHT KYOKO ...

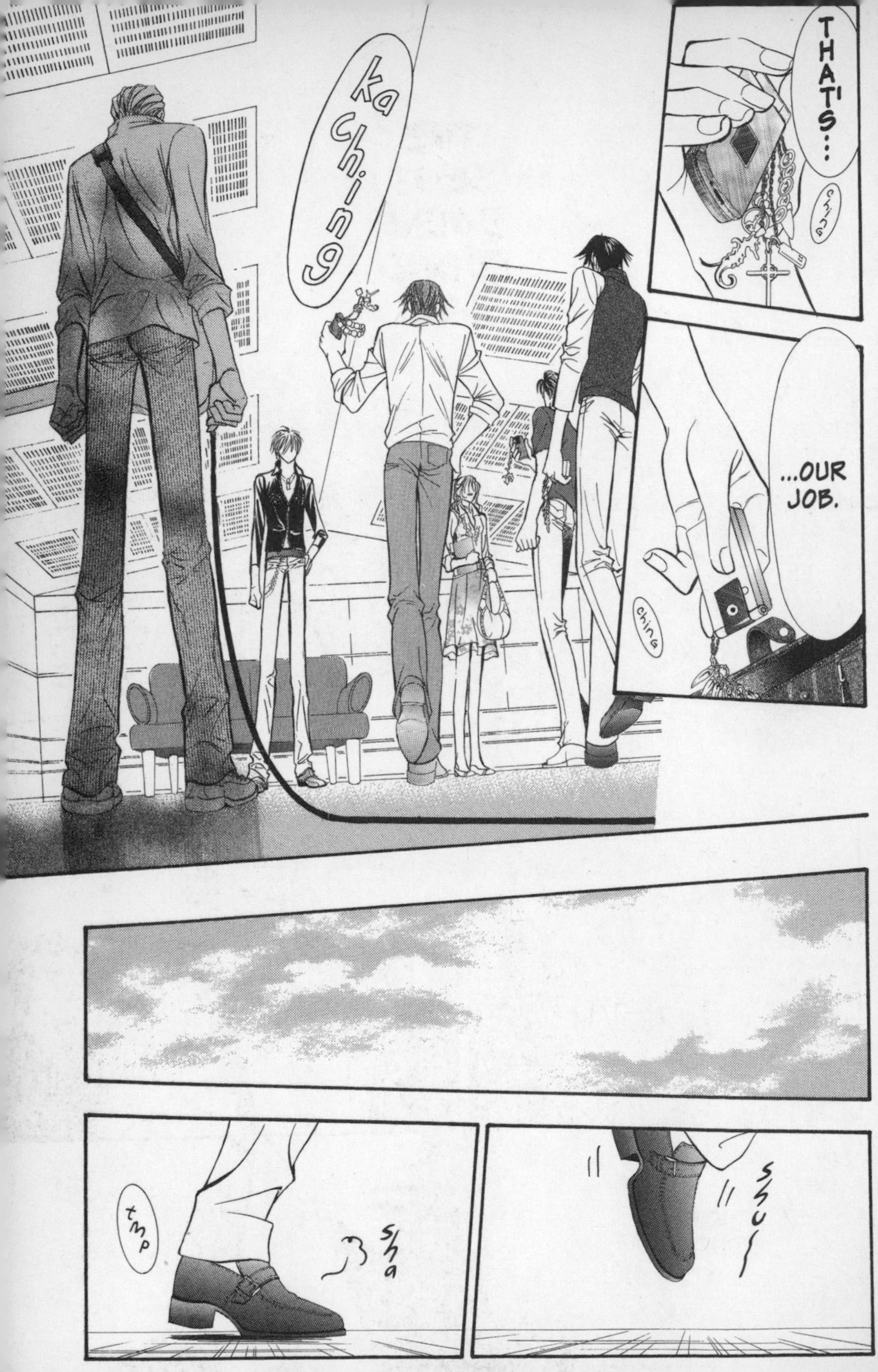
THAT'S...
ching
...OUR JOB.
ching
ka ching
shu
tmp
sha

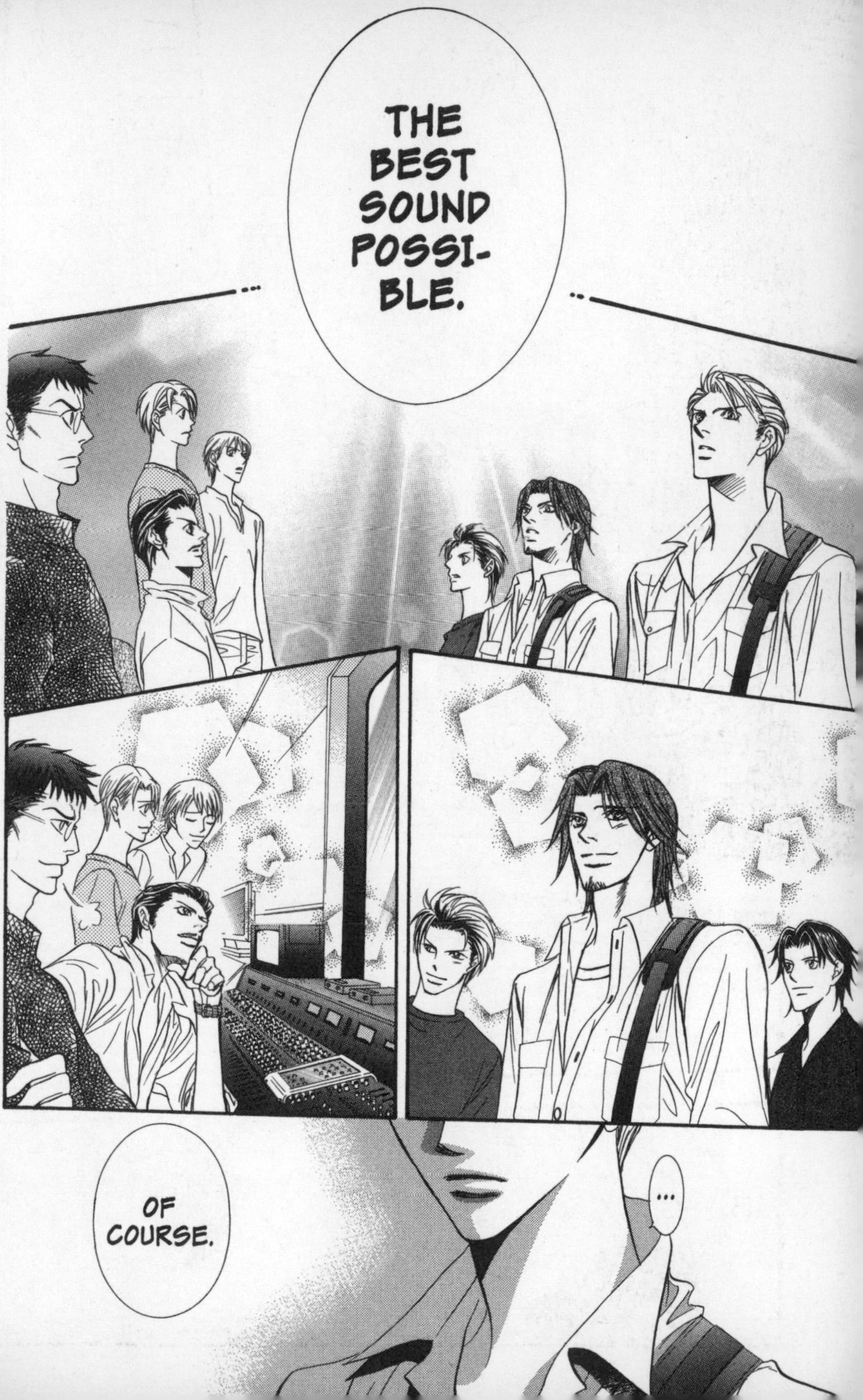
THE BEST SOUND POSSI-BLE.
...
OF COURSE.

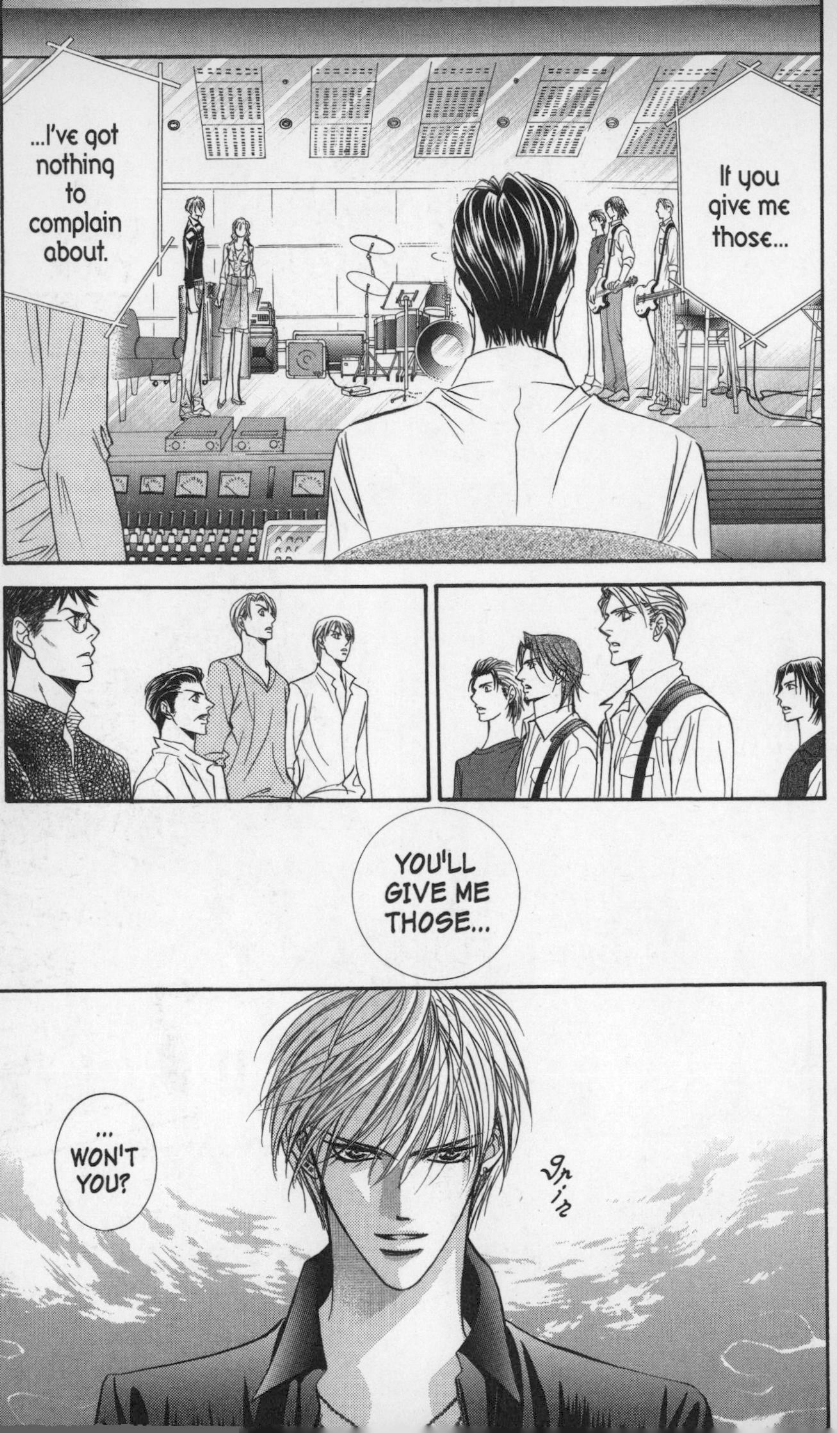
If you give me those...
...I've got nothing to complain about.
YOU'LL GIVE ME THOSE...
... WON'T YOU?
grin

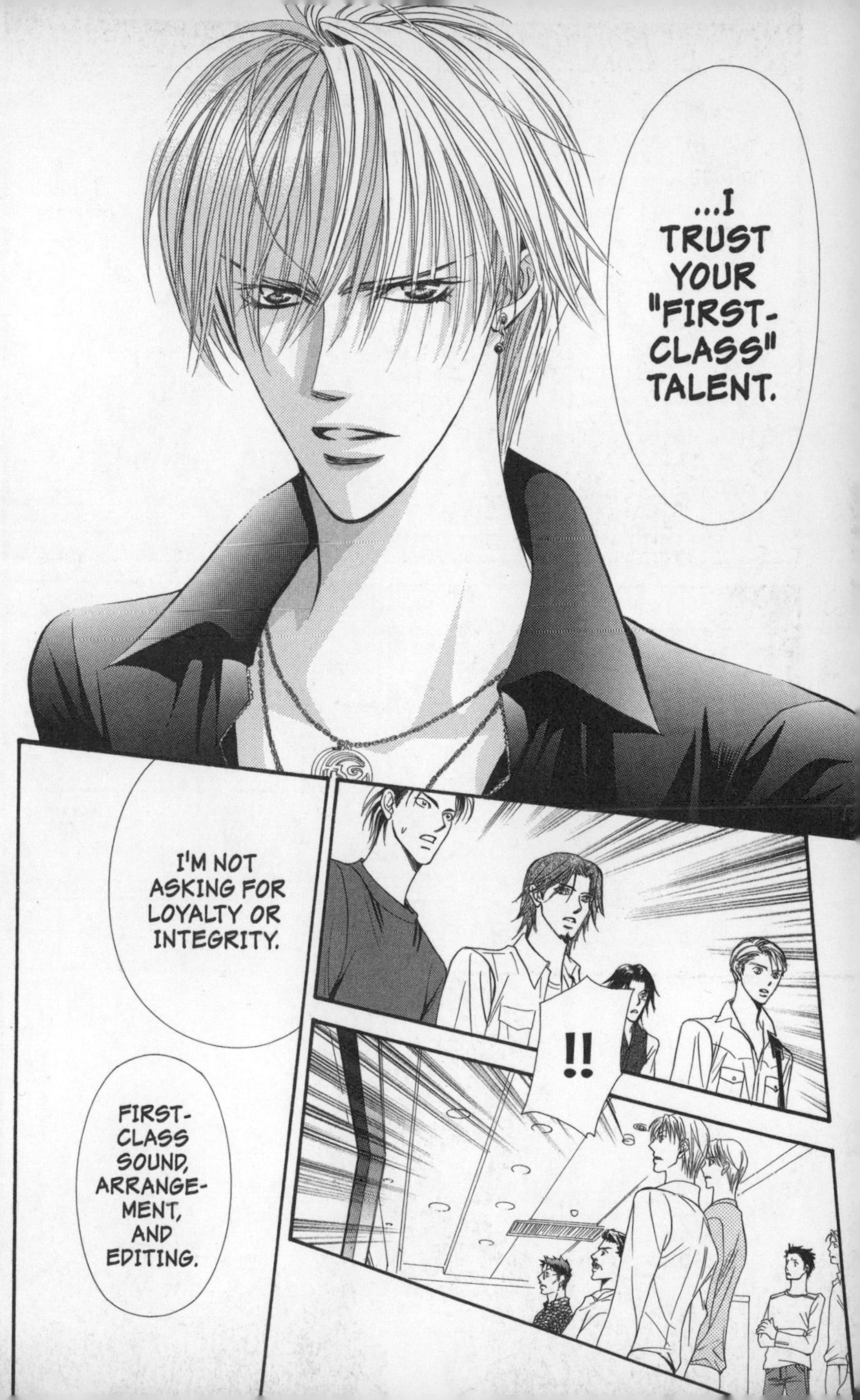
...I TRUST YOUR "FIRST-CLASS" TALENT.
!!
I'M NOT ASKING FOR LOYALTY OR INTEGRITY.
FIRST-CLASS SOUND, ARRANGEMENT, AND EDITING.

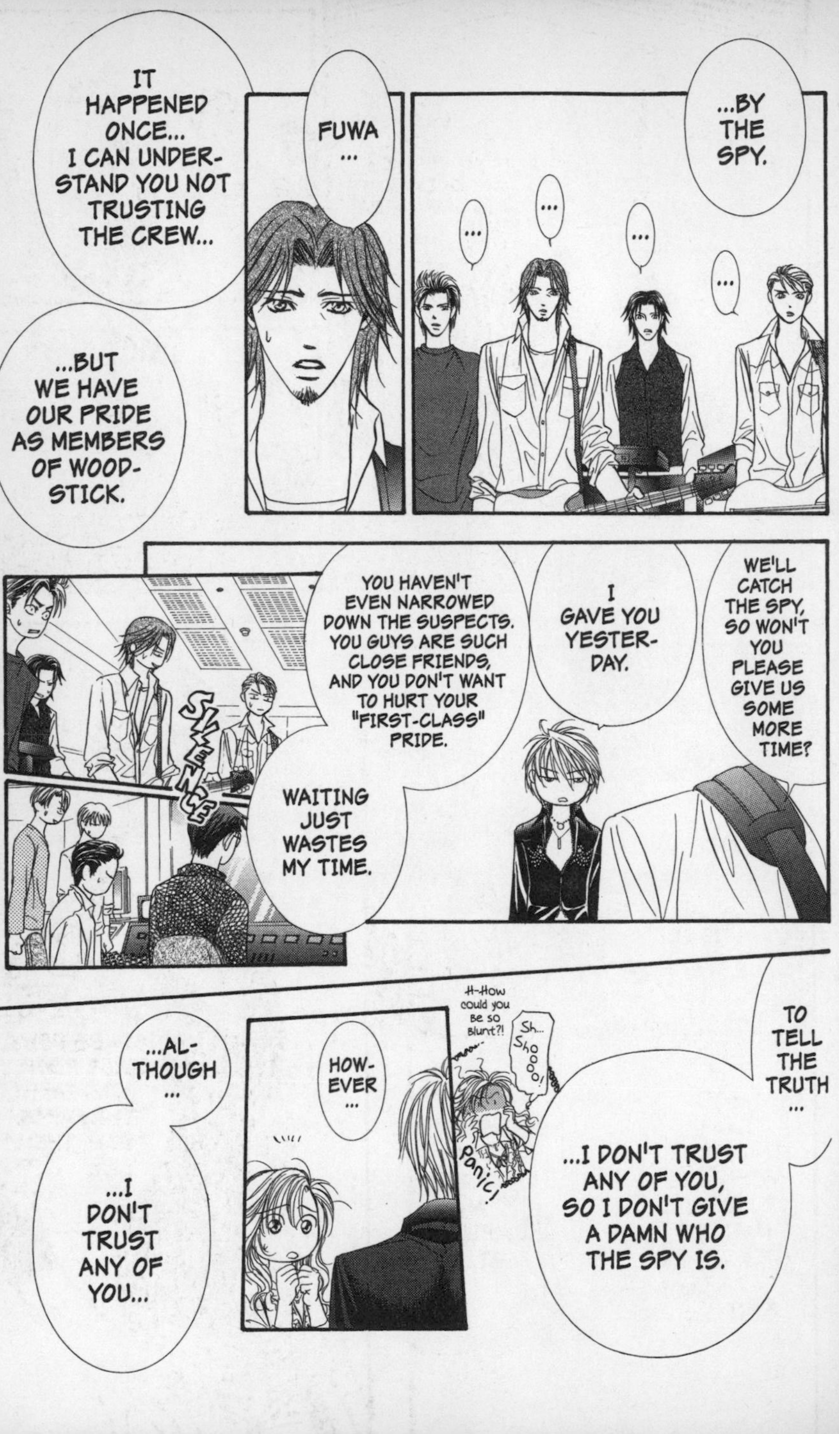

...BY THE SPY.
...
...
...
...
FUWA ...
IT HAPPENED ONCE... I CAN UNDERSTAND YOU NOT TRUSTING THE CREW...
...BUT WE HAVE OUR PRIDE AS MEMBERS OF WOODSTICK.
WE'LL CATCH THE SPY, SO WON'T YOU PLEASE GIVE US SOME MORE TIME?
I GAVE YOU YESTERDAY.
YOU HAVEN'T EVEN NARROWED DOWN THE SUSPECTS. YOU GUYS ARE SUCH CLOSE FRIENDS, AND YOU DON'T WANT TO HURT YOUR "FIRST-CLASS" PRIDE.
WAITING JUST WASTES MY TIME.
SILENCE
TO TELL THE TRUTH ...
...I DON'T TRUST ANY OF YOU, SO I DON'T GIVE A DAMN WHO THE SPY IS.
Sh... Shoooo!
H-How could you be so Blunt?!
Panic!
HOW-EVER ...
...AL-THOUGH ...
...I DON'T TRUST ANY OF YOU...

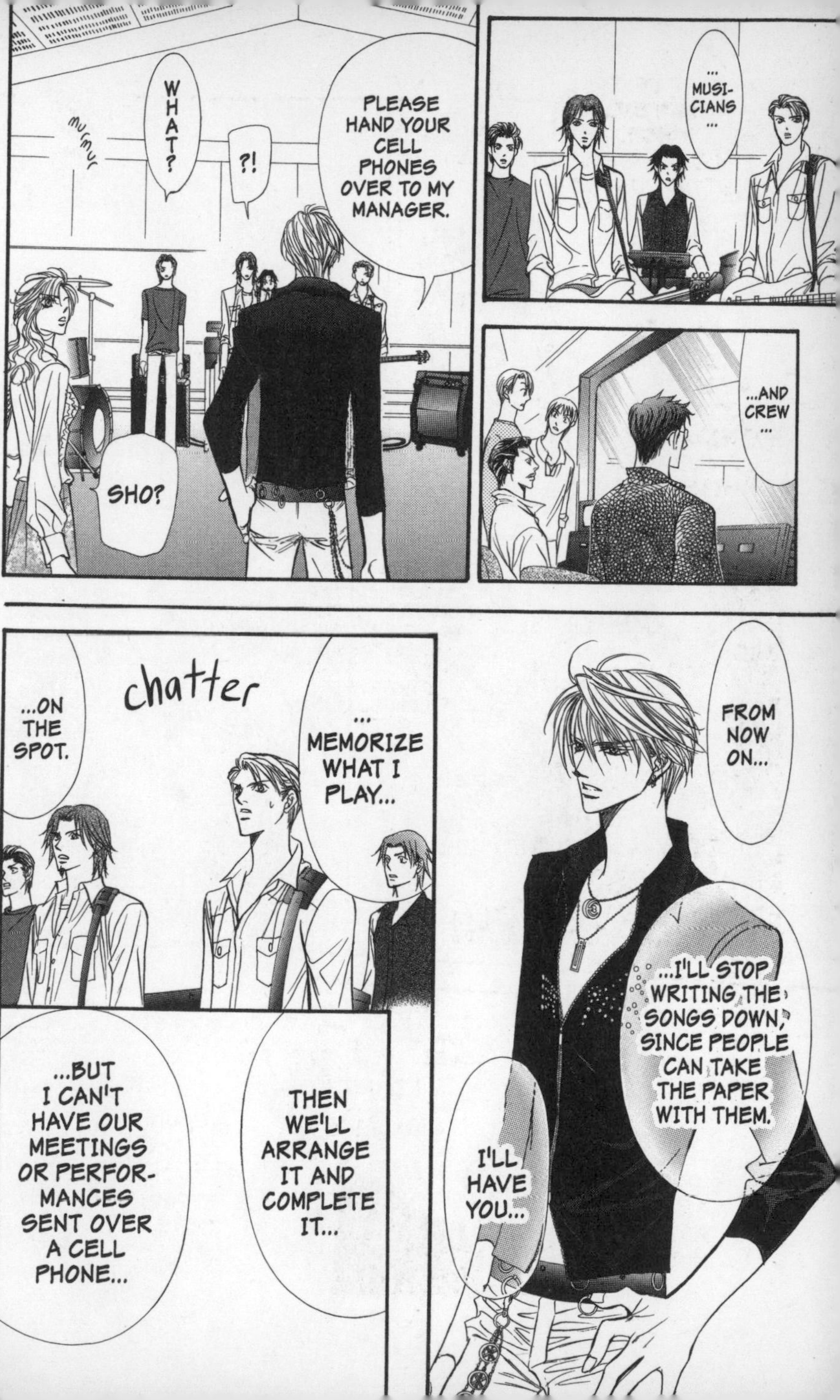
... MUSI- CIANS ...
...AND CREW ...
PLEASE HAND YOUR CELL PHONES OVER TO MY MANAGER.
?!
WHAT?
murmur
SHO?
FROM NOW ON...
...I'LL STOP WRITING THE SONGS DOWN, SINCE PEOPLE CAN TAKE THE PAPER WITH THEM.
I'LL HAVE YOU...
... MEMORIZE WHAT I PLAY...
chatter
...ON THE SPOT.
THEN WE'LL ARRANGE IT AND COMPLETE IT...
...BUT I CAN'T HAVE OUR MEETINGS OR PERFOR- MANCES SENT OVER A CELL PHONE...

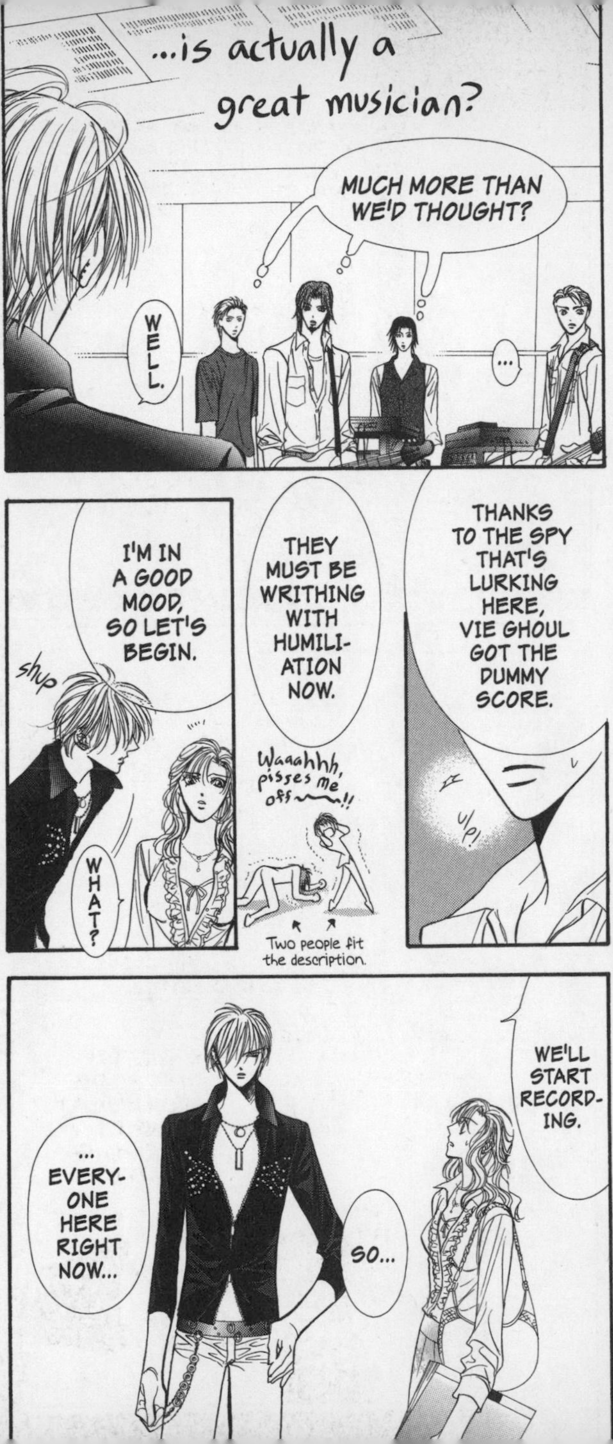
...is actually a great musician?
MUCH MORE THAN WE'D THOUGHT?
...
WELL.
THANKS TO THE SPY THAT'S LURKING HERE, VIE GHOUL GOT THE DUMMY SCORE.
u/p!
THEY MUST BE WRITHING WITH HUMILI-ATION NOW.
Waaahhh, pisses me off~!!
Two people fit the description.
I'M IN A GOOD MOOD, SO LET'S BEGIN.
shup
WHAT?
WE'LL START RECORD-ING.
SO...
...EVERY-ONE HERE RIGHT NOW...

Secret stories about Reino -continued-

"You-know-who"..."Rei no otoko"..."Reino"... "Reino"...?...it suddenly came to me during the storyboard meet-ing, and I blurted out "This is fine...I'll go with that name...it sounds like a visual-kei name too"...so with my super-simplistic (could be called irrespon-sible...) proposal, he was named "Reino"...

...There's...just no love for him at all...

...So Reino doesn't come from "psychic" ("reinoryokusha")...and it's pure coincidence that he became some-thing like a fighting hero, "Super-psychic Reino" I didn't aim to make things that way...

...By the way...while I'm on the topic of "I didn't aim to make"... ...the Reino I drew for the cover of the previous volume...I guess a lot of readers think that Reino's hair is light blue... ...But...with that...I haven't used any...light blue in Reino's hair...I can think of many reasons why it turned out that way...in any case, what I was going for was not light blue... but platinum hair...? The beauty of it is that I do not call it silver.

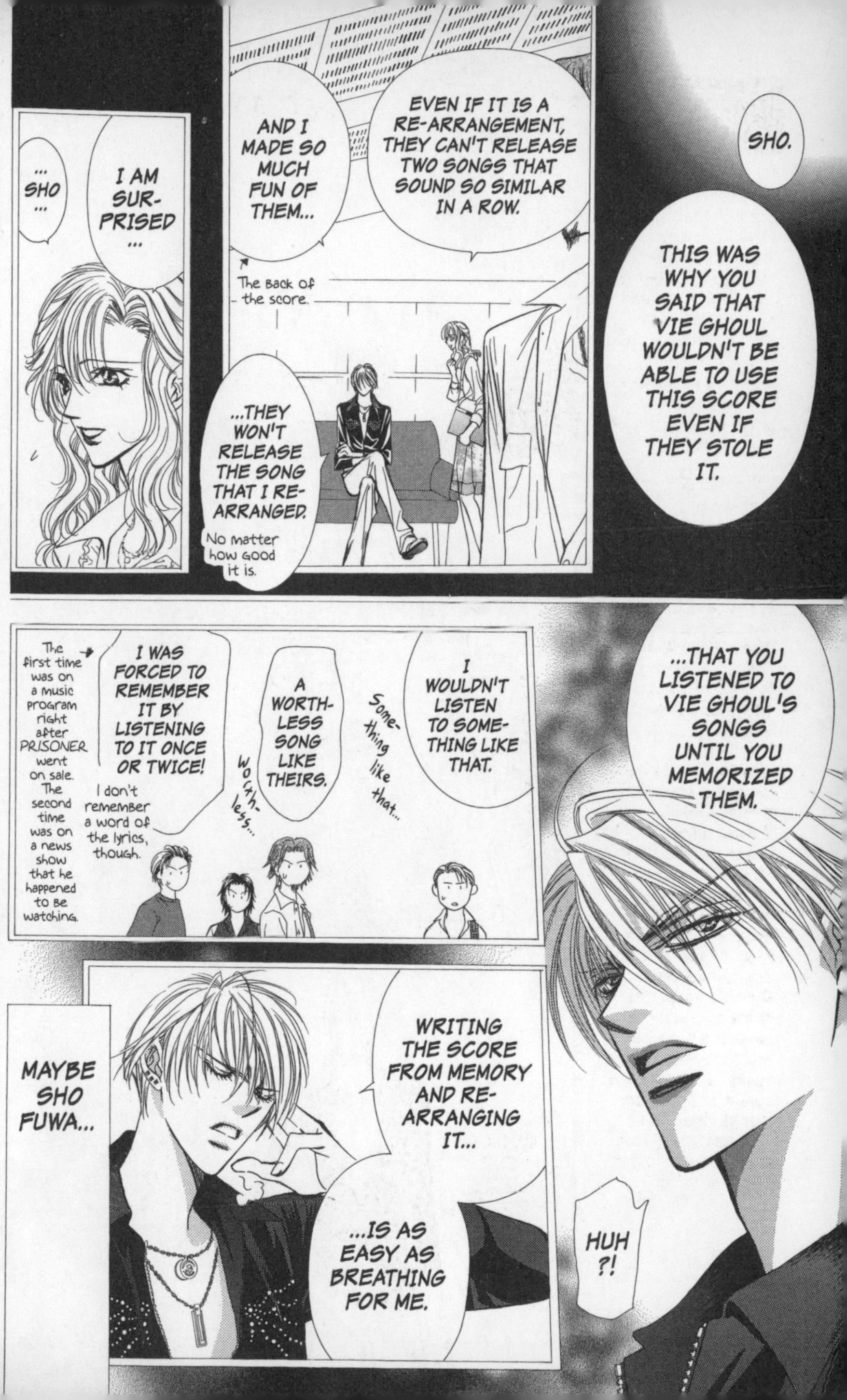
SHO.
THIS WAS WHY YOU SAID THAT VIE GHOUL WOULDN'T BE ABLE TO USE THIS SCORE EVEN IF THEY STOLE IT.
EVEN IF IT IS A RE-ARRANGEMENT, THEY CAN'T RELEASE TWO SONGS THAT SOUND SO SIMILAR IN A ROW.
AND I MADE SO MUCH FUN OF THEM...
The Back of the score.
...THEY WON'T RELEASE THE SONG THAT I RE-ARRANGED.
No matter how good it is.
I AM SUR-PRISED...
...SHO...
...THAT YOU LISTENED TO VIE GHOUL'S SONGS UNTIL YOU MEMORIZED THEM.
HUH?!
I WOULDN'T LISTEN TO SOME-THING LIKE THAT.
Some-thing like that...
A WORTH-LESS SONG LIKE THEIRS.
Worth-less...
I WAS FORCED TO REMEMBER IT BY LISTENING TO IT ONCE OR TWICE!
I don't remember a word of the lyrics, though.
The first time was on a music program right after PRISONER went on sale. The second time was on a news show that he happened to be watching.
WRITING THE SCORE FROM MEMORY AND RE-ARRANGING IT...
...IS AS EASY AS BREATHING FOR ME.
MAYBE SHO FUWA...

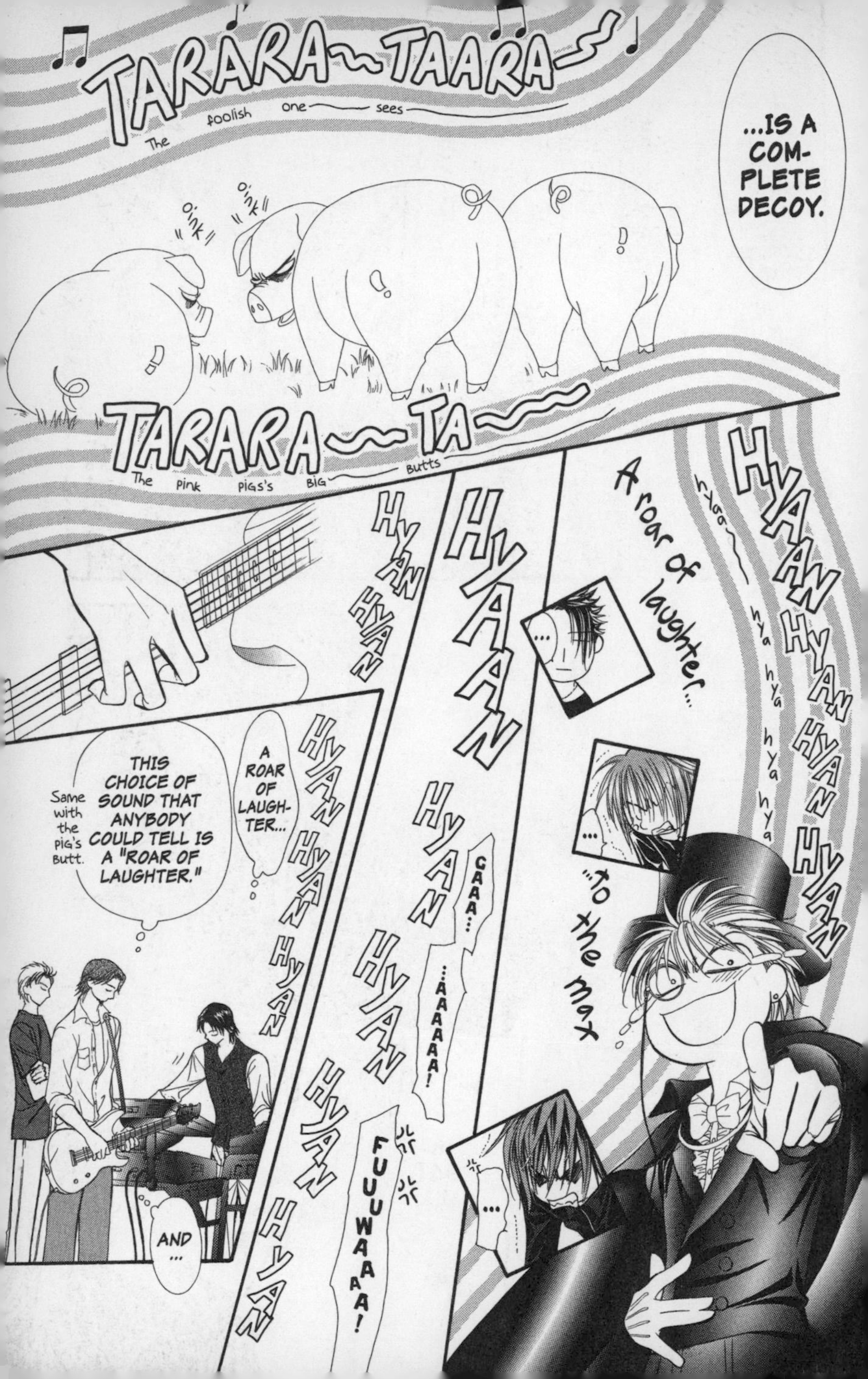
TARARA~TAARA~
The foolish one sees
TARARA~TA~
The pink pigs's BIG butts
...IS A COMPLETE DECOY.
oink
oink
HYAAN HYAN HYAN HYAN
hyaa~ hya hya hya hya hya
A roar of laughter...
...
...
...to the mat
...
HYAAN
HYAN
HYAN
HYAN
HYAN
GAAA...
...AAAAAA!
FUUUWAAAAA!
HYAN HYAN HYAN
HYAN HYAN HYAN HYAN HYAN HYAN HYAN
A ROAR OF LAUGHTER...
THIS CHOICE OF SOUND THAT ANYBODY COULD TELL IS A "ROAR OF LAUGHTER."
Same with the pig's butt.
AND...

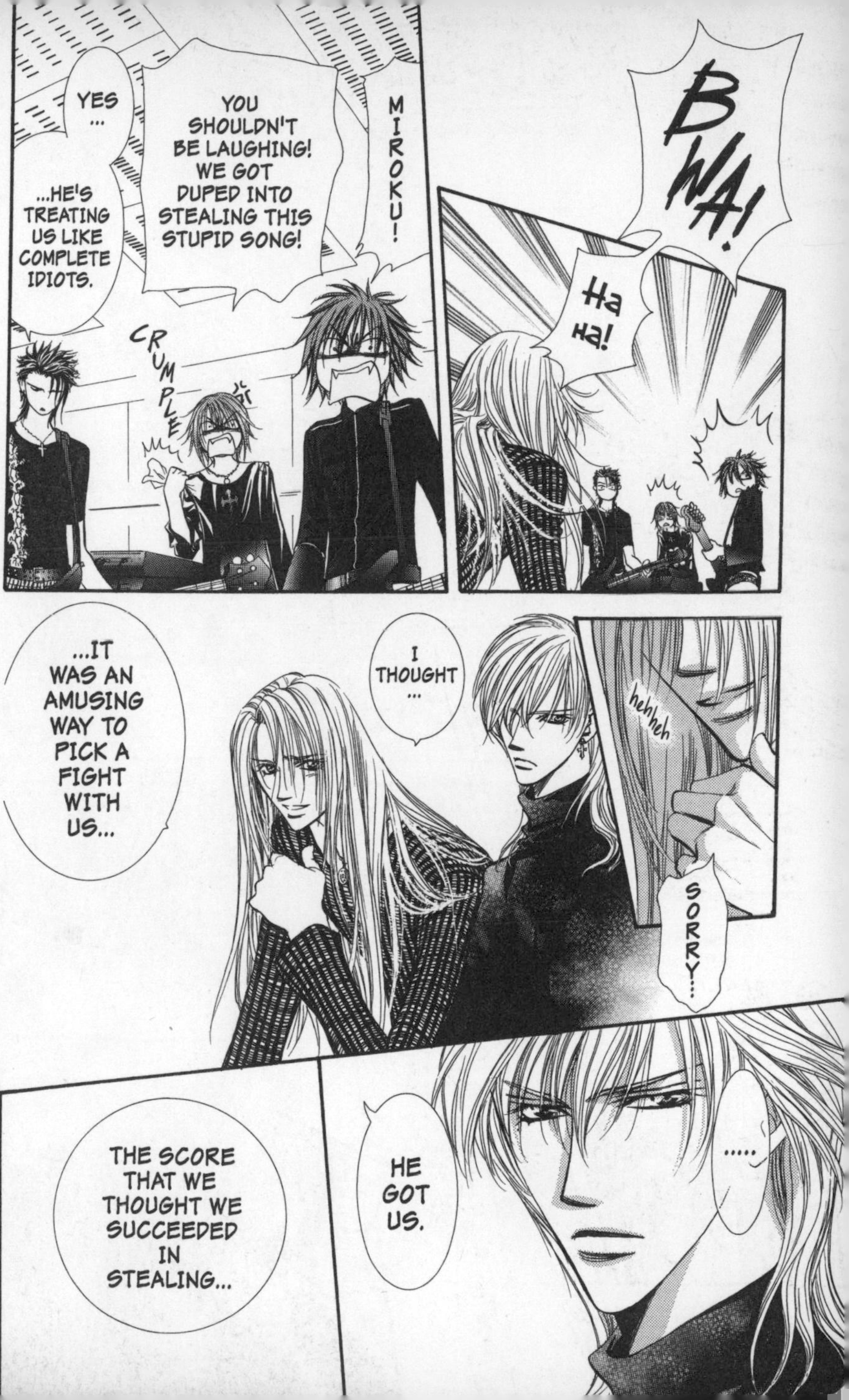
BWA!
Ha ha!
MIROKU!
YOU SHOULDN'T BE LAUGHING! WE GOT DUPED INTO STEALING THIS STUPID SONG!
CRUMPLE
YES ...
...HE'S TREATING US LIKE COMPLETE IDIOTS.
heh heh
SORRY...
I THOUGHT ...
...IT WAS AN AMUSING WAY TO PICK A FIGHT WITH US...
.....
HE GOT US.
THE SCORE THAT WE THOUGHT WE SUCCEEDED IN STEALING...

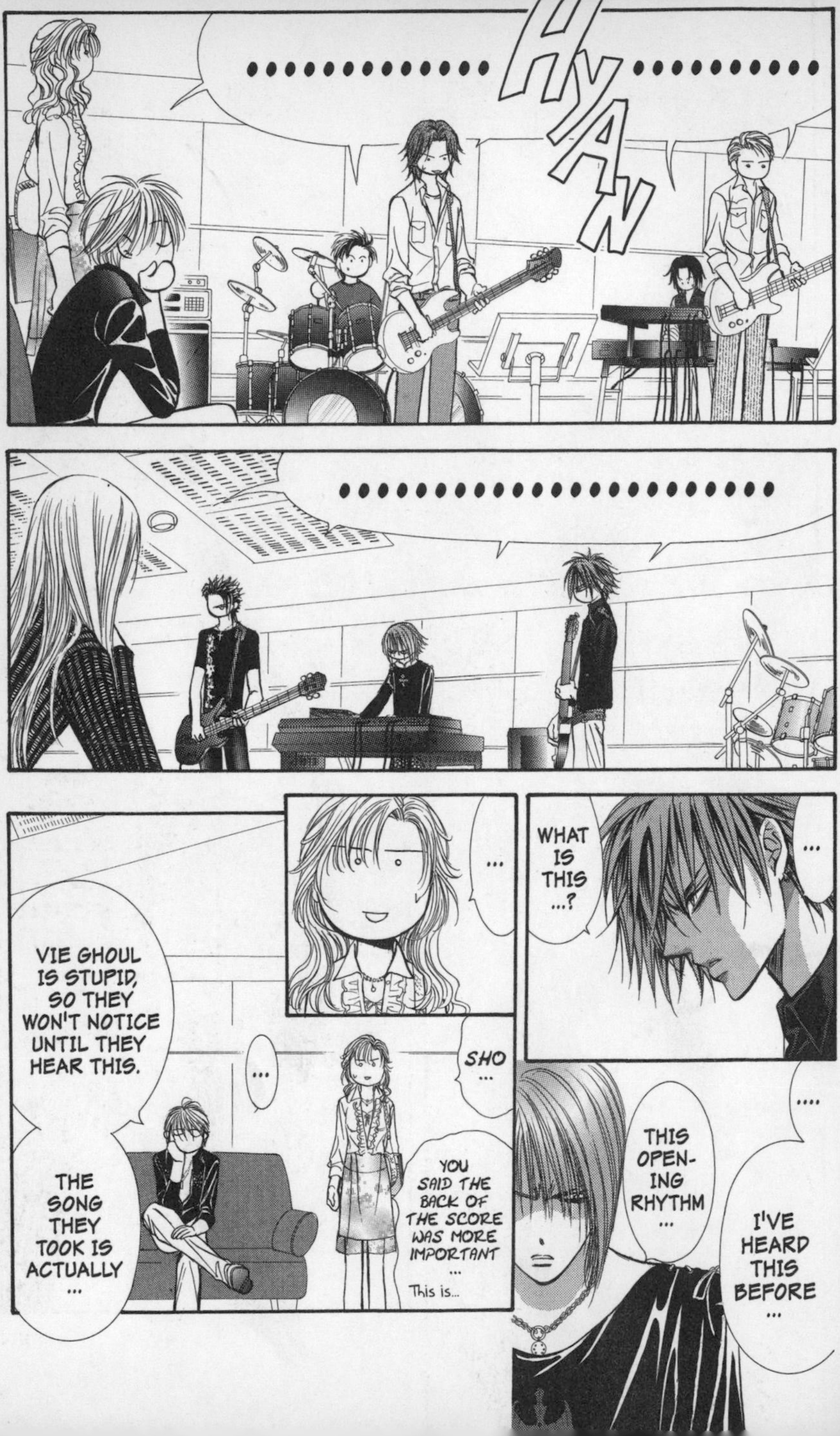
....
HYAN
....
....
...
WHAT IS THIS ...?
....
THIS OPENING RHYTHM ...
I'VE HEARD THIS BEFORE ...
...
VIE GHOUL IS STUPID, SO THEY WON'T NOTICE UNTIL THEY HEAR THIS.
SHO ...
...
YOU SAID THE BACK OF THE SCORE WAS MORE IMPORTANT ...
This is...
THE SONG THEY TOOK IS ACTUALLY ...

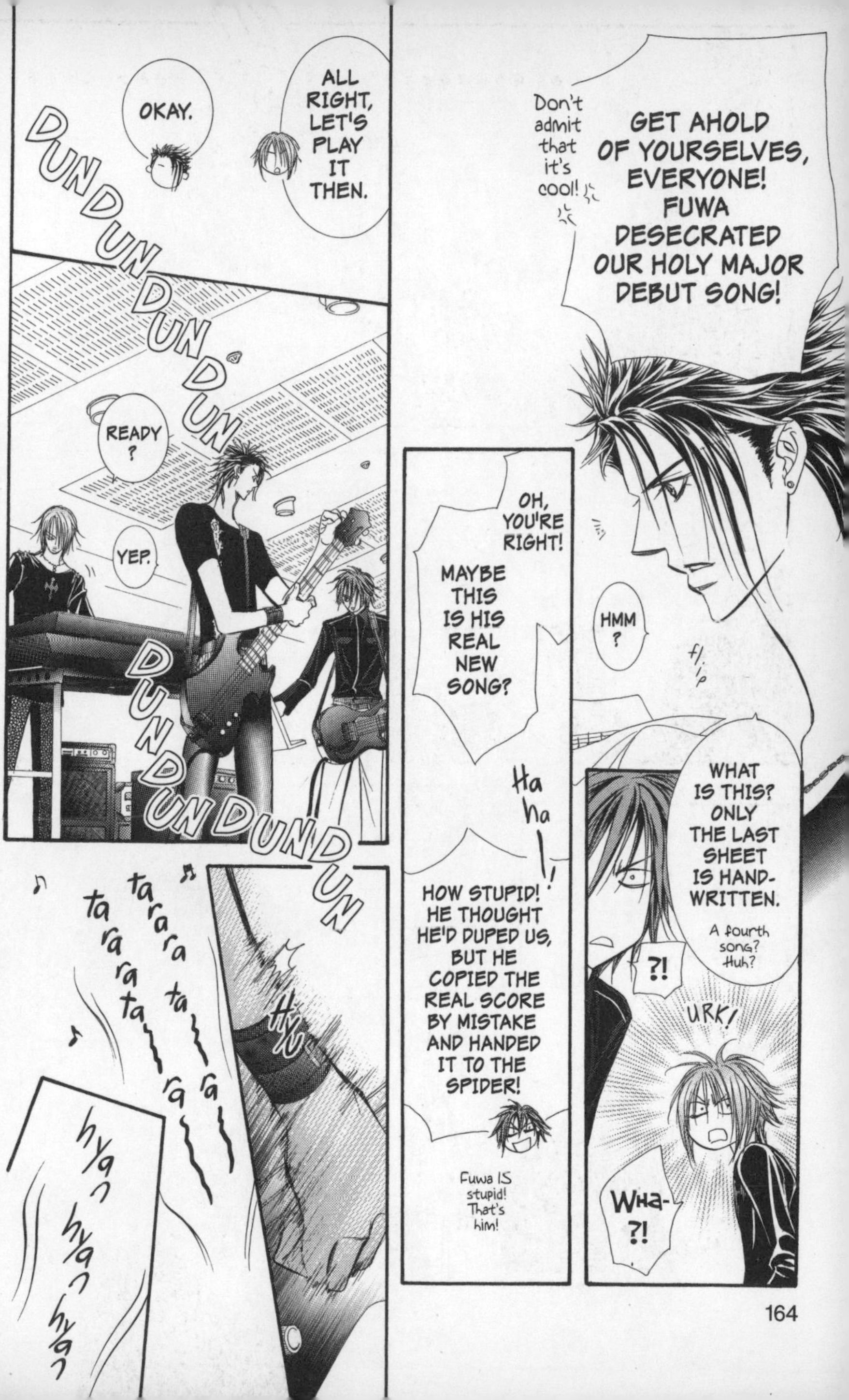
GET AHOLD OF YOURSELVES, EVERYONE! FUWA DESECRATED OUR HOLY MAJOR DEBUT SONG!
Don't admit that it's cool!
HMM?
flip
WHAT IS THIS? ONLY THE LAST SHEET IS HAND-WRITTEN.
A fourth song? Huh?
?!
URK!
WHA-?!
OH, YOU'RE RIGHT!
MAYBE THIS IS HIS REAL NEW SONG?
Ha ha!
HOW STUPID! HE THOUGHT HE'D DUPED US, BUT HE COPIED THE REAL SCORE BY MISTAKE AND HANDED IT TO THE SPIDER!
Fuwa IS stupid! That's him!
ALL RIGHT, LET'S PLAY IT THEN.
OKAY.
DUNDUNDUNDUN
READY?
YEP.
DUNDUNDUNDUN
tarara ta~ra~
tararata~ra~
hyan hyan hyan hyan

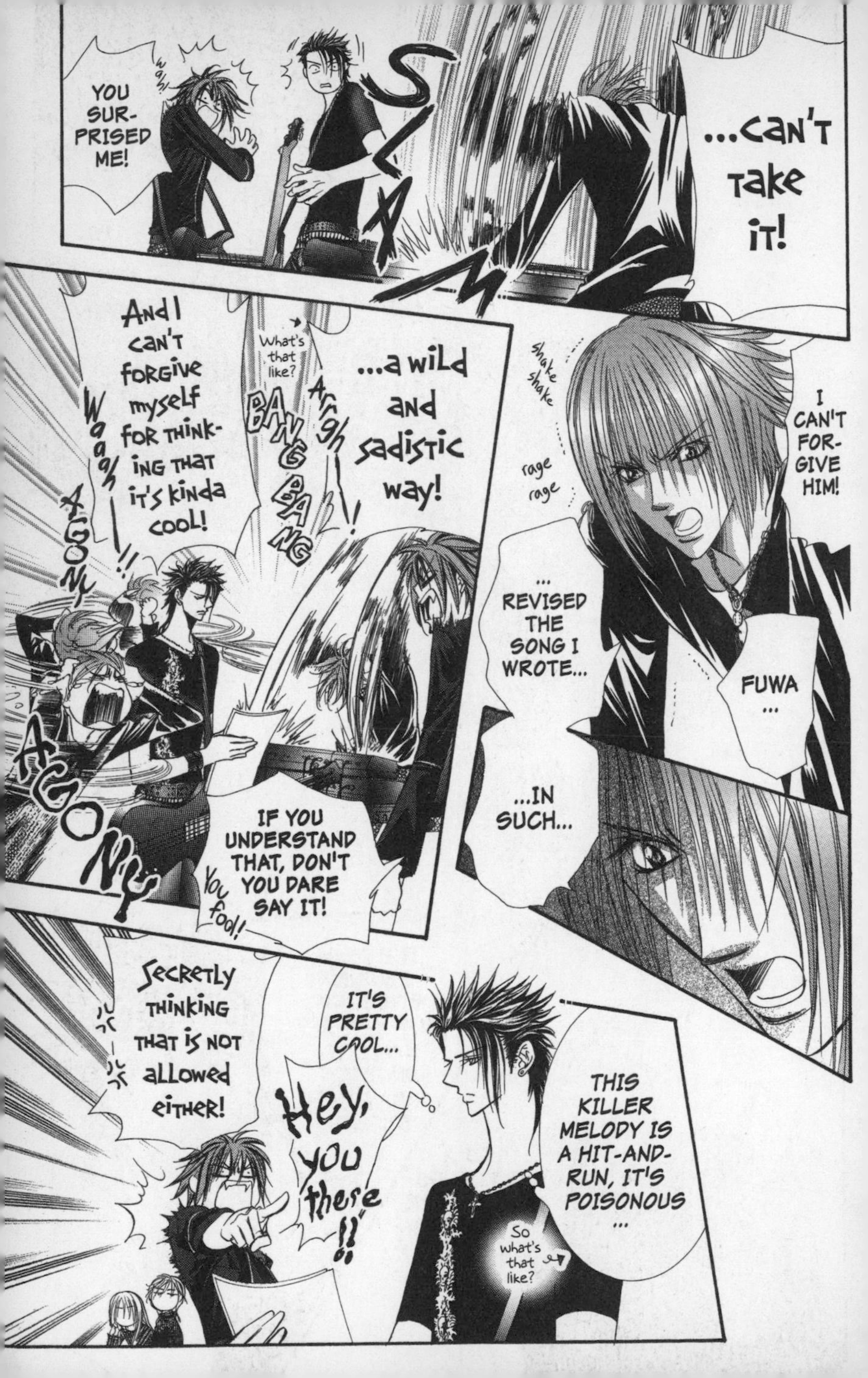
...can't take it!
SLAM
YOU SUR-PRISED ME!
wah!
I CAN'T FOR-GIVE HIM!
shake shake
rage rage
FUWA ...
... REVISED THE SONG I WROTE...
...IN SUCH...
...a wild and sadistic way!
What's that like?
Arrgh!
BANG BANG
And I can't forgive myself for think-ing that it's kinda cool!
Waaah!!
AGONY
AGONY
IF YOU UNDERSTAND THAT, DON'T YOU DARE SAY IT!
You fool!
THIS KILLER MELODY IS A HIT-AND-RUN, IT'S POISONOUS ...
So what's that like?
IT'S PRETTY COOL...
Secretly thinking that is not allowed either!
Hey, you there!!

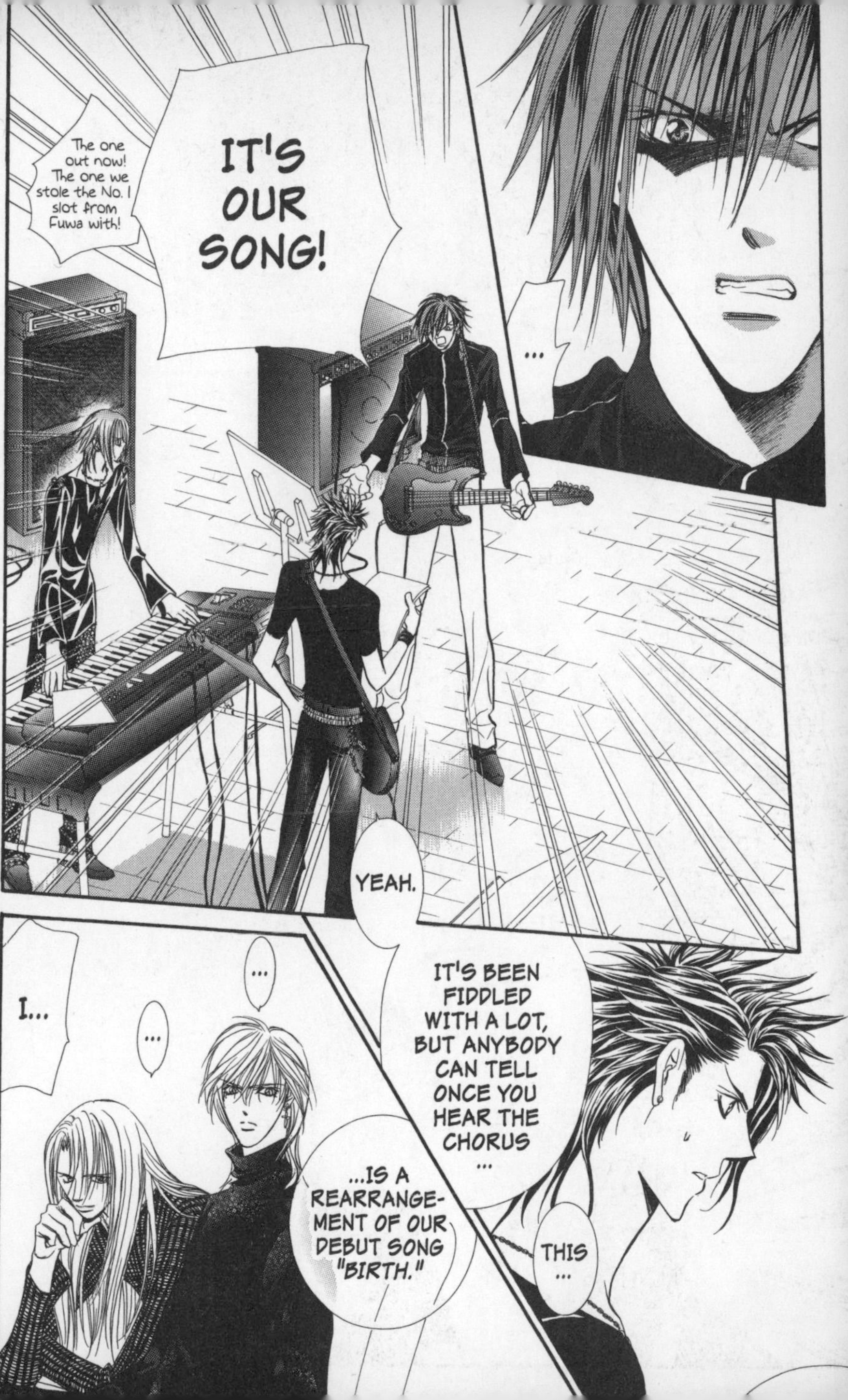
...
IT'S OUR SONG!
The one out now! The one we stole the No. 1 slot from Fuwa with!
YEAH.
IT'S BEEN FIDDLED WITH A LOT, BUT ANYBODY CAN TELL ONCE YOU HEAR THE CHORUS ...
THIS ...
...IS A REARRANGEMENT OF OUR DEBUT SONG "BIRTH."
...
...
I...

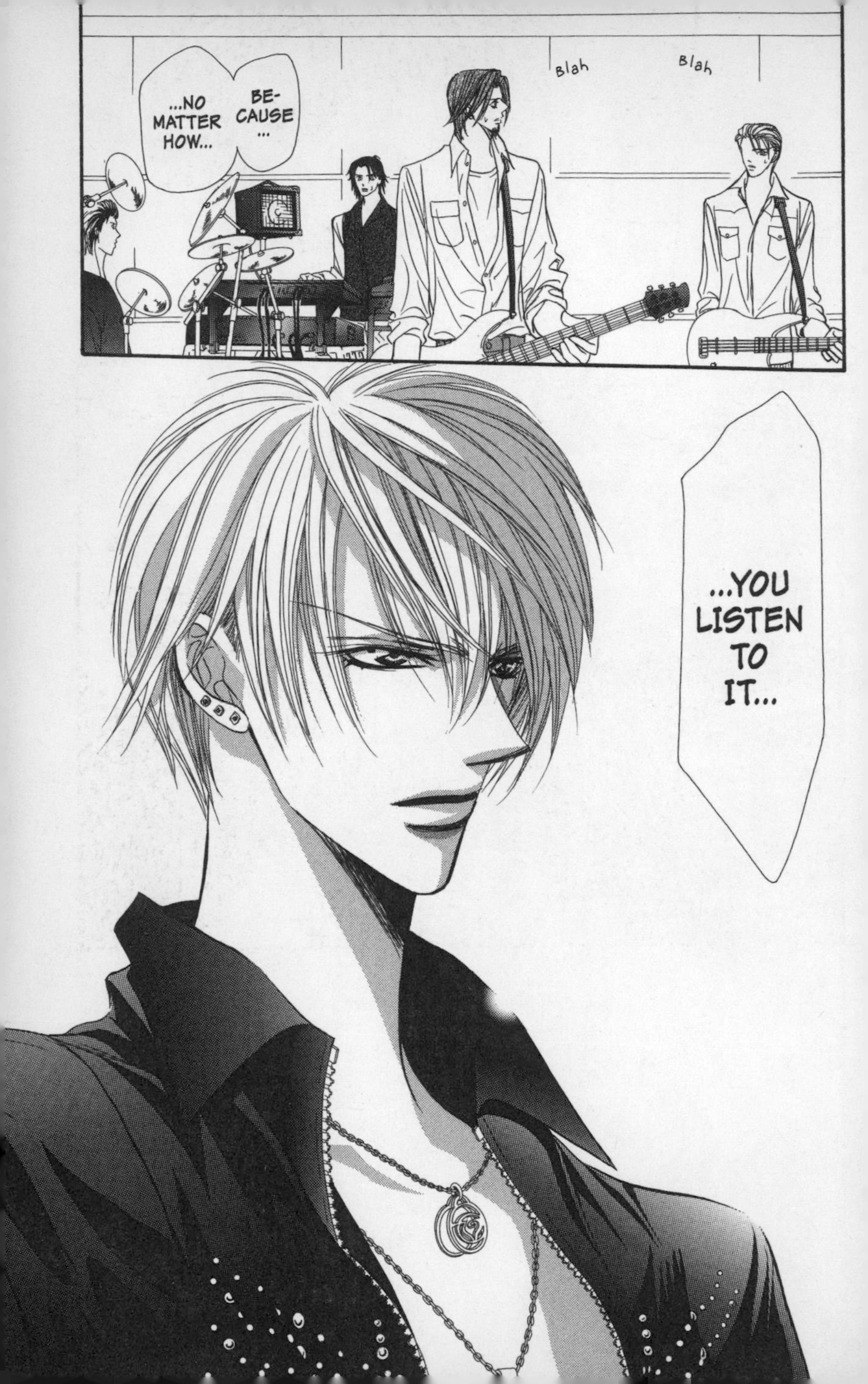

Blah
Blah
BE-CAUSE...
...NO MATTER HOW...
...YOU LISTEN TO IT...

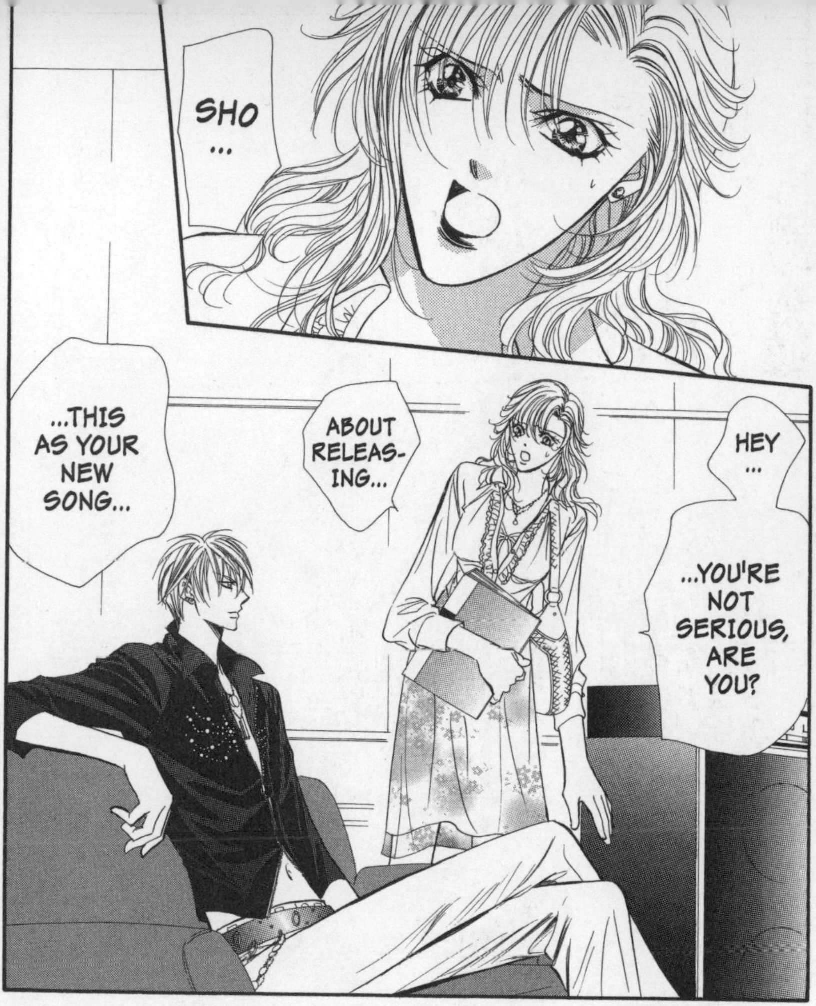
SHO ...
HEY ...
...YOU'RE NOT SERIOUS, ARE YOU?
ABOUT RELEAS-ING...
...THIS AS YOUR NEW SONG...
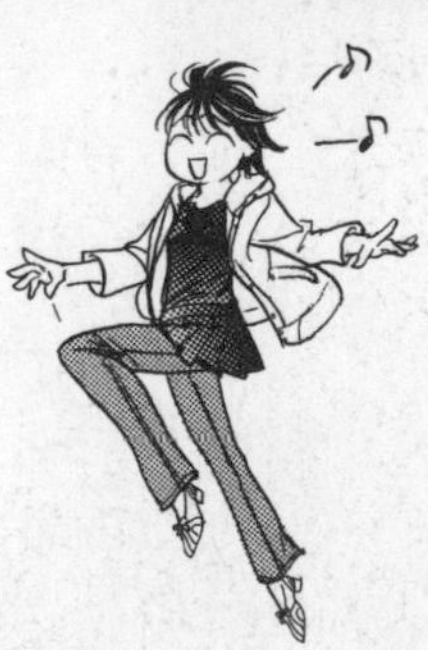

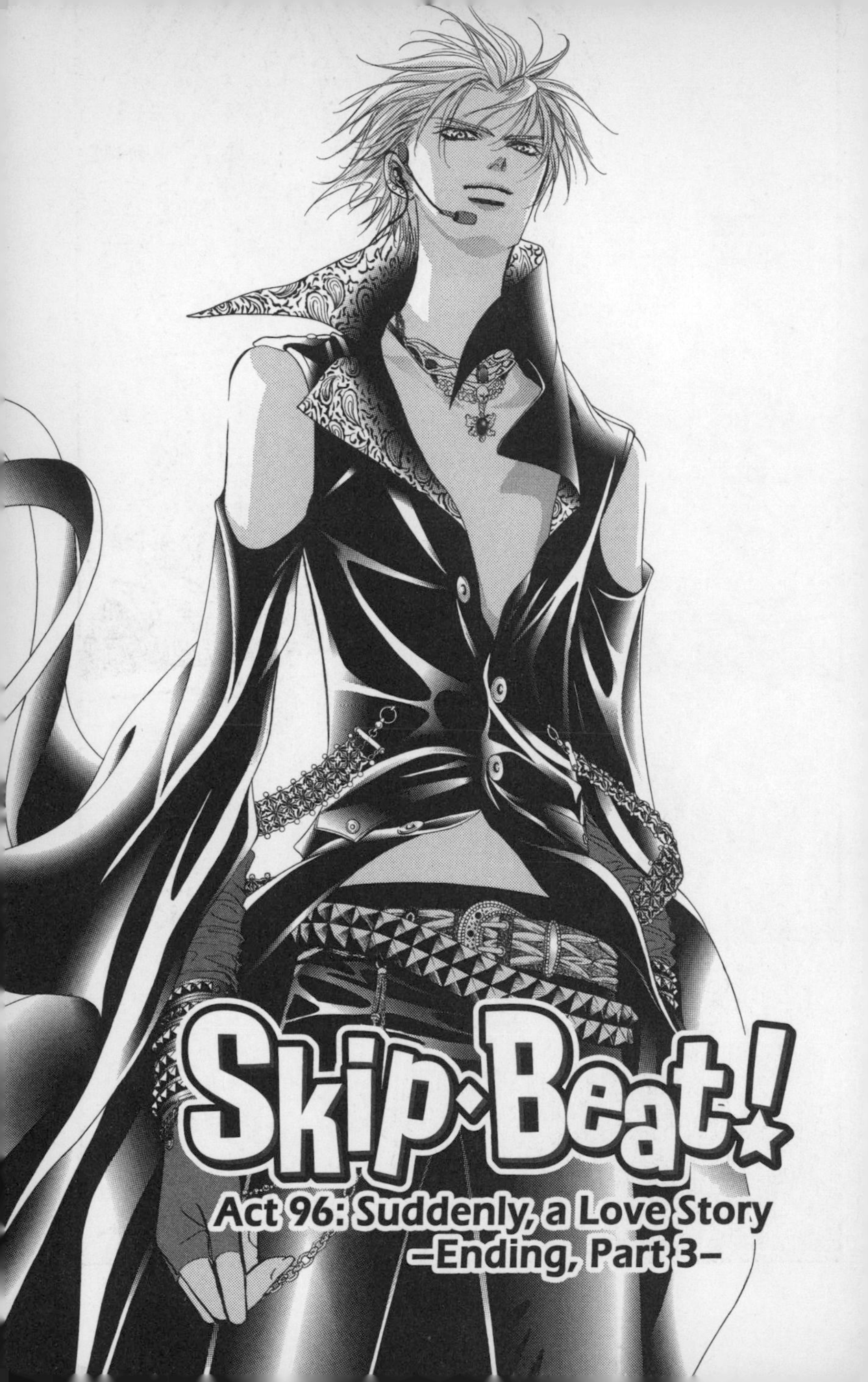
Skip·Beat!
Act 96: Suddenly, a Love Story
–Ending, Part 3–

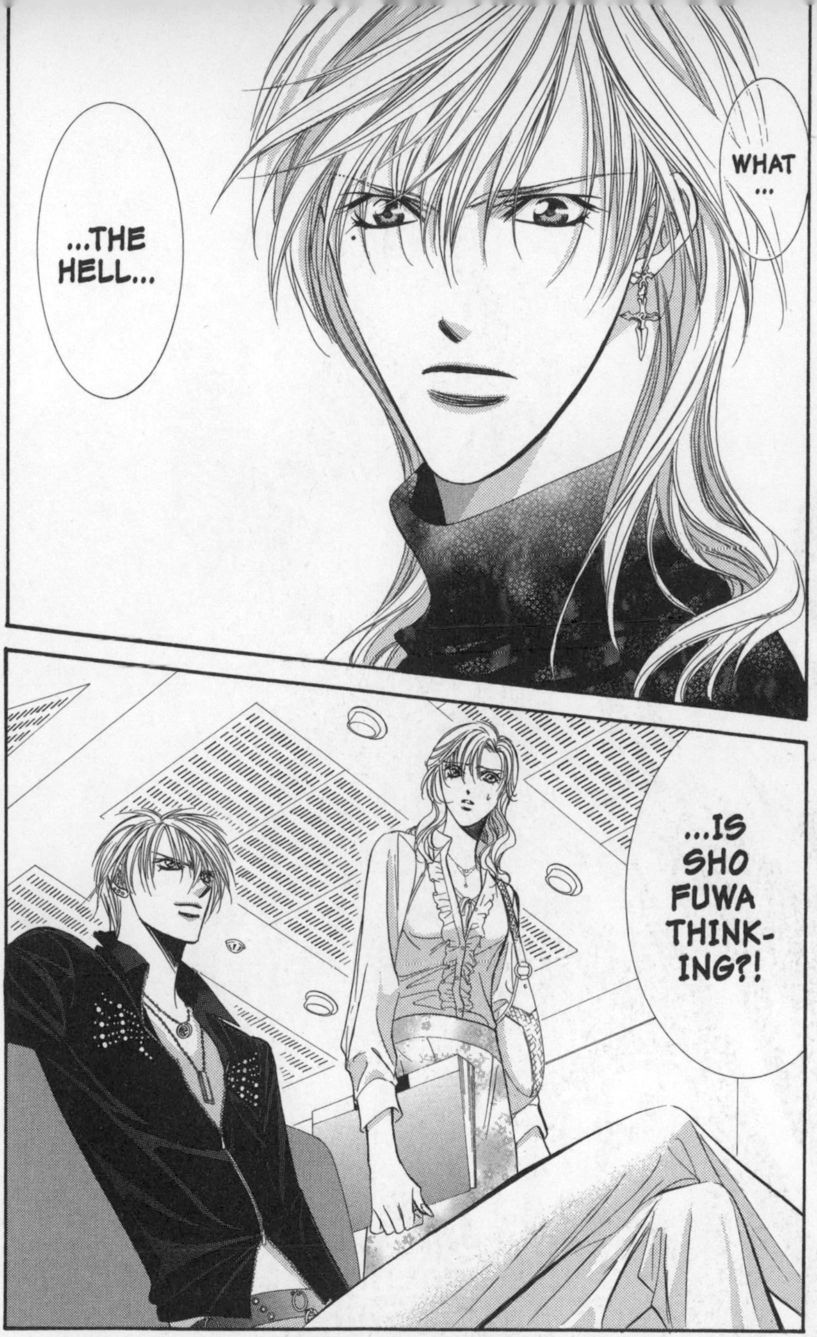
WHAT ...
...THE HELL...
...IS SHO FUWA THINKING?!

End of Act 95

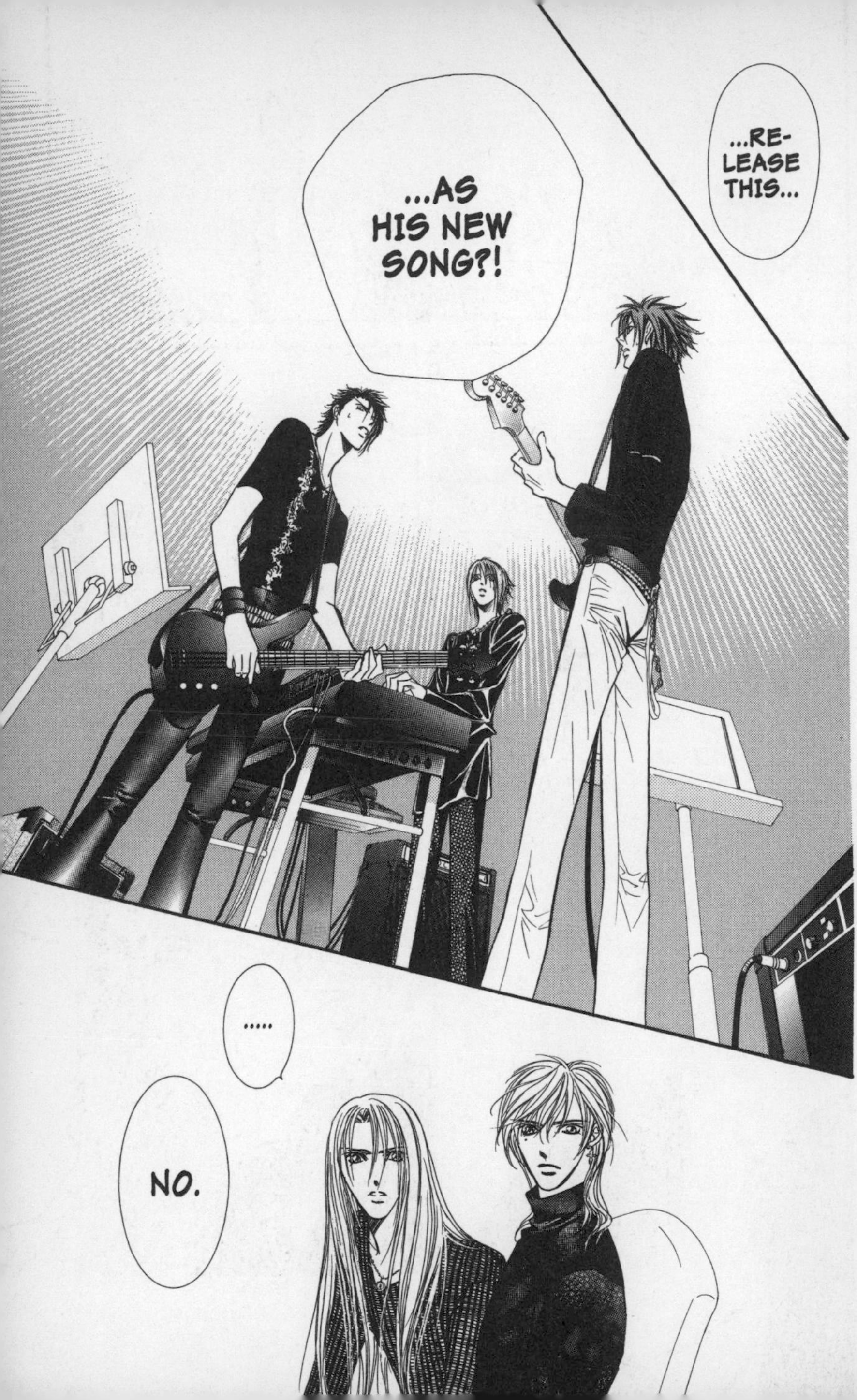
...RE-LEASE THIS...
...AS HIS NEW SONG?!
......
NO.

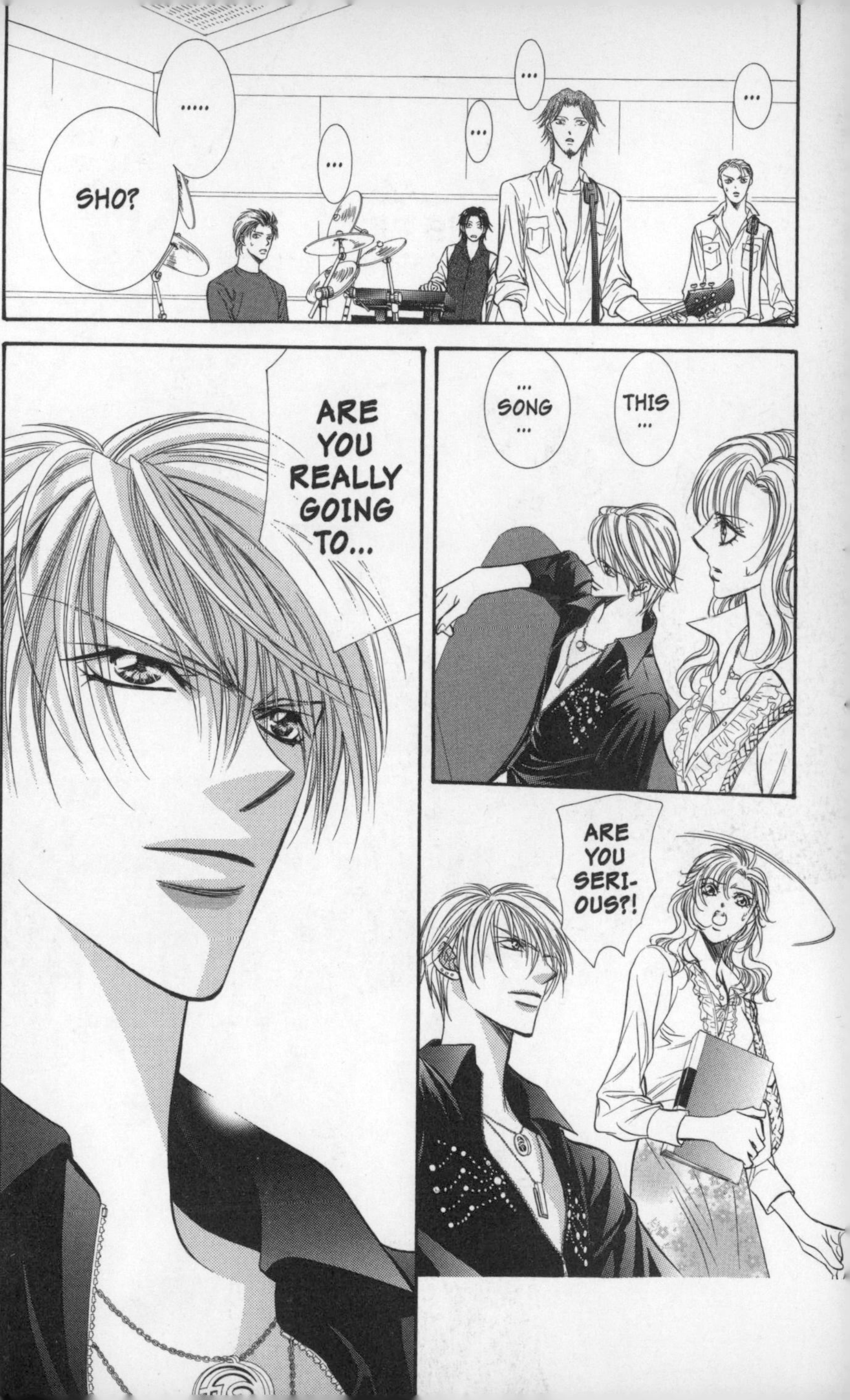
...
...
...
...
.....
SHO?
THIS ...
... SONG ...
ARE YOU SERI-OUS?!
ARE YOU REALLY GOING TO...

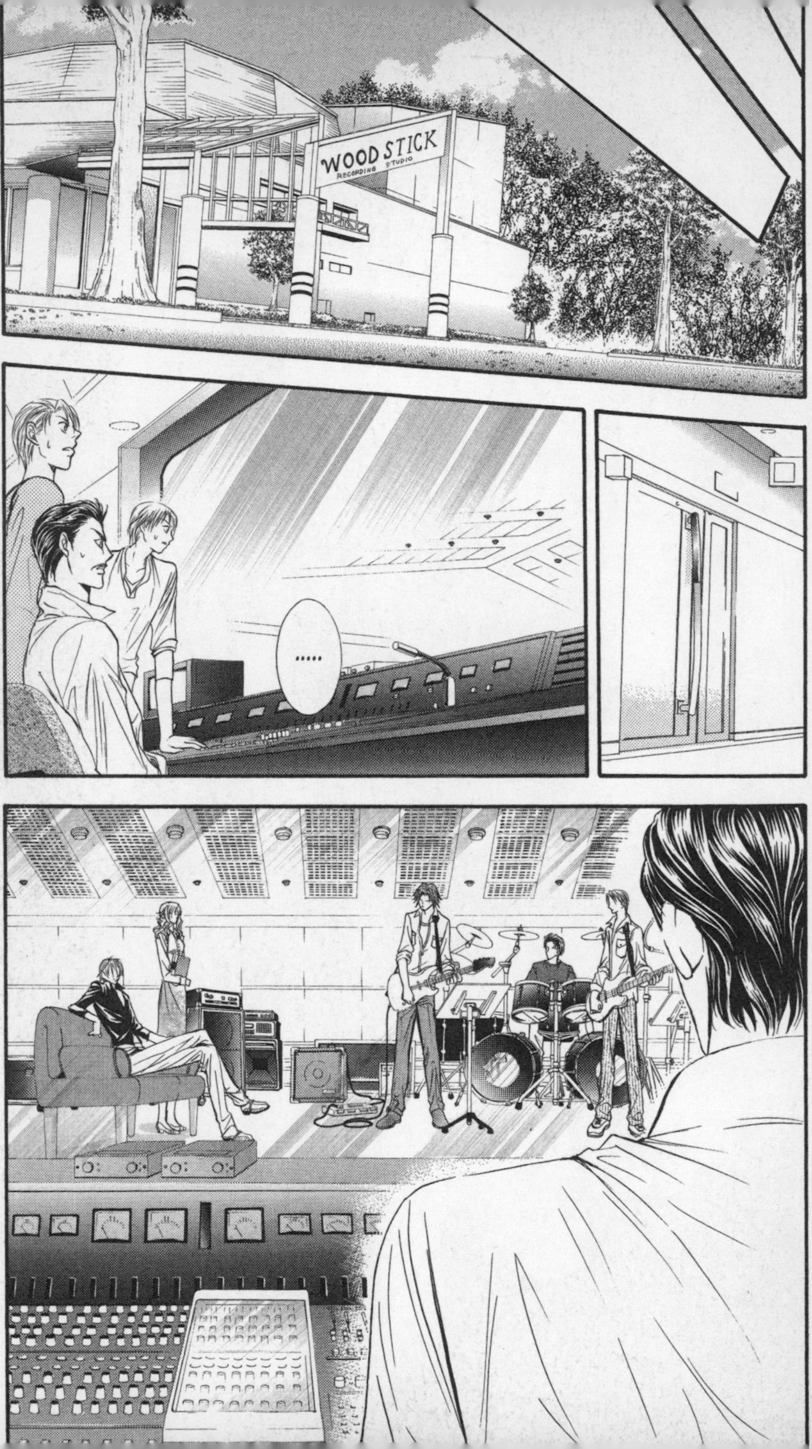
WOOD STICK
RECORDING STUDIO
......

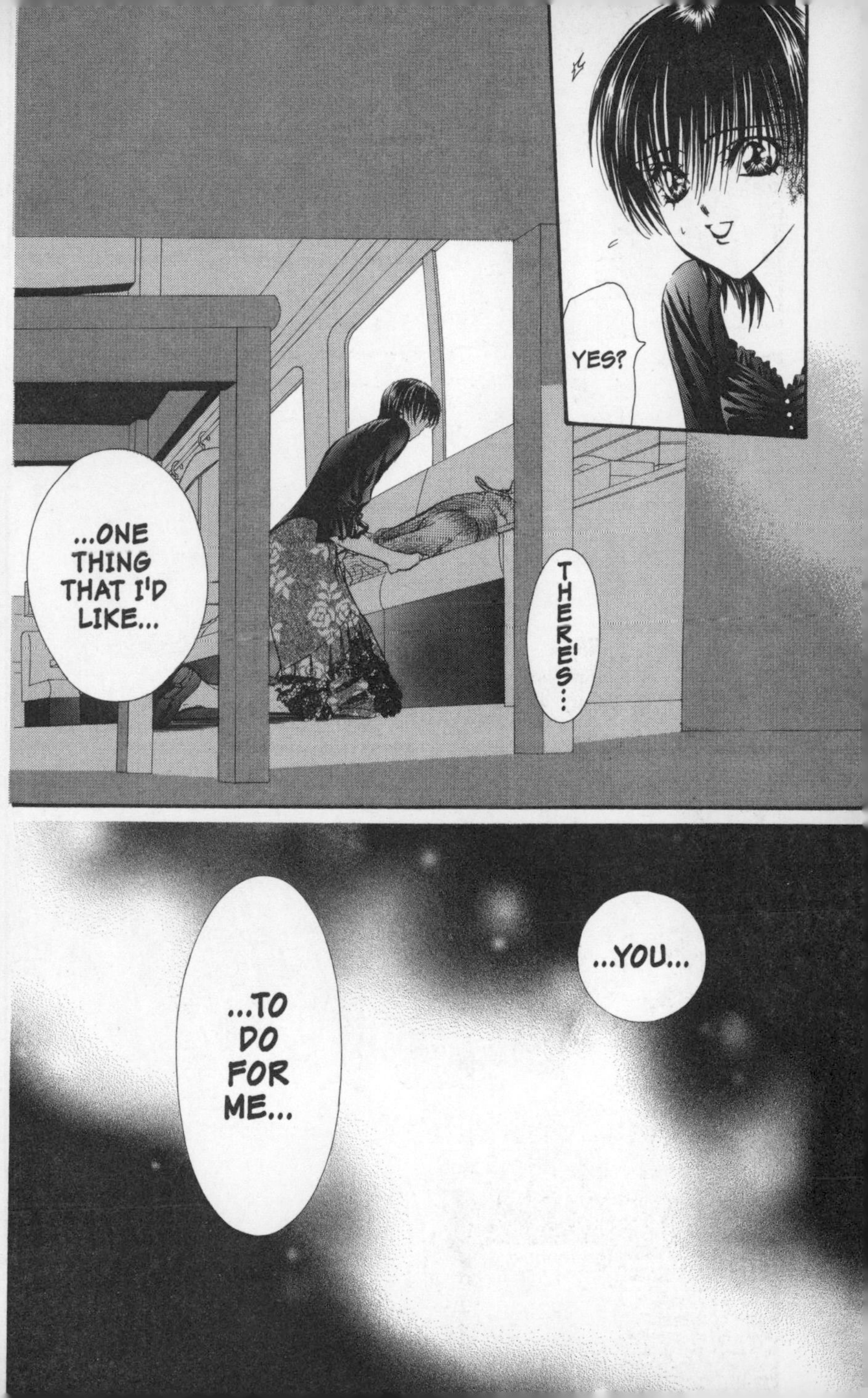
YES?
THERE'S...
...ONE THING THAT I'D LIKE...
...YOU...
...TO DO FOR ME...

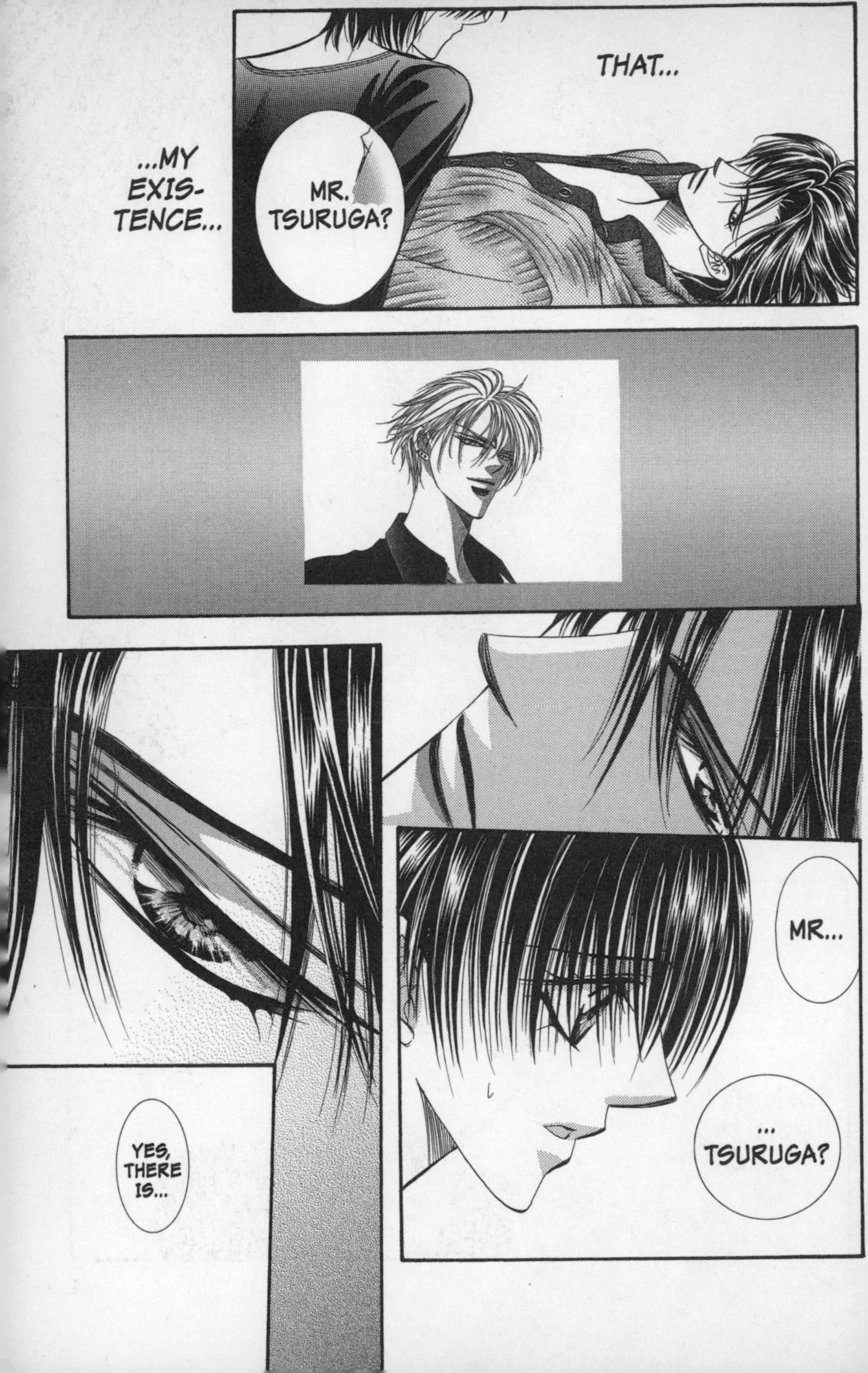
THAT...
MR. TSURUGA?
...MY EXIS-TENCE...
MR...
...TSURUGA?
YES, THERE IS...

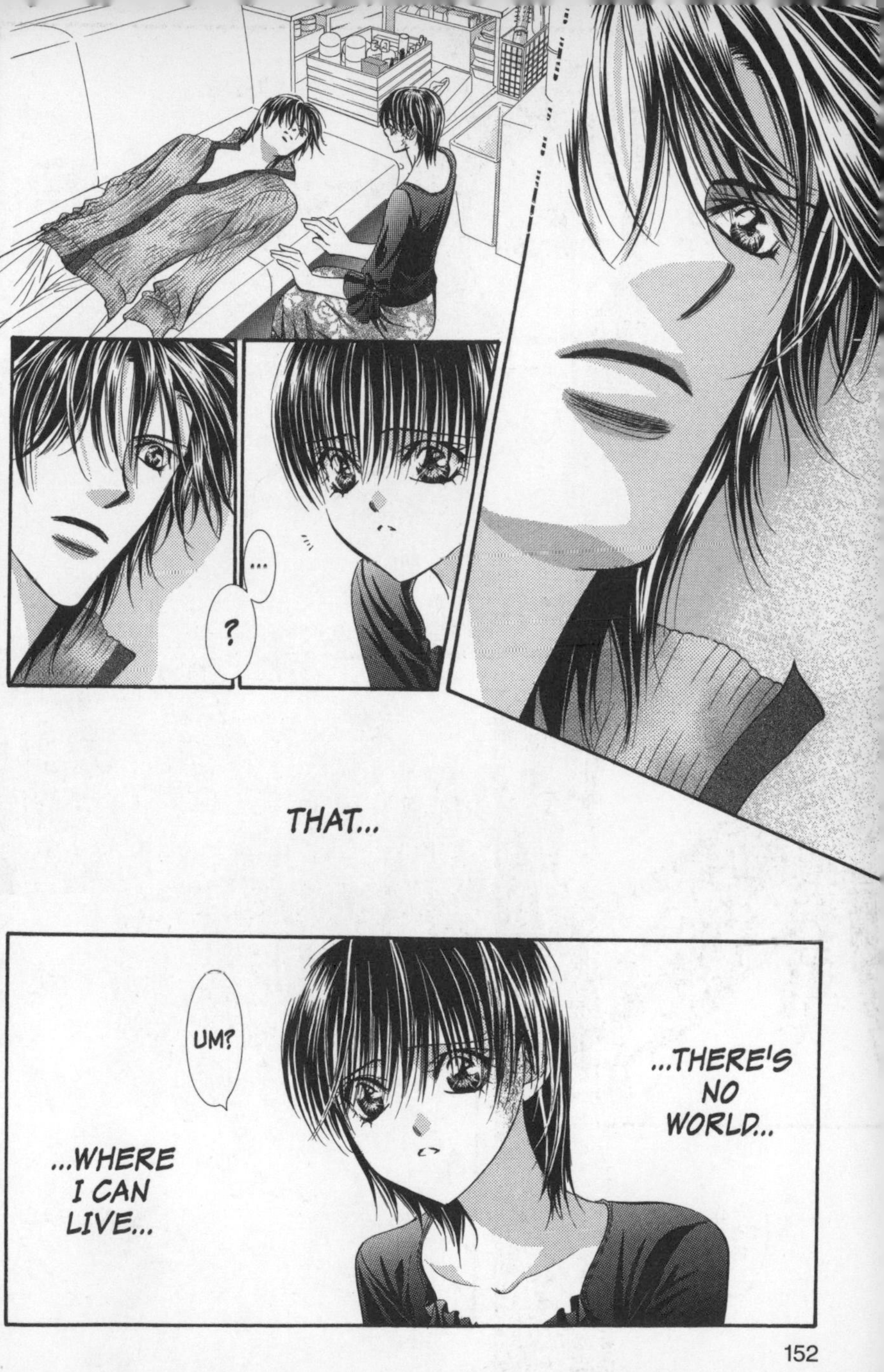
...
?
THAT...
...THERE'S NO WORLD...
UM?
...WHERE I CAN LIVE...

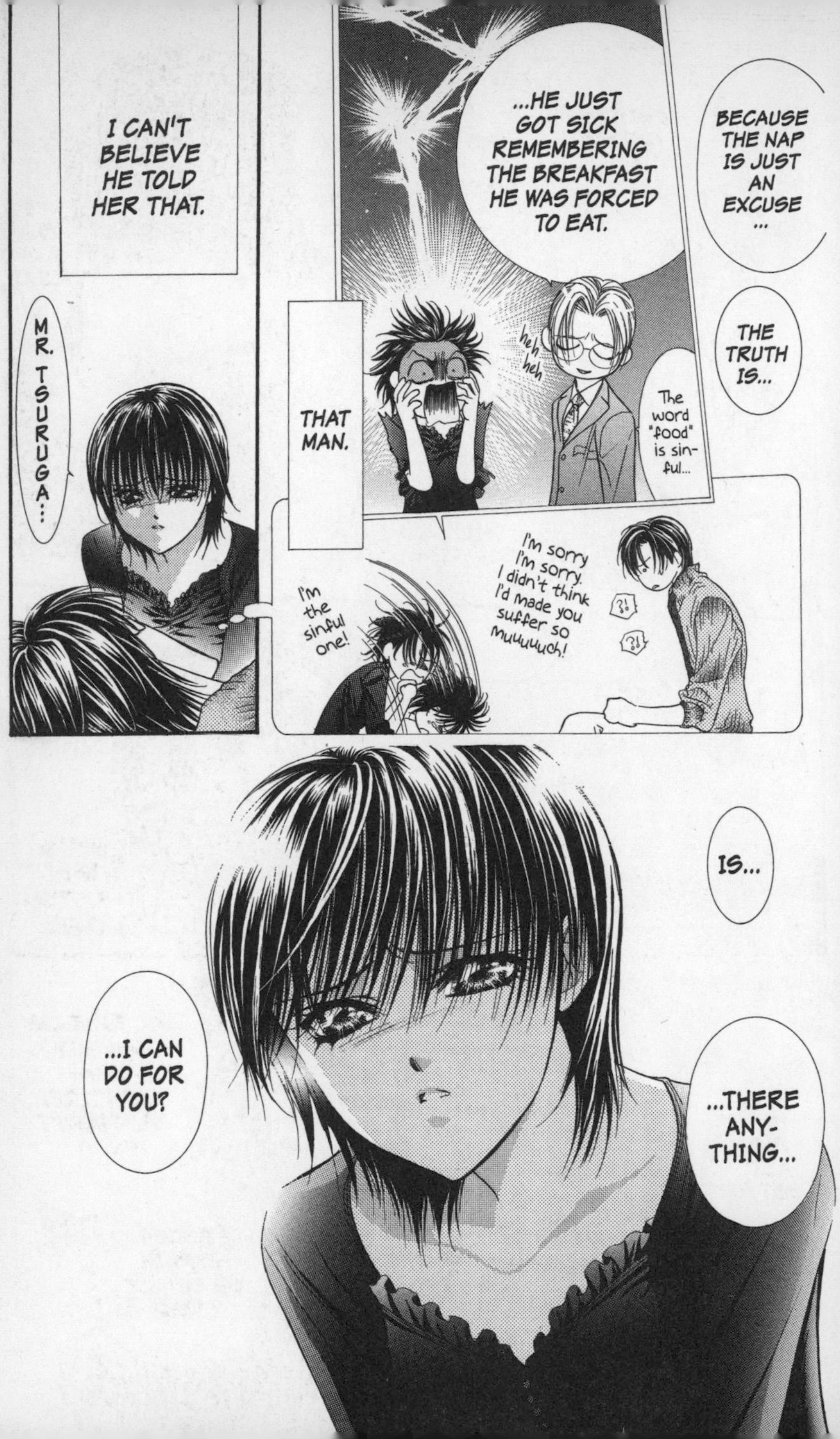
BECAUSE THE NAP IS JUST AN EXCUSE...
...HE JUST GOT SICK REMEMBERING THE BREAKFAST HE WAS FORCED TO EAT.
THE TRUTH IS...
heh heh
The word "food" is sinful...
THAT MAN.
I'm sorry I'm sorry. I didn't think I'd made you suffer so muuuuuch!
?!
?!
I'm the sinful one!
I CAN'T BELIEVE HE TOLD HER THAT.
MR. TSURUGA...
IS...
...THERE ANYTHING...
...I CAN DO FOR YOU?

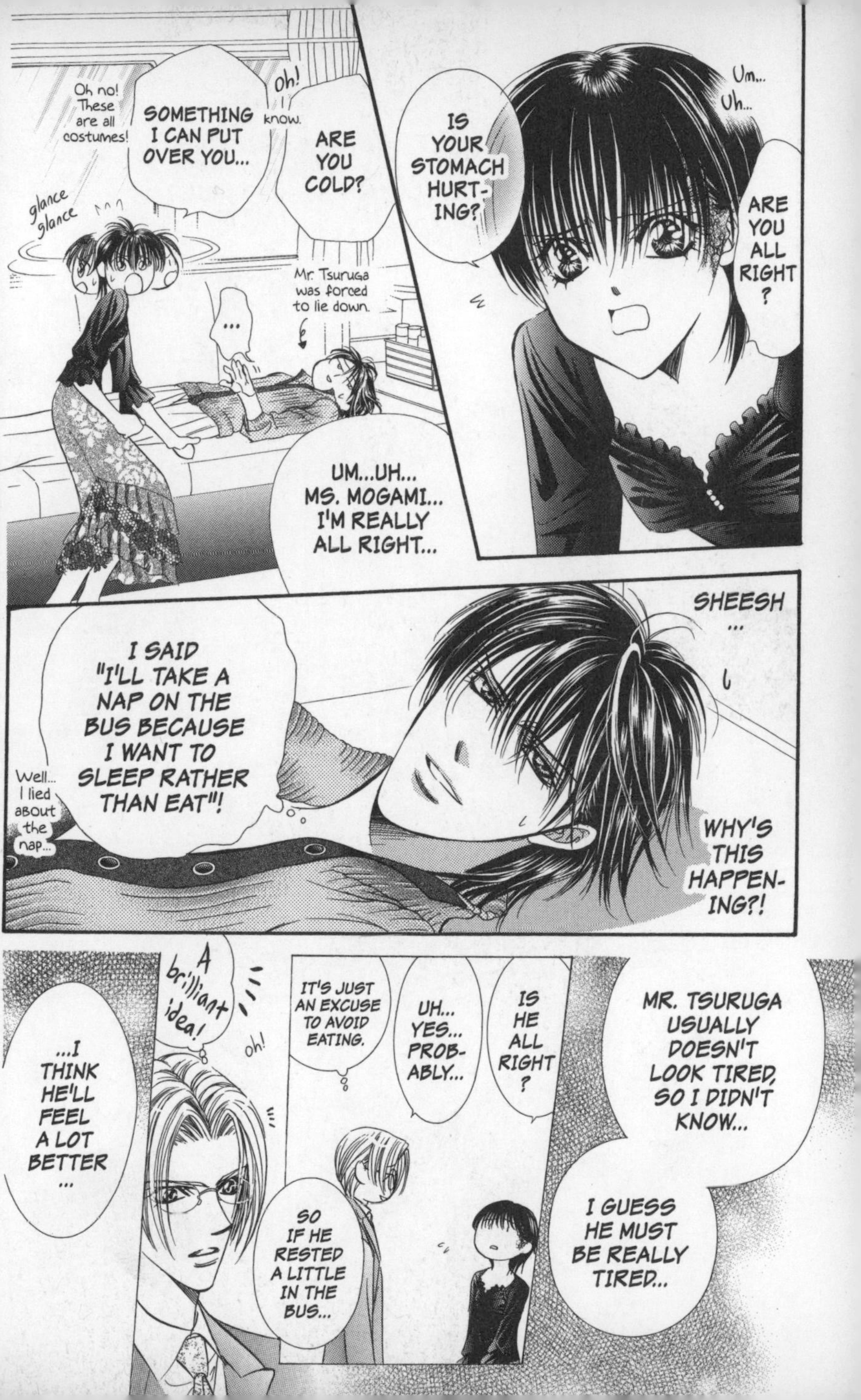
Um... Uh...
ARE YOU ALL RIGHT?
IS YOUR STOMACH HURTING?
Oh!
know.
ARE YOU COLD?
SOMETHING I CAN PUT OVER YOU...
Oh no! These are all costumes!
glance glance
Mr. Tsuruga was forced to lie down.
...
UM...UH... MS. MOGAMI... I'M REALLY ALL RIGHT...
SHEESH...
WHY'S THIS HAPPENING?!
I SAID "I'LL TAKE A NAP ON THE BUS BECAUSE I WANT TO SLEEP RATHER THAN EAT"!
Well... I lied about the nap...
MR. TSURUGA USUALLY DOESN'T LOOK TIRED, SO I DIDN'T KNOW...
I GUESS HE MUST BE REALLY TIRED...
IS HE ALL RIGHT?
UH... YES... PROBABLY...
IT'S JUST AN EXCUSE TO AVOID EATING.
SO IF HE RESTED A LITTLE IN THE BUS...
A brilliant idea!
oh!
...I THINK HE'LL FEEL A LOT BETTER...

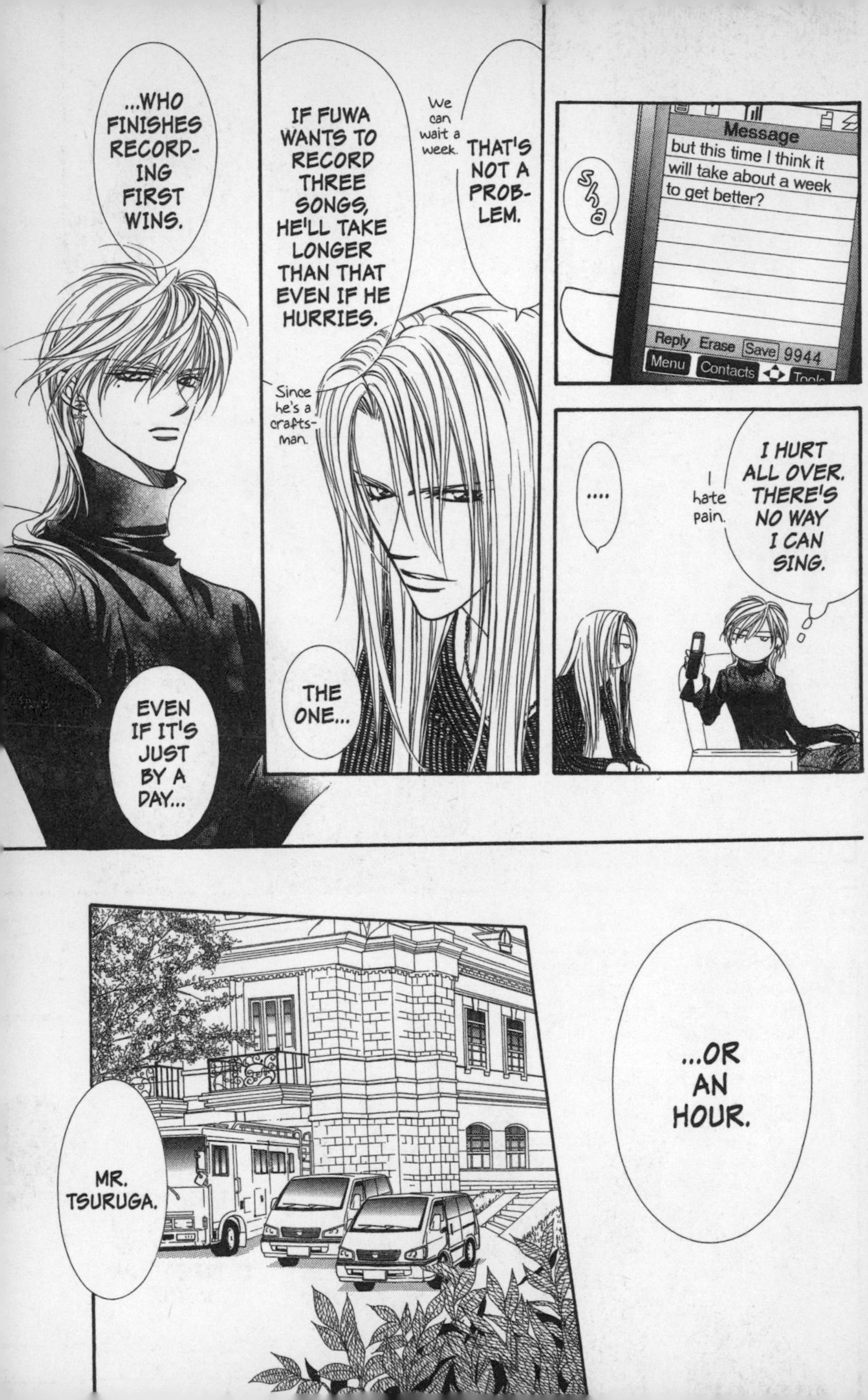
Message
but this time I think it will take about a week to get better?
Reply Erase Save 9944
Menu Contacts Tools
Sha
I HURT ALL OVER. THERE'S NO WAY I CAN SING.
I hate pain.
....
THAT'S NOT A PROBLEM.
We can wait a week.
IF FUWA WANTS TO RECORD THREE SONGS, HE'LL TAKE LONGER THAN THAT EVEN IF HE HURRIES.
Since he's a craftsman.
THE ONE...
...WHO FINISHES RECORDING FIRST WINS.
EVEN IF IT'S JUST BY A DAY...
...OR AN HOUR.
MR. TSURUGA.

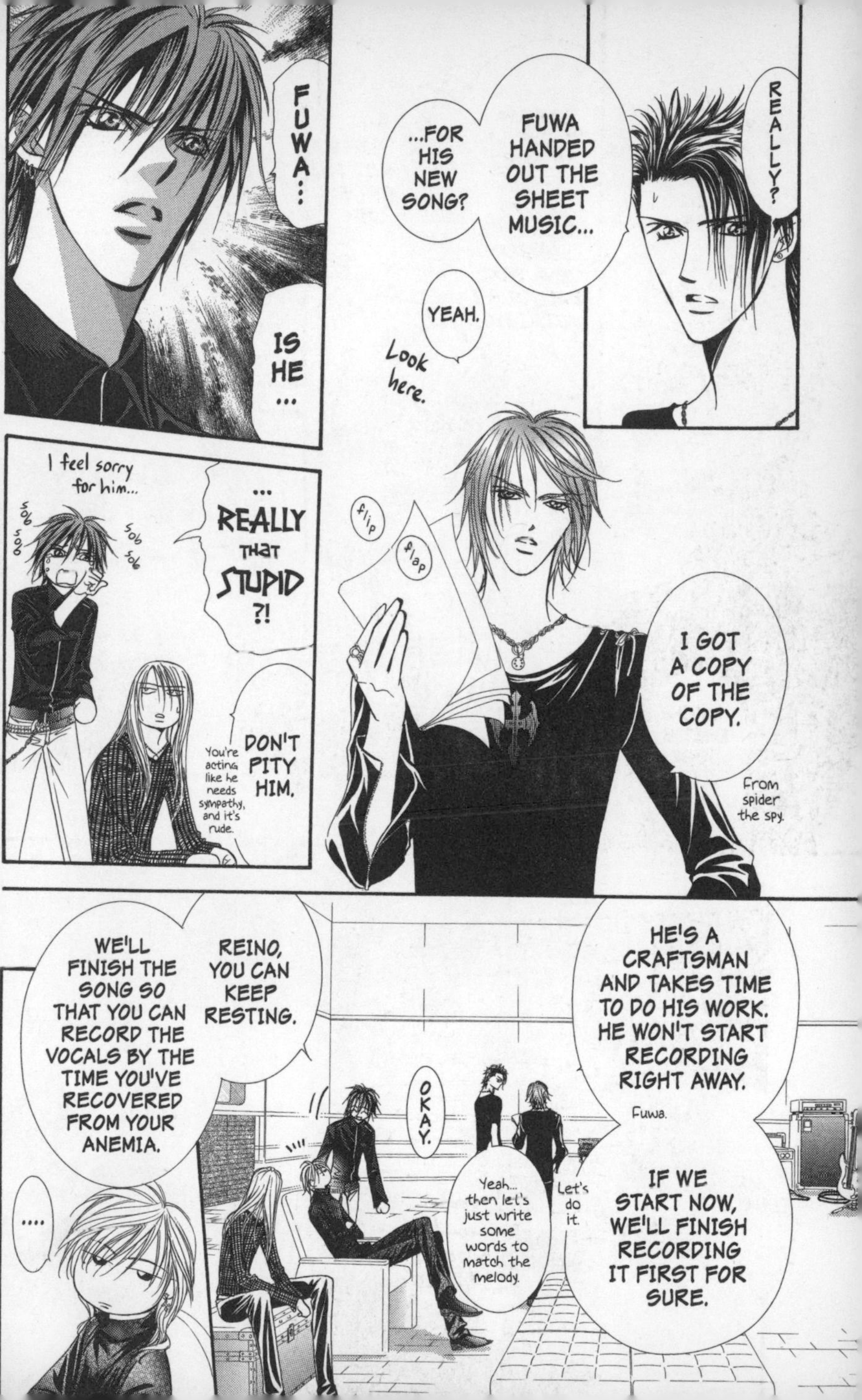
REALLY?
FUWA HANDED OUT THE SHEET MUSIC...
...FOR HIS NEW SONG?
YEAH.
Look here.
flip
flap
I GOT A COPY OF THE COPY.
From spider the spy.
FUWA...
IS HE...
...REALLY THAT STUPID?!
I feel sorry for him...
sob sob
sob sob
DON'T PITY HIM.
You're acting like he needs sympathy, and it's rude.
HE'S A CRAFTSMAN AND TAKES TIME TO DO HIS WORK. HE WON'T START RECORDING RIGHT AWAY.
Fuwa.
IF WE START NOW, WE'LL FINISH RECORDING IT FIRST FOR SURE.
Let's do it.
Yeah... then let's just write some words to match the melody.
OKAY.
REINO, YOU CAN KEEP RESTING.
WE'LL FINISH THE SONG SO THAT YOU CAN RECORD THE VOCALS BY THE TIME YOU'VE RECOVERED FROM YOUR ANEMIA.
....

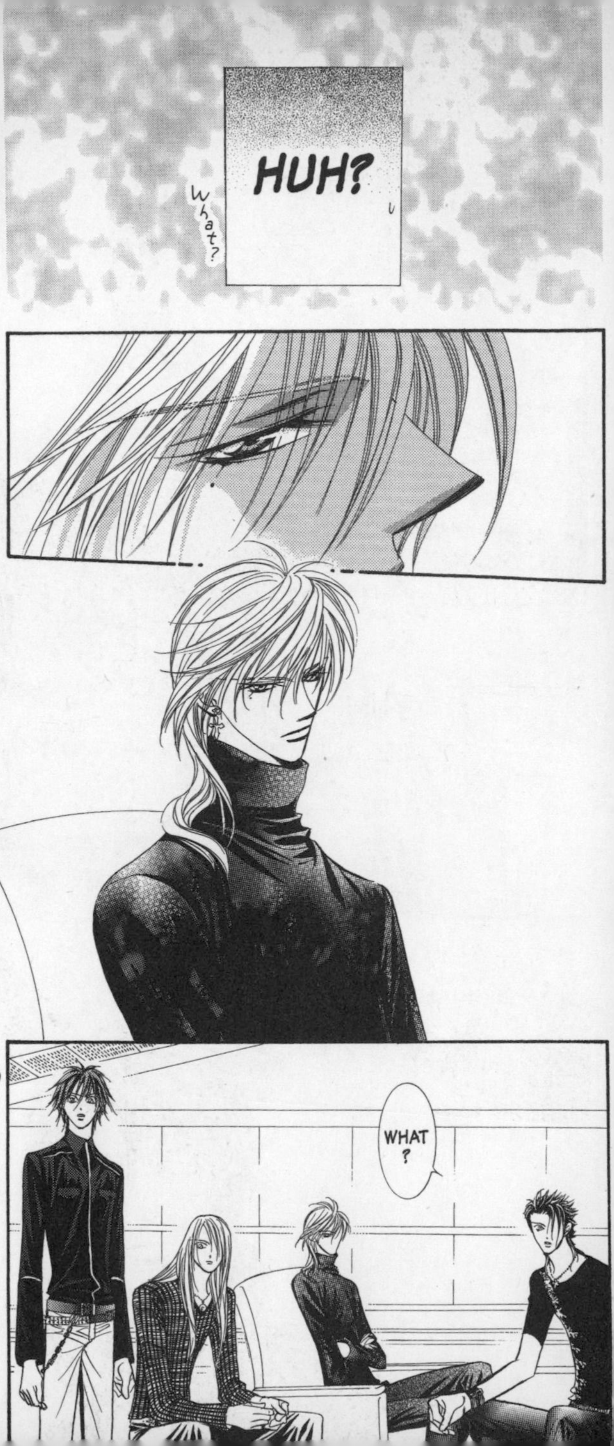
HUH?
What?
WHAT?

Various secret stories about Reino

I made Reino psychic because I felt that an ordinary guy wasn't enough to make Kyoko scared from the bottom of her heart... She can use the grudge Kyokos to cause paranormal phenomena (beat guys she doesn't like to a pulp, or give them a sound thrashing ♪). Kyoko is invincible(?), so there's no way an ordinary guy can win against her...

So the guy had to be someone who has the powers to seal Kyoko's weapon, the grudge Kyokos... ♪ ...Therefore, it was decided that Reino was a psychic quite early on...but what wasn't decided until I was forced to...was his name... until then, I didn't feel any special love for him, and I was wearing out time and energy every chapter, so I found it a bother to think of a name, and I'd just neglected it. (how terrible)

One day, his name was suddenly decided...my editor was the godparent...(a godparent?... ♪) The cue was that I noticed that my editor kept calling him "you-know-who"* when we were discussing the storyboards... ♪(I was also calling him that...)

* "You-know-who" is "Rei no otoko" in Japanese.

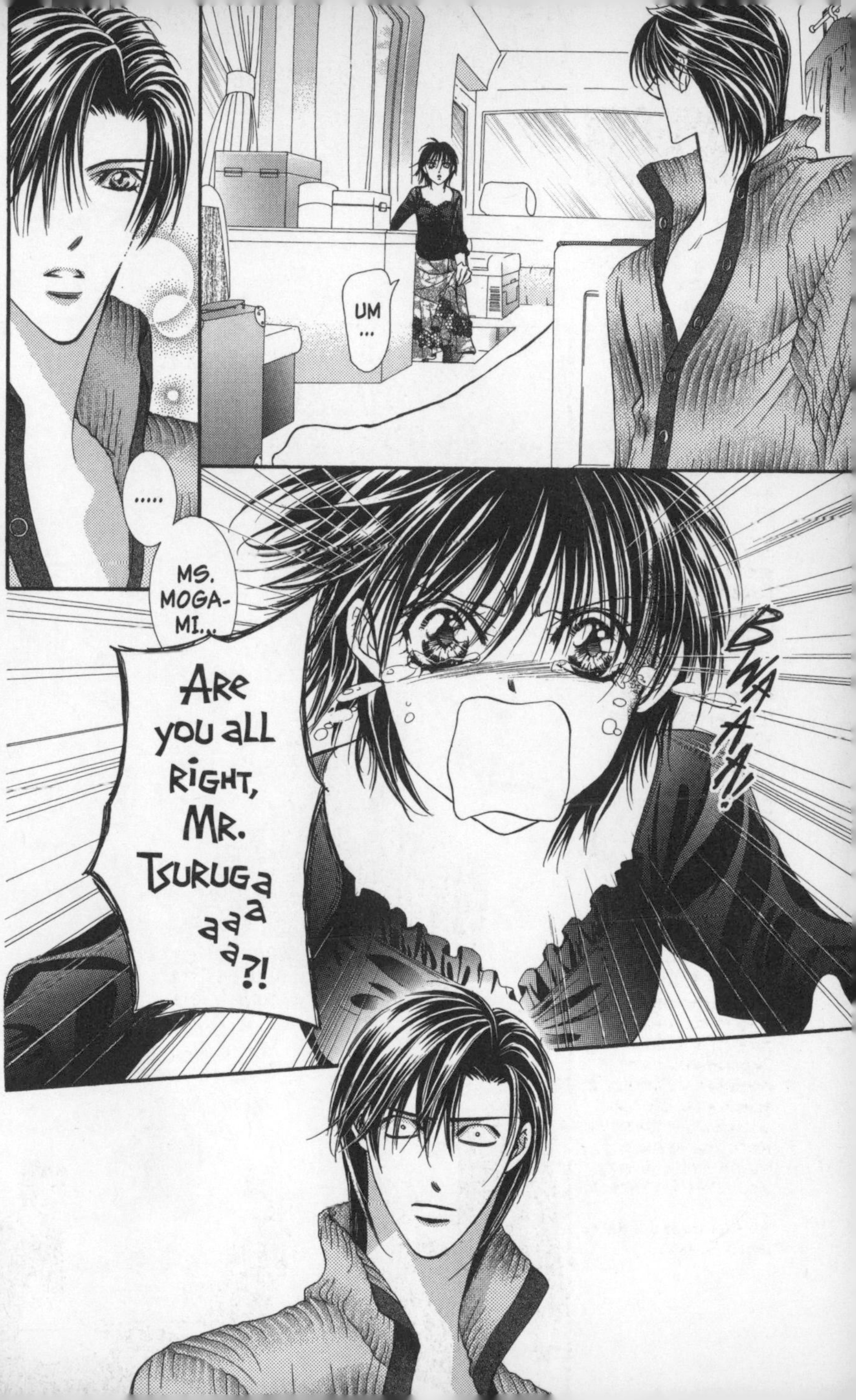
UM ...
.....
MS. MOGA-MI...
BWAAAA!!
Are you all RIGHT, MR. TSURUGaaaaa?!

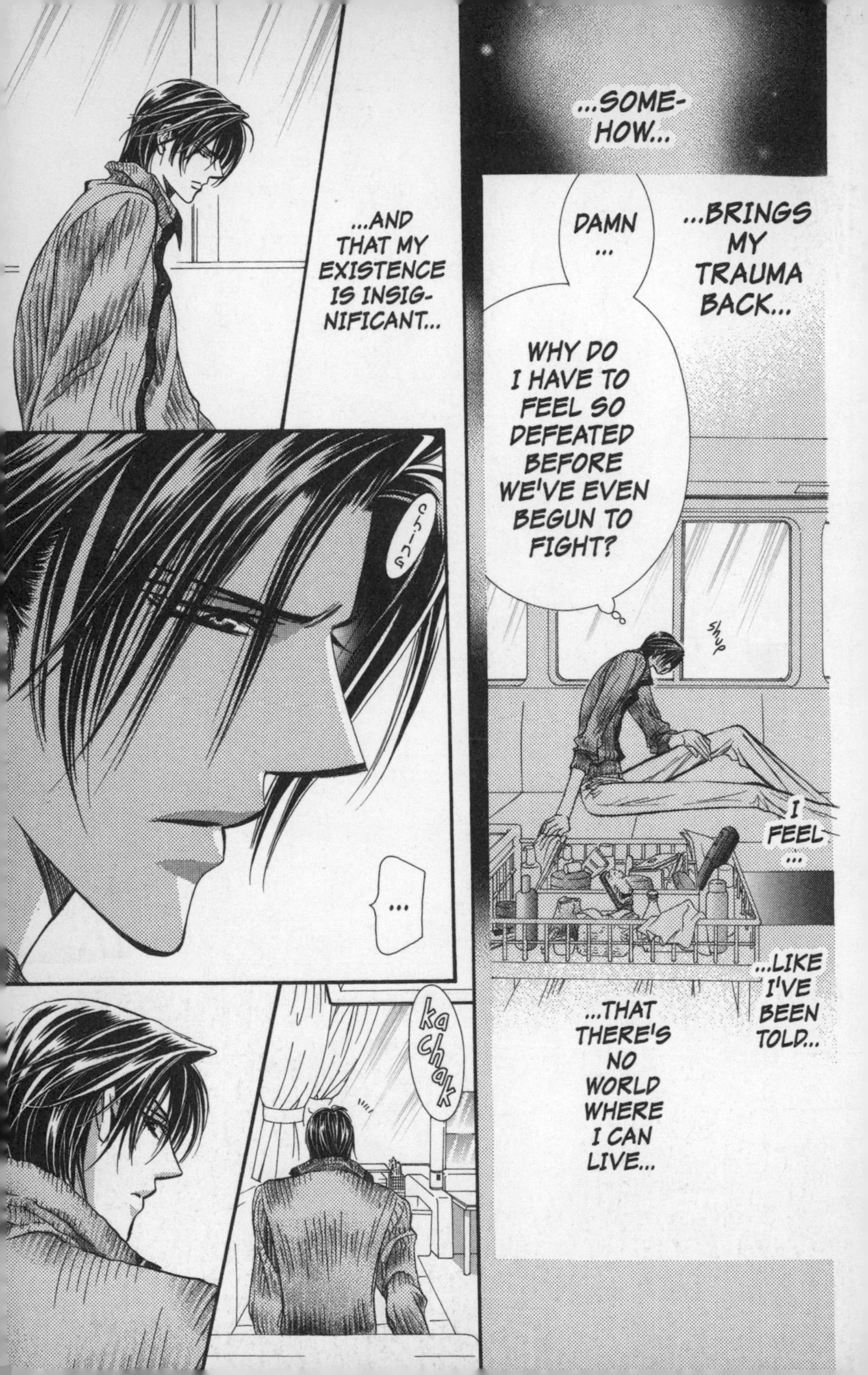
...SOME-HOW...
...BRINGS MY TRAUMA BACK...
DAMN...
WHY DO I HAVE TO FEEL SO DEFEATED BEFORE WE'VE EVEN BEGUN TO FIGHT?
shup
I FEEL...
...LIKE I'VE BEEN TOLD...
...THAT THERE'S NO WORLD WHERE I CAN LIVE...
...AND THAT MY EXISTENCE IS INSIG-NIFICANT...
ching
...
ka chak

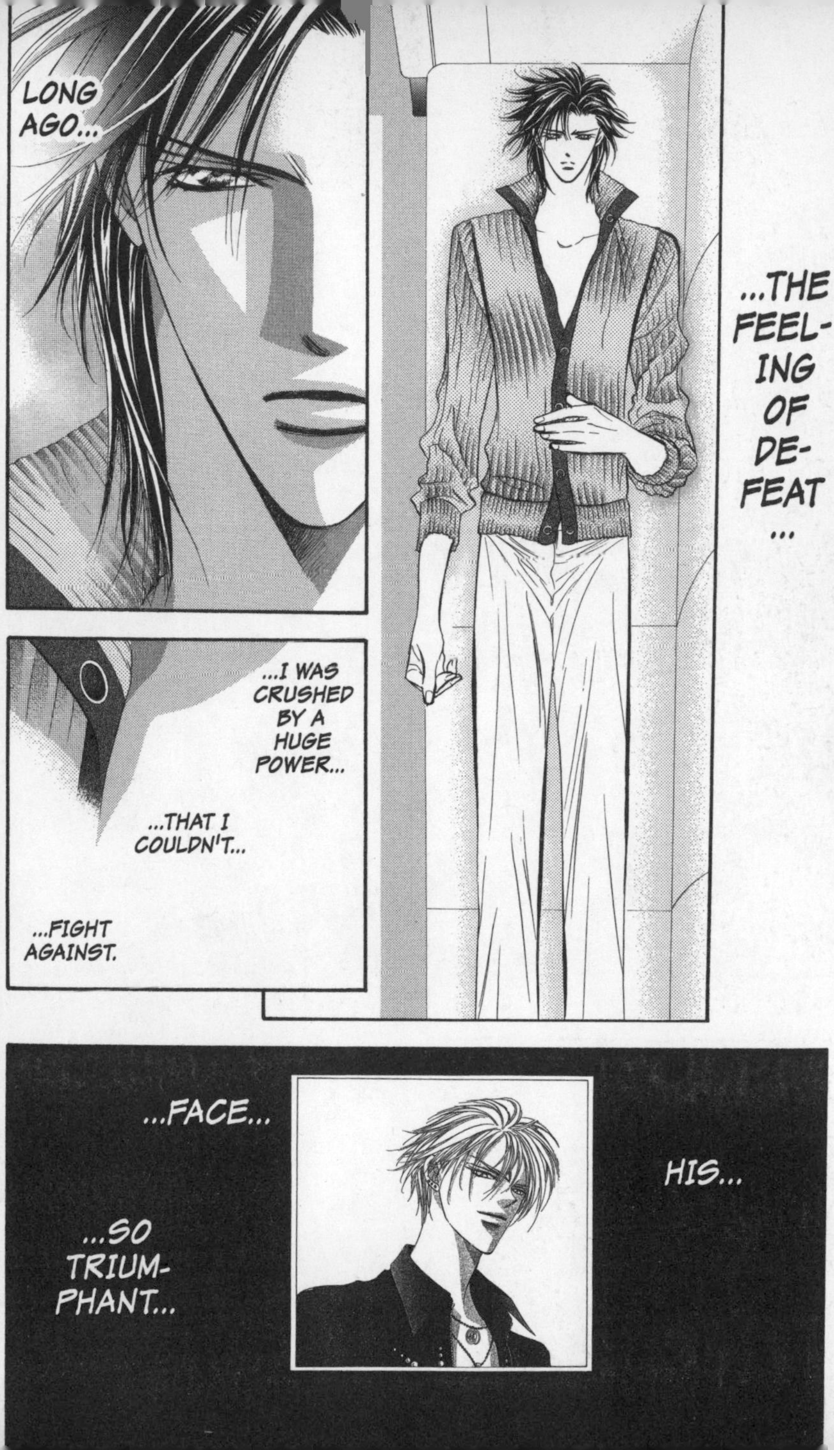
...THE FEEL-ING OF DE-FEAT...
LONG AGO...
...I WAS CRUSHED BY A HUGE POWER...
...THAT I COULDN'T...
...FIGHT AGAINST.
HIS...
...FACE...
...SO TRIUM-PHANT...

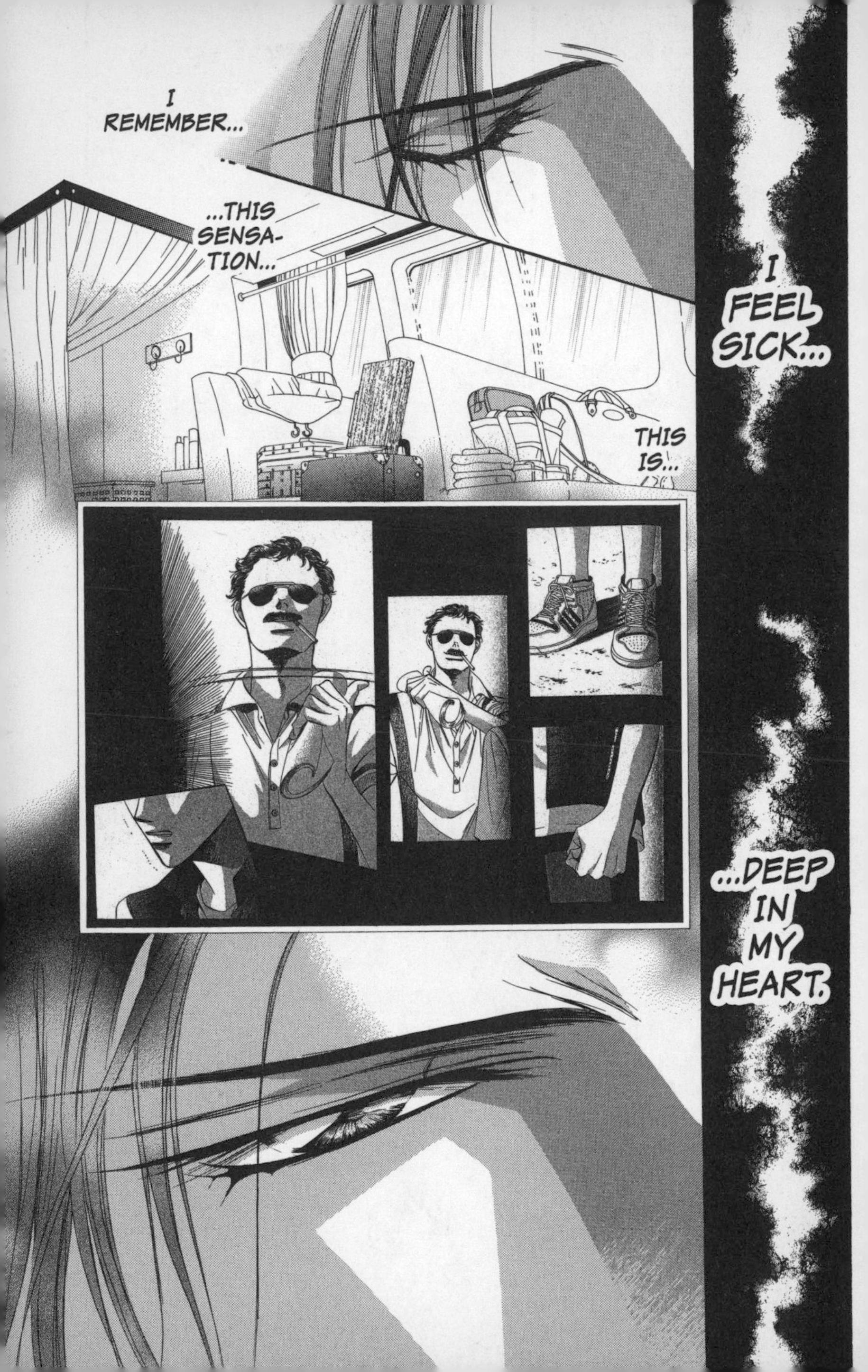
I FEEL SICK...
...DEEP IN MY HEART.
I REMEMBER...
...THIS SENSA-TION...
THIS IS...

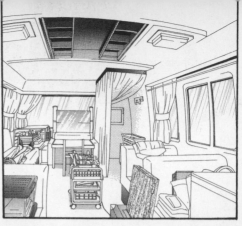

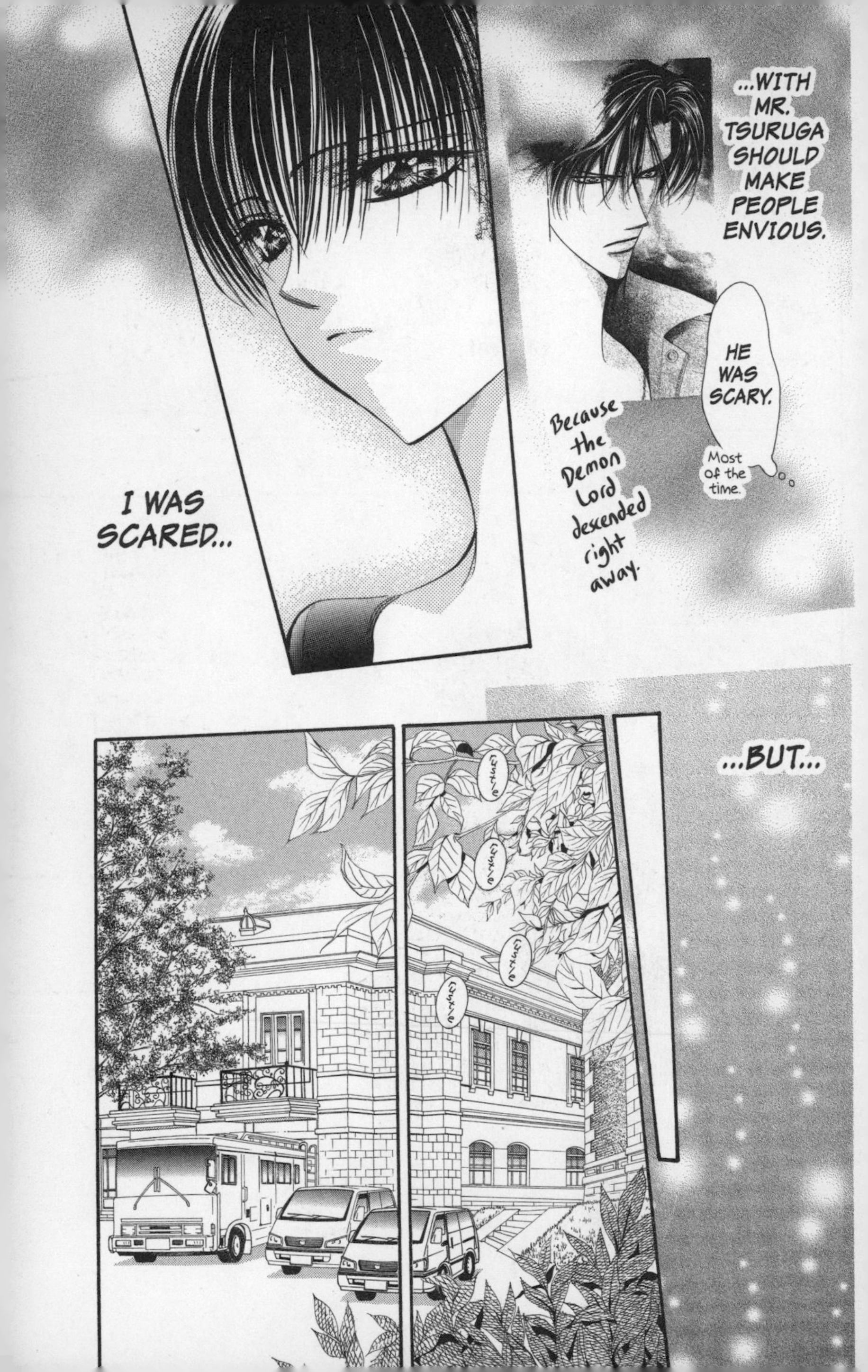
...WITH MR. TSURUGA SHOULD MAKE PEOPLE ENVIOUS.
HE WAS SCARY.
Most of the time.
Because the Demon Lord descended right away.
I WAS SCARED...
...BUT...
Rustle
Rustle
Rustle
Rustle

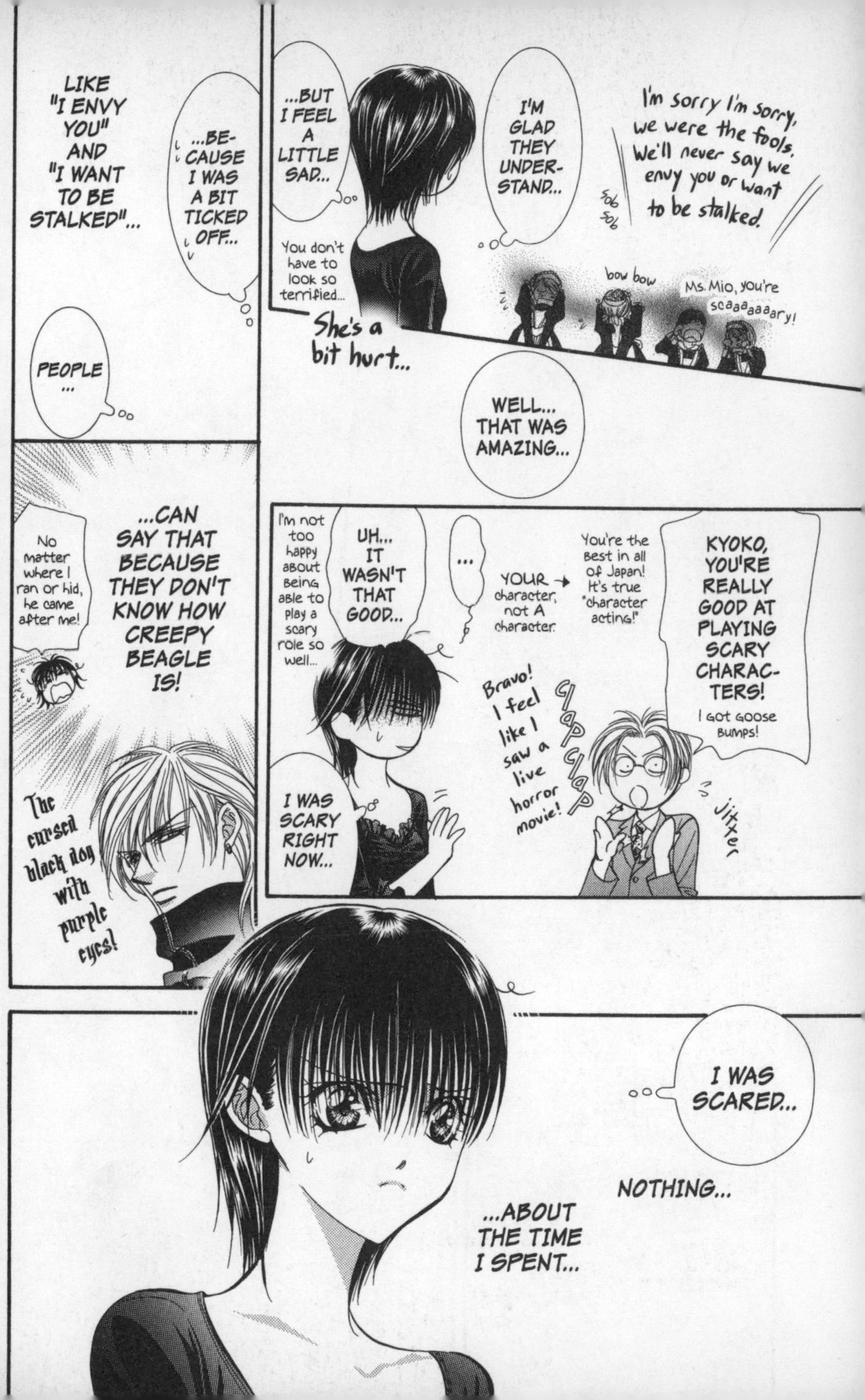
I'M GLAD THEY UNDERSTAND...
I'm sorry I'm sorry, we were the fools. We'll never say we envy you or want to be stalked.
sob sob
bow bow
Ms. Mio, you're scaaaaaaary!
...BUT I FEEL A LITTLE SAD...
You don't have to look so terrified...
She's a bit hurt...
...BECAUSE I WAS A BIT TICKED OFF...
LIKE "I ENVY YOU" AND "I WANT TO BE STALKED"...
PEOPLE ...
WELL... THAT WAS AMAZING...
KYOKO, YOU'RE REALLY GOOD AT PLAYING SCARY CHARACTERS!
I got goose bumps!
jitter
You're the best in all of Japan! It's true "character acting!"
YOUR → character, not A character.
Bravo! I feel like I saw a live horror movie!
clap clap
...
UH... IT WASN'T THAT GOOD...
I'm not too happy about being able to play a scary role so well...
I WAS SCARY RIGHT NOW...
...CAN SAY THAT BECAUSE THEY DON'T KNOW HOW CREEPY BEAGLE IS!
No matter where I ran or hid, he came after me!
The cursed black dog with purple eyes!
I WAS SCARED...
NOTHING...
...ABOUT THE TIME I SPENT...

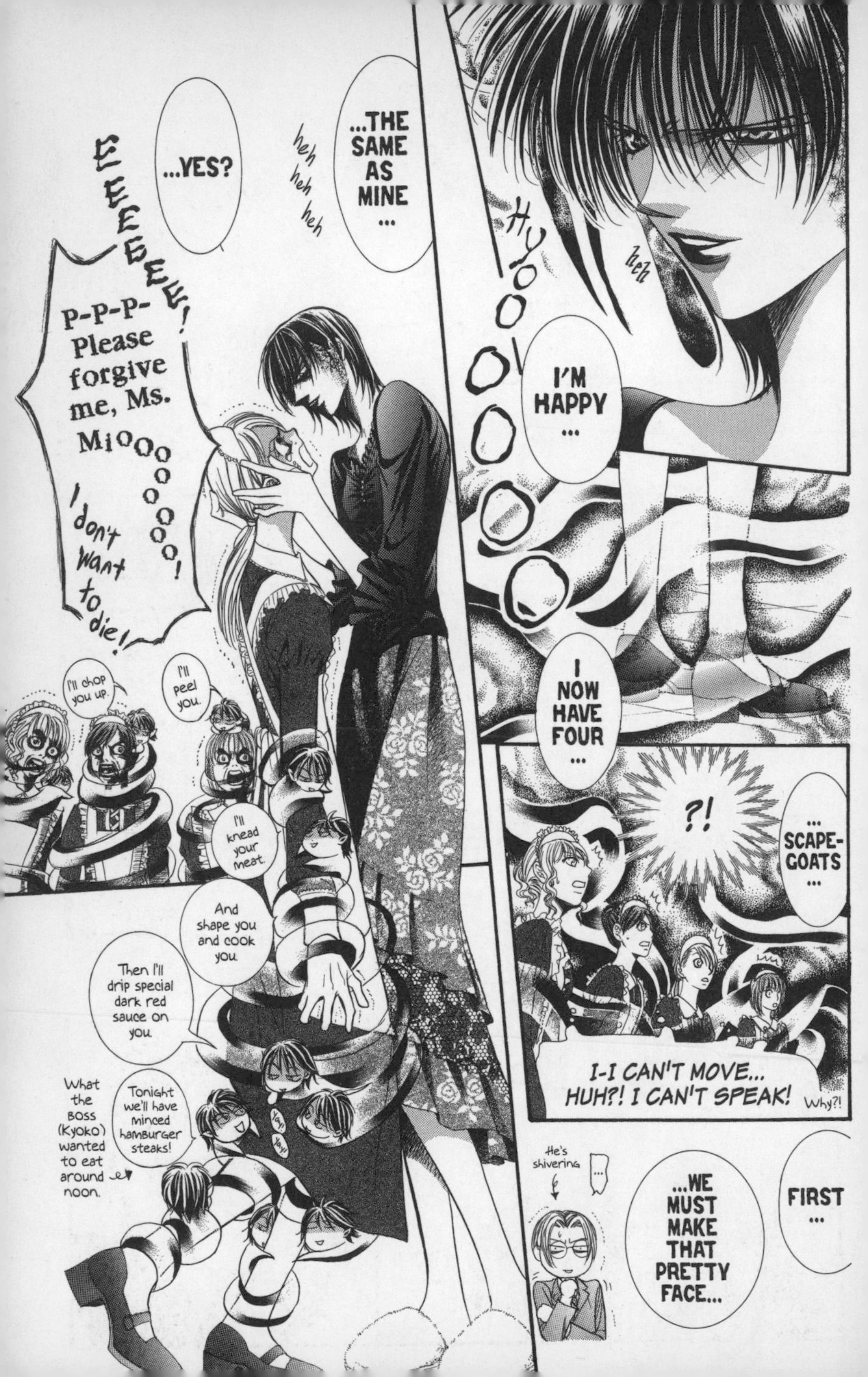
heh
HYOOOOOOOO
I'M HAPPY...
I NOW HAVE FOUR...
...SCAPE-GOATS...
?!
I-I CAN'T MOVE... HUH?! I CAN'T SPEAK!
Why?!
FIRST...
...WE MUST MAKE THAT PRETTY FACE...
He's shivering
...
...THE SAME AS MINE...
heh heh heh
...YES?
EEEEEE!
P-P-P-Please forgive me, Ms. Mioooooooooo! I don't want to die!
I'll peel you.
I'll chop you up.
I'll knead your meat.
And shape you and cook you.
Then I'll drip special dark red sauce on you.
Tonight we'll have minced hamburger steaks!
Yay! Yay!
What the boss (Kyoko) wanted to eat around noon.

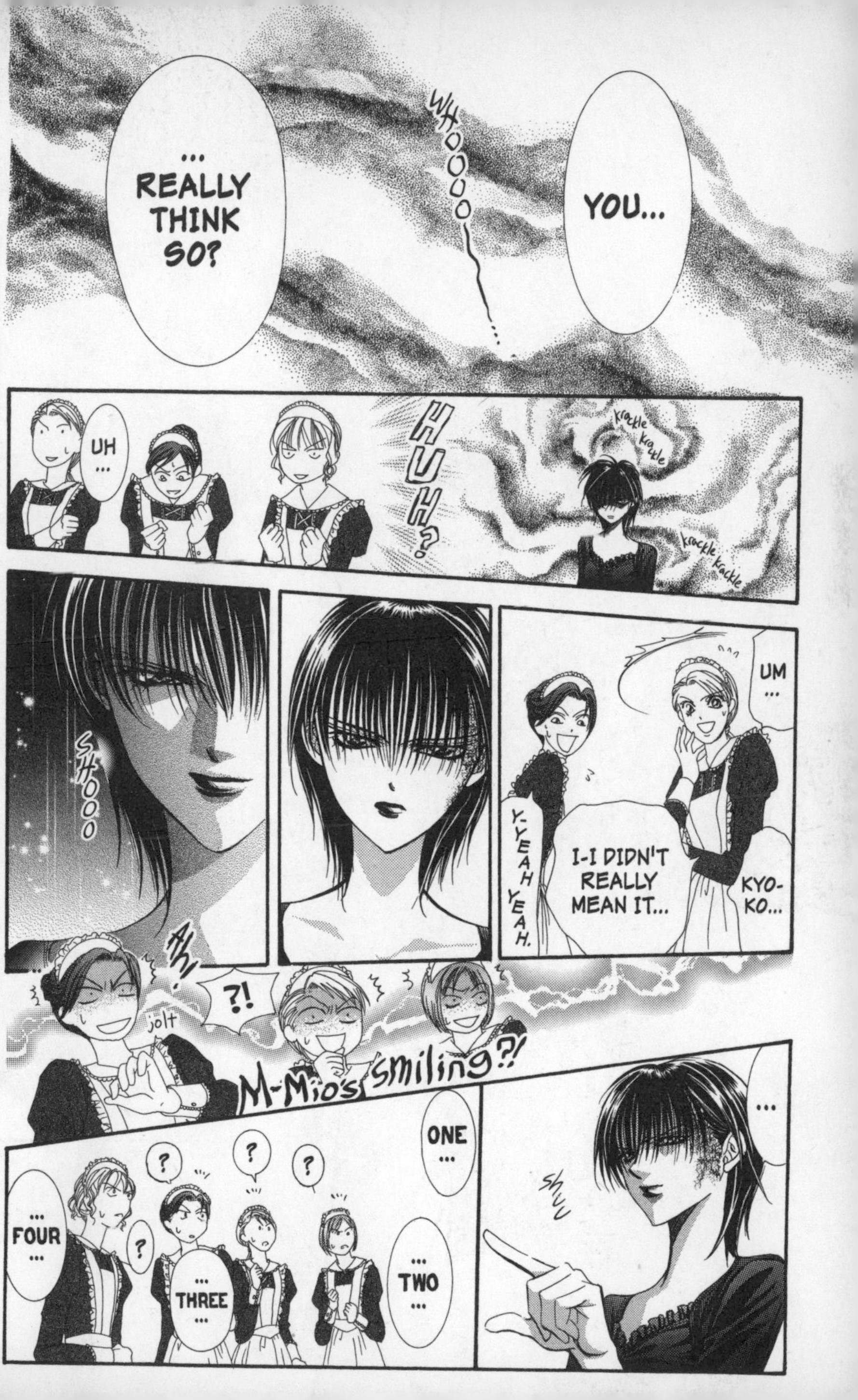
YOU...
WHOOOO
... REALLY THINK SO?
krackle krackle
krackle krackle
HUH?
UH ...
UM ...
KYO-KO...
I-I DIDN'T REALLY MEAN IT...
Y-YEAH YEAH.
SHOOOO
AK!
?!
jolt
M-Mio's smiling?!
...
shu
ONE ...
... TWO ...
?
?
?
... THREE ...
?
... FOUR ...

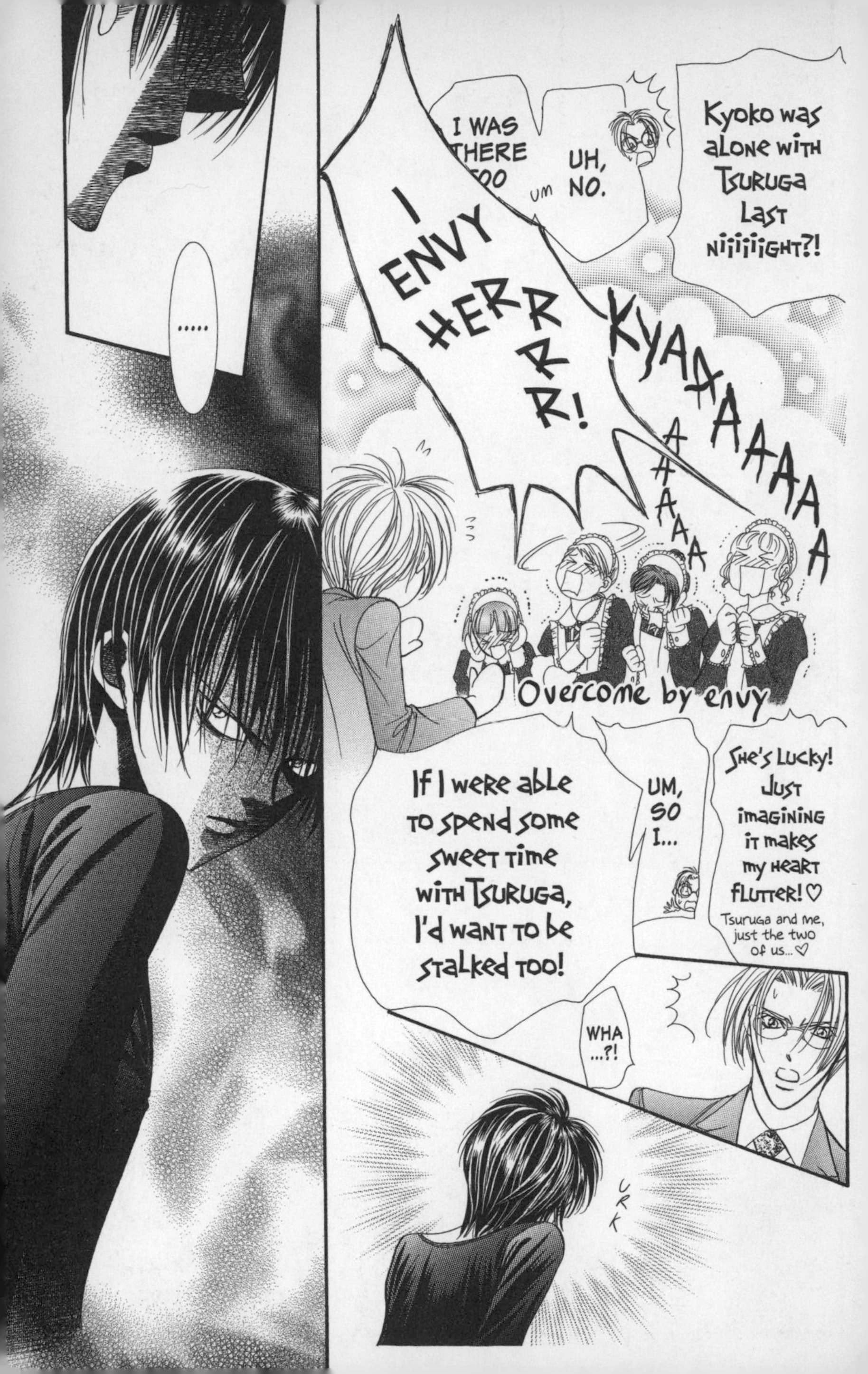
Kyoko was alone with Tsuruga last niiiiiight?!
UH, NO.
um
I WAS THERE TOO
I ENVY HERRRR!
KYAAAAAAAAAA
Overcome by envy
She's lucky! Just imagining it makes my heart flutter! ♡
Tsuruga and me, just the two of us... ♡
UM, SO I...
If I were able to spend some sweet time with Tsuruga, I'd want to be stalked too!
WHA ...?!
URK
.....

Shojo Beat

Skip·Beat!

16
Story & Art by Yoshiki Nakamura

Skip·Beat!
Volume 16

CONTENTS

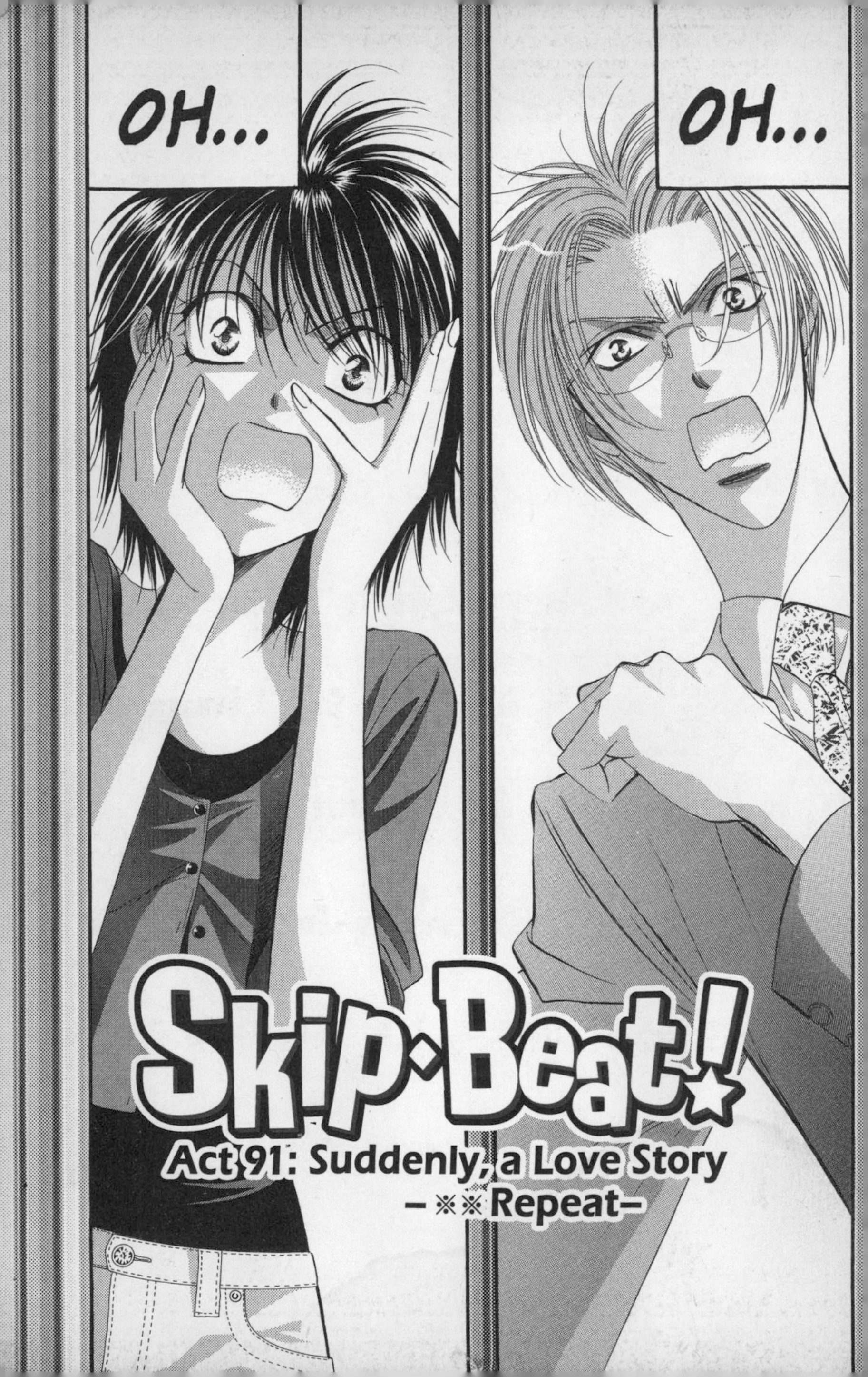
OH...
OH...
Skip·Beat!
Act 91: Suddenly, a Love Story
–※※Repeat–

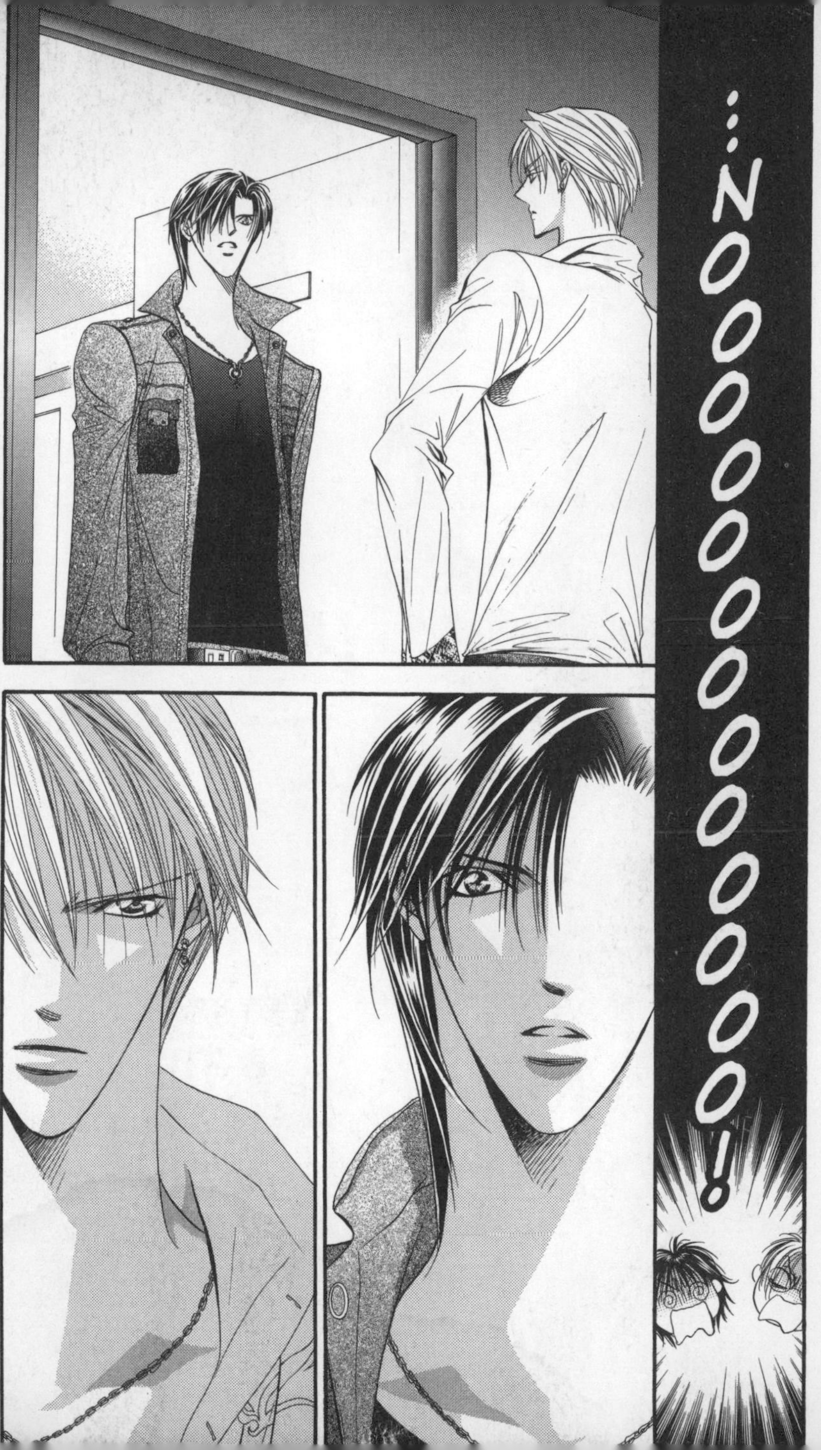
...NOOOOOOOOOOOOO!

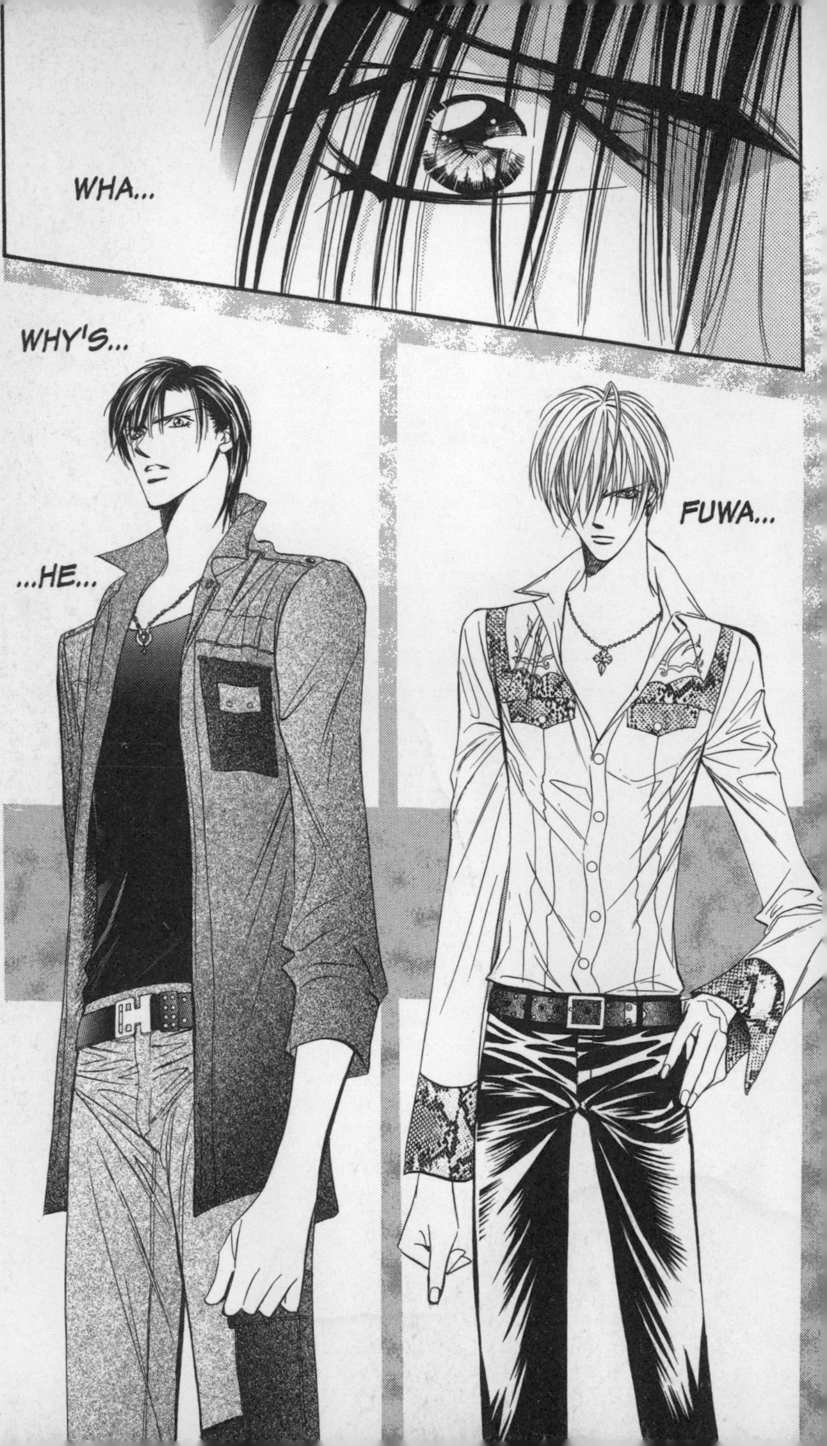
WHA...
FUWA...
WHY'S...
...HE...

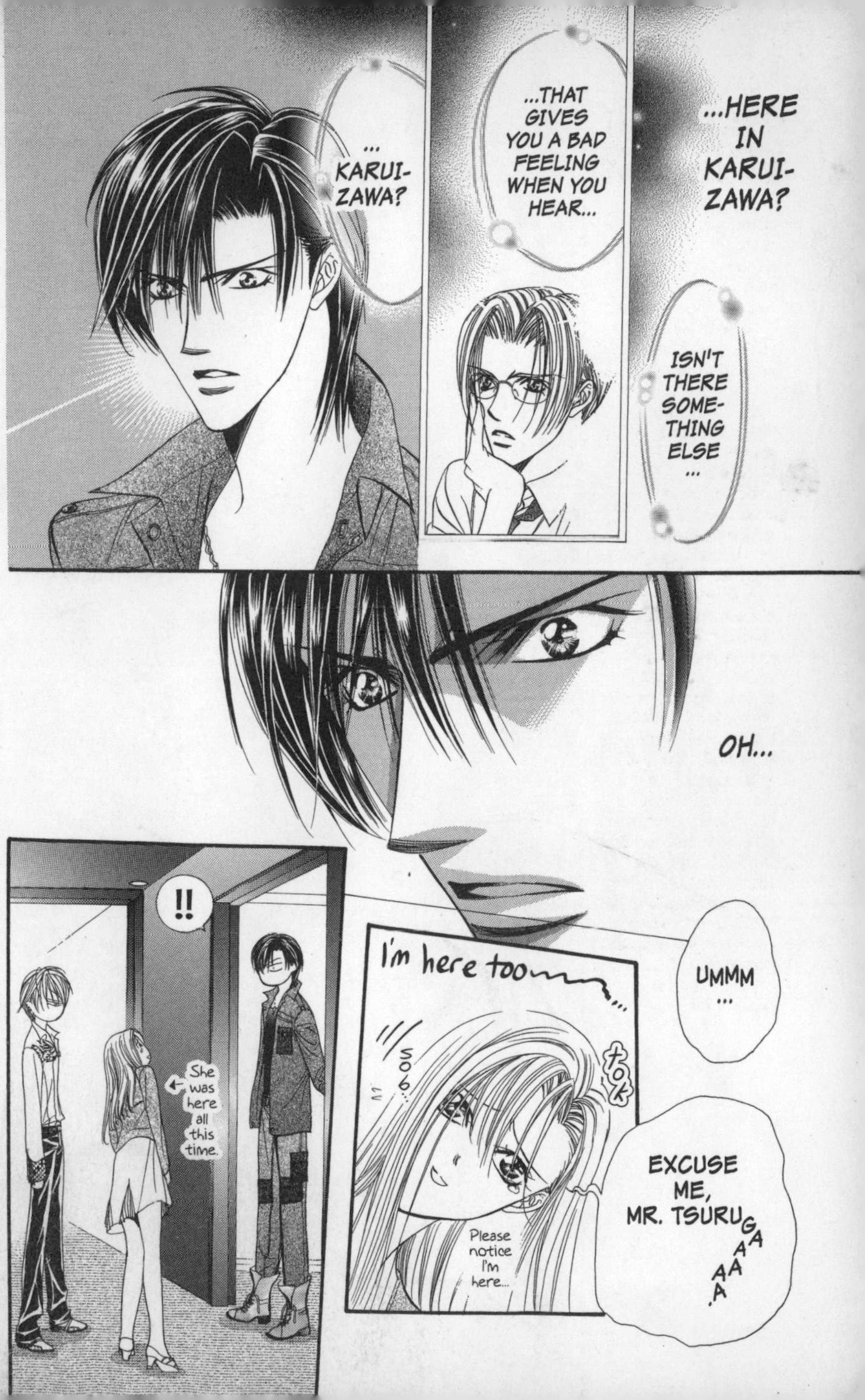
ISN'T THERE SOMETHING ELSE...
...THAT GIVES YOU A BAD FEELING WHEN YOU HEAR...
...HERE IN KARUI-ZAWA?
...KARUI-ZAWA?
OH...
UMMM...
I'm here too...
sob...
tok
EXCUSE ME, MR. TSURUGAAAAA
Please notice I'm here...
!!
She was here all this time.

Wood Stick Recording Studio

In *Skip•Beat*, this studio was created in association with a world-famous drummer who's called Mr. Wood Stick (because he handles his drumsticks unbelievably and miraculously) ← Oh really...

...so in the "Precious Gallery" of this studio (this is where Kyoko says "There're lots of antique-looking instruments" in Act 84), instruments that Mr. Wood Stick received from musician friends all over the world (as tokens of their friendship) are displayed. With tight security of course. For collectors, this would be a treasure hoard.. Maybe VIE GHOUL's Miroku looks up to Mr. Wood Stick, since he's a drummer too...maybe...is he that sort of guy?...no... well...anyway... There is a studio called Woodstock Recording Studio in Karuizawa. I most humbly borrowed the name from them.

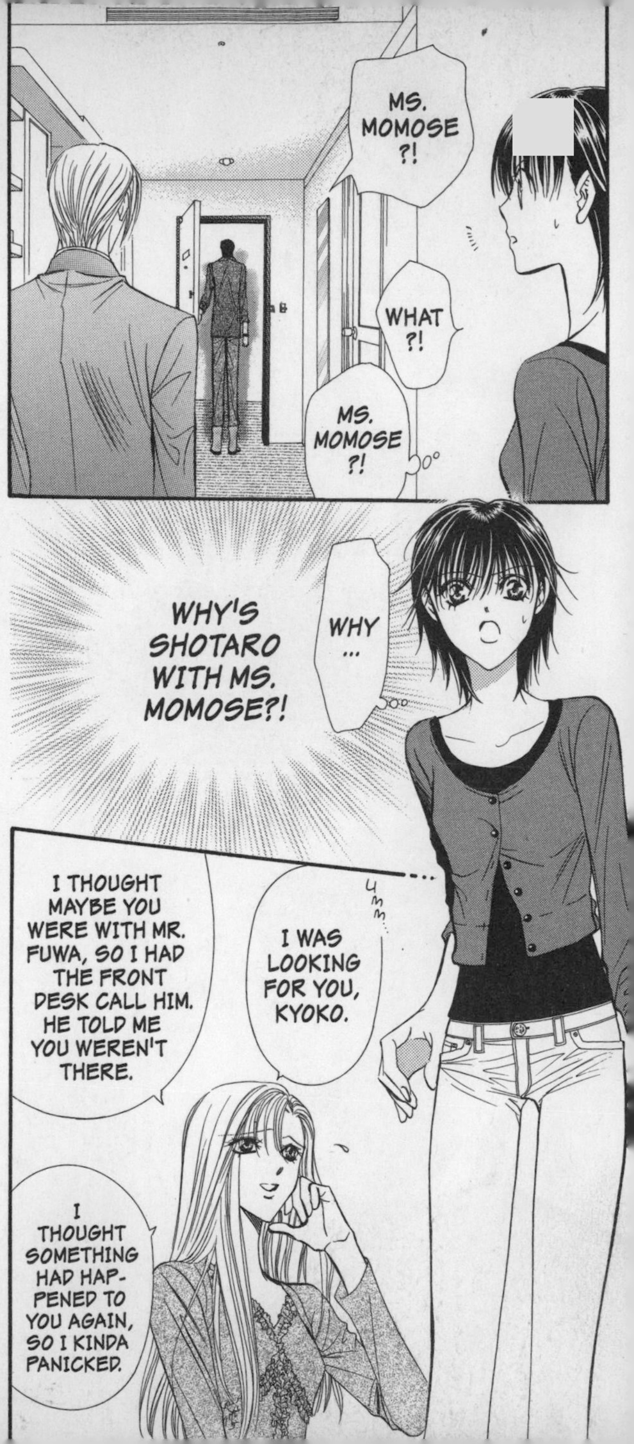
MS. MOMOSE ?!
WHAT ?!
MS. MOMOSE ?!
WHY ...
WHY'S SHOTARO WITH MS. MOMOSE?!
I WAS LOOKING FOR YOU, KYOKO.
I THOUGHT MAYBE YOU WERE WITH MR. FUWA, SO I HAD THE FRONT DESK CALL HIM. HE TOLD ME YOU WEREN'T THERE.
Umm...
I THOUGHT SOMETHING HAD HAPPENED TO YOU AGAIN, SO I KINDA PANICKED.

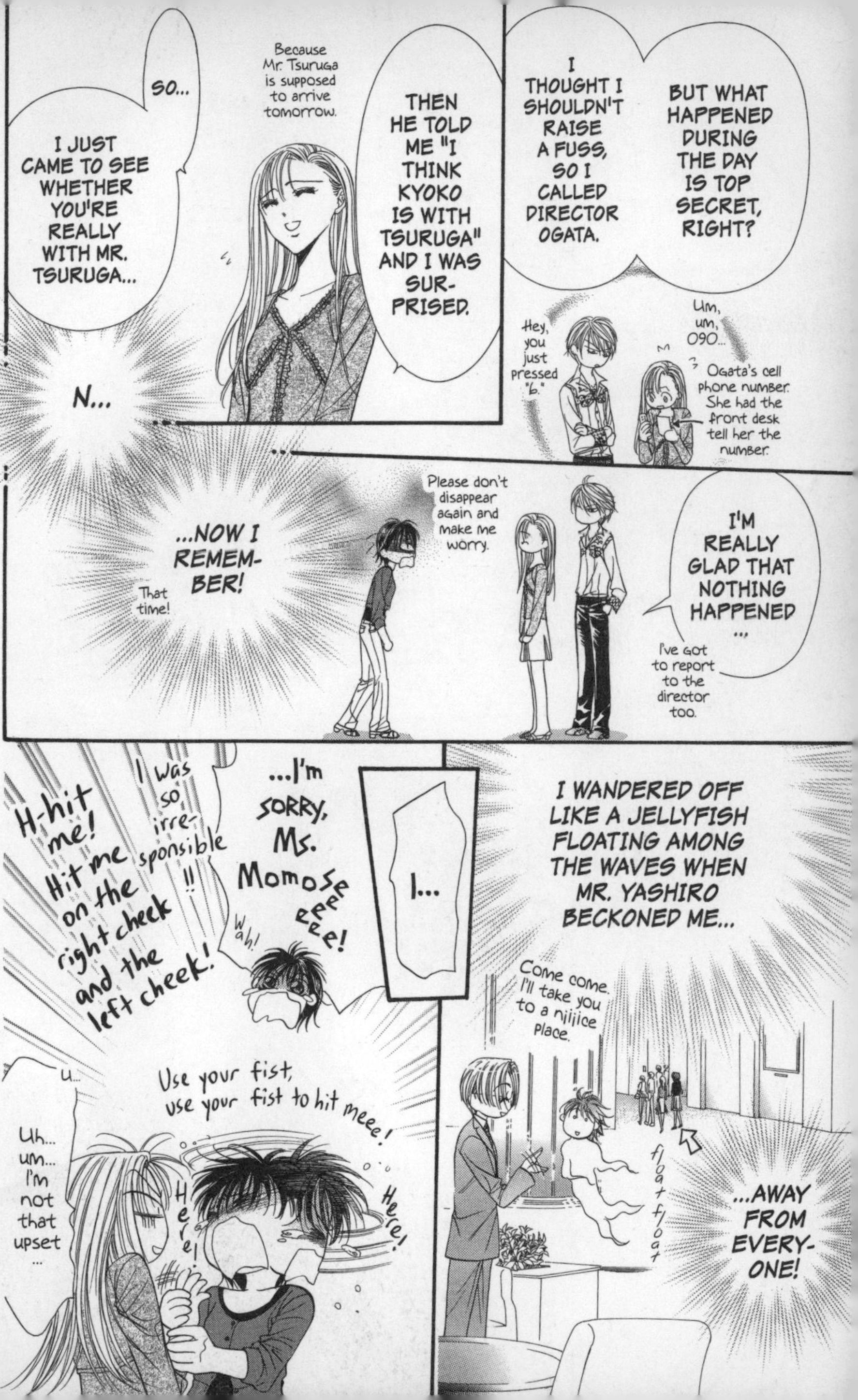
BUT WHAT HAPPENED DURING THE DAY IS TOP SECRET, RIGHT?
I THOUGHT I SHOULDN'T RAISE A FUSS, SO I CALLED DIRECTOR OGATA.
Um, um, 090...
Ogata's cell phone number. She had the front desk tell her the number.
Hey, you just pressed "6."
THEN HE TOLD ME "I THINK KYOKO IS WITH TSURUGA" AND I WAS SURPRISED.
Because Mr. Tsuruga is supposed to arrive tomorrow.
SO...
I JUST CAME TO SEE WHETHER YOU'RE REALLY WITH MR. TSURUGA...
N...
I'M REALLY GLAD THAT NOTHING HAPPENED...
I've got to report to the director too.
Please don't disappear again and make me worry.
...NOW I REMEMBER!
That time!
I WANDERED OFF LIKE A JELLYFISH FLOATING AMONG THE WAVES WHEN MR. YASHIRO BECKONED ME...
Come come. I'll take you to a niiiice place.
float float
...AWAY FROM EVERYONE!
I...
...I'm SORRY, Ms. Momoseeeeee!
Wah!
I was so irresponsible!!
H-hit me! Hit me on the right cheek and the left cheek!
Use your fist, use your fist to hit meee!
Here! Here!
u...
Uh... um... I'm not that upset...

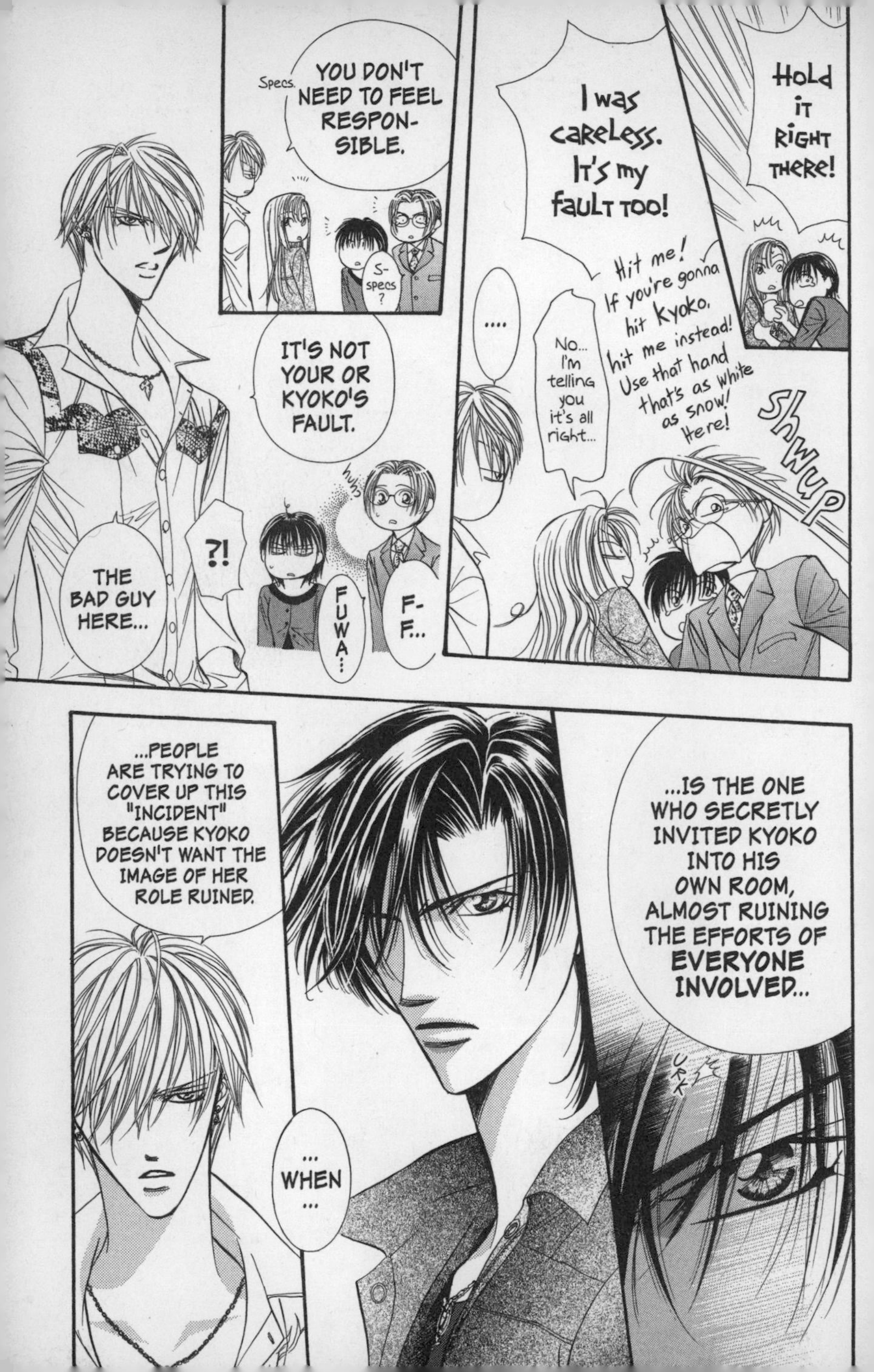
Hold it right there!
I was careless. It's my fault too!
Hit me! If you're gonna hit Kyoko, hit me instead! Use that hand that's as white as snow! Here!
SHWUP
No... I'm telling you it's all right...
....
Specs.
YOU DON'T NEED TO FEEL RESPON-SIBLE.
S-specs?
IT'S NOT YOUR OR KYOKO'S FAULT.
huh
F-F...
FUWA...
?!
THE BAD GUY HERE...
...IS THE ONE WHO SECRETLY INVITED KYOKO INTO HIS OWN ROOM, ALMOST RUINING THE EFFORTS OF EVERYONE INVOLVED...
URK
...WHEN...
...PEOPLE ARE TRYING TO COVER UP THIS "INCIDENT" BECAUSE KYOKO DOESN'T WANT THE IMAGE OF HER ROLE RUINED.

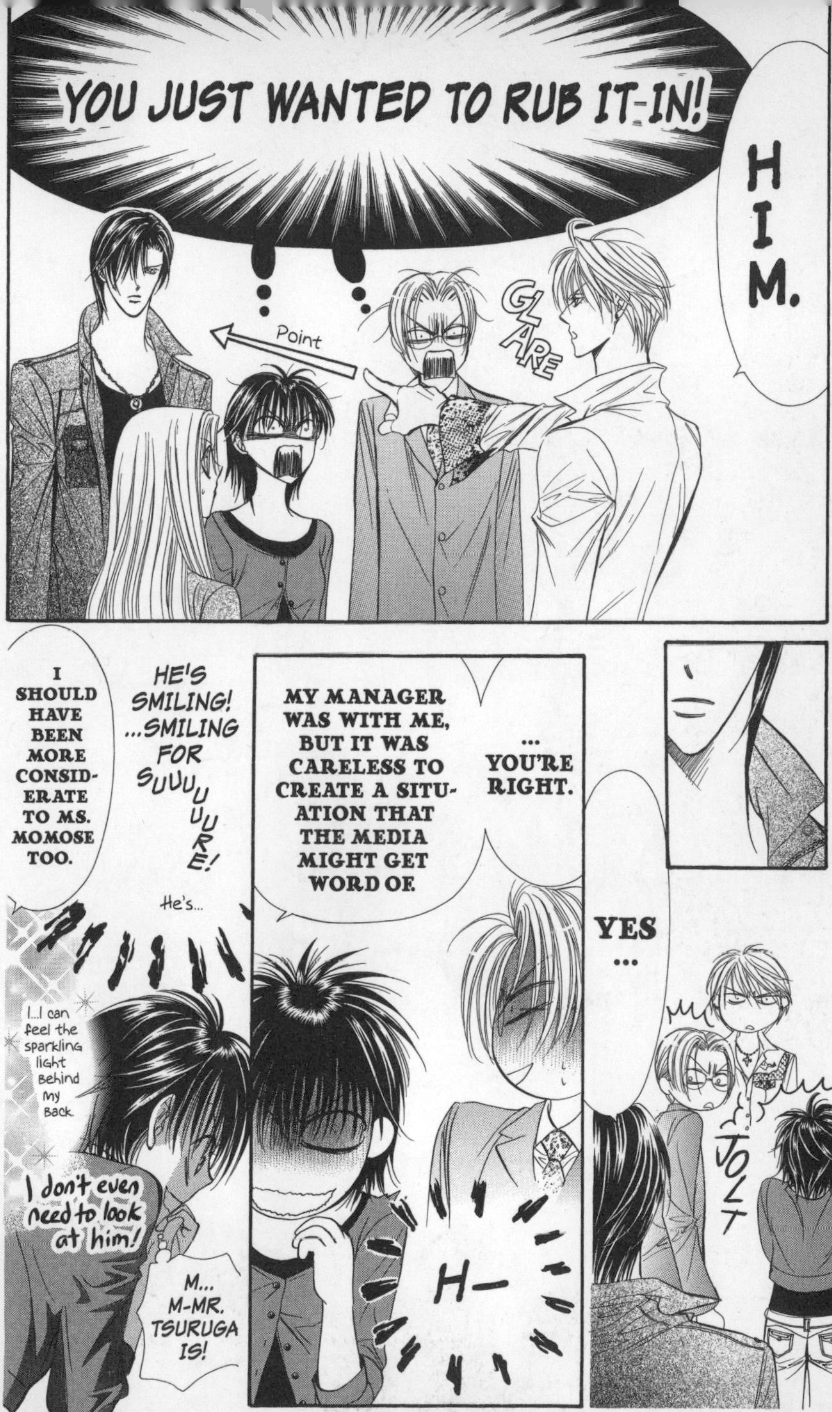
HIM.
YOU JUST WANTED TO RUB IT-IN!
GLARE
Point
YES ...
JOLT
... YOU'RE RIGHT.
MY MANAGER WAS WITH ME, BUT IT WAS CARELESS TO CREATE A SITUATION THAT THE MEDIA MIGHT GET WORD OF.
H—
I SHOULD HAVE BEEN MORE CONSIDERATE TO MS. MOMOSE TOO.
HE'S SMILING! ...SMILING FOR SUUUUUURE!
He's...
I...I can feel the sparkling light behind my back.
I don't even need to look at him!
M... M-MR. TSURUGA IS!

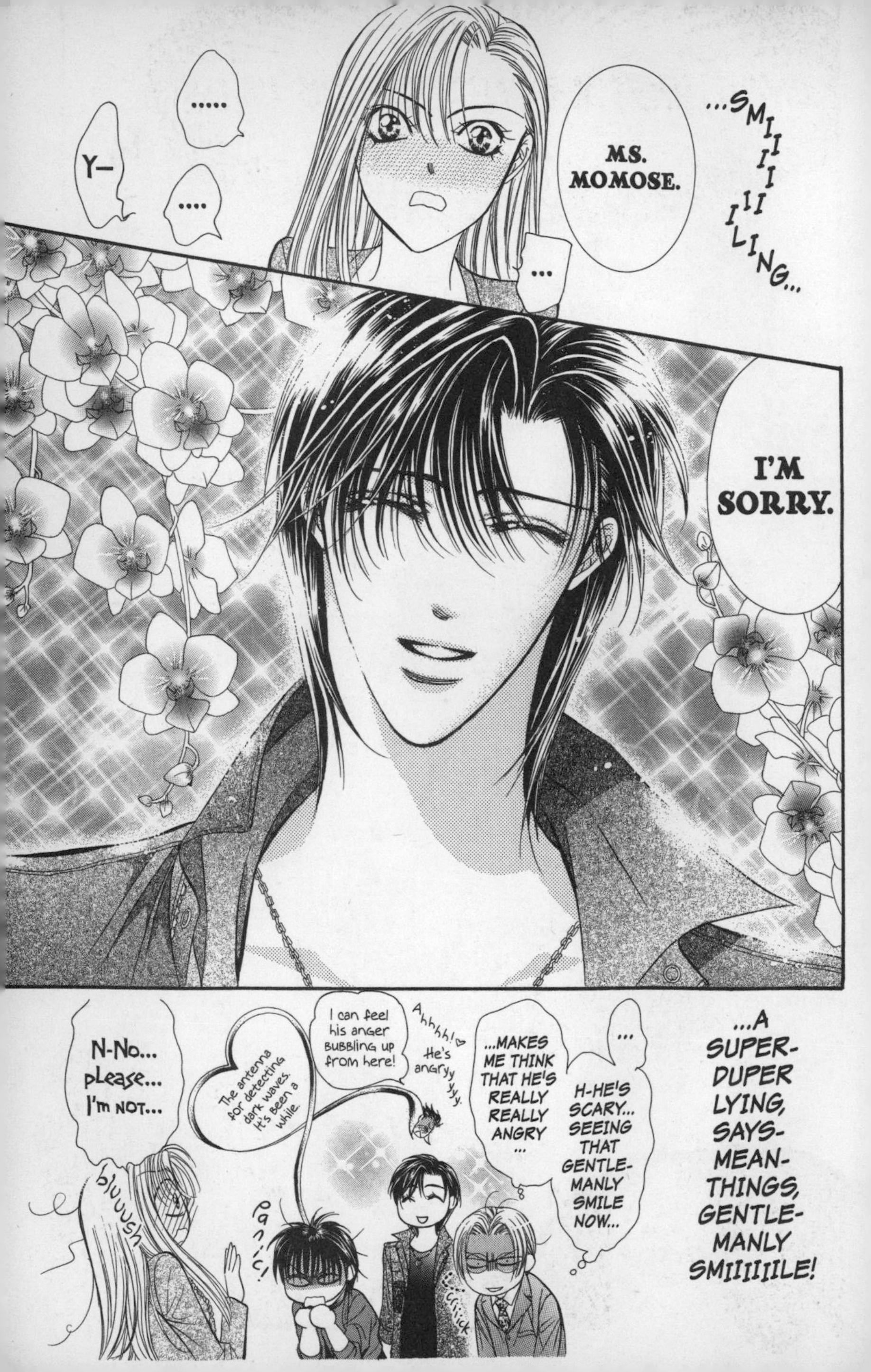
...SMIIIIIIIIILING...
MS. MOMOSE.
...
......
....
Y—
I'M SORRY.
...A SUPER-DUPER LYING, SAYS-MEAN-THINGS, GENTLEMANLY SMIIIIIIILE!
...
H-HE'S SCARY... SEEING THAT GENTLEMANLY SMILE NOW...
...MAKES ME THINK THAT HE'S REALLY REALLY ANGRY ...
Ahhhh!♡ He's angryyyyy.
I can feel his anger bubbling up from here!
The antenna for detecting dark waves. It's been a while.
N-No... please... I'm NOT...
bluuush
panic!
criiick

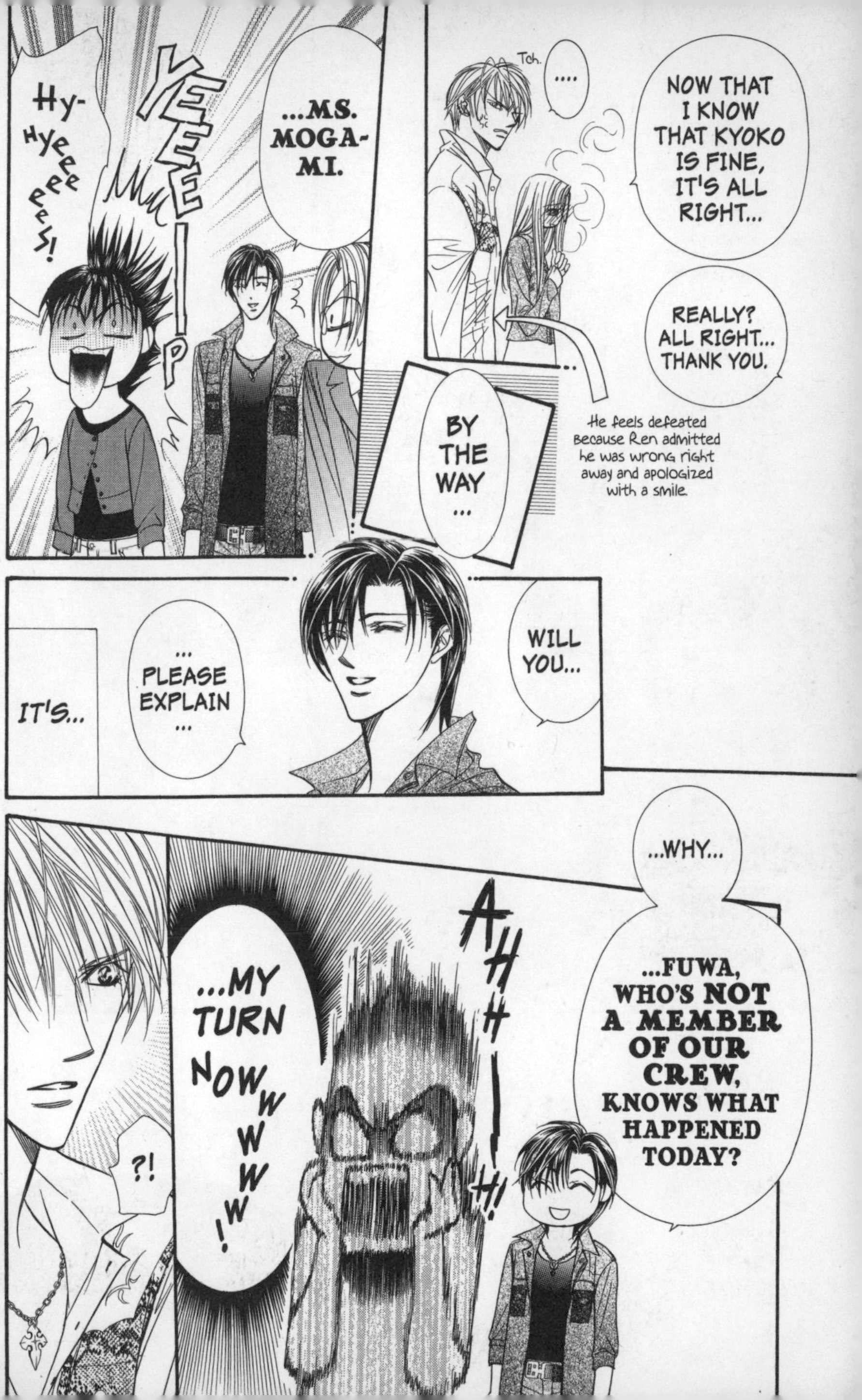

Tch.
....
NOW THAT I KNOW THAT KYOKO IS FINE, IT'S ALL RIGHT...
REALLY? ALL RIGHT... THANK YOU.
He feels defeated because Ren admitted he was wrong right away and apologized with a smile.
BY THE WAY...
...MS. MOGA-MI.
YEEEEIP
Hy- Hyeeeeeees!
WILL YOU...
...PLEASE EXPLAIN...
IT'S...
...WHY...
...FUWA, WHO'S NOT A MEMBER OF OUR CREW, KNOWS WHAT HAPPENED TODAY?
AHHH!!
...MY TURN NOWWWWW!
?!

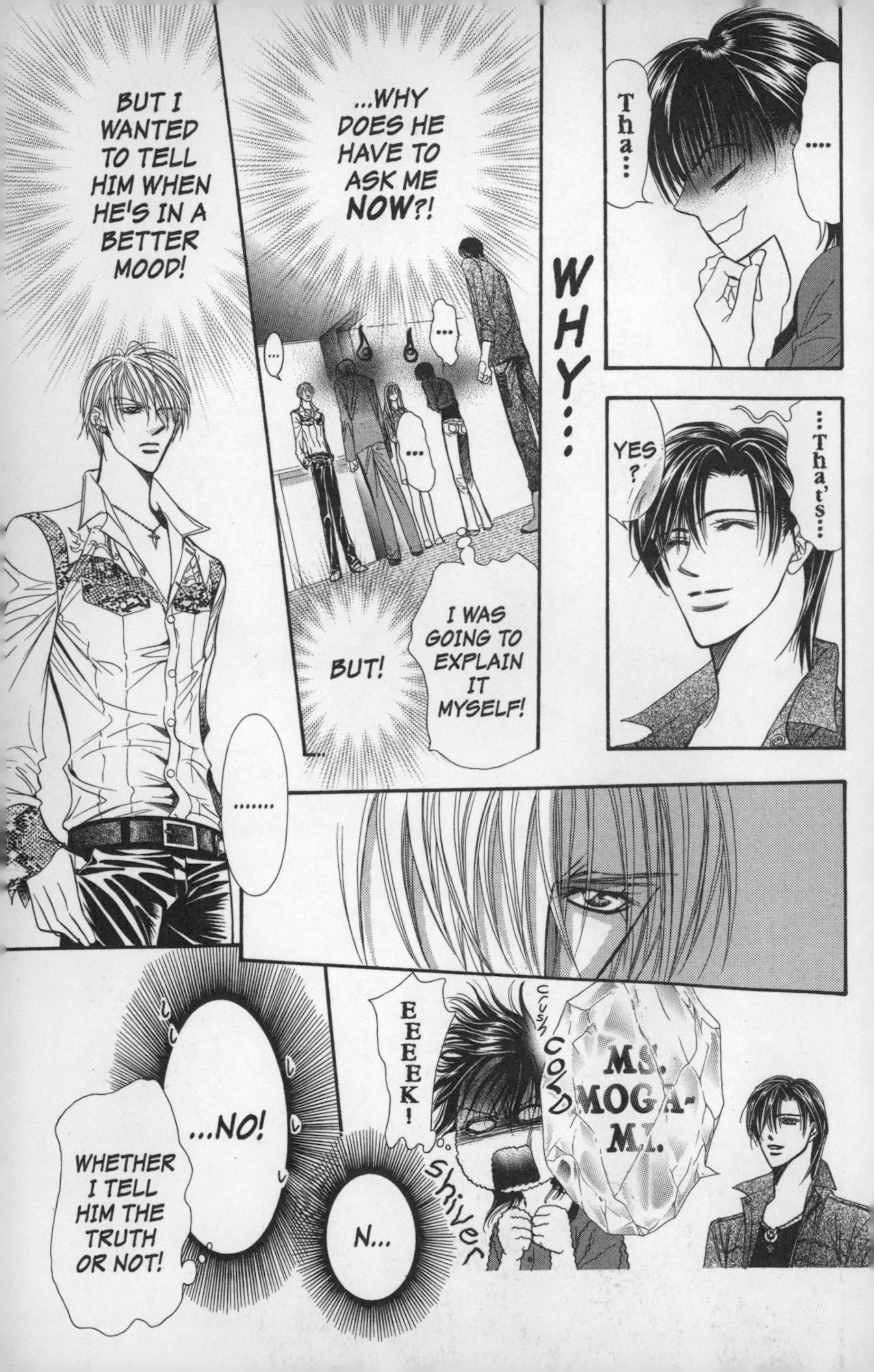
....
Tha...
...That's...
YES?
WHY...
...WHY DOES HE HAVE TO ASK ME NOW?!
...
...
...
I WAS GOING TO EXPLAIN IT MYSELF!
BUT!
...
BUT I WANTED TO TELL HIM WHEN HE'S IN A BETTER MOOD!
....
MS. MOGA-MI.
crush
COLD
EEEEK!
shiver
...NO!
N...
WHETHER I TELL HIM THE TRUTH OR NOT!

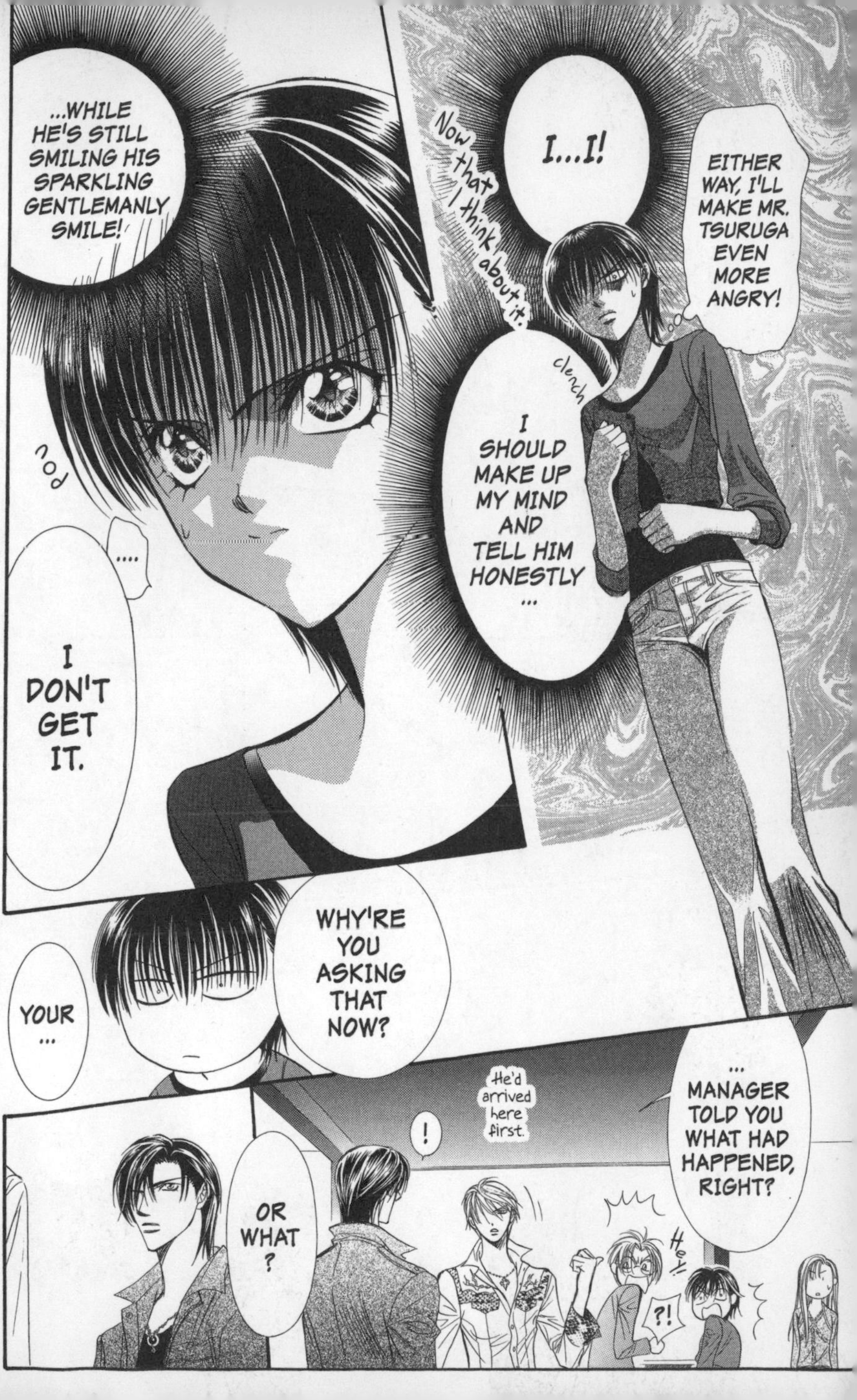
EITHER WAY, I'LL MAKE MR. TSURUGA EVEN MORE ANGRY!
I...I!
Now that I think about it.
clench
I SHOULD MAKE UP MY MIND AND TELL HIM HONESTLY...
...WHILE HE'S STILL SMILING HIS SPARKLING GENTLEMANLY SMILE!
pou
....
I DON'T GET IT.
WHY'RE YOU ASKING THAT NOW?
YOUR...
...MANAGER TOLD YOU WHAT HAD HAPPENED, RIGHT?
He'd arrived here first.
Hey!
?!
!
OR WHAT?

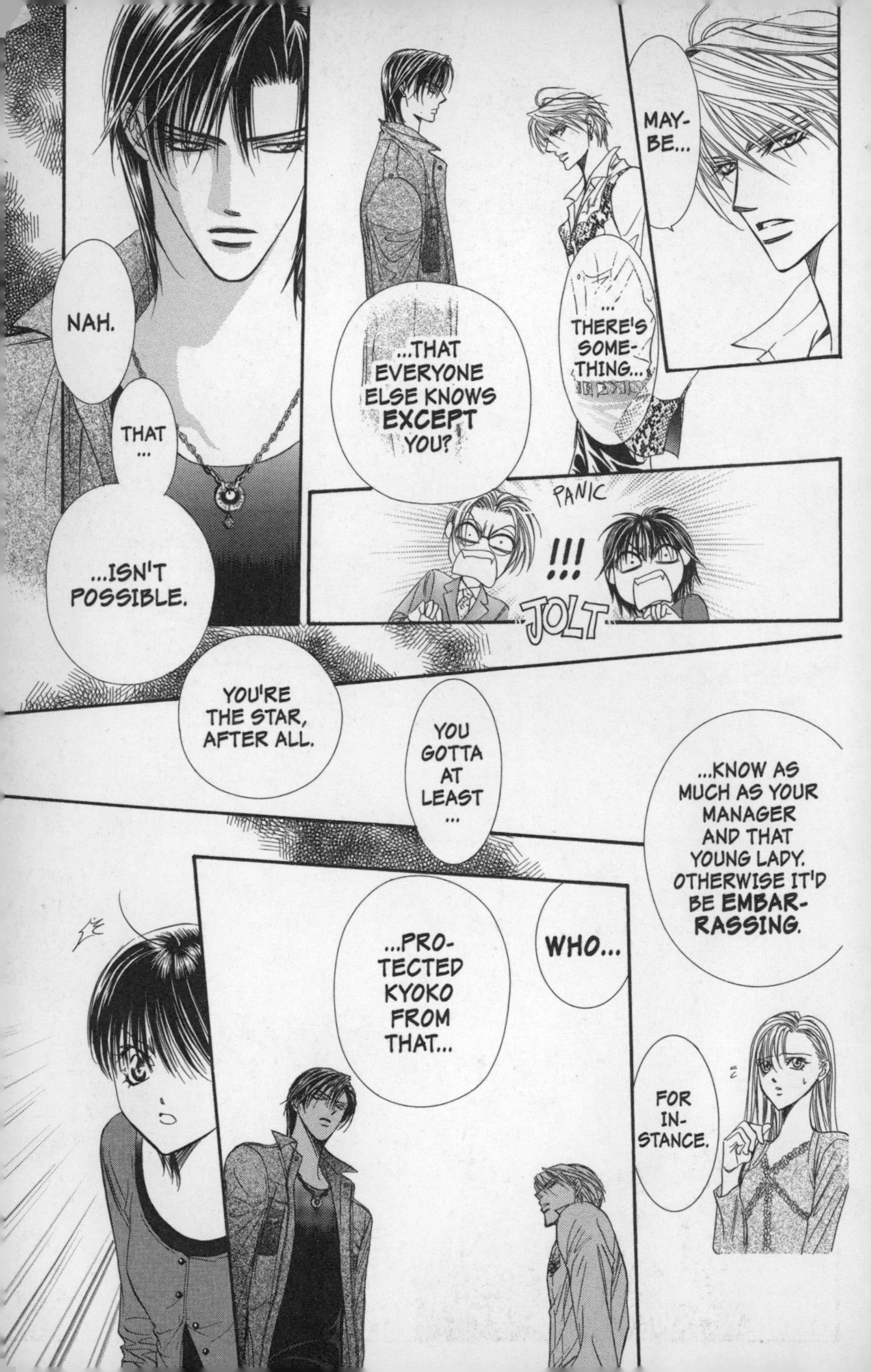
MAY-BE...
...THERE'S SOME-THING...
...THAT EVERYONE ELSE KNOWS EXCEPT YOU?
PANIC
!!!
JOLT
NAH.
THAT...
...ISN'T POSSIBLE.
YOU'RE THE STAR, AFTER ALL.
YOU GOTTA AT LEAST...
...KNOW AS MUCH AS YOUR MANAGER AND THAT YOUNG LADY. OTHERWISE IT'D BE EMBAR-RASSING.
FOR IN-STANCE.
WHO...
...PRO-TECTED KYOKO FROM THAT...

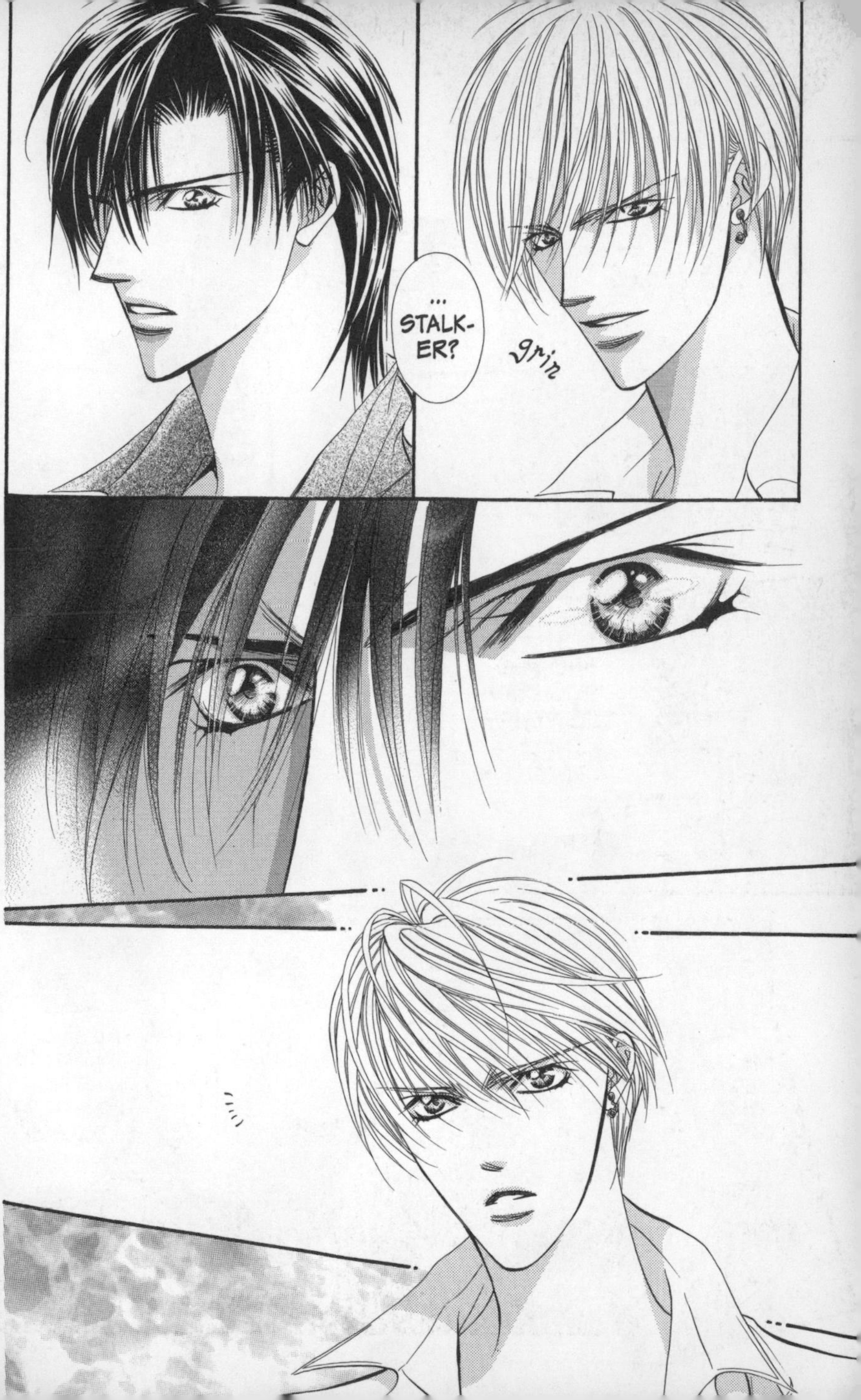
... STALK-ER?
grin

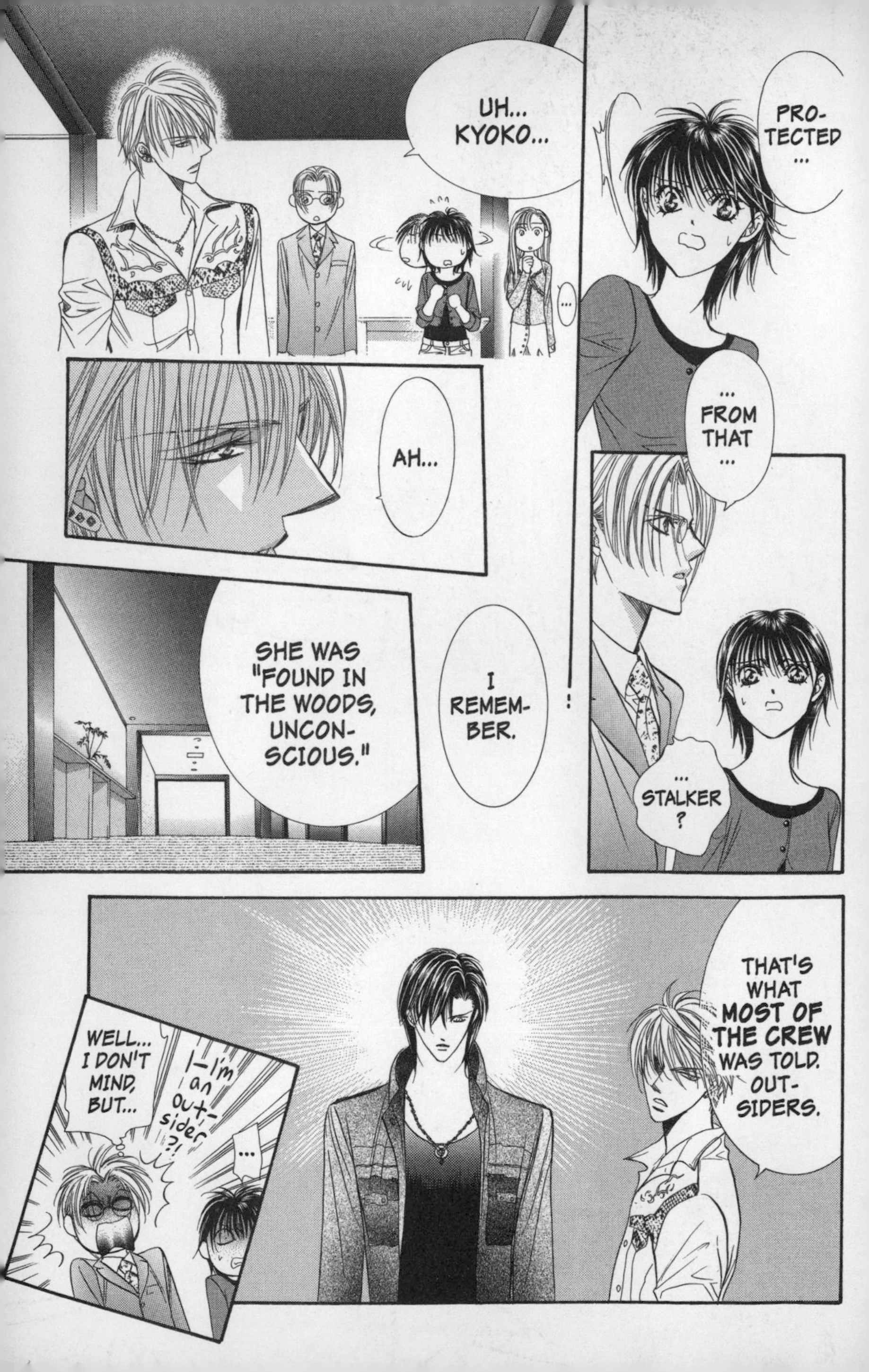
PRO-TECTED...
... FROM THAT ...
... STALKER?
!
UH... KYOKO...
AH...
...
I REMEMBER.
SHE WAS "FOUND IN THE WOODS, UNCONSCIOUS."
THAT'S WHAT MOST OF THE CREW WAS TOLD. OUTSIDERS.
...
I-I'm an outsider?!
WELL... I DON'T MIND, BUT...

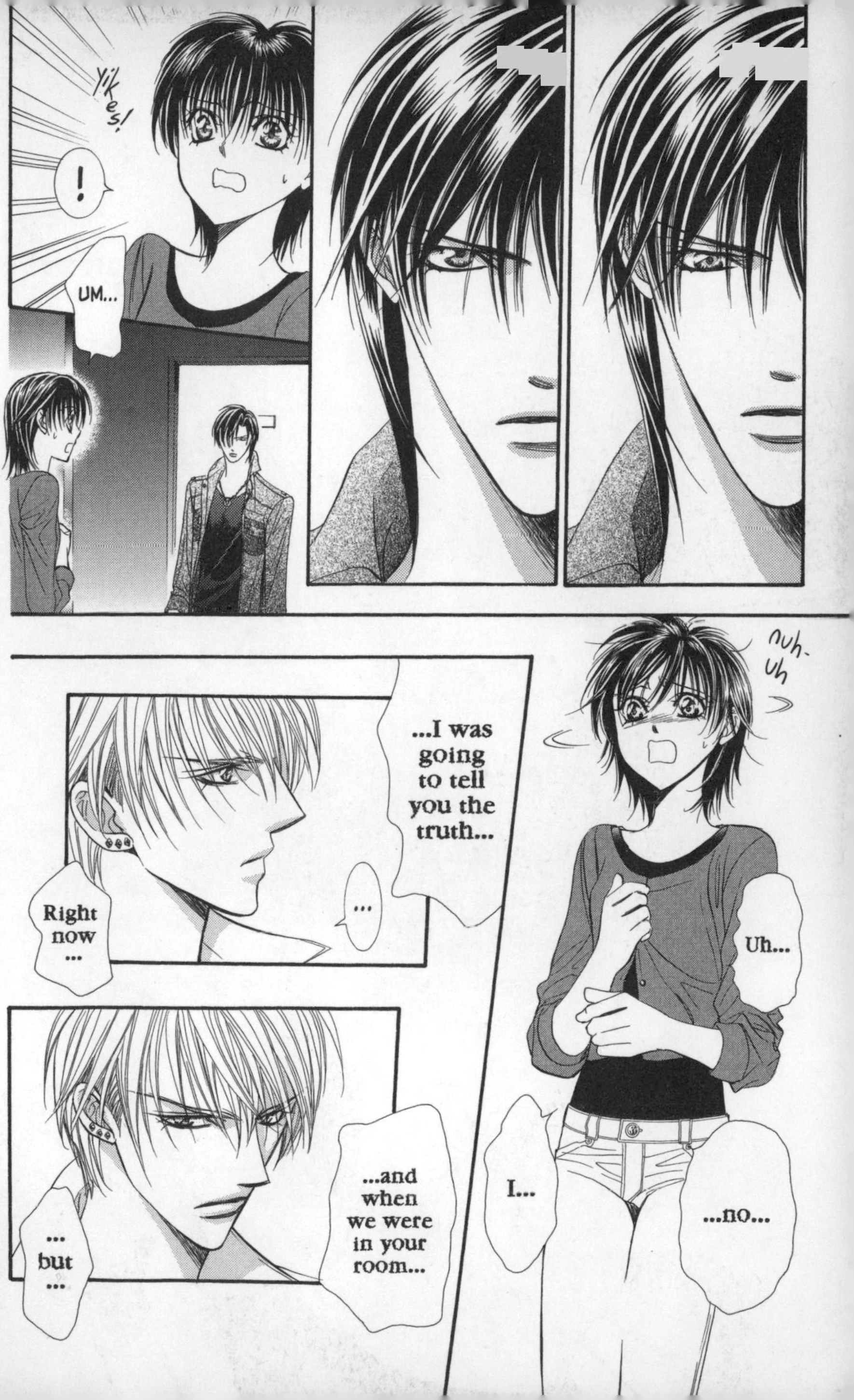
Yikes!
!
UM...
nuh-uh
Uh...
...no...
I...
...I was going to tell you the truth...
...
Right now ...
...and when we were in your room...
... but ...

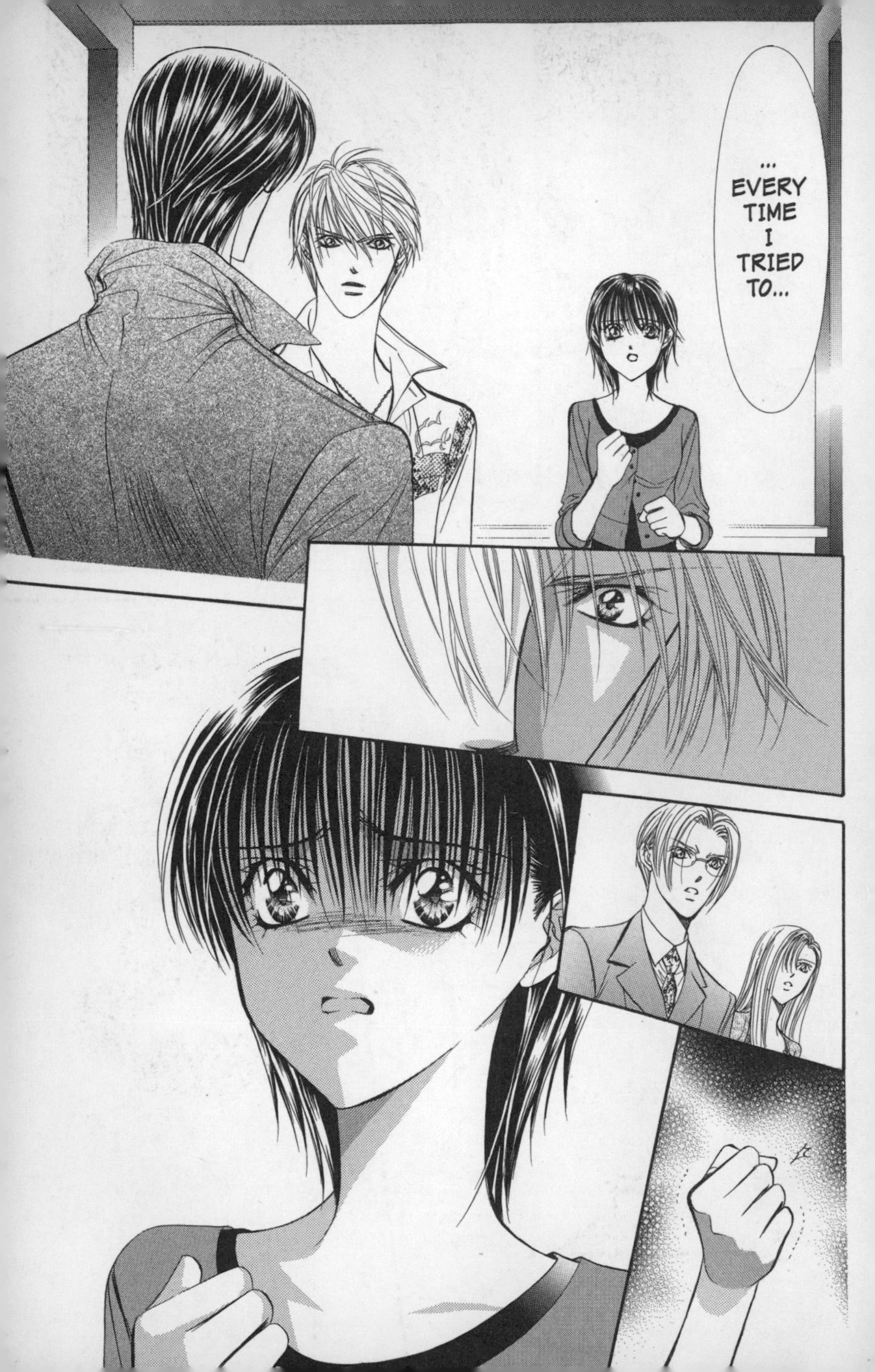
...EVERY TIME I TRIED TO...

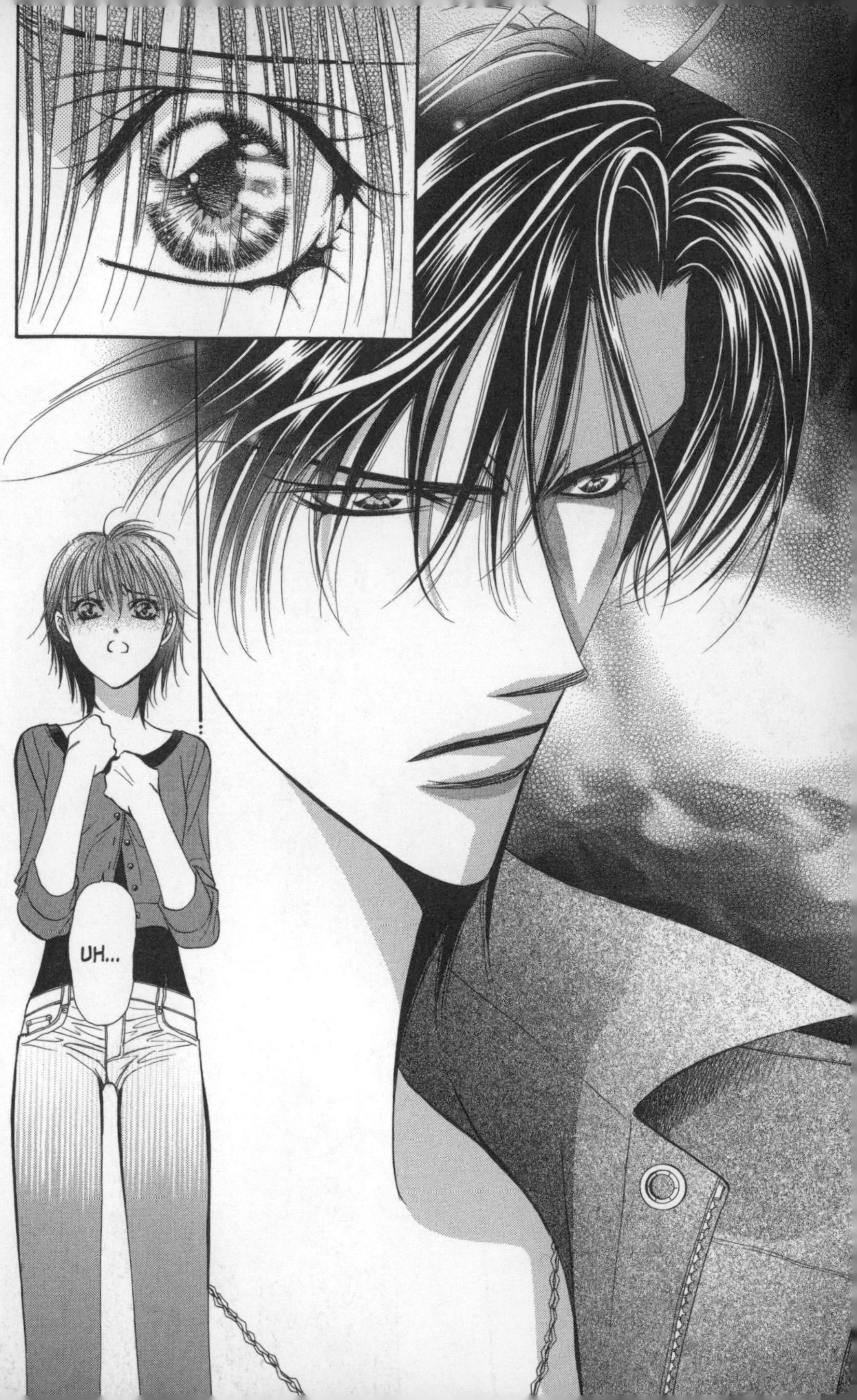
UH...

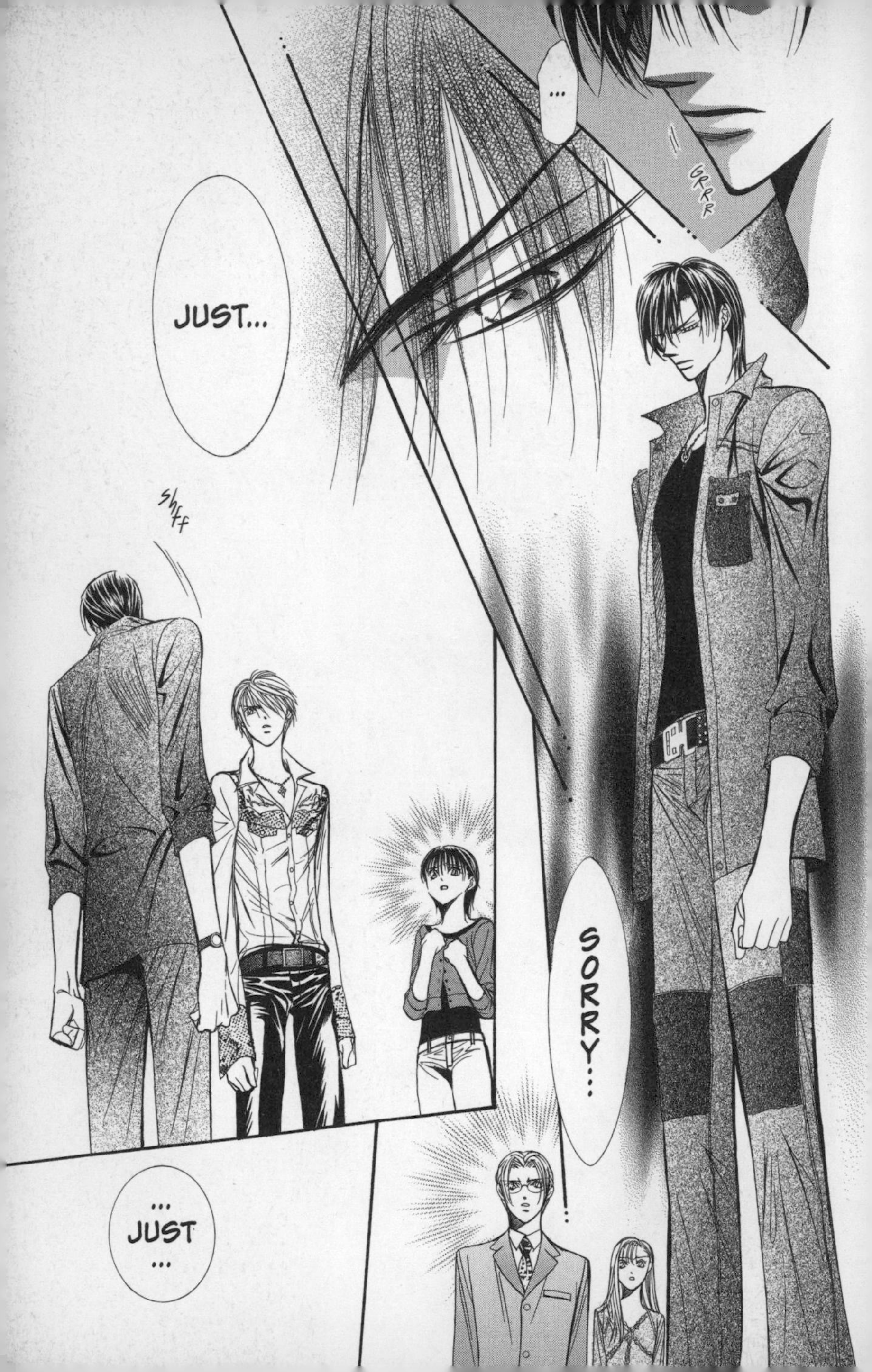
...
GRRR
SORRY...
JUST...
shff
...JUST...

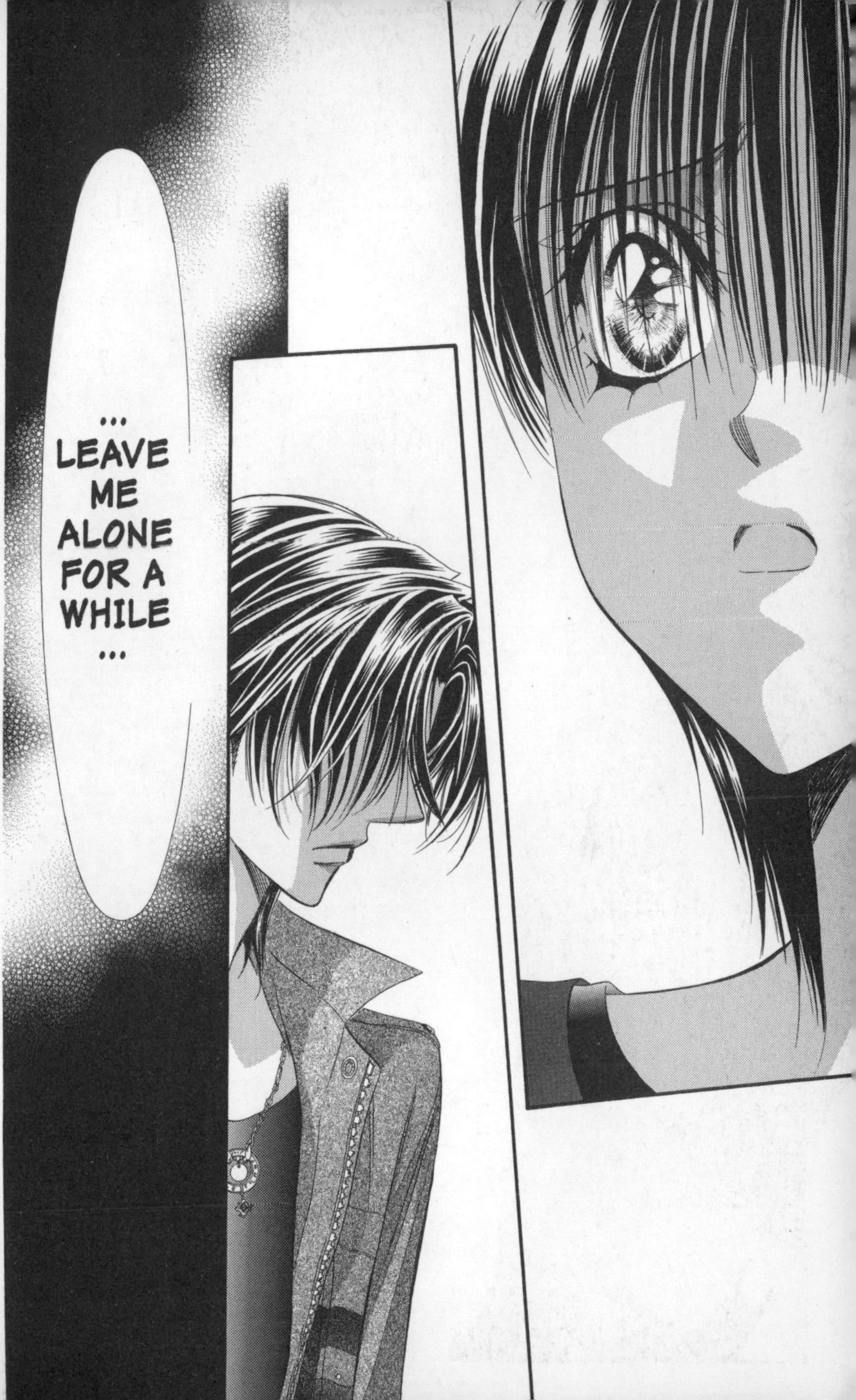
...LEAVE ME ALONE FOR A WHILE...

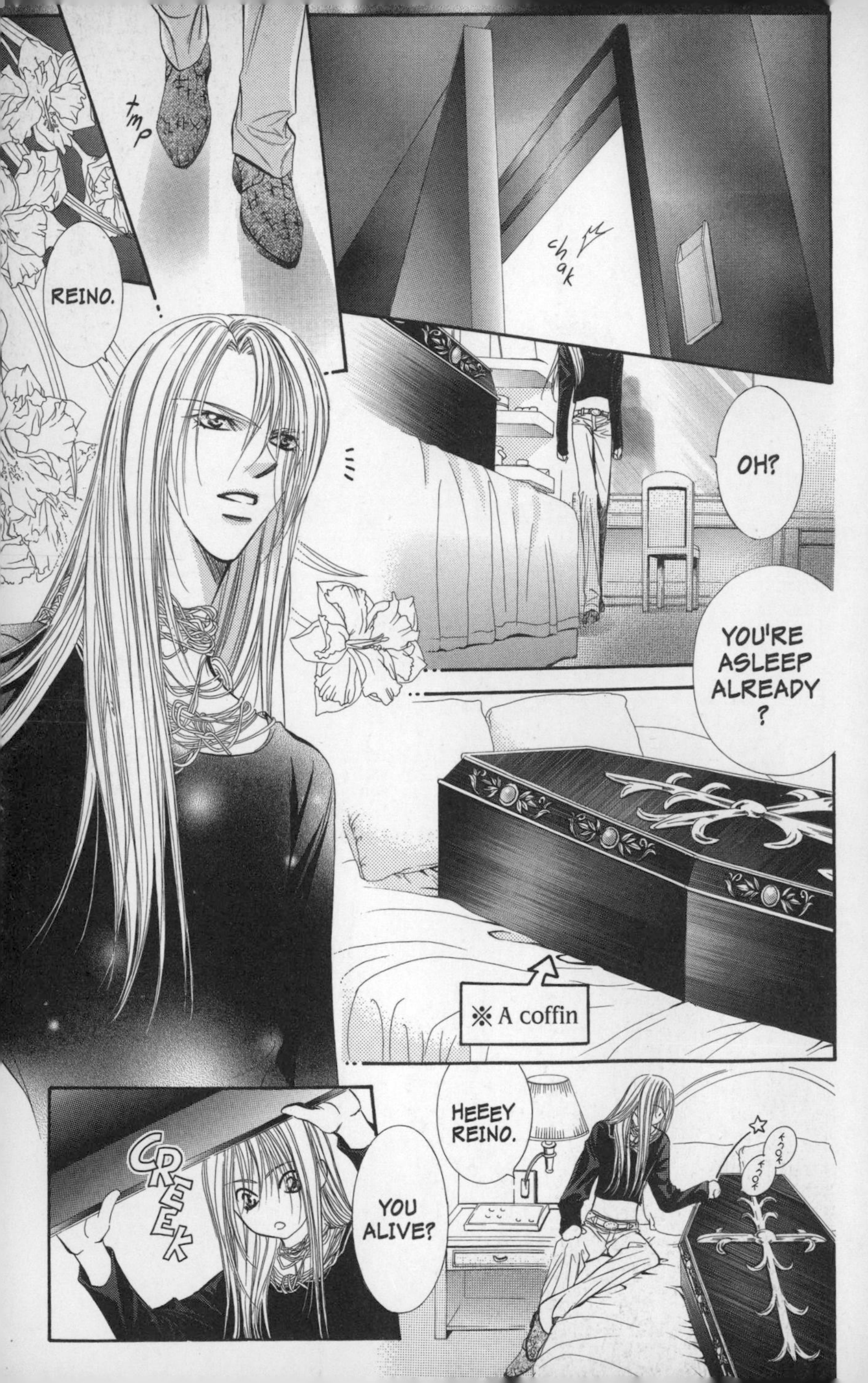
chak
tmp
REINO.
OH?
YOU'RE ASLEEP ALREADY?
※ A coffin
HEEEY REINO.
YOU ALIVE?
CREEK

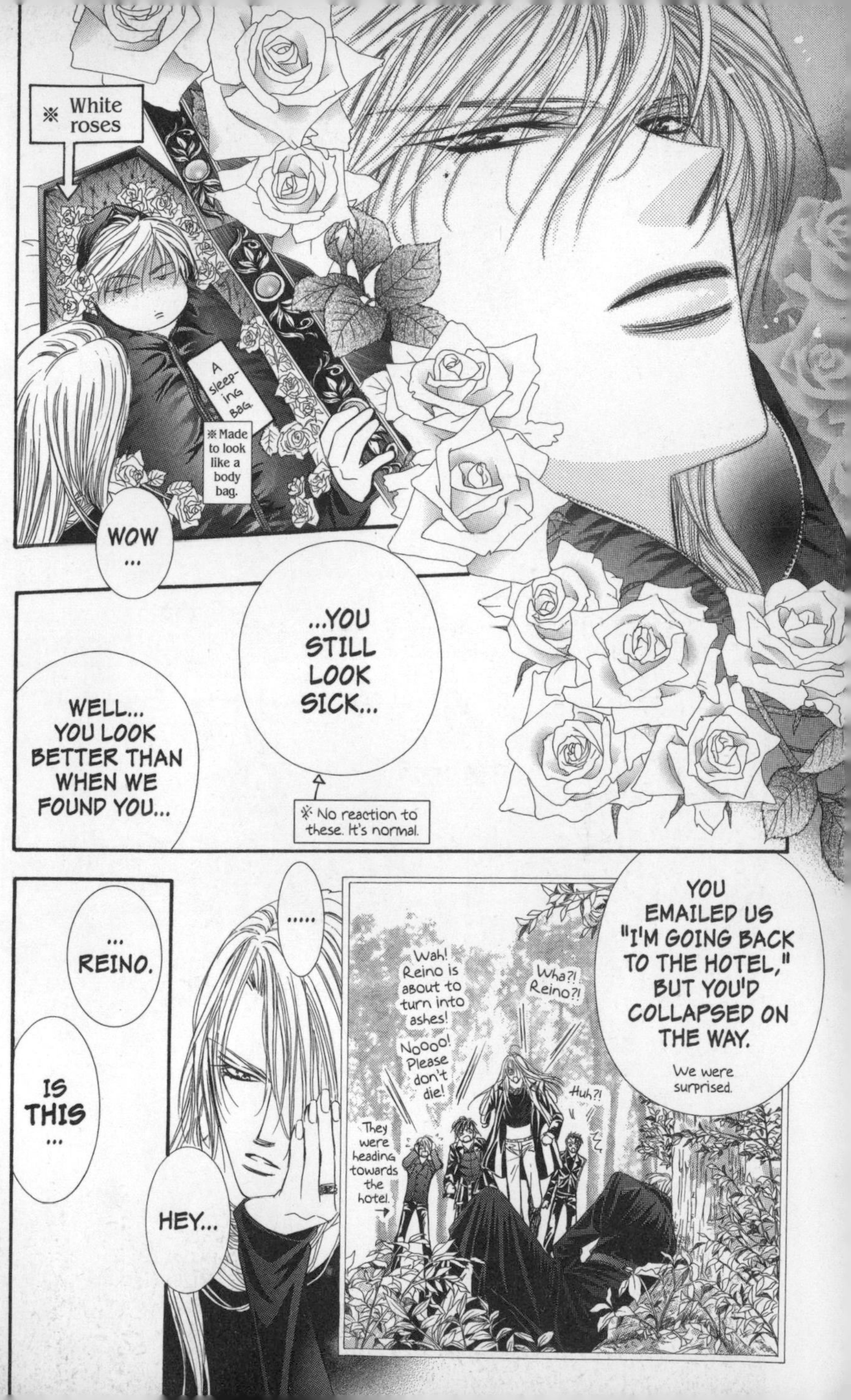
※ White roses
A sleeping bag.
※ Made to look like a body bag.
WOW ...
...YOU STILL LOOK SICK...
WELL... YOU LOOK BETTER THAN WHEN WE FOUND YOU...
※ No reaction to these. It's normal.
YOU EMAILED US "I'M GOING BACK TO THE HOTEL," BUT YOU'D COLLAPSED ON THE WAY.
We were surprised.
Wha?! Reino?!
Wah! Reino is about to turn into ashes!
Noooo! Please don't die!
Huh?!
They were heading towards the hotel.
.....
... REINO.
IS THIS ...
HEY...

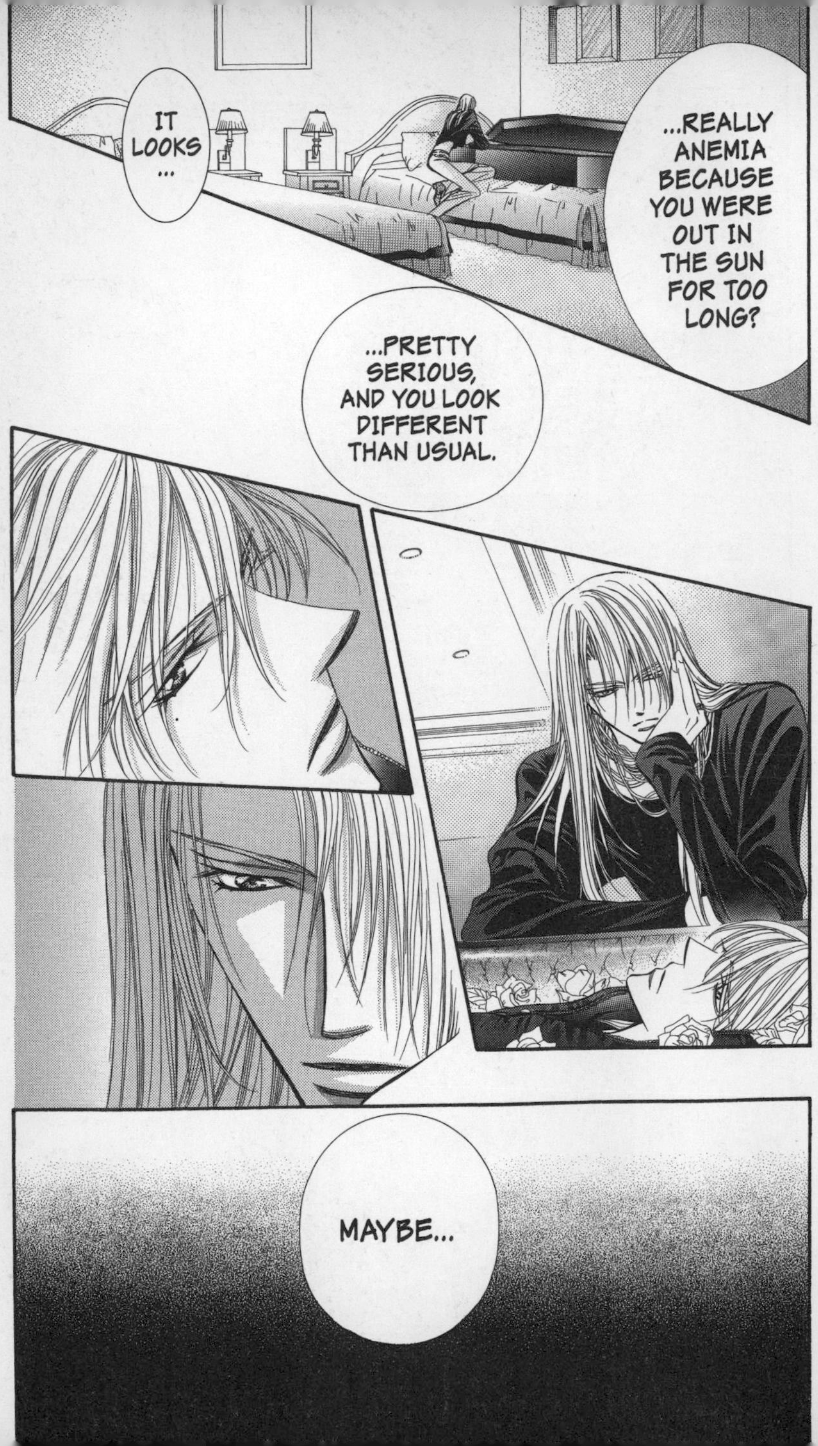
...REALLY ANEMIA BECAUSE YOU WERE OUT IN THE SUN FOR TOO LONG?
IT LOOKS ...
...PRETTY SERIOUS, AND YOU LOOK DIFFERENT THAN USUAL.
MAYBE...

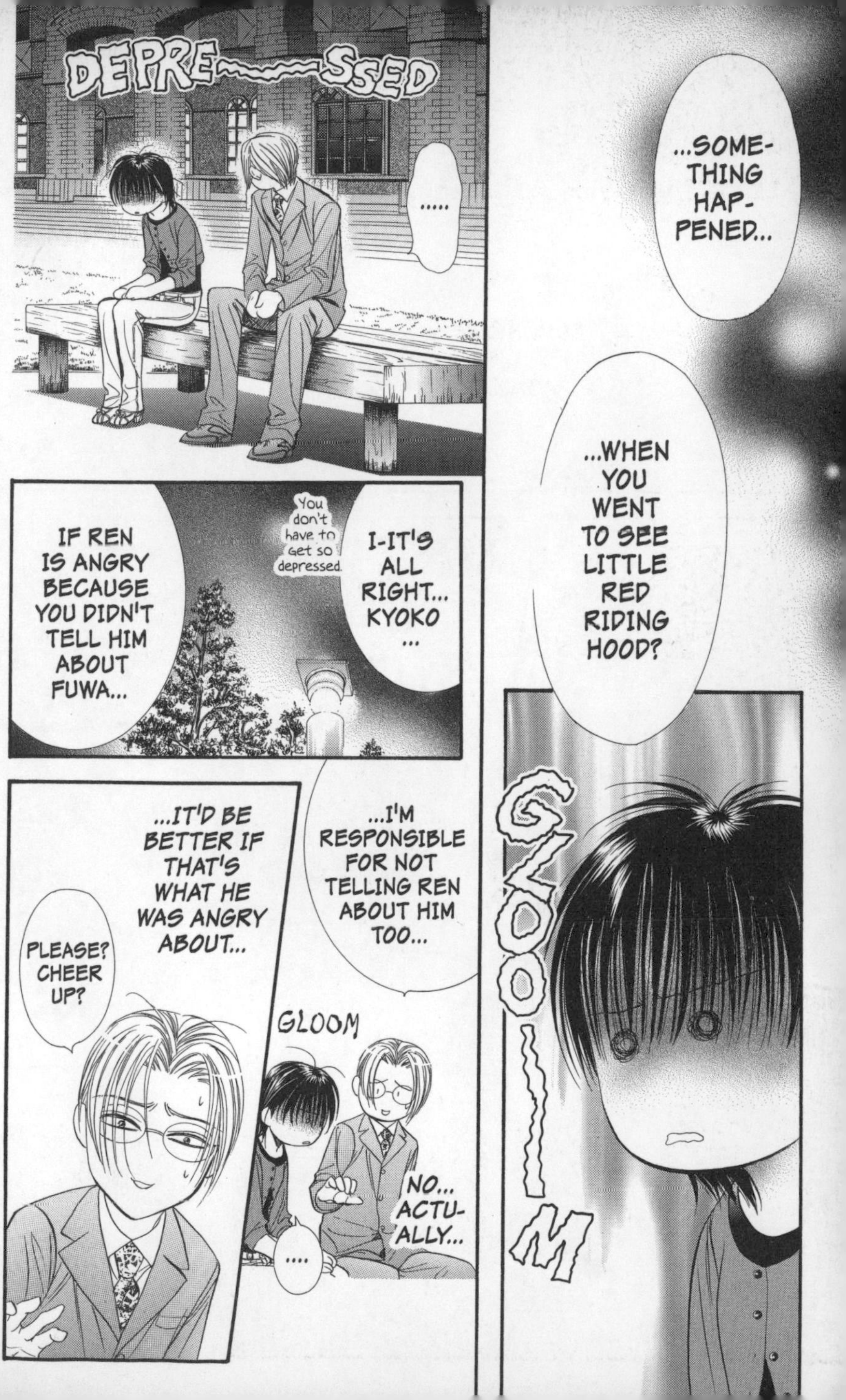
...SOME-THING HAP-PENED...
...WHEN YOU WENT TO SEE LITTLE RED RIDING HOOD?
GLOOO—M
DEPRE——SSED
.....
I-IT'S ALL RIGHT... KYOKO ...
You don't have to get so depressed.
IF REN IS ANGRY BECAUSE YOU DIDN'T TELL HIM ABOUT FUWA...
...I'M RESPONSIBLE FOR NOT TELLING REN ABOUT HIM TOO...
...IT'D BE BETTER IF THAT'S WHAT HE WAS ANGRY ABOUT...
PLEASE? CHEER UP?
GLOOM
NO... ACTU-ALLY...
....

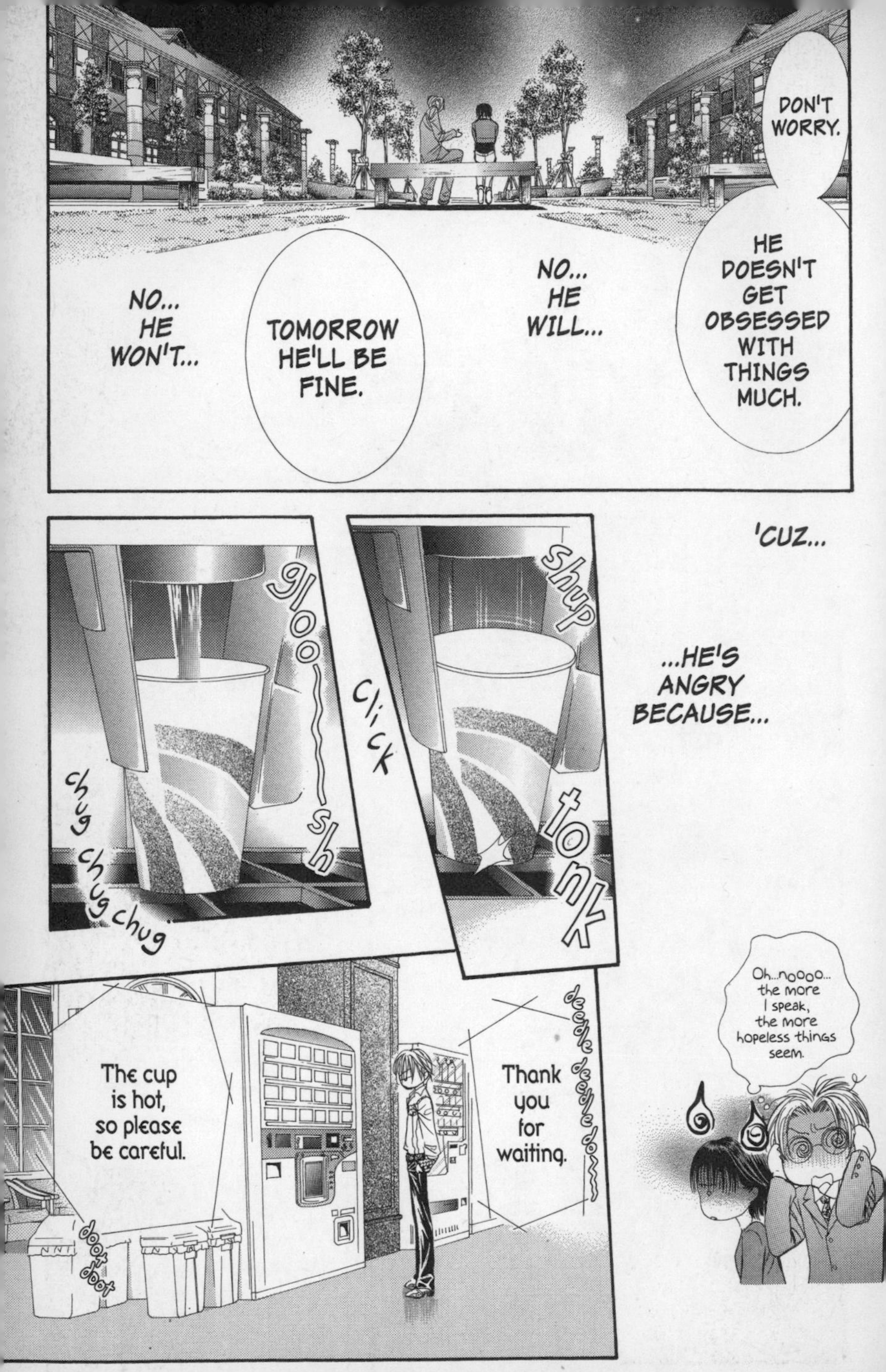
DON'T WORRY.
HE DOESN'T GET OBSESSED WITH THINGS MUCH.
NO... HE WILL...
TOMORROW HE'LL BE FINE.
NO... HE WON'T...
'CUZ...
...HE'S ANGRY BECAUSE...
shup
tonk
gloo—sh
click
chug chug chug chug
Oh...noooo... the more I speak, the more hopeless things seem.
deedle deedle deedle do~
Thank you for waiting.
The cup is hot, so please be careful.
doot doot

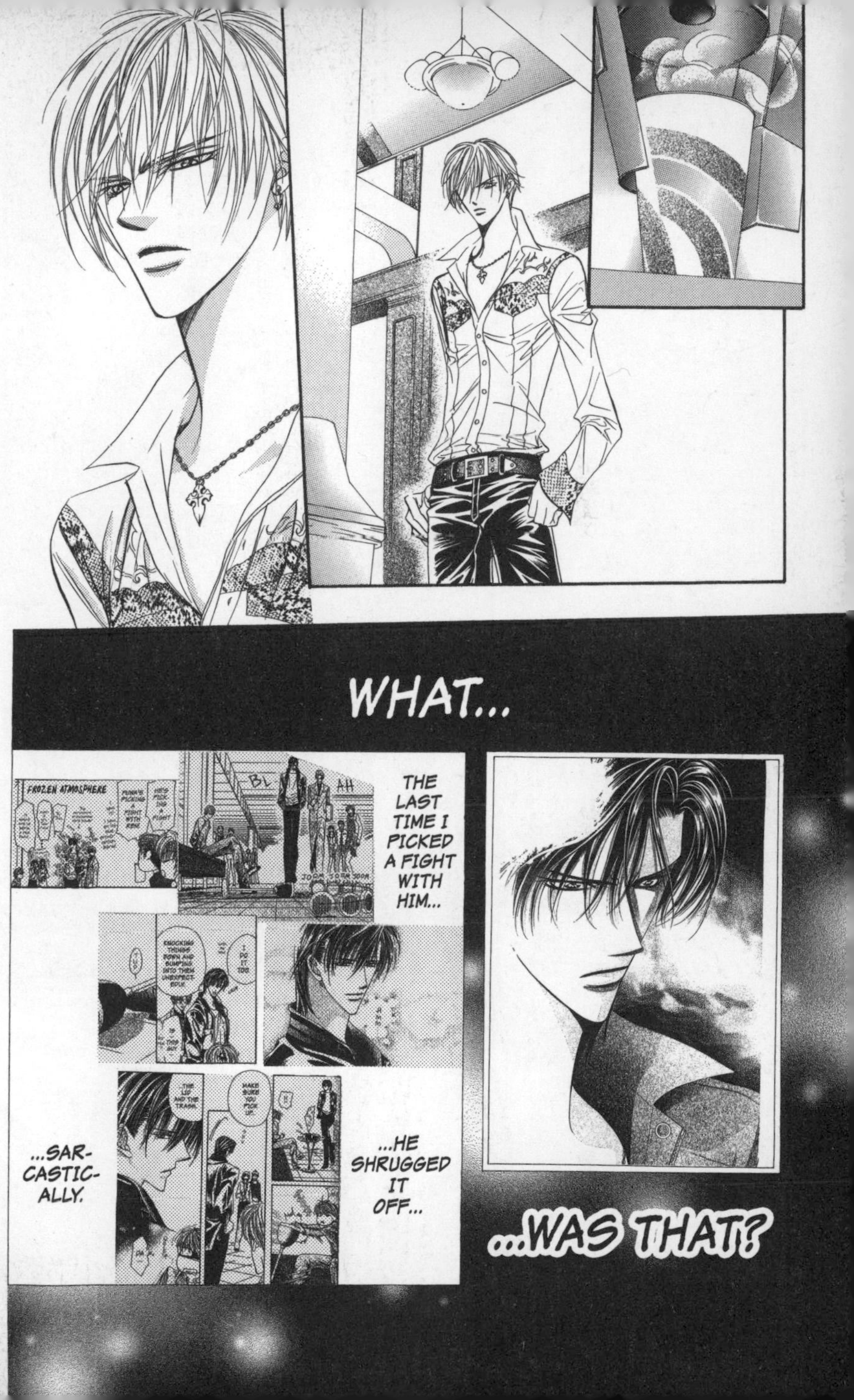
WHAT...
FROZEN ATMOSPHERE
THE LAST TIME I PICKED A FIGHT WITH HIM...
...HE SHRUGGED IT OFF...
...SAR-CASTIC-ALLY.
...WAS THAT?

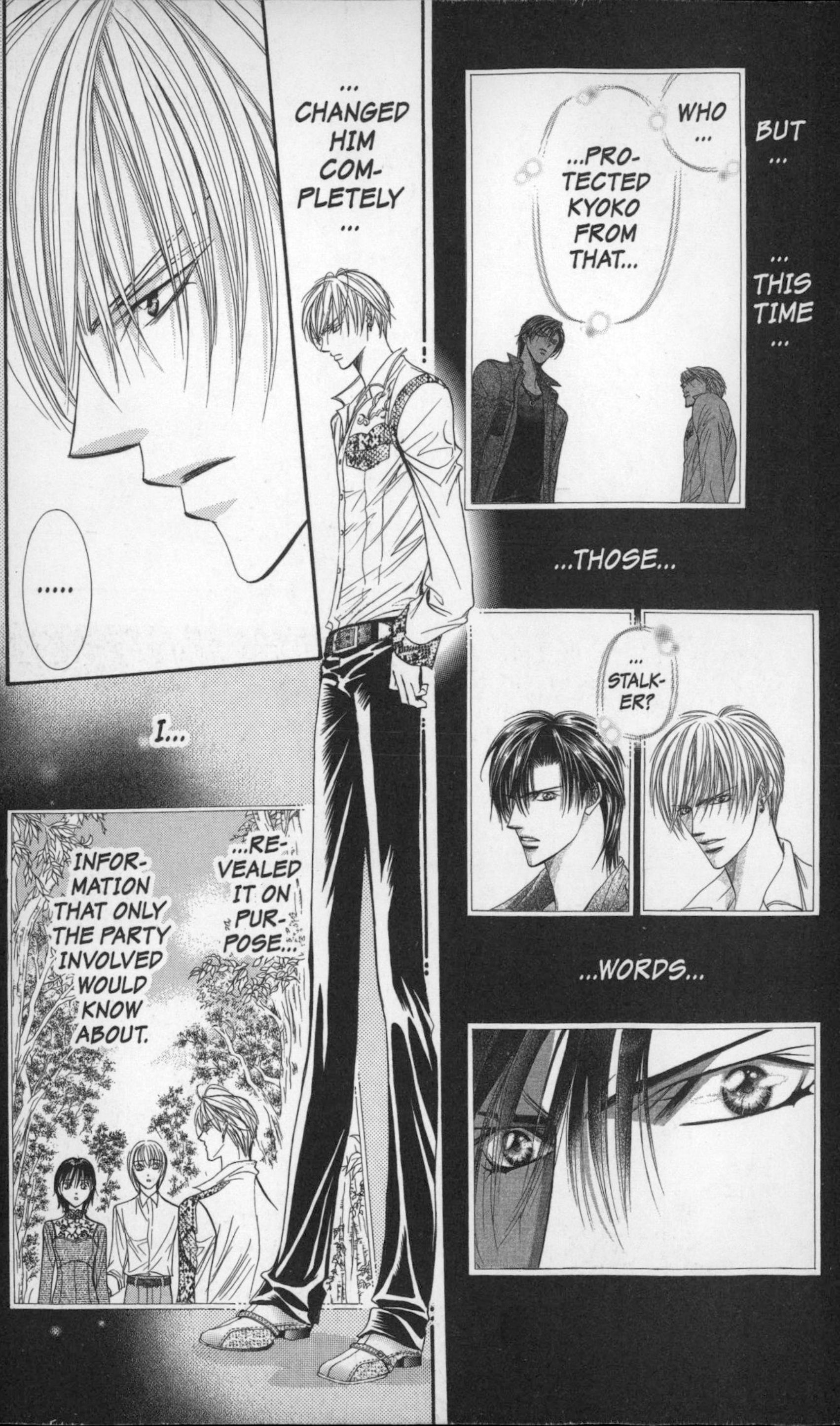
BUT ...
... THIS TIME ...
WHO ...
...PROTECTED KYOKO FROM THAT...
...THOSE...
... STALKER?
...WORDS...
... CHANGED HIM COMPLETELY ...
.....
I...
...REVEALED IT ON PURPOSE...
INFORMATION THAT ONLY THE PARTY INVOLVED WOULD KNOW ABOUT.

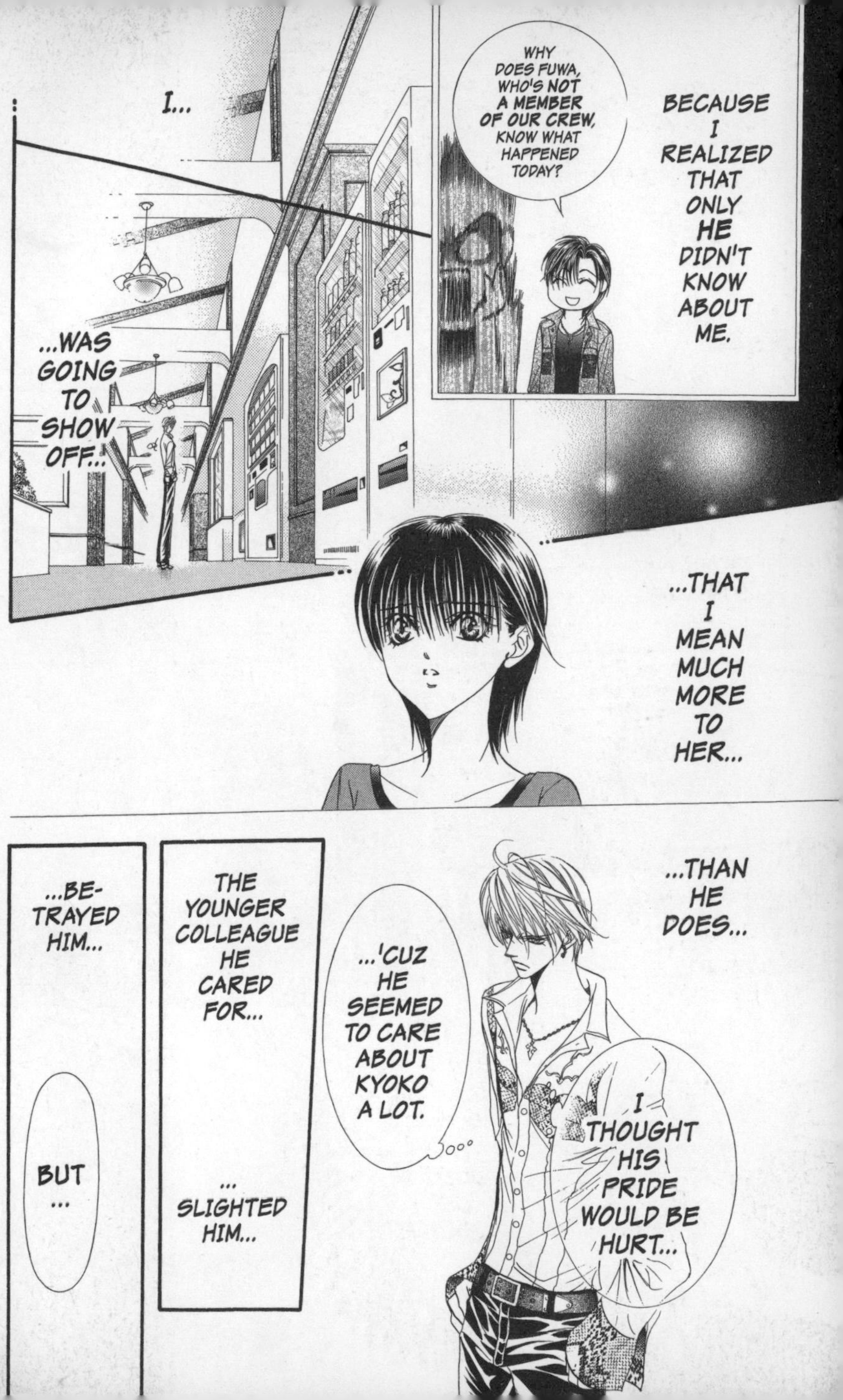
WHY DOES FUWA, WHO'S NOT A MEMBER OF OUR CREW, KNOW WHAT HAPPENED TODAY?
BECAUSE I REALIZED THAT ONLY HE DIDN'T KNOW ABOUT ME.
I...
...WAS GOING TO SHOW OFF...
...THAT I MEAN MUCH MORE TO HER...
...THAN HE DOES...
...'CUZ HE SEEMED TO CARE ABOUT KYOKO A LOT.
I THOUGHT HIS PRIDE WOULD BE HURT...
THE YOUNGER COLLEAGUE HE CARED FOR...
...SLIGHTED HIM...
...BE-TRAYED HIM...
BUT...

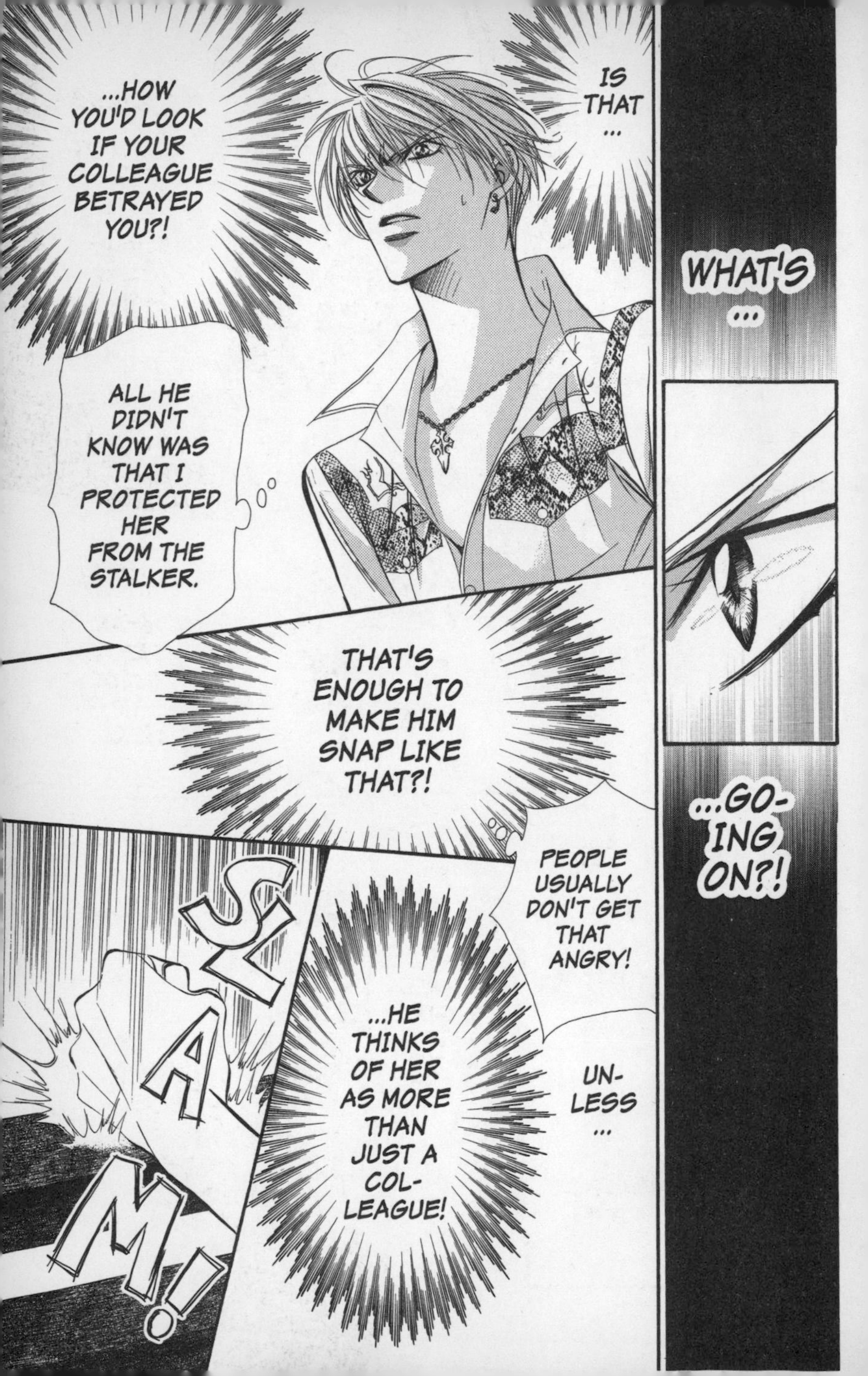
WHAT'S ...
...GO-ING ON?!
IS THAT ...
...HOW YOU'D LOOK IF YOUR COLLEAGUE BETRAYED YOU?!
ALL HE DIDN'T KNOW WAS THAT I PROTECTED HER FROM THE STALKER.
THAT'S ENOUGH TO MAKE HIM SNAP LIKE THAT?!
PEOPLE USUALLY DON'T GET THAT ANGRY!
UN-LESS ...
...HE THINKS OF HER AS MORE THAN JUST A COL-LEAGUE!
SLAM!

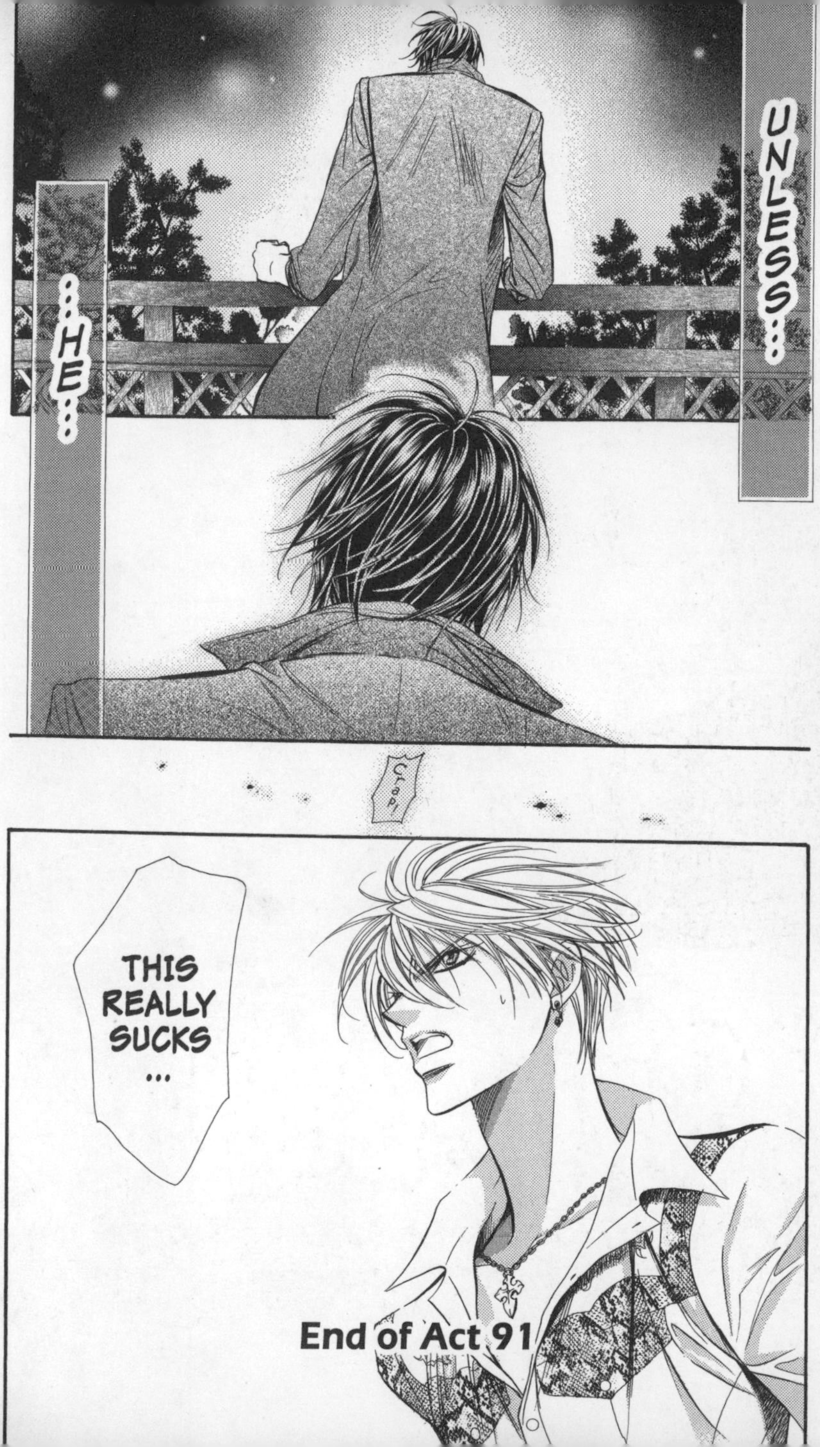
UNLESS...
...HE...
Crap!
THIS REALLY SUCKS ...
End of Act 91

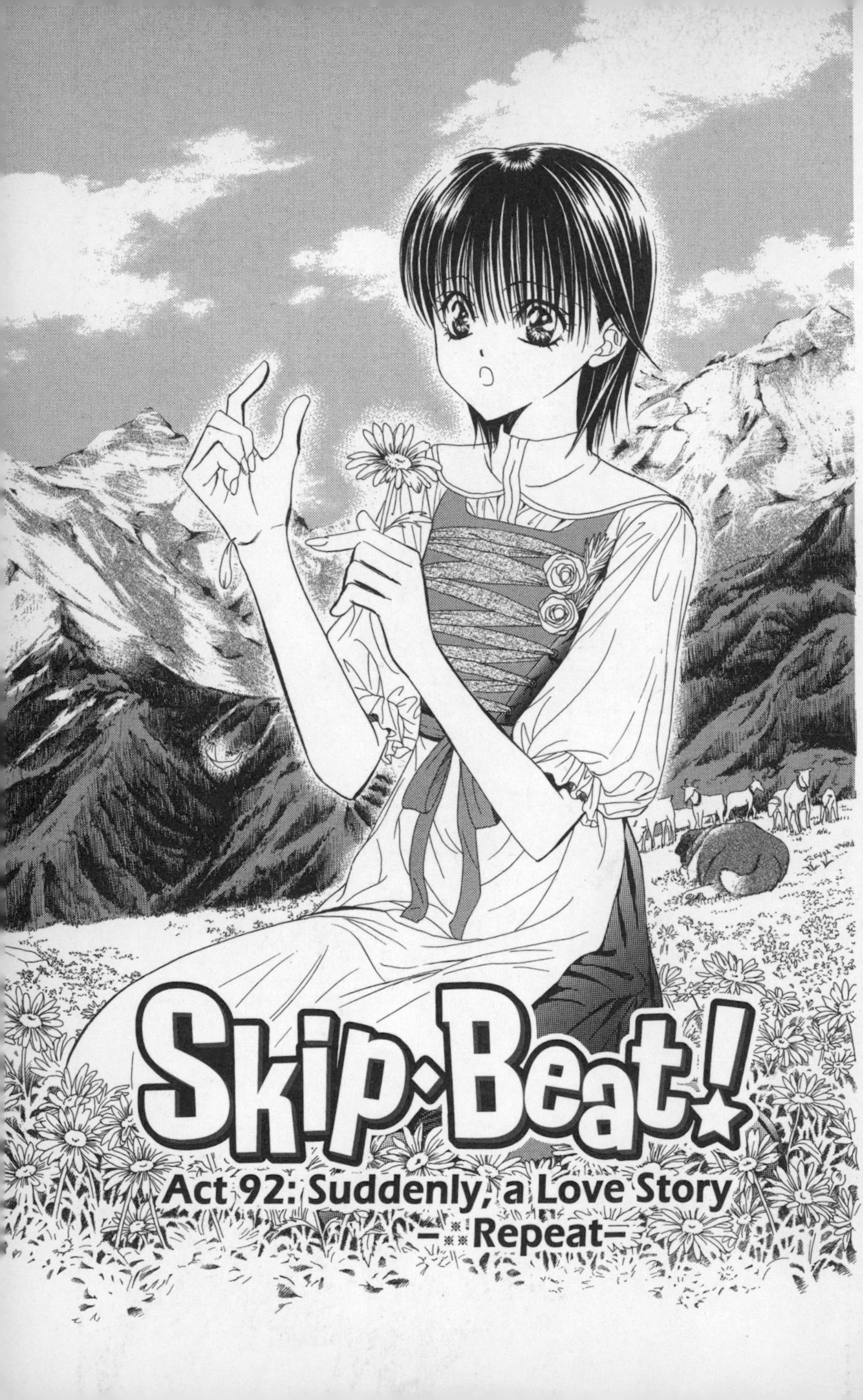
Skip·Beat!
Act 92: Suddenly, a Love Story
—※※Repeat—

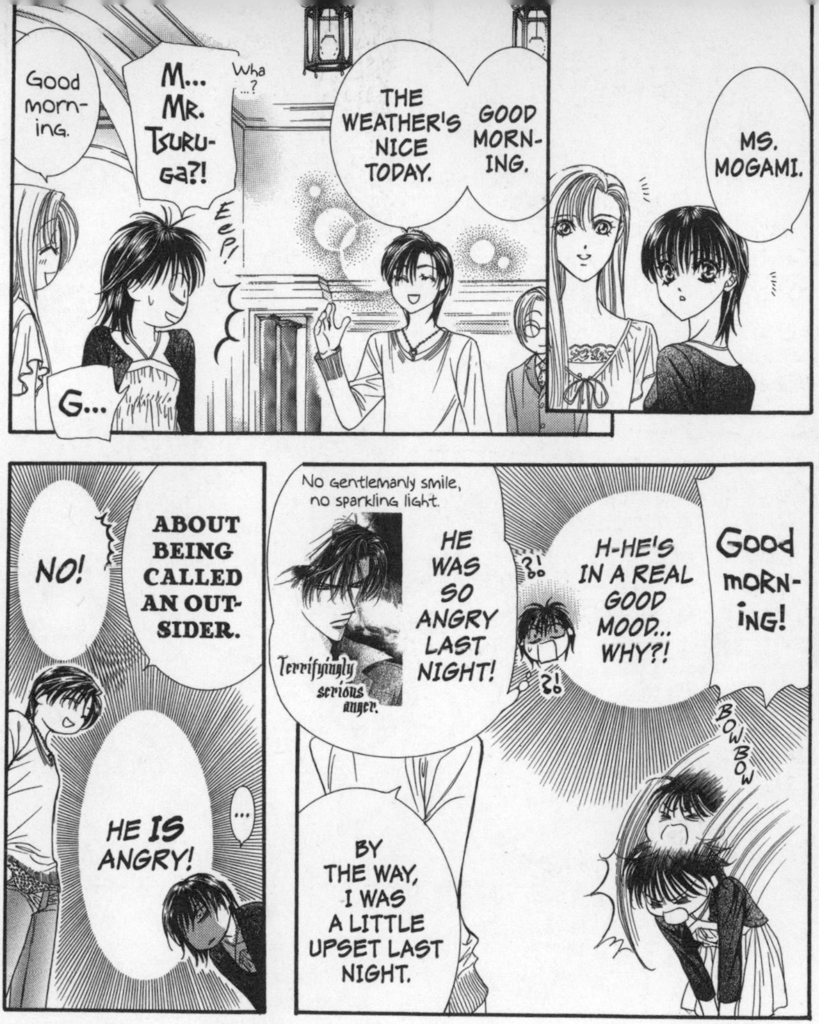
MS. MOGAMI.
GOOD MORNING.
THE WEATHER'S NICE TODAY.
Wha ...?
M... MR. TSURUga?!
Good morning.
EEP!
G...
Good morning!
H-HE'S IN A REAL GOOD MOOD... WHY?!
?!
?!
BOW BOW
HE WAS SO ANGRY LAST NIGHT!
No gentlemanly smile, no sparkling light.
Terrifyingly serious anger.
BY THE WAY, I WAS A LITTLE UPSET LAST NIGHT.
ABOUT BEING CALLED AN OUTSIDER.
NO!
...
HE IS ANGRY!

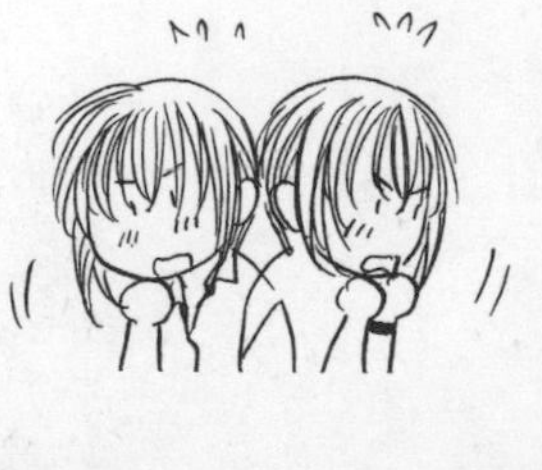

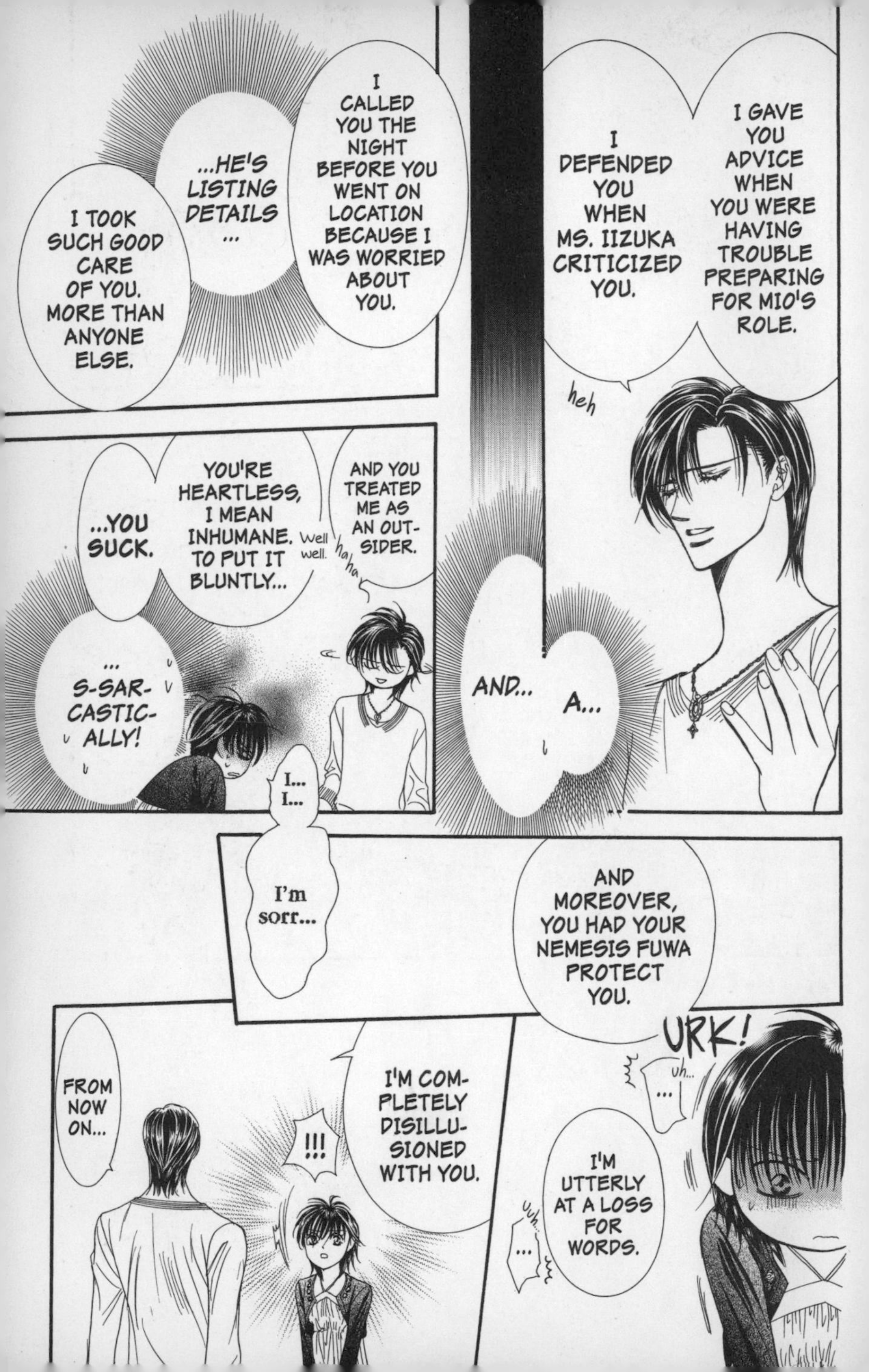
I GAVE YOU ADVICE WHEN YOU WERE HAVING TROUBLE PREPARING FOR MIO'S ROLE.
I DEFENDED YOU WHEN MS. IIZUKA CRITICIZED YOU.
heh
A...
AND...
I CALLED YOU THE NIGHT BEFORE YOU WENT ON LOCATION BECAUSE I WAS WORRIED ABOUT YOU.
...HE'S LISTING DETAILS...
I TOOK SUCH GOOD CARE OF YOU. MORE THAN ANYONE ELSE.
AND YOU TREATED ME AS AN OUT-SIDER.
haha
Well well.
YOU'RE HEARTLESS, I MEAN INHUMANE. TO PUT IT BLUNTLY...
...YOU SUCK.
... S-SAR-CASTIC-ALLY!
I... I...
I'm sorr...
AND MOREOVER, YOU HAD YOUR NEMESIS FUWA PROTECT YOU.
URK!
uh...
...
I'M UTTERLY AT A LOSS FOR WORDS.
uuh...
...
I'M COM-PLETELY DISILLU-SIONED WITH YOU.
!!!
FROM NOW ON...

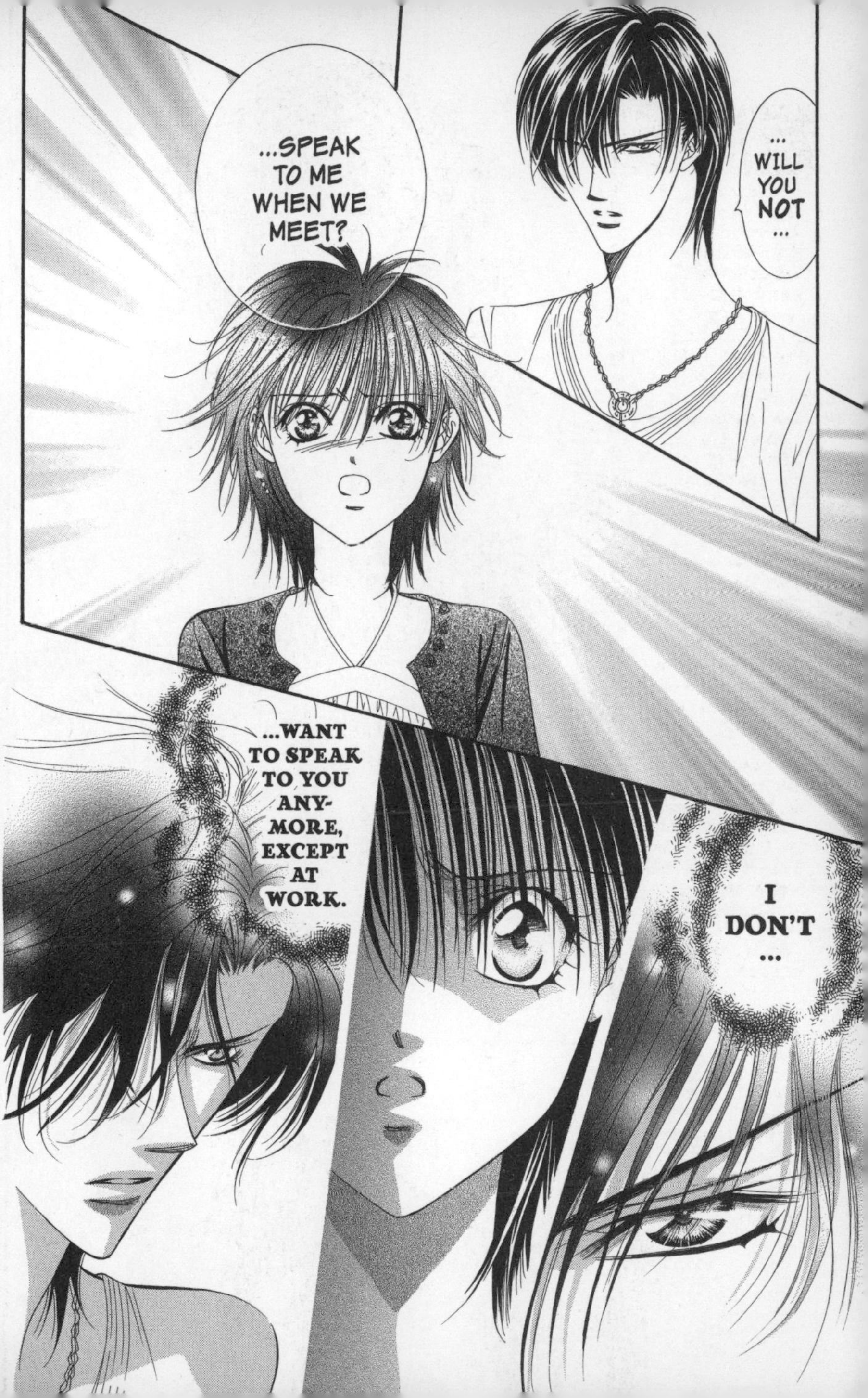
...WILL YOU NOT...
...SPEAK TO ME WHEN WE MEET?
I DON'T...
...WANT TO SPEAK TO YOU ANYMORE, EXCEPT AT WORK.

Super-evil VIE GHOUL

...My ideal band name was a name in the Roman letters with a gothic image and with the name meaning something like a typical villain. But my Japanese vocabulary is poor to begin with, and so there was no way I could think up a foreign name... I didn't have time, so I couldn't spend a lot of time looking for words that fit my image. I just looked up the words that happened to catch my eye then. VIE = "life, existence". GHOUL = "little devil, a cold-blooded person"... and this was too gruesome, so I left it out - "a demon that opens graves and eats the corpses, a grave-robber"...so I decided on this name right away, thinking it was perfect...

Well...I had VIE GHOUL appear as the really bad guys who are beyond redemption, so I could have revealed the meanings "eats corpses" or "grave-robber"...but this is a shojo manga after all...and I felt that the girls would find it gross, so I decided not to use those meanings...

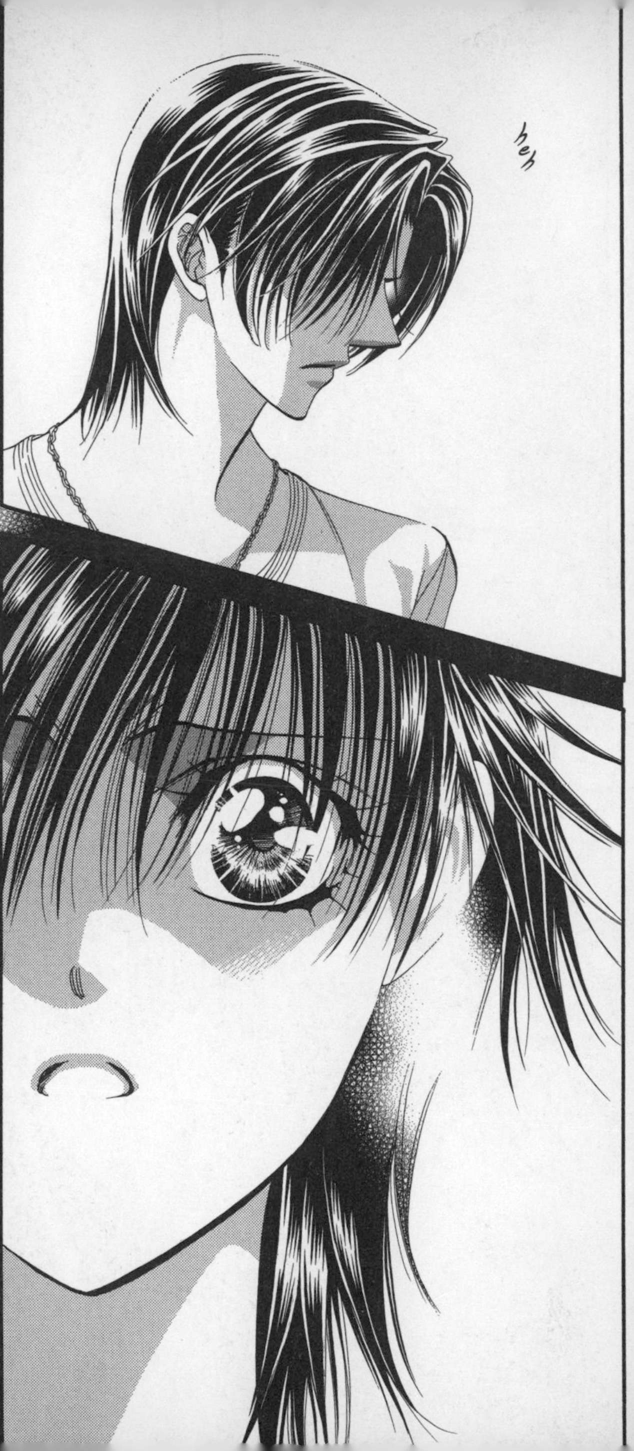
heh

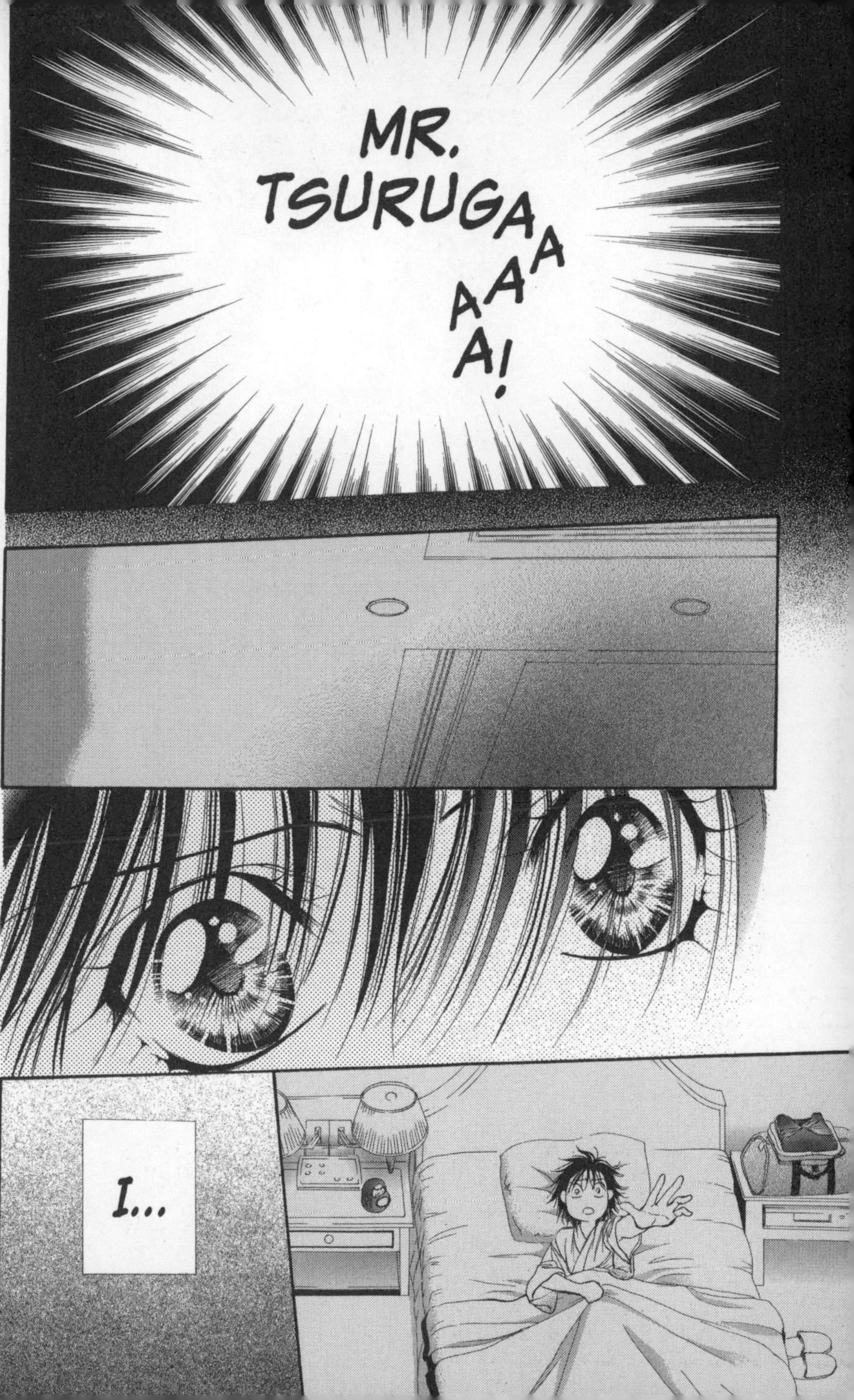
MR. TSURUGAAAAAA!
I...

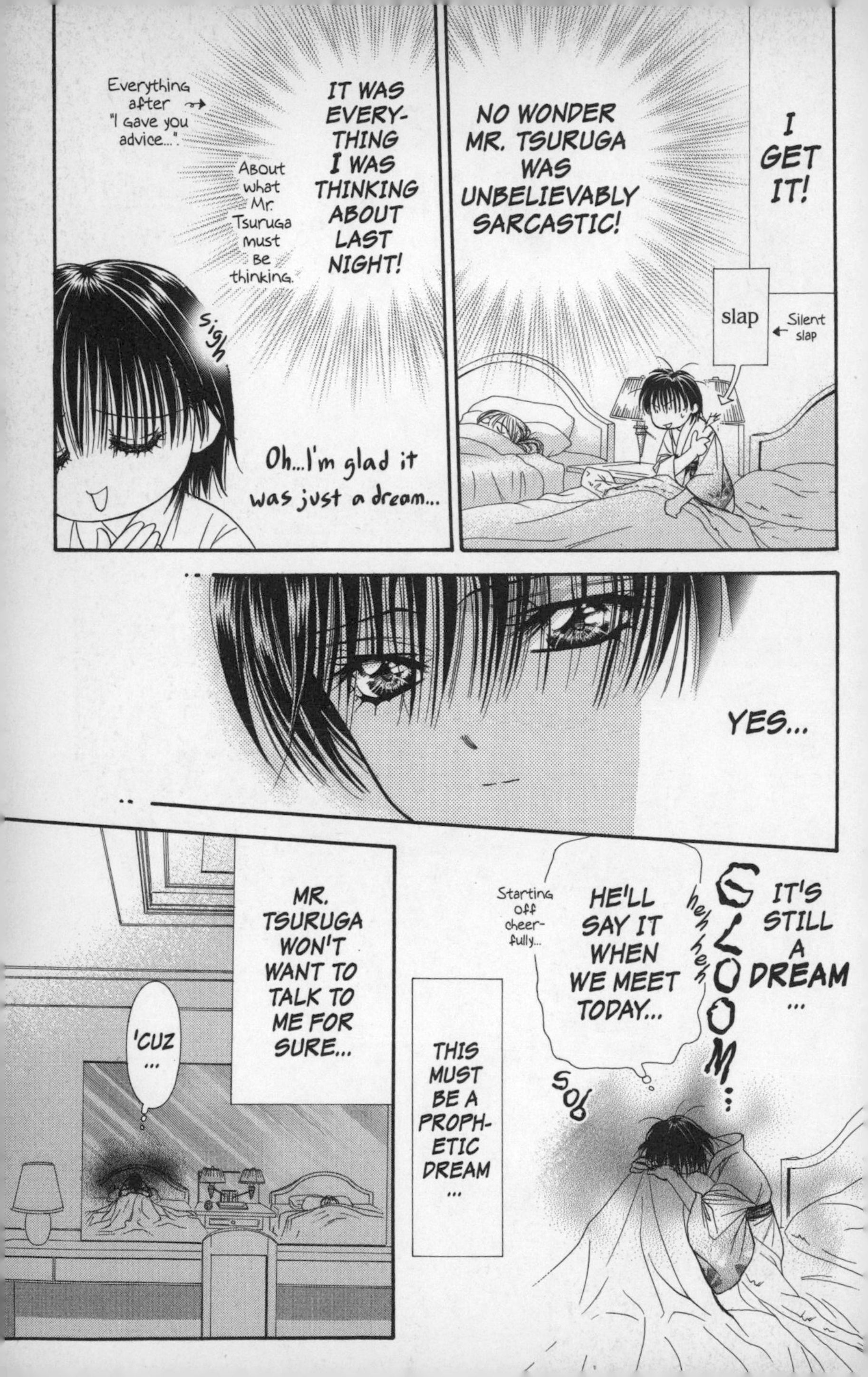
I GET IT!
NO WONDER MR. TSURUGA WAS UNBELIEVABLY SARCASTIC!
slap
Silent slap
IT WAS EVERY-THING I WAS THINKING ABOUT LAST NIGHT!
About what Mr. Tsuruga must be thinking.
Everything after "I gave you advice..."
sigh
Oh...I'm glad it was just a dream...
YES...
IT'S STILL A DREAM...
GLOOM...
heh heh
HE'LL SAY IT WHEN WE MEET TODAY...
Starting off cheer-fully...
sob
THIS MUST BE A PROPH-ETIC DREAM...
MR. TSURUGA WON'T WANT TO TALK TO ME FOR SURE...
'CUZ...

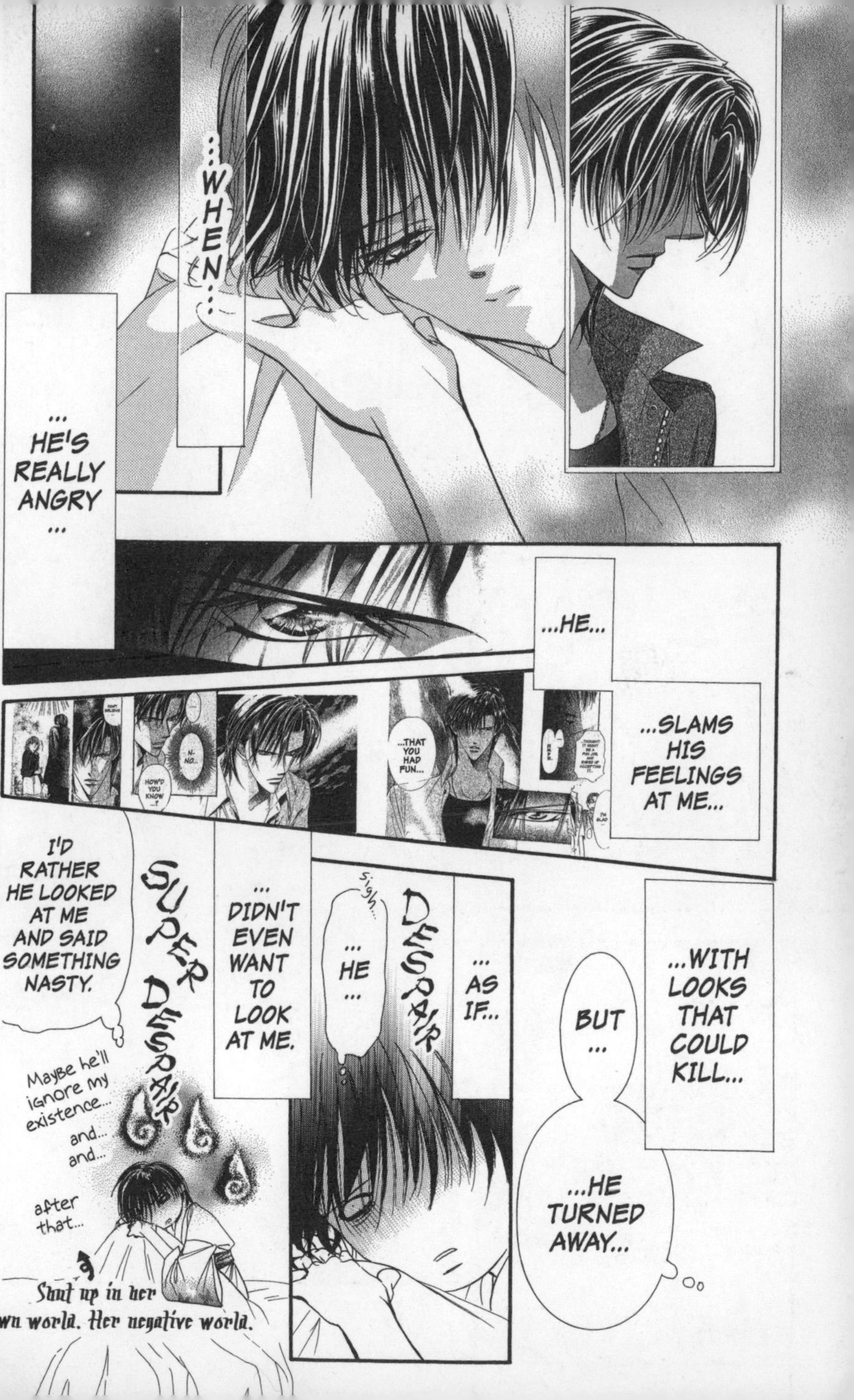
...WHEN...
... HE'S REALLY ANGRY ...
...HE...
...SLAMS HIS FEELINGS AT ME...
...THAT YOU HAD FUN...
N-NO...
HOW'D YOU KNOW ...?
...WITH LOOKS THAT COULD KILL...
BUT ... ...HE TURNED AWAY...
... AS IF...
DESPAIR
sigh...
... HE ...
... DIDN'T EVEN WANT TO LOOK AT ME.
I'D RATHER HE LOOKED AT ME AND SAID SOMETHING NASTY.
SUPER DESPAIR
Maybe he'll ignore my existence...
and... and...
after that...
Shut up in her own world. Her negative world.

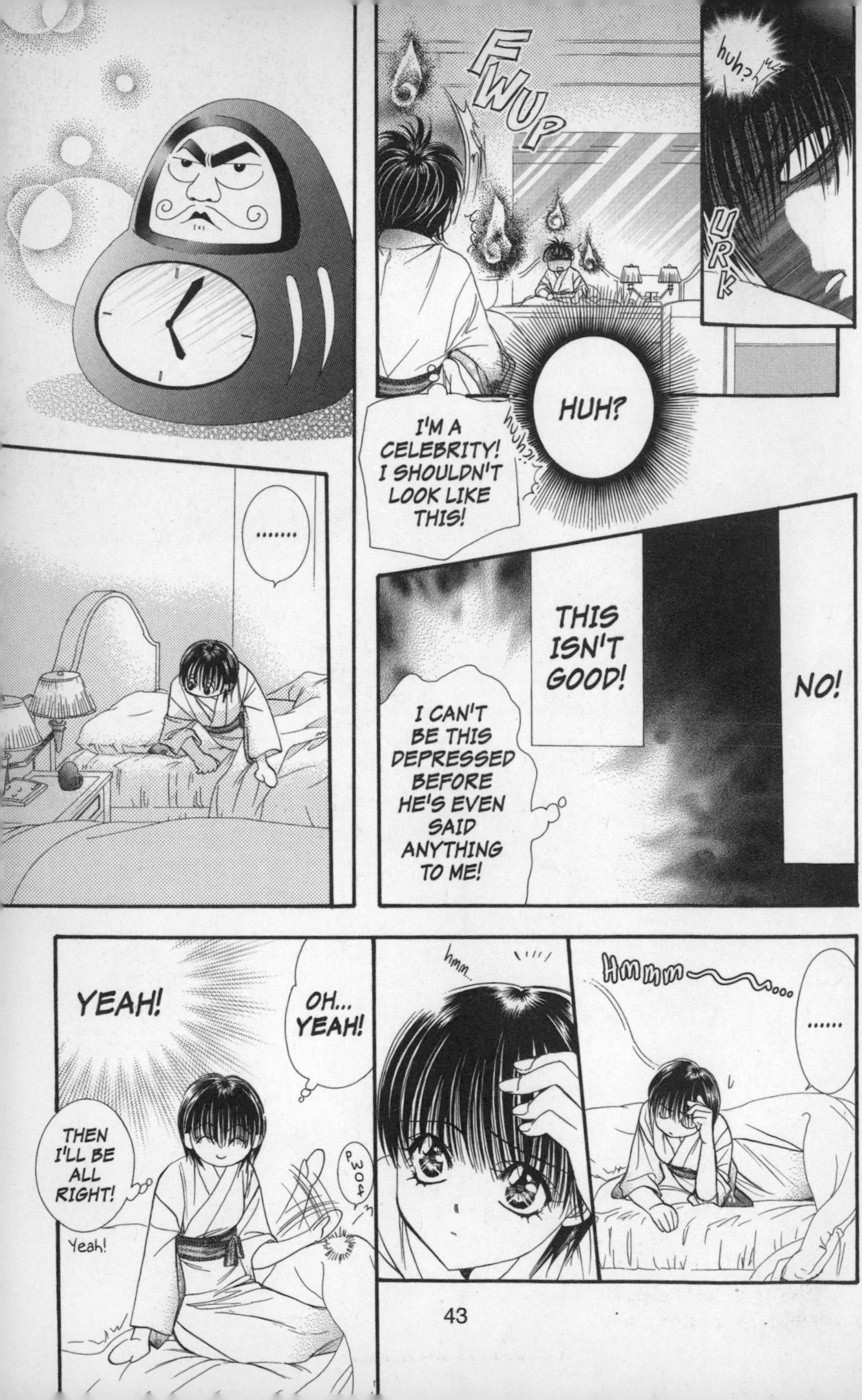
huh?
URK
FWUP
HUH?
huh?
I'M A CELEBRITY! I SHOULDN'T LOOK LIKE THIS!
NO!
THIS ISN'T GOOD!
I CAN'T BE THIS DEPRESSED BEFORE HE'S EVEN SAID ANYTHING TO ME!
....
Hmmm~~ooo
......
hmm...
OH... YEAH!
YEAH!
PWOF
THEN I'LL BE ALL RIGHT!
Yeah!

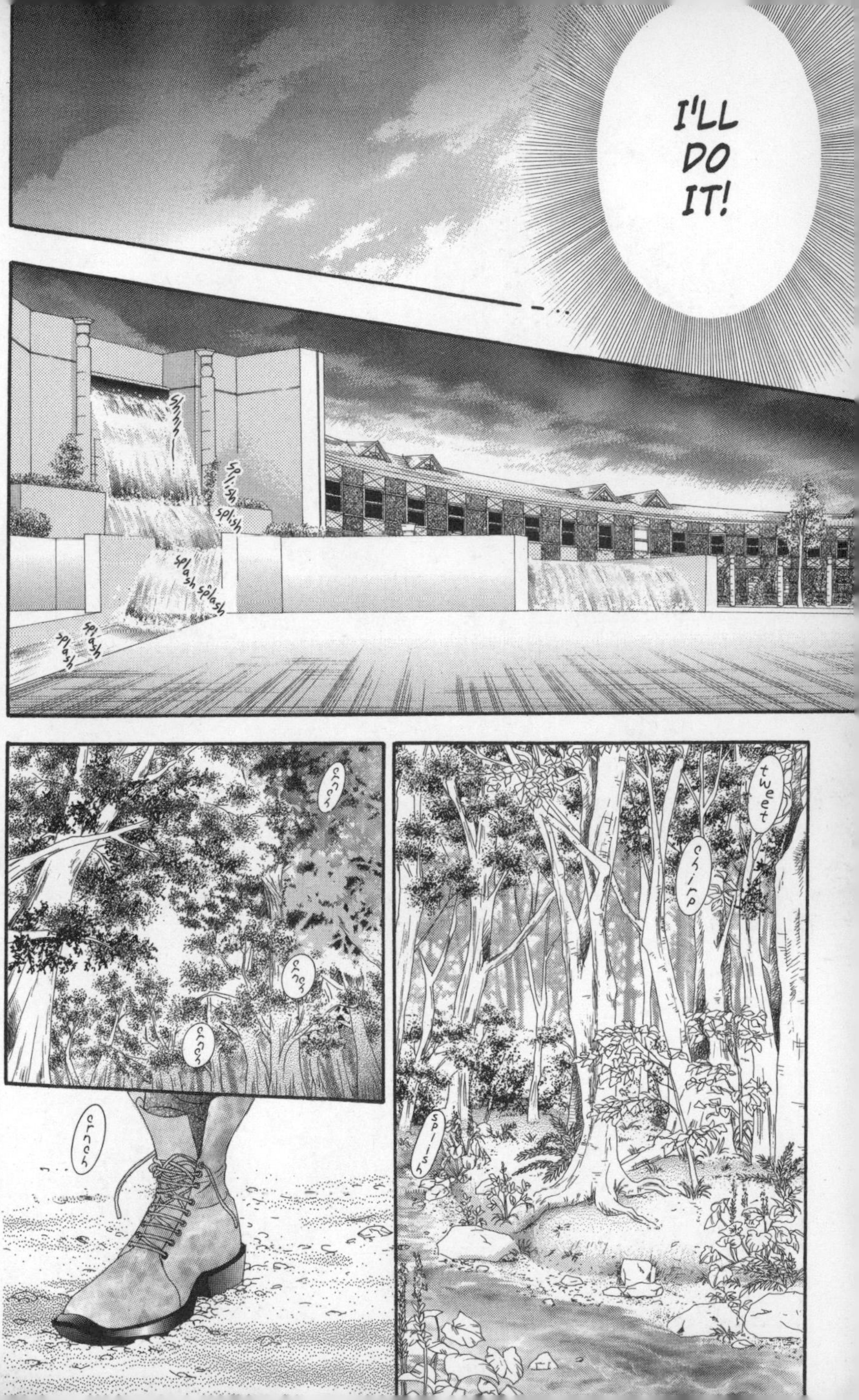
I'LL DO IT!
————–...
Shhhh—
splish
splish
splash
splash
splash
splash
tweet
chirp
splish
crnch
crnch
crnch
crnch
...

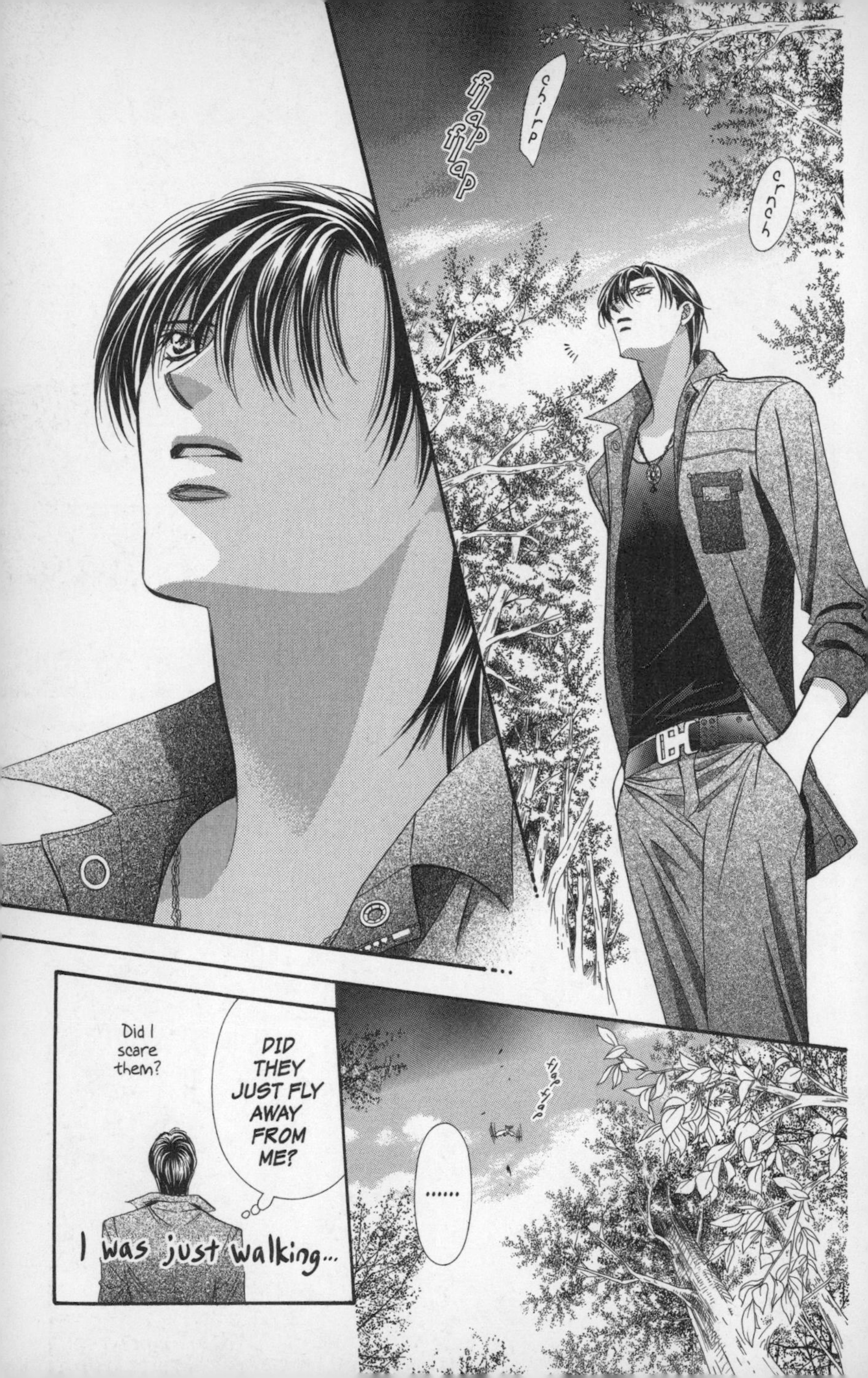
chirp
flap flap
crnch
......
flap flap
DID THEY JUST FLY AWAY FROM ME?
Did I scare them?
I was just walking...

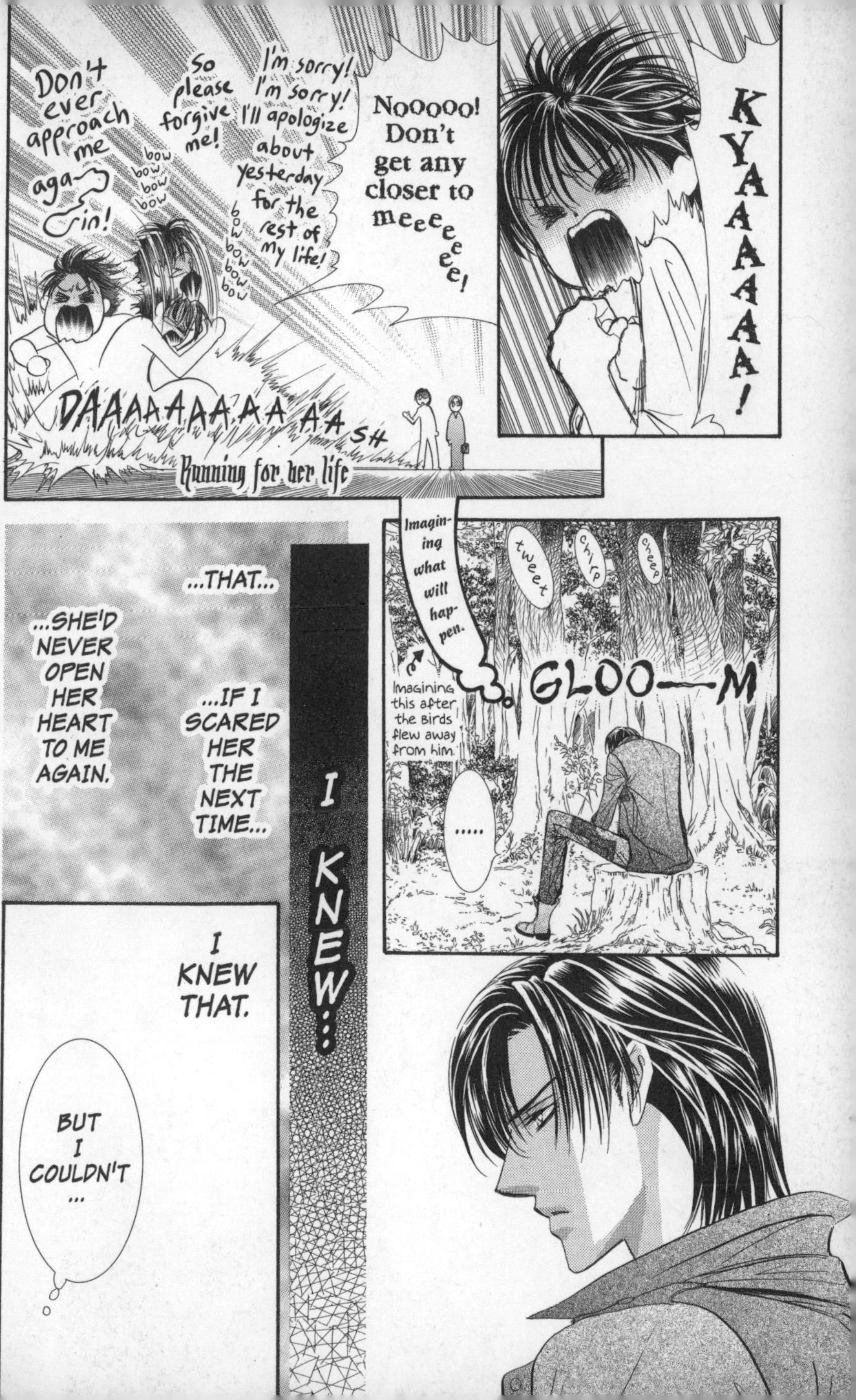
KYAAAAAA!
Nooooo! Don't get any closer to meeeeeee!
I'm sorry! I'm sorry! I'll apologize about yesterday for the rest of my life!
So please forgive me!
Don't ever approach me aga—in!
bow bow bow bow
bow bow bow bow
DAAAAAAAA AA AASH
Running for her life
Imagining what will happen.
tweet
chirp
cheep
GLOO—M
Imagining this after the birds flew away from him.
.....
...THAT...
...SHE'D NEVER OPEN HER HEART TO ME AGAIN.
...IF I SCARED HER THE NEXT TIME...
I KNEW...
I KNEW THAT.
BUT I COULDN'T ...

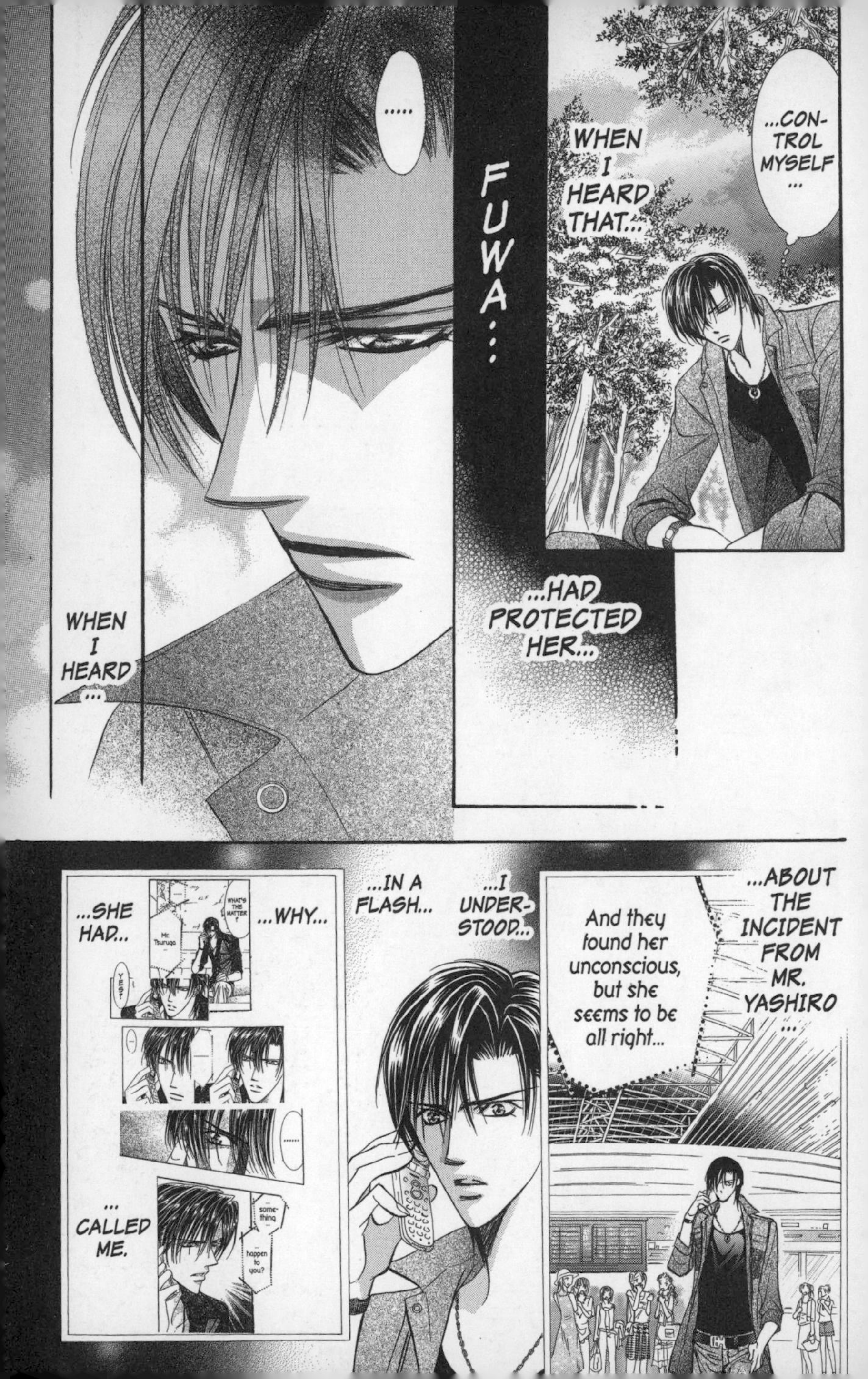

...CON-TROL MYSELF ...
WHEN I HEARD THAT...
FUWA...
...HAD PROTECTED HER...
.....
WHEN I HEARD ...
...ABOUT THE INCIDENT FROM MR. YASHIRO ...
And they found her unconscious, but she seems to be all right...
...I UNDER-STOOD...
...IN A FLASH...
...WHY...
...SHE HAD...
WHAT'S THE MATTER?
Mr. Tsuruga ...
YES?
...CALLED ME.
...something...
...happen to you?

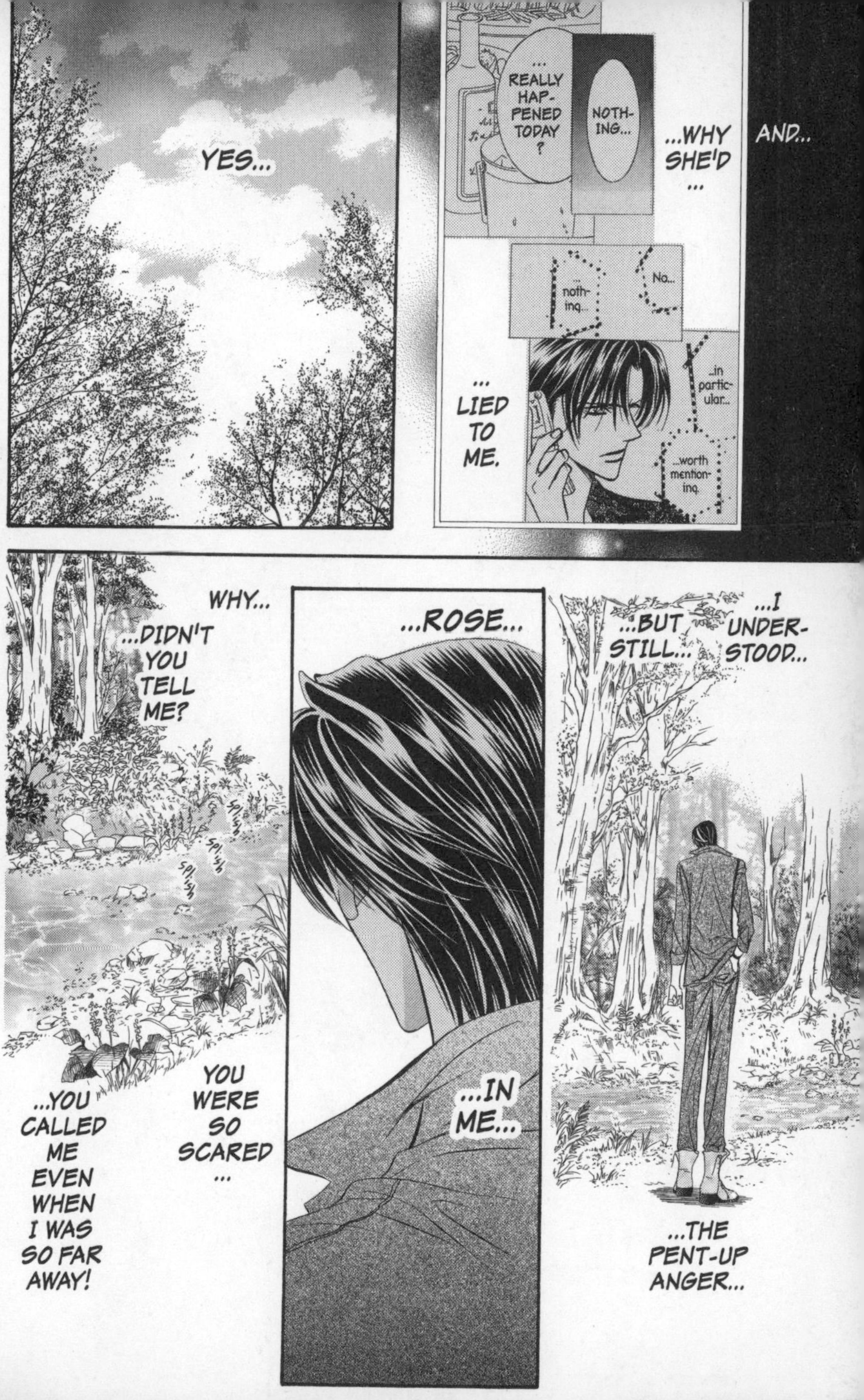
AND...
...WHY SHE'D ...
... REALLY HAP-PENED TODAY ?
NOTH-ING...
Na...
noth-ing...
...in partic-ular...
...worth mention-ing.
... LIED TO ME.
YES...
...I UNDER-STOOD...
...BUT STILL...
...THE PENT-UP ANGER...
...ROSE...
...IN ME...
WHY...
...DIDN'T YOU TELL ME?
splish
splish
splish
YOU WERE SO SCARED ...
...YOU CALLED ME EVEN WHEN I WAS SO FAR AWAY!

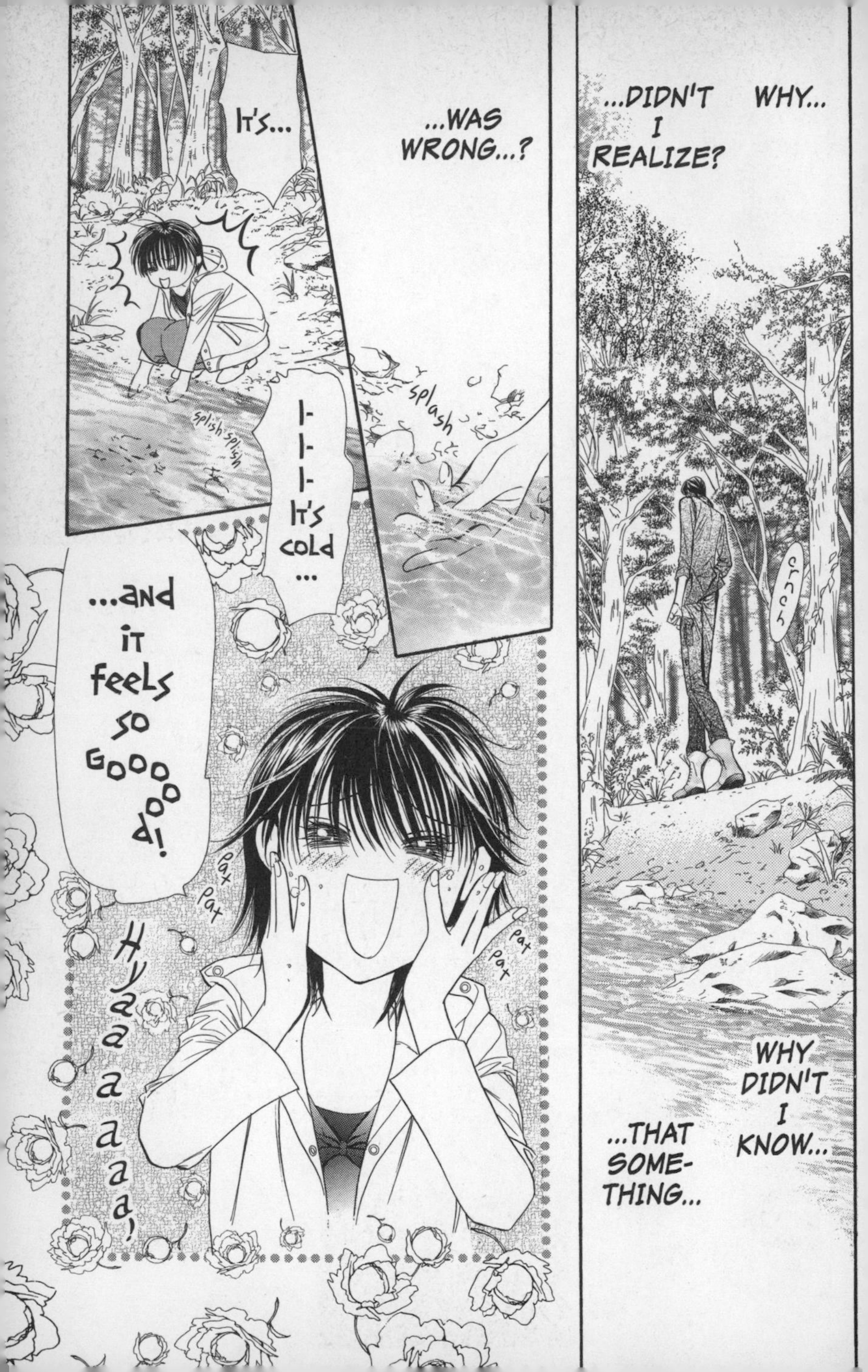

WHY...
...DIDN'T I REALIZE?
WHY DIDN'T I KNOW...
...THAT SOME-THING...
...WAS WRONG...?
splash
It's...
splish splish
I- I- I- It's cold...
...and it feels so gooooood!
Pat pat
Hyaaaaaaaaa!
Pat pat

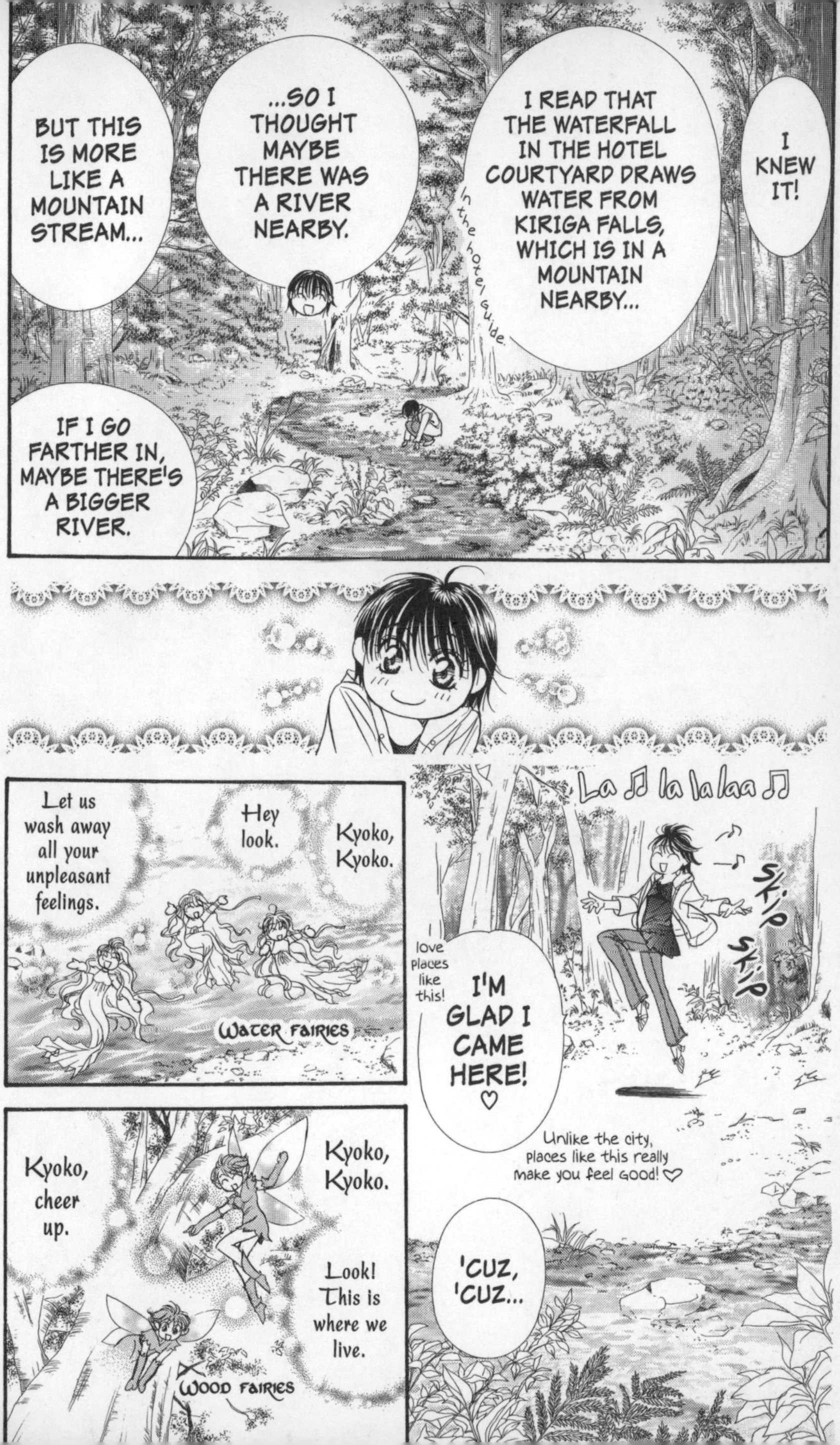
I KNEW IT!
I READ THAT THE WATERFALL IN THE HOTEL COURTYARD DRAWS WATER FROM KIRIGA FALLS, WHICH IS IN A MOUNTAIN NEARBY...
In the hotel guide.
...SO I THOUGHT MAYBE THERE WAS A RIVER NEARBY.
BUT THIS IS MORE LIKE A MOUNTAIN STREAM...
IF I GO FARTHER IN, MAYBE THERE'S A BIGGER RIVER.
La ♫ la la laa ♫
SKIP SKIP
I'M GLAD I CAME HERE! ♡
I love places like this!
Unlike the city, places like this really make you feel good! ♡
Kyoko, Kyoko.
Hey look.
Let us wash away all your unpleasant feelings.
WATER FAIRIES
'CUZ, 'CUZ...
Kyoko, Kyoko.
Kyoko, cheer up.
Look! This is where we live.
WOOD FAIRIES

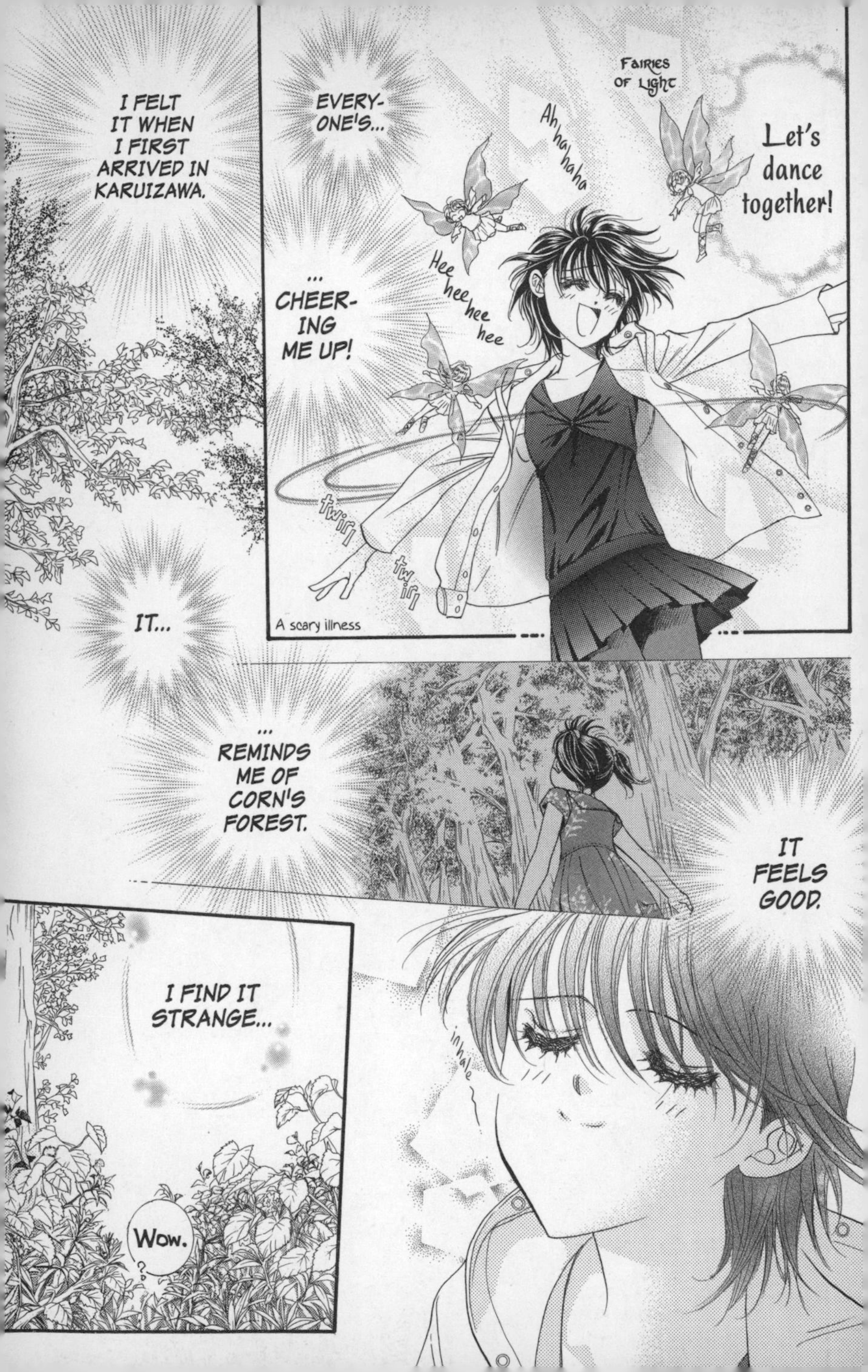
Fairies of Light
Let's dance together!
Ah hahaha
EVERY-ONE'S...
Hee hee hee hee
... CHEERING ME UP!
twirl
twirl
A scary illness
I FELT IT WHEN I FIRST ARRIVED IN KARUIZAWA.
IT...
... REMINDS ME OF CORN'S FOREST.
IT FEELS GOOD.
inhale
I FIND IT STRANGE...
Wow.
?

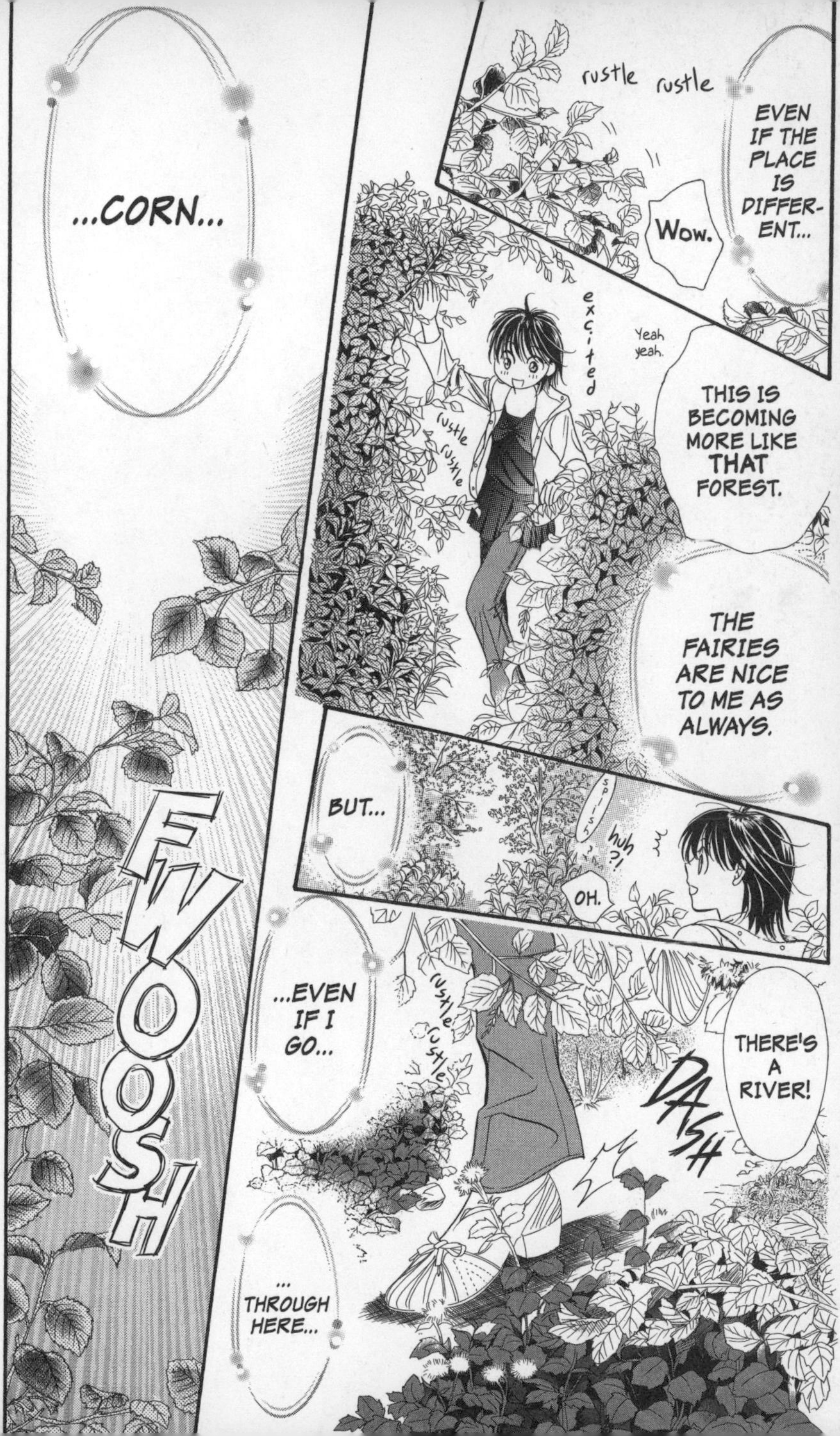
EVEN IF THE PLACE IS DIFFERENT...
rustle rustle
Wow.
Yeah yeah.
THIS IS BECOMING MORE LIKE THAT FOREST.
excited
rustle rustle
THE FAIRIES ARE NICE TO ME AS ALWAYS.
huh ?!
splish
BUT...
OH.
THERE'S A RIVER!
DASH
rustle rustle
...EVEN IF I GO...
... THROUGH HERE...
...CORN...
FWOOSH

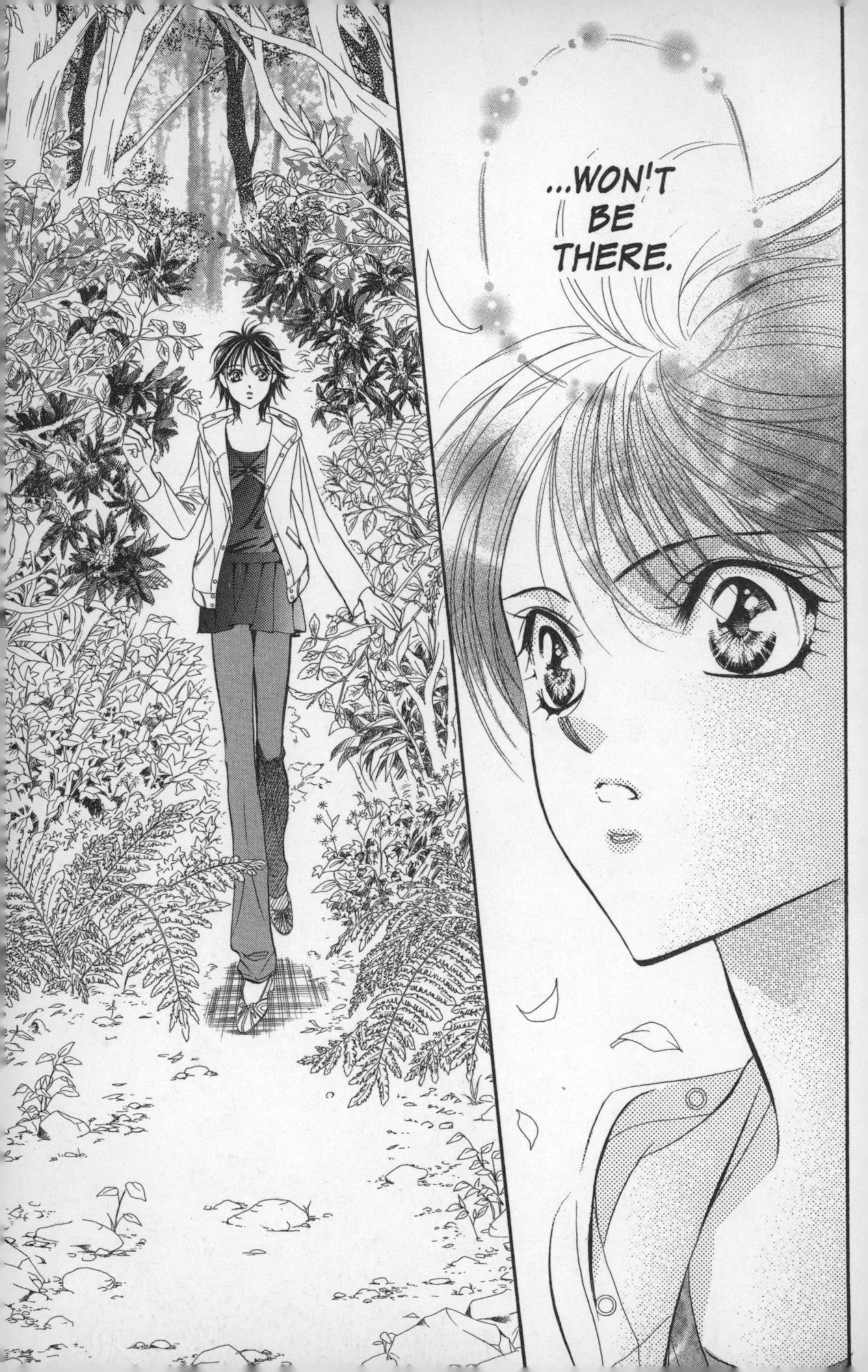
...WON'T BE THERE.

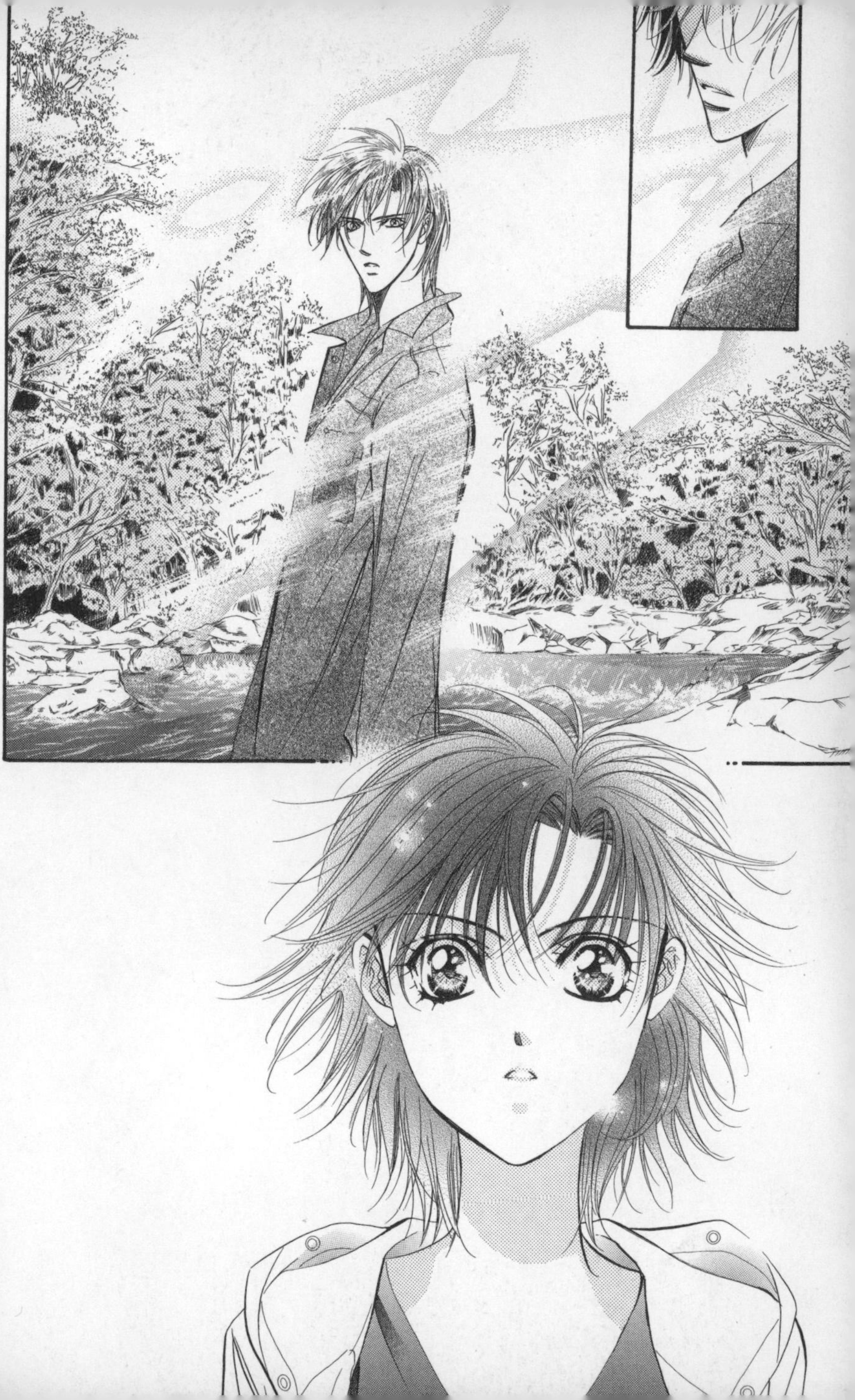

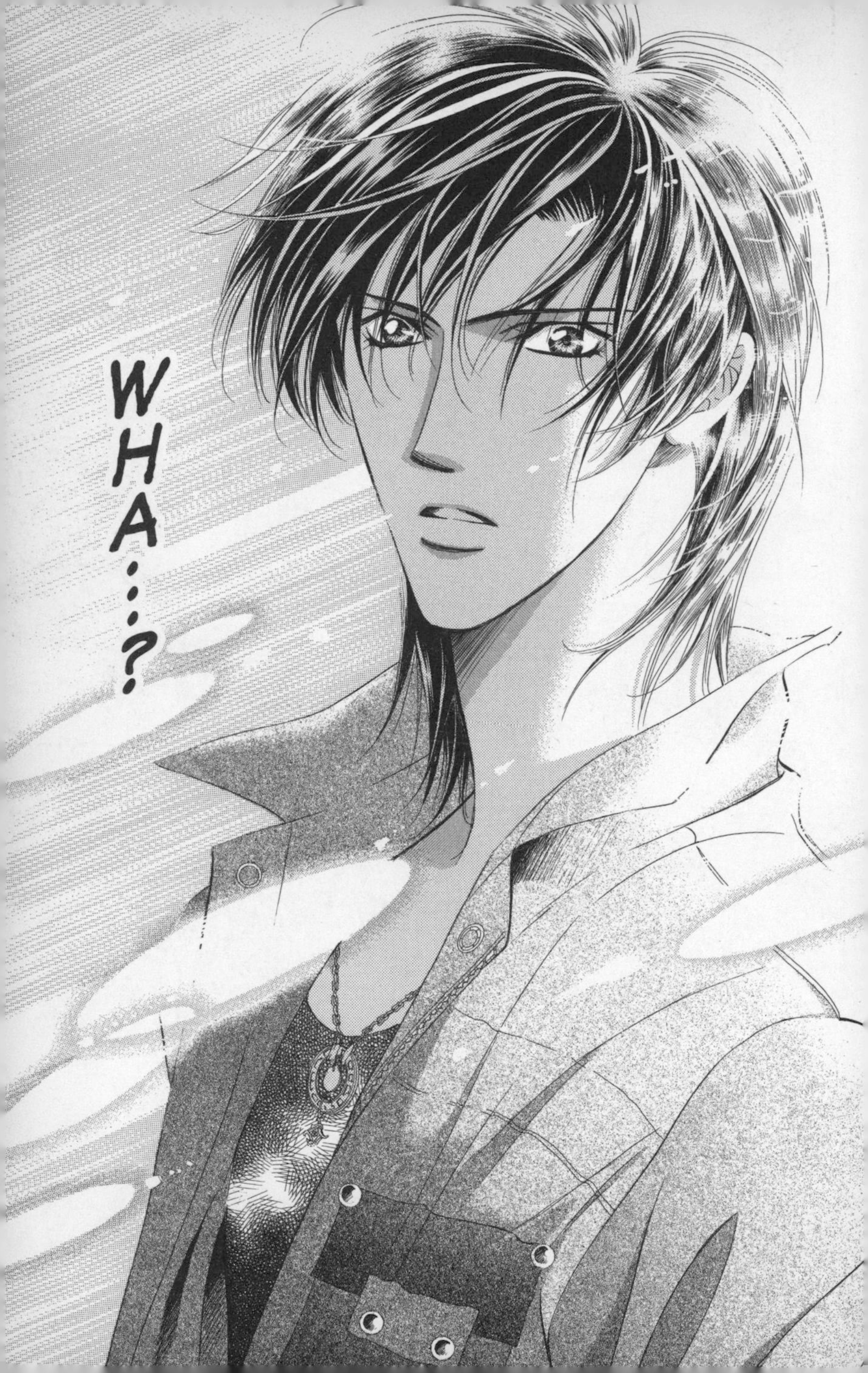
WHA...?

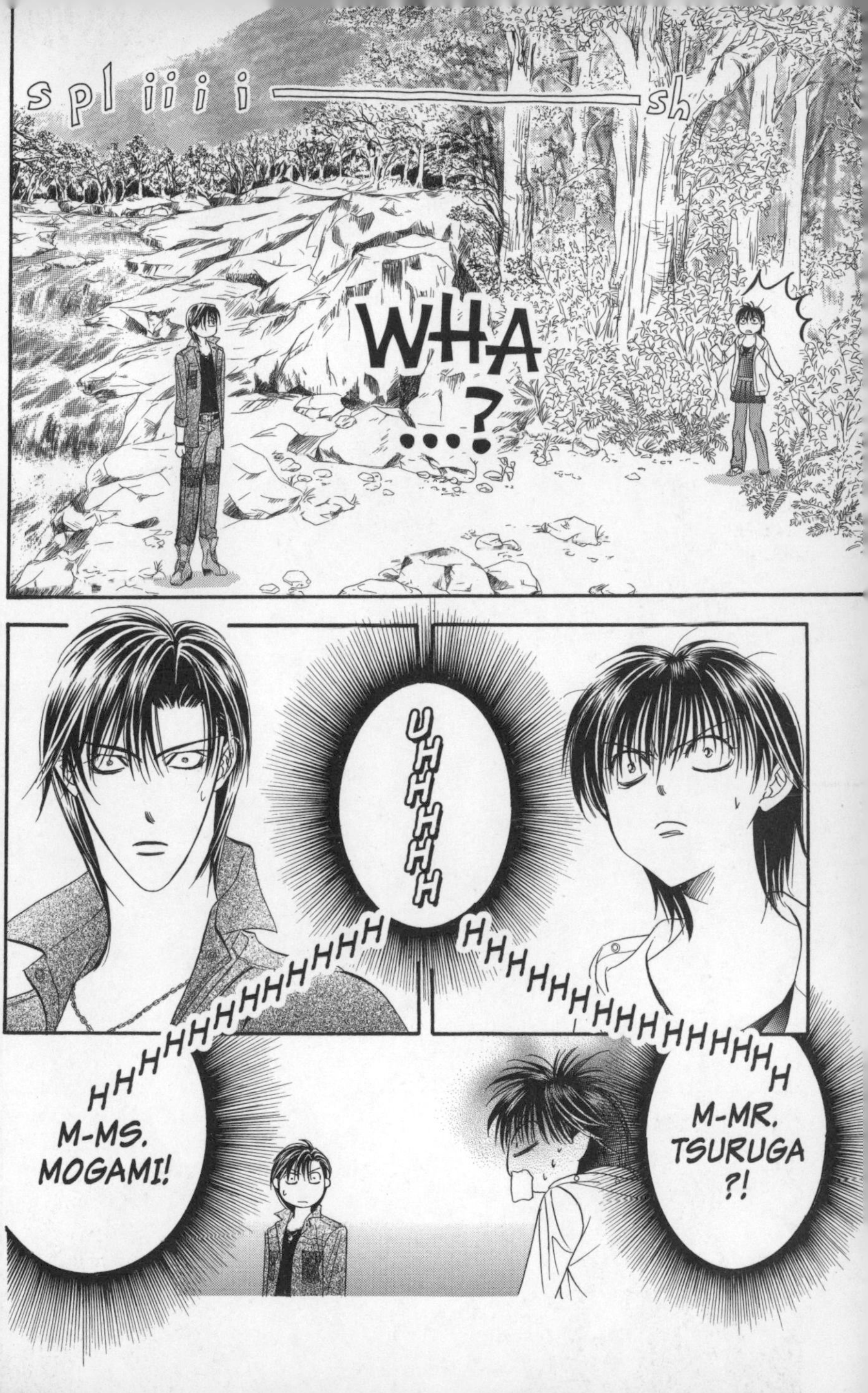
splii i i i—————sh
WHA...?
UHHHHHHH
HHHHHHHHHHHHHHH
HHHHHHHHHHHHHH
M-MR. TSURUGA?!
M-MS. MOGAMI!

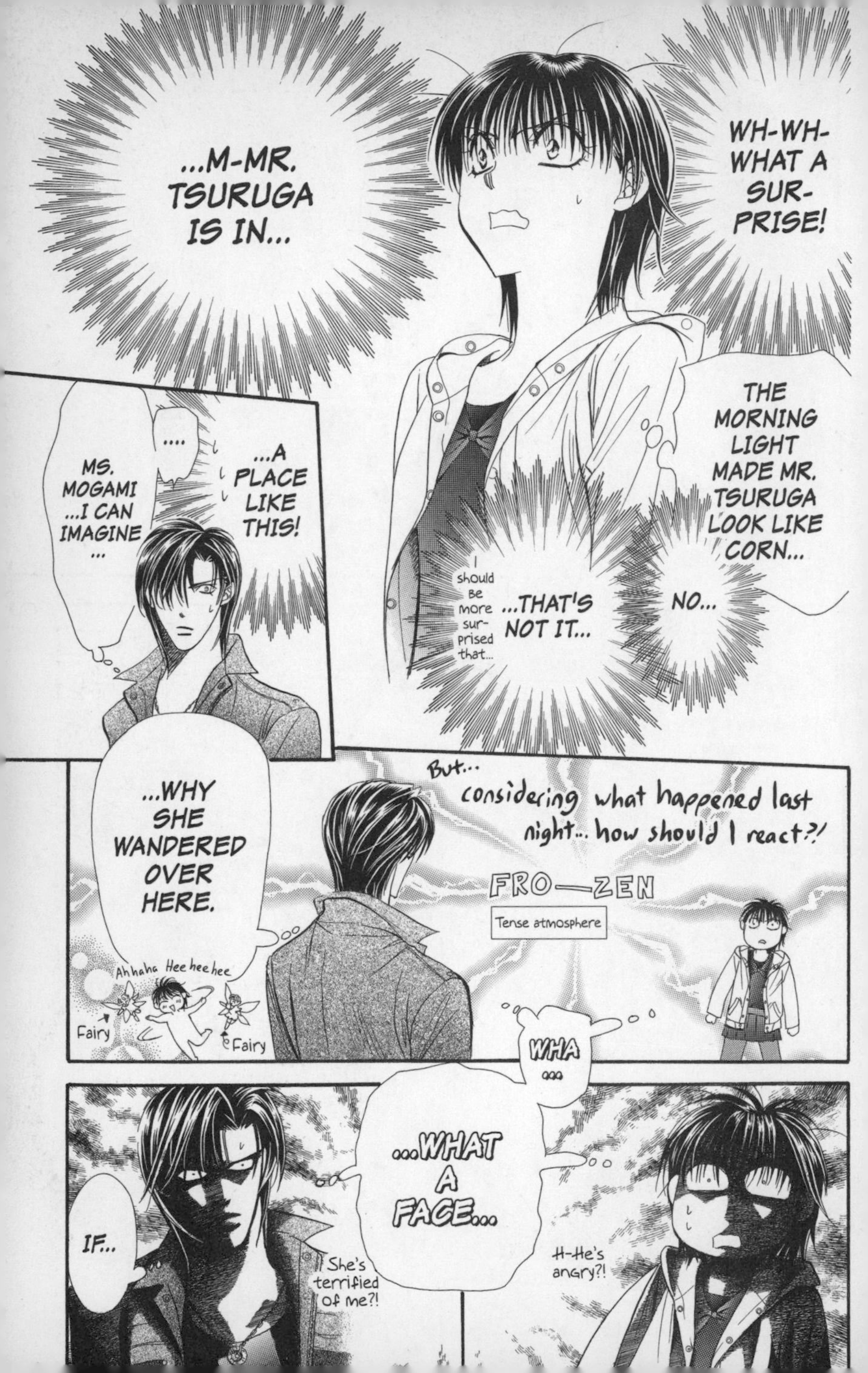
WH-WH-WHAT A SUR-PRISE!
...M-MR. TSURUGA IS IN...
THE MORNING LIGHT MADE MR. TSURUGA LOOK LIKE CORN...
NO...
...THAT'S NOT IT...
I should be more surprised that...
...A PLACE LIKE THIS!
....
MS. MOGAMI ...I CAN IMAGINE ...
But... considering what happened last night... how should I react?!
FRO—ZEN
Tense atmosphere
WHA...
...WHY SHE WANDERED OVER HERE.
Ahhaha Heeheehee
Fairy
Fairy
H-He's angry?!
...WHAT A FACE...
She's terrified of me?!
IF...

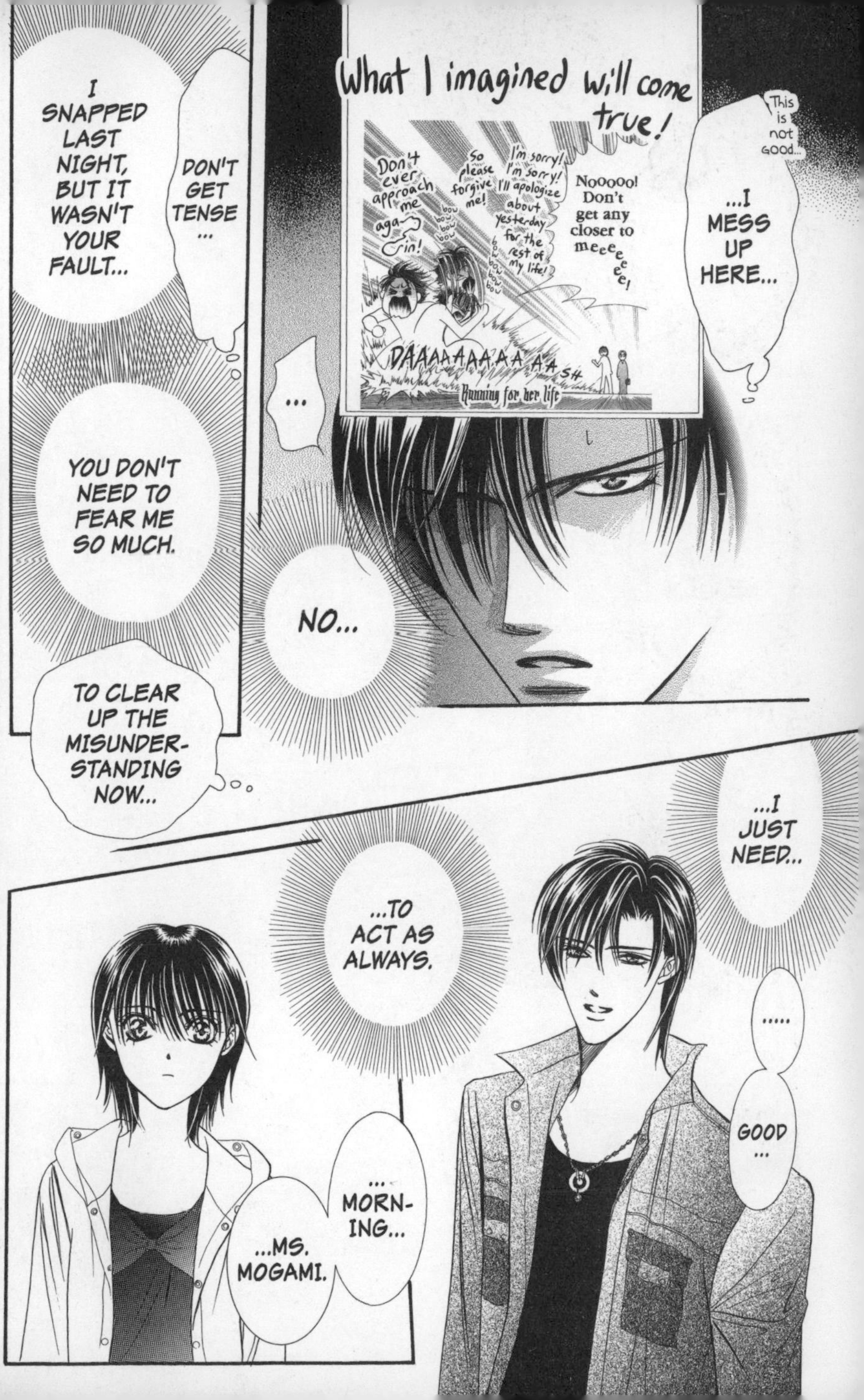
What I imagined will come true!
This is not good...
...I MESS UP HERE...
Nooooo! Don't get any closer to meeeeeee!
I'm sorry! I'm sorry! I'll apologize about yesterday for the rest of my life!
So please forgive me!
Don't ever approach me aga~in!
bow bow bow bow
bow bow bow bow
DAAAAAAAAAASH
Running for her life
...
NO...
DON'T GET TENSE ...
I SNAPPED LAST NIGHT, BUT IT WASN'T YOUR FAULT...
YOU DON'T NEED TO FEAR ME SO MUCH.
TO CLEAR UP THE MISUNDERSTANDING NOW...
...I JUST NEED...
...TO ACT AS ALWAYS.
.....
GOOD ...
... MORNING...
...MS. MOGAMI.

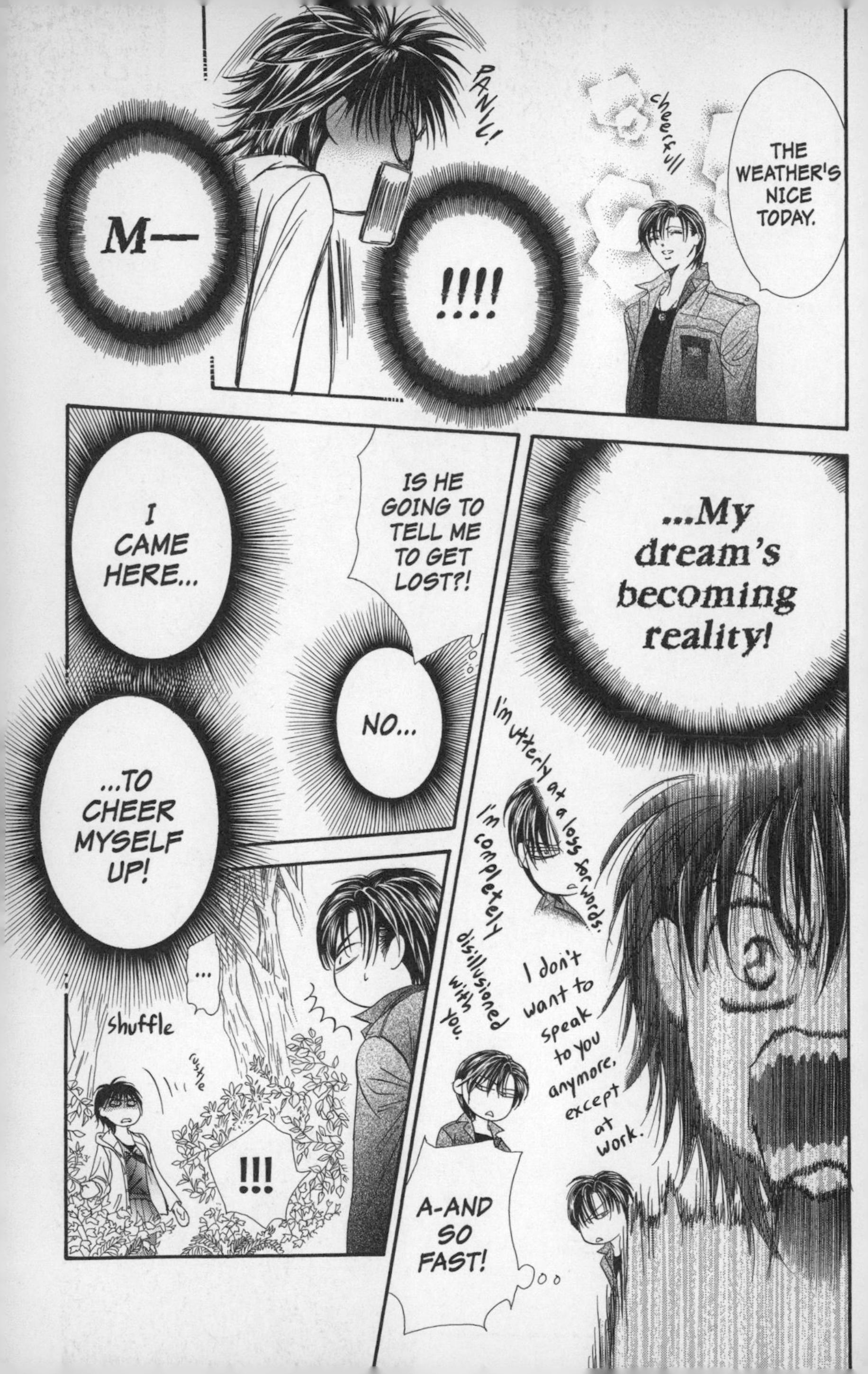
THE WEATHER'S NICE TODAY.
cheerful!
PANIC!
M—
!!!!
...My dream's becoming reality!
I'm utterly at a loss for words.
I'm completely disillusioned with you.
I don't want to speak to you anymore, except at work.
A-AND SO FAST!
IS HE GOING TO TELL ME TO GET LOST?!
I CAME HERE...
NO...
...TO CHEER MYSELF UP!
...
shuffle
rustle
!!!

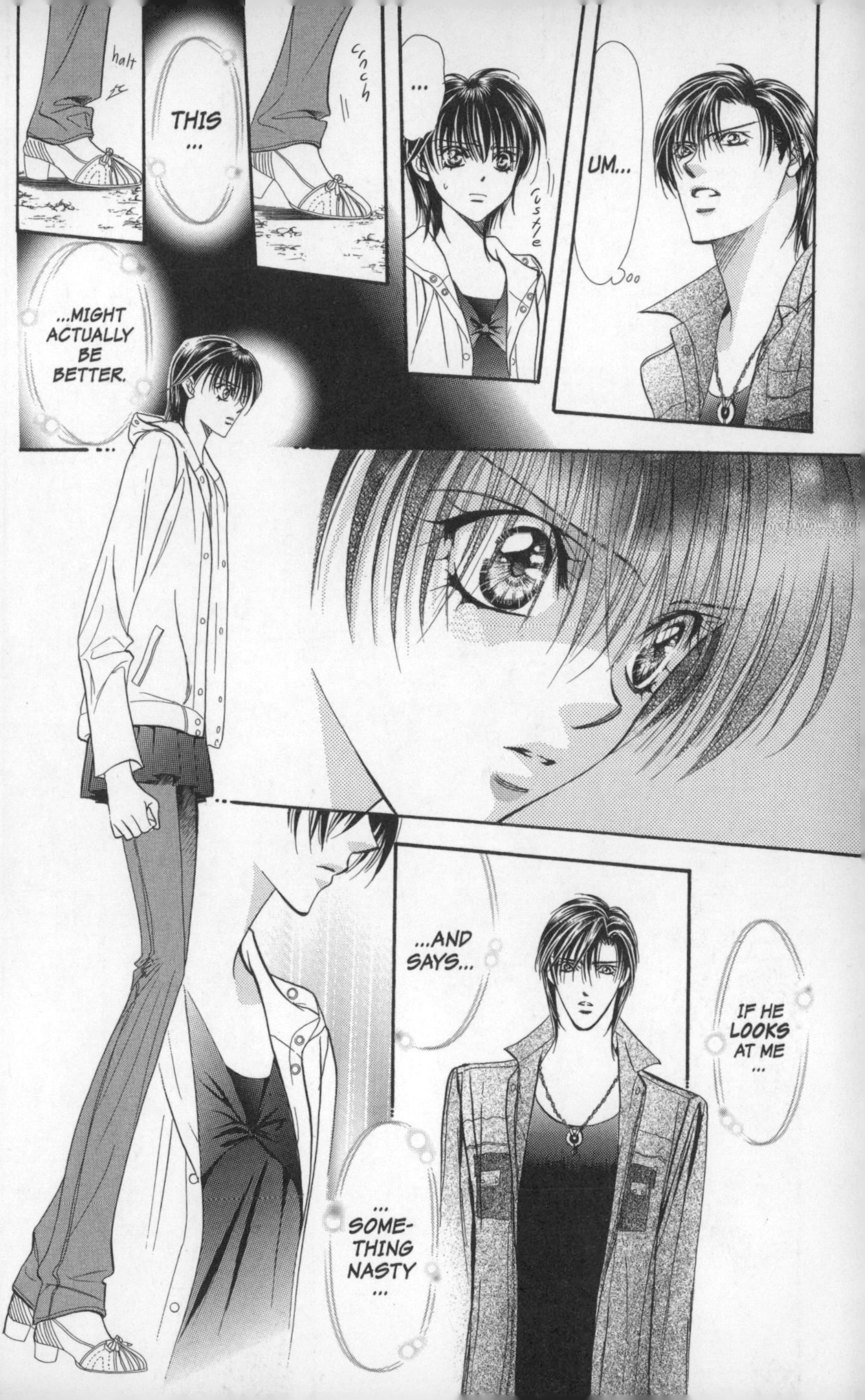
UM...
...
rustle
crnch
THIS ...
halt
...MIGHT ACTUALLY BE BETTER.
IF HE LOOKS AT ME ...
...AND SAYS...
... SOME-THING NASTY ...

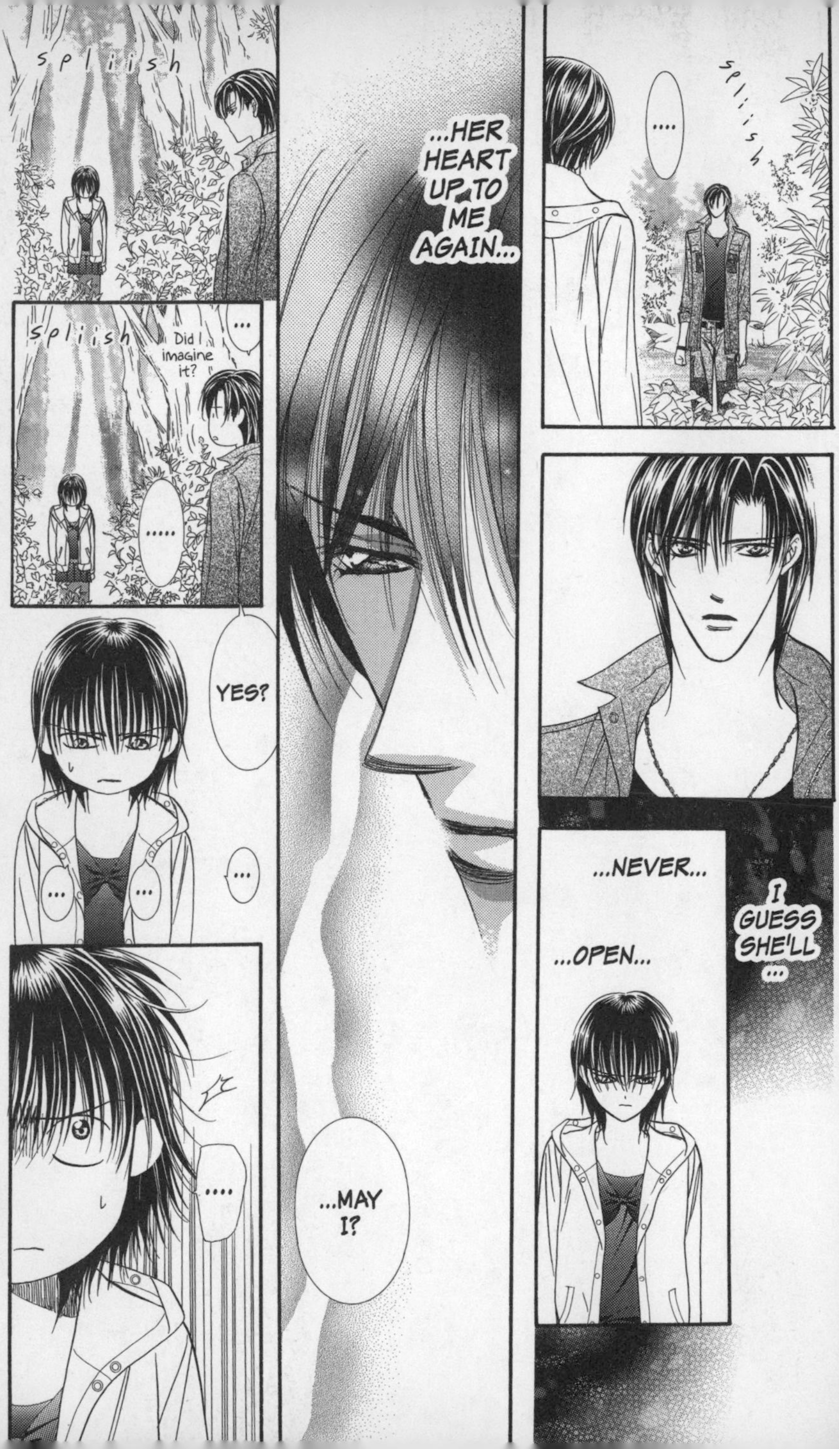
splish
....
...
I GUESS SHE'LL ...
...NEVER...
...OPEN...
...HER HEART UP TO ME AGAIN...
...MAY I?
splish
...
Did I imagine it?
splish
......
YES?
...
...
...
....

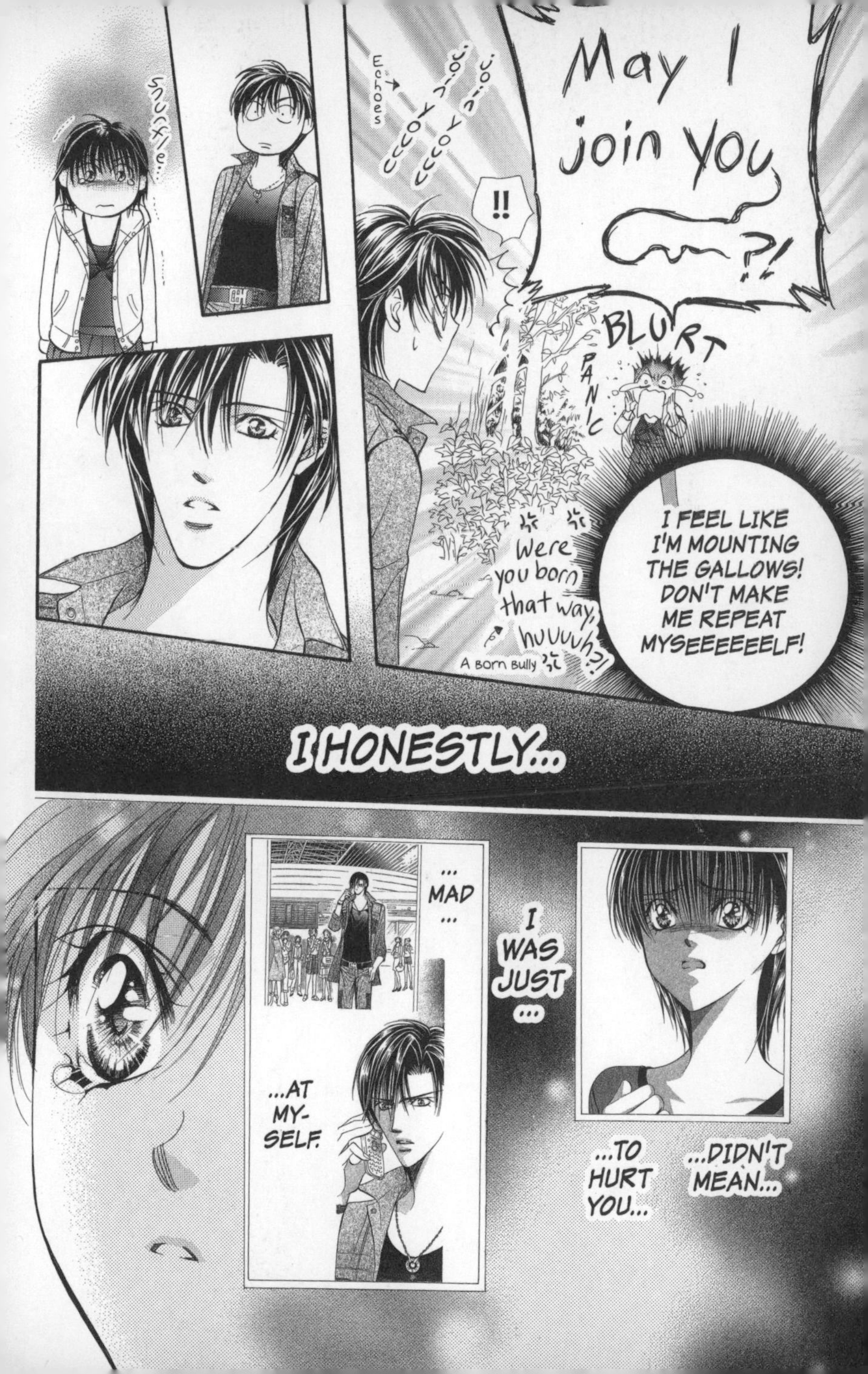

May I join you ~~~?!
!!
BLURT
PANIC
I FEEL LIKE I'M MOUNTING THE GALLOWS! DON'T MAKE ME REPEAT MYSEEEEEEELF!
Were you born that way, huuuuh?!
A Born Bully
Join youuuu
Join youuuu
Echoes
snurfle...
I HONESTLY...
...DIDN'T MEAN...
...TO HURT YOU...
I WAS JUST...
...MAD...
...AT MYSELF.

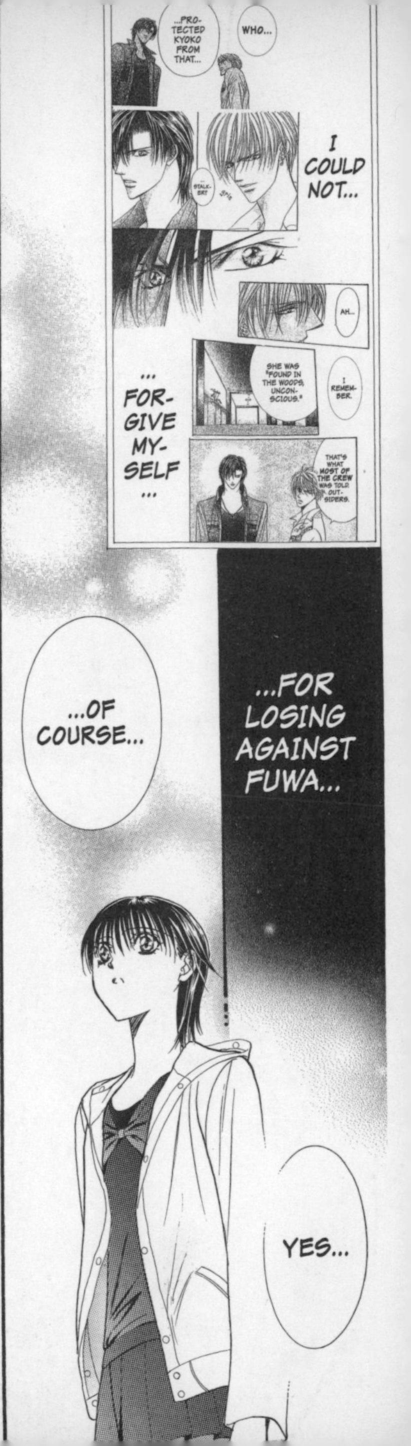
WHO...
...PROTECTED KYOKO FROM THAT...
...STALKER
I COULD NOT...
AH...
I REMEMBER.
SHE WAS "FOUND IN THE WOODS, UNCONSCIOUS."
...FORGIVE MYSELF...
THAT'S WHAT MOST OF THE CREW WAS TOLD. OUTSIDERS.
...FOR LOSING AGAINST FUWA...
...OF COURSE...
YES...
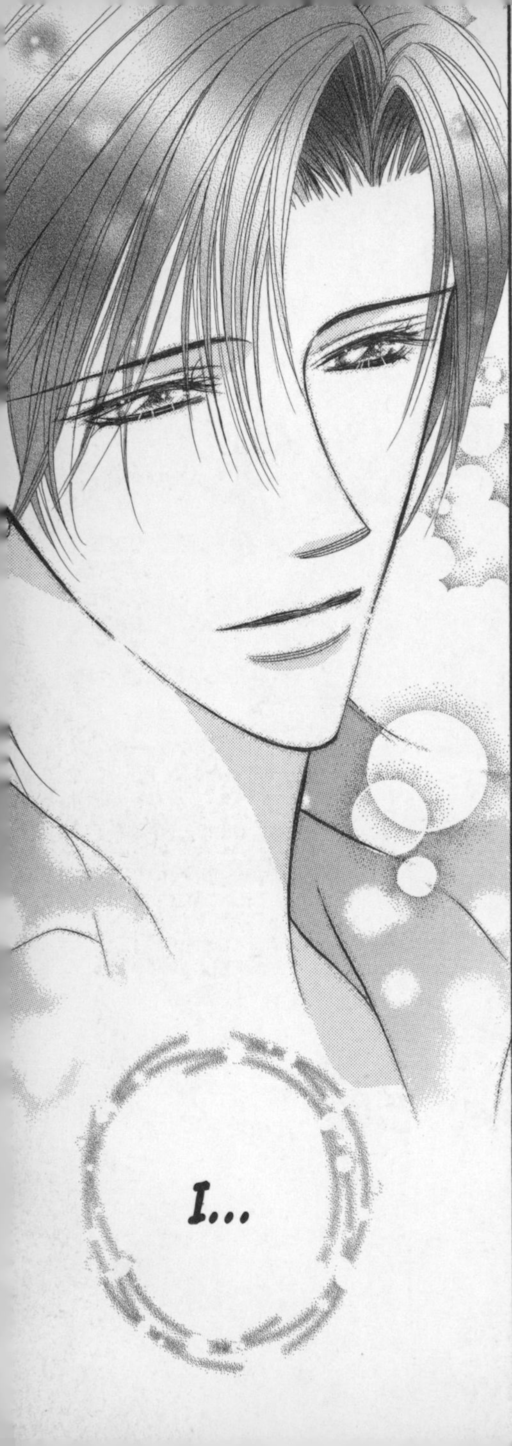
I...

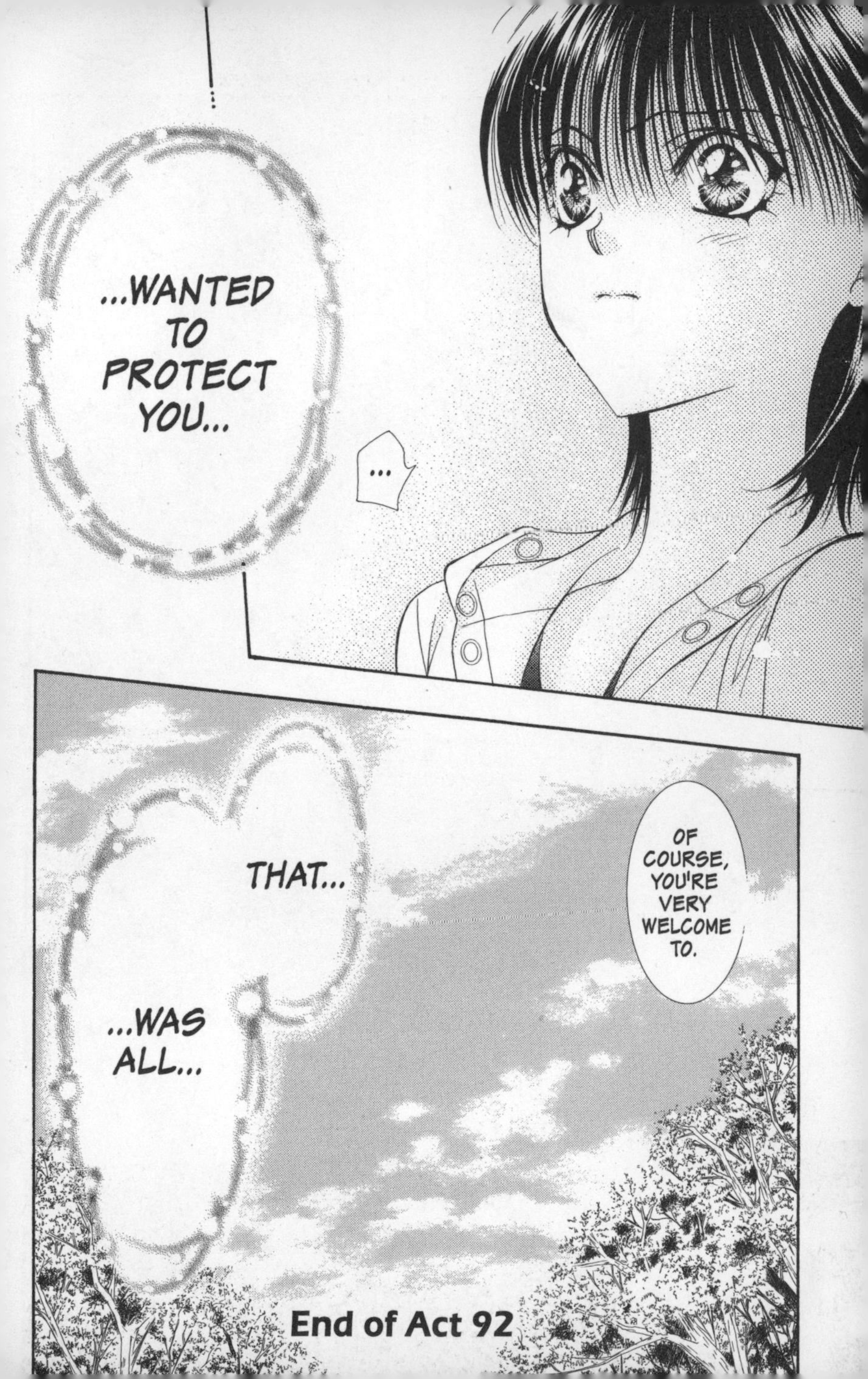
...WANTED TO PROTECT YOU...
...
OF COURSE, YOU'RE VERY WELCOME TO.
THAT...
...WAS ALL...

End of Act 92

Skip•Beat! 16 "Her First Experience"

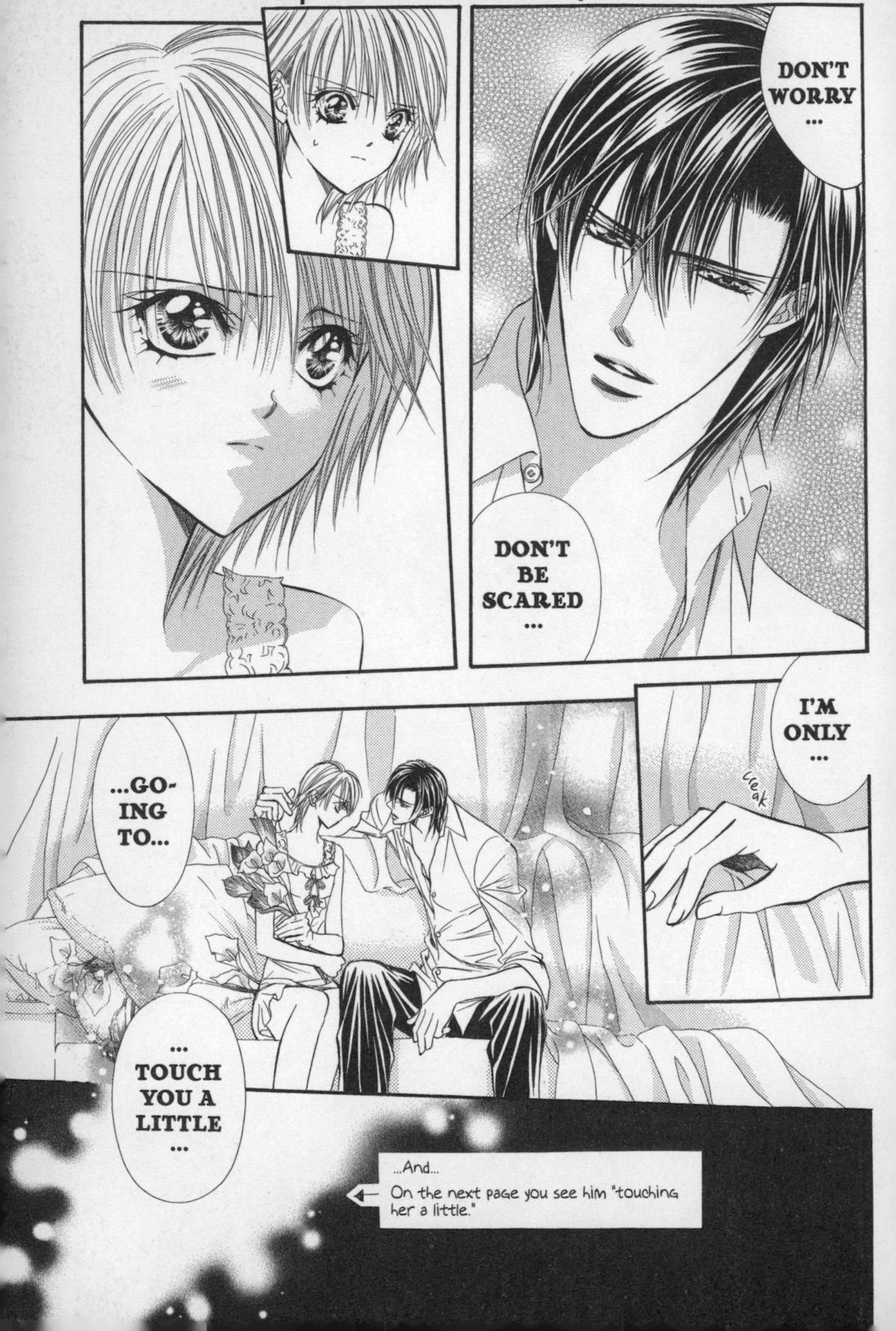

DON'T WORRY ...
DON'T BE SCARED ...
I'M ONLY ...
creak
...GO-ING TO...
... TOUCH YOU A LITTLE ...
...And...
On the next page you see him "touching her a little."

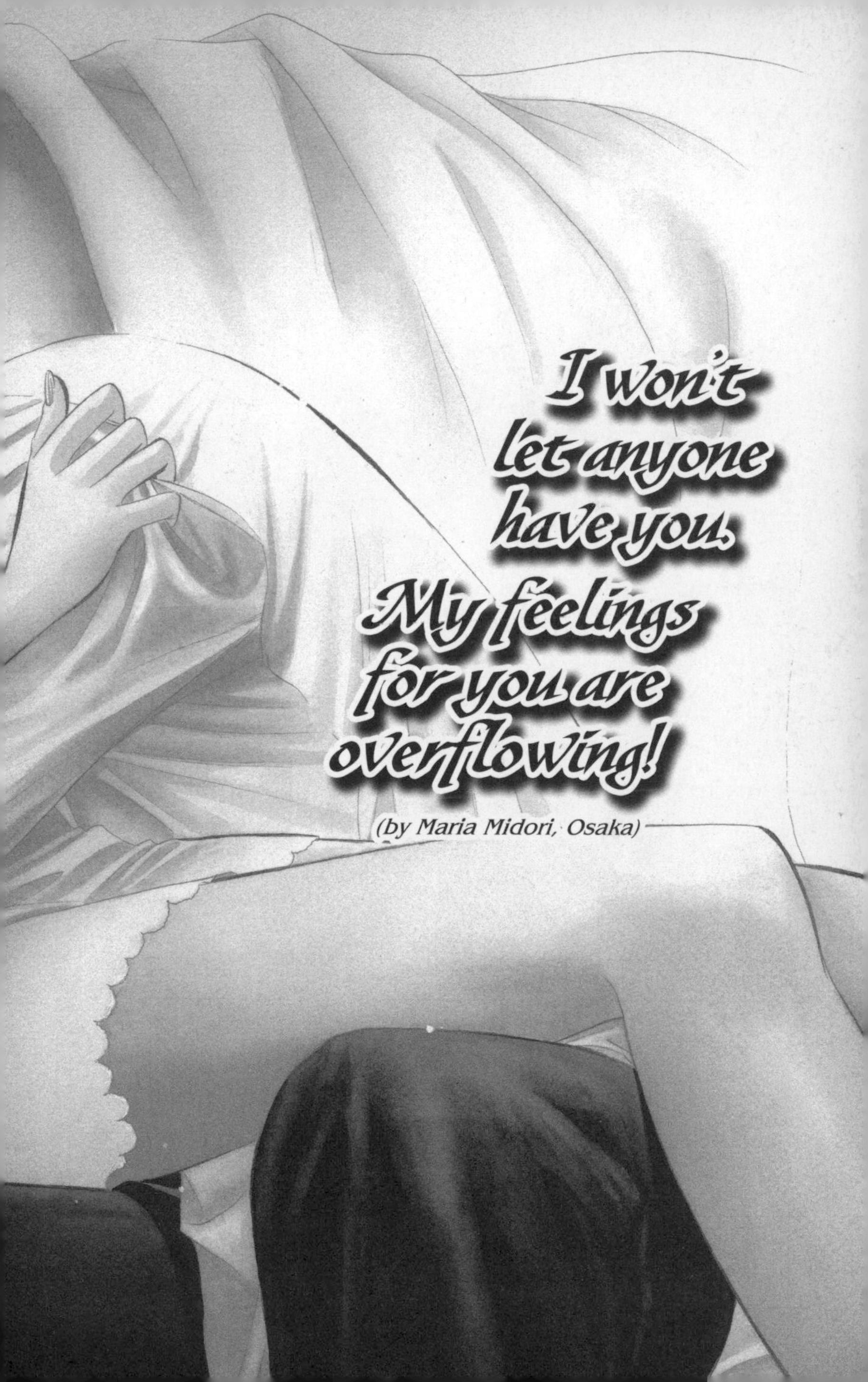
I won't let anyone have you. My feelings for you are overflowing!
(by Maria Midori, Osaka)

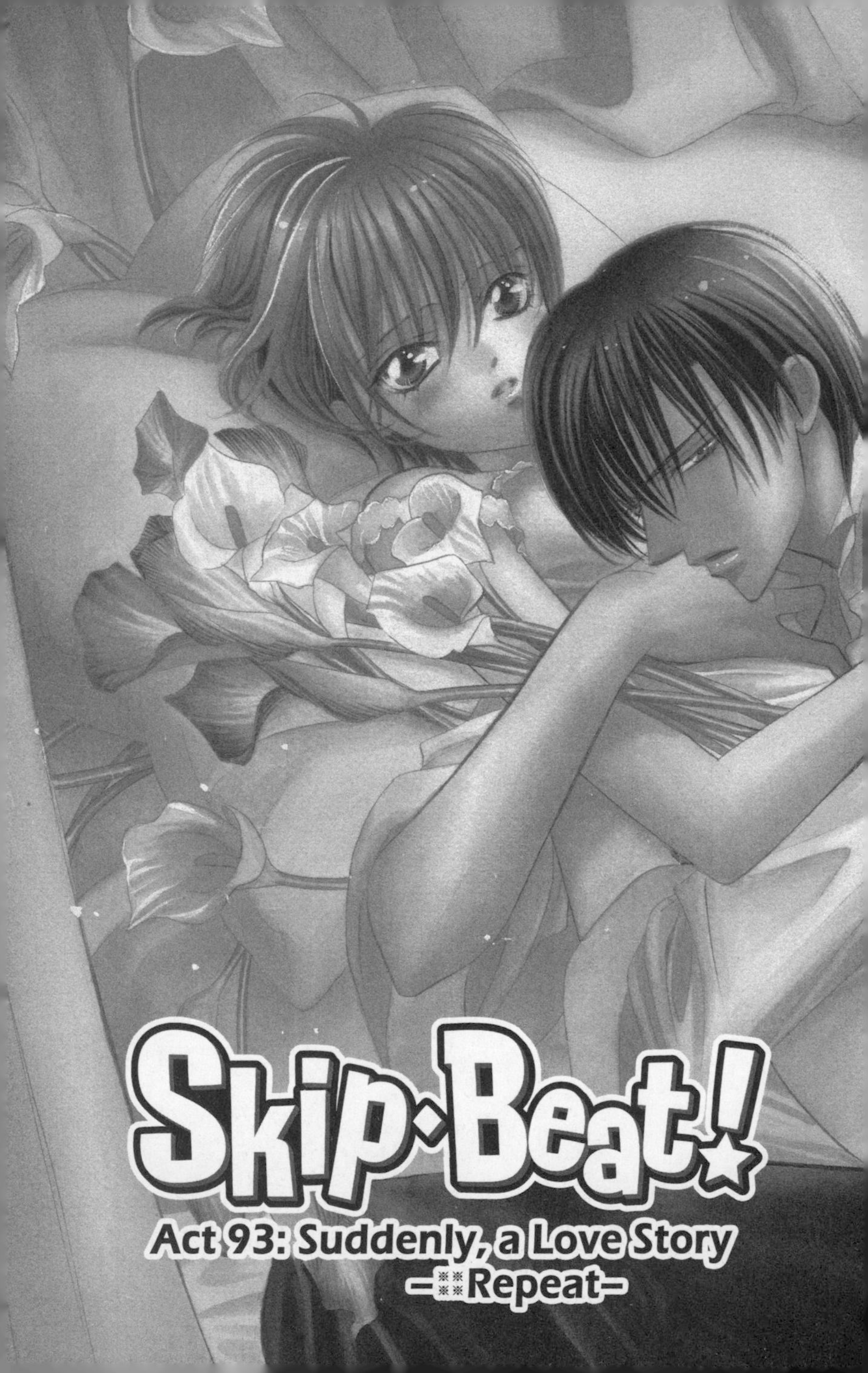
Skip·Beat!
Act 93: Suddenly, a Love Story
-Repeat-

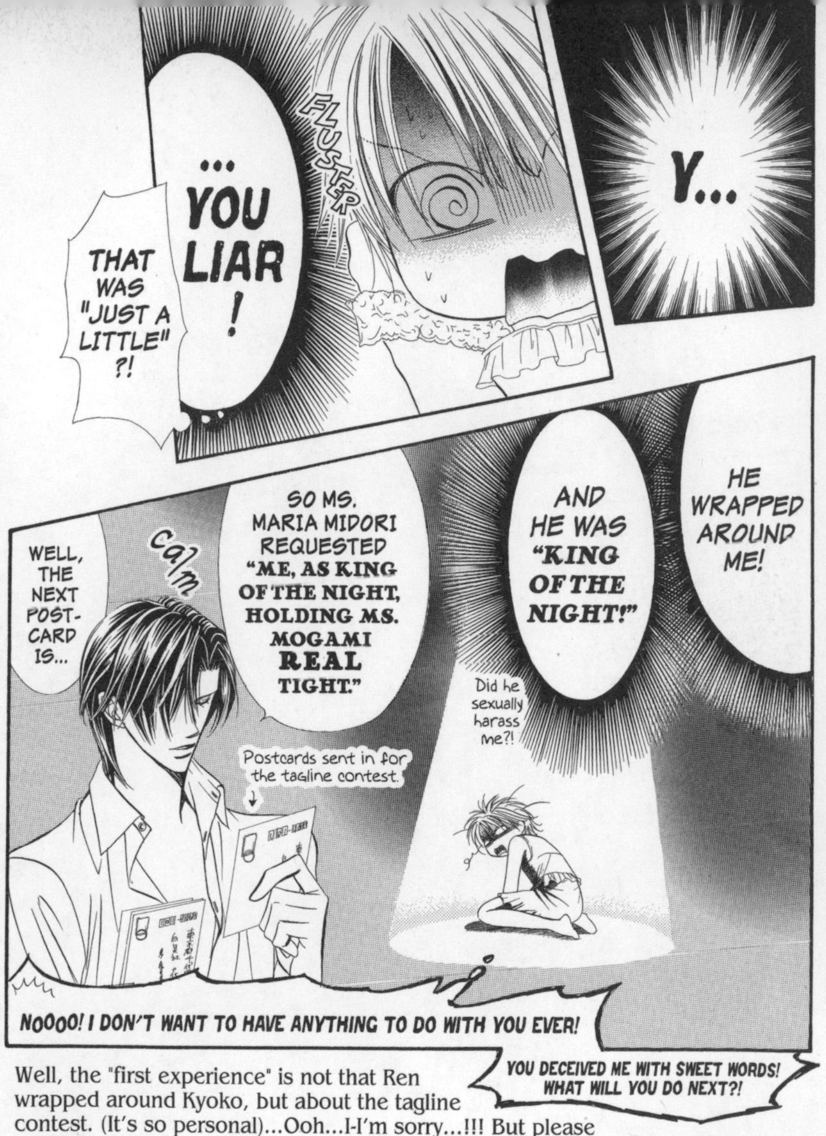
Y...
FLUSTER
...YOU LIAR!
THAT WAS "JUST A LITTLE"?!
HE WRAPPED AROUND ME!
AND HE WAS "KING OF THE NIGHT!"
Did he sexually harass me?!
SO MS. MARIA MIDORI REQUESTED "ME, AS KING OF THE NIGHT, HOLDING MS. MOGAMI REAL TIGHT."
calm
WELL, THE NEXT POST-CARD IS...
Postcards sent in for the tagline contest.
NOOOO! I DON'T WANT TO HAVE ANYTHING TO DO WITH YOU EVER!
YOU DECEIVED ME WITH SWEET WORDS! WHAT WILL YOU DO NEXT?!

Well, the "first experience" is not that Ren wrapped around Kyoko, but about the tagline contest. (It's so personal)...Ooh...I-I'm sorry...!!! But please indulge me...

I've been a mangaka for over ten years. I've drawn two long series, but this is the first time a magazine sponsored a contest like this, so I was really happy!! When I heard about the contest, I really felt..."Oh...so *Skip•Beat*...is a manga that everyone really likes..."...(wry smile) Everybody sent in their passionate thoughts, and the results were announced in Act 93. The grand prize went to the line that's included in the cover illustration (usually, my editor writes the copy). Thank you everyone for sending in so many phrases!! Nakamura is overwhelmed!!

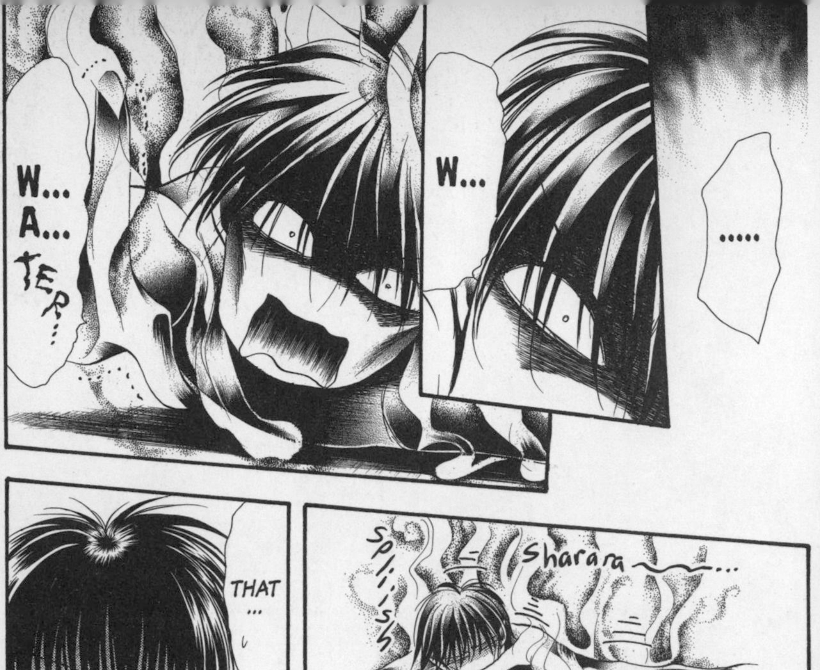
.....
W...
W...
A...
TER...
Sharara~~...
Spliish
Shriveled up
SCATTERED
Sha rarara
THA...
sharara
Sound of it being exorcised.
THAT...
... SCARED ME...

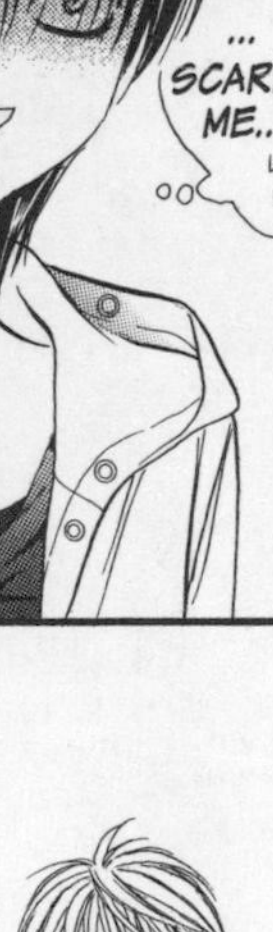

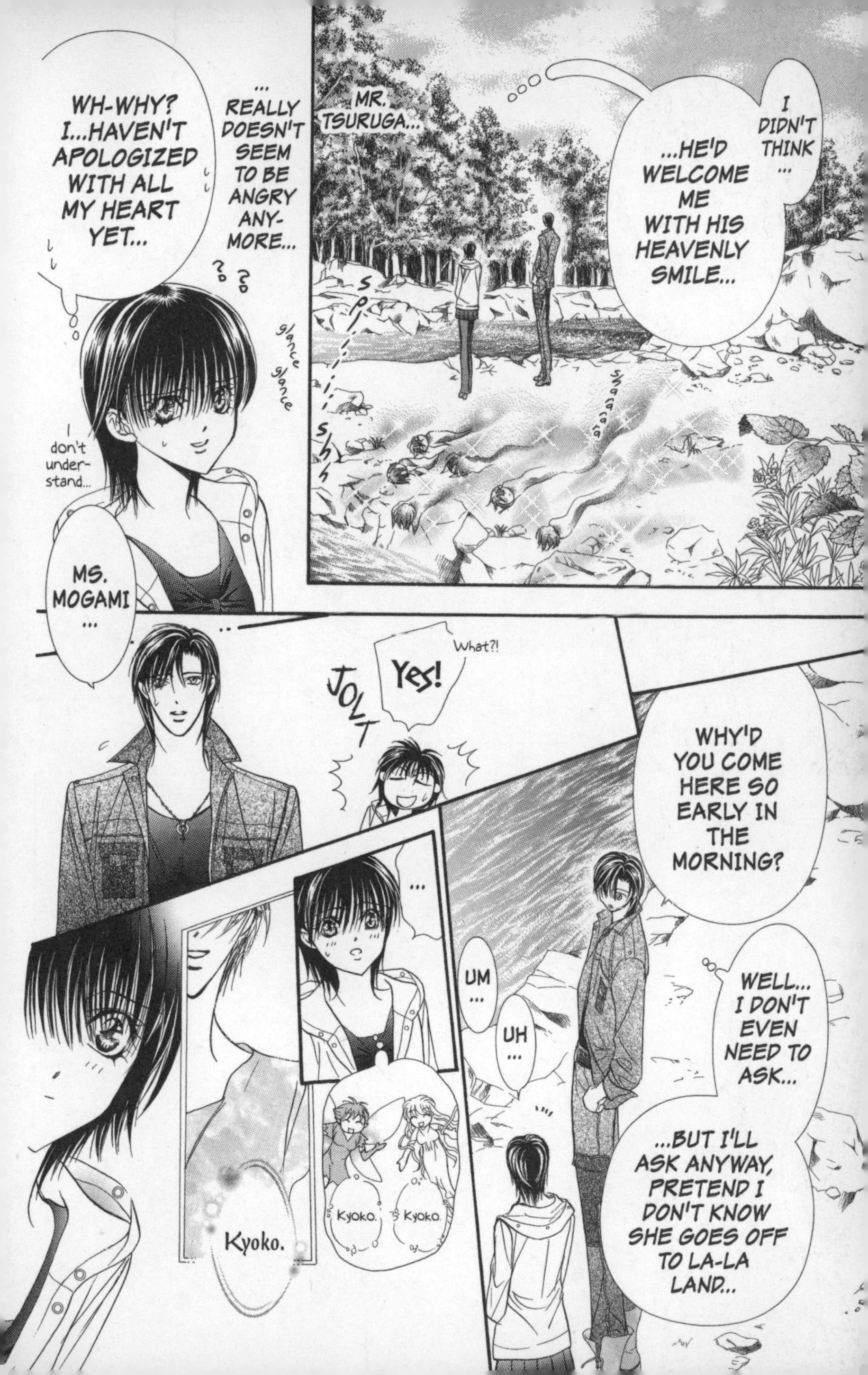

I DIDN'T THINK...
...HE'D WELCOME ME WITH HIS HEAVENLY SMILE...
MR. TSURUGA...
shararara
SPI...SHH
...REALLY DOESN'T SEEM TO BE ANGRY ANYMORE...
WH-WHY? I...HAVEN'T APOLOGIZED WITH ALL MY HEART YET...
glance glance
I don't under-stand...
WHY'D YOU COME HERE SO EARLY IN THE MORNING?
UM...
UH...
WELL... I DON'T EVEN NEED TO ASK...
...BUT I'LL ASK ANYWAY, PRETEND I DON'T KNOW SHE GOES OFF TO LA-LA LAND...
...
Kyoko.
Kyoko.
Kyoko.
MS. MOGAMI...
Yes!
What?!
JOLT

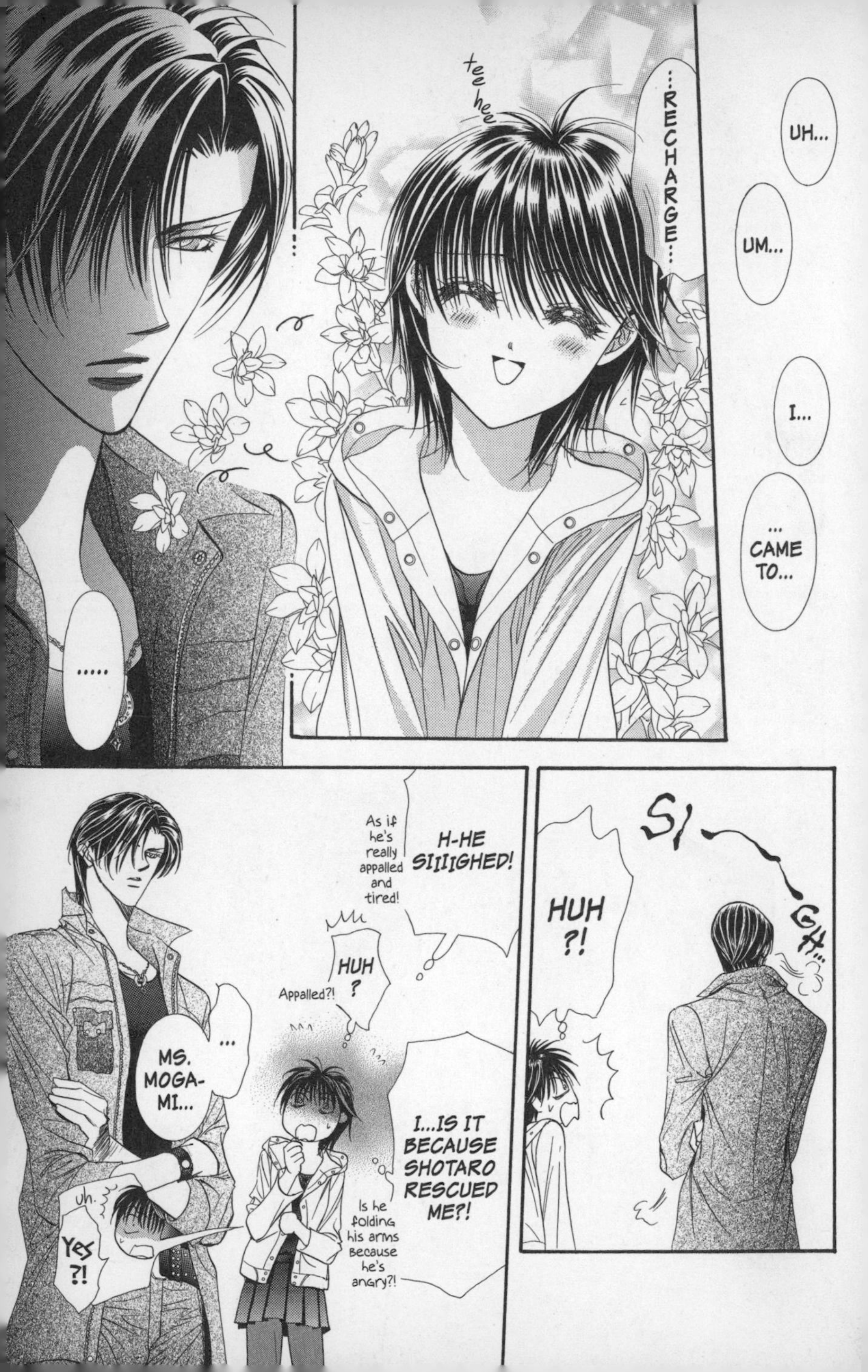
UH...
UM...
I...
...CAME TO...
...RECHARGE...
tee hee
.....
SI—GH...
HUH?!
H-HE SIIIIGHED!
As if he's really appalled and tired!
HUH?
Appalled?!
I...IS IT BECAUSE SHOTARO RESCUED ME?!
Is he folding his arms because he's angry?!
...
MS. MOGA-MI...
uh.
Yes?!

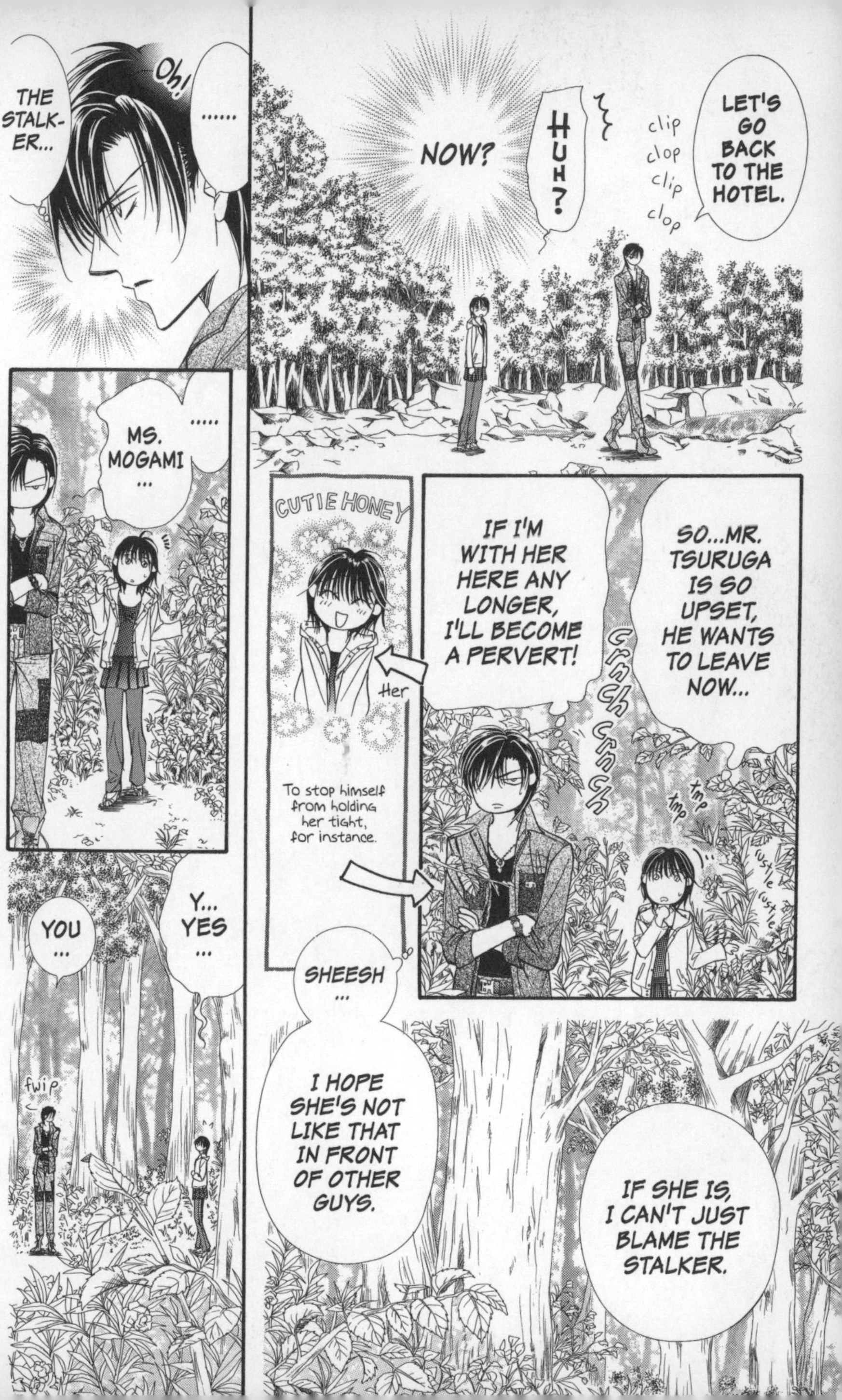
LET'S GO BACK TO THE HOTEL.
clip clop clip clop
HUH?
NOW?
SO...MR. TSURUGA IS SO UPSET, HE WANTS TO LEAVE NOW...
tmp tmp
rustle rustle
crnch crnch
IF I'M WITH HER HERE ANY LONGER, I'LL BECOME A PERVERT!
CUTIE HONEY
Her
To stop himself from holding her tight, for instance.
SHEESH...
I HOPE SHE'S NOT LIKE THAT IN FRONT OF OTHER GUYS.
IF SHE IS, I CAN'T JUST BLAME THE STALKER.
Oh!
......
THE STALKER...
......
MS. MOGAMI...
Y... YES...
YOU...
fwip

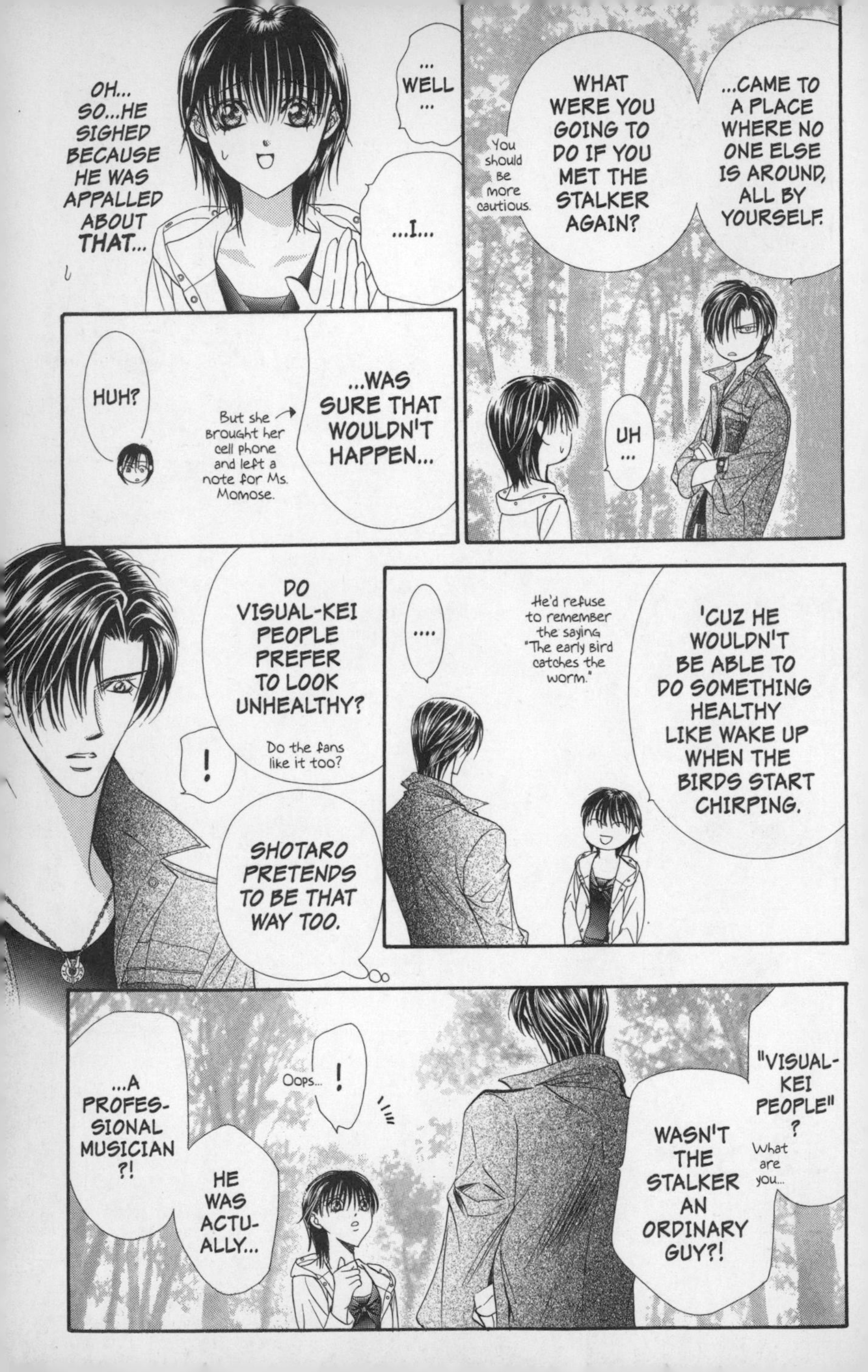
...CAME TO A PLACE WHERE NO ONE ELSE IS AROUND, ALL BY YOURSELF.
WHAT WERE YOU GOING TO DO IF YOU MET THE STALKER AGAIN?
You should be more cautious.
UH ...
... WELL ...
OH... SO...HE SIGHED BECAUSE HE WAS APPALLED ABOUT THAT...
...I...
...WAS SURE THAT WOULDN'T HAPPEN...
But she brought her cell phone and left a note for Ms. Momose.
HUH?
'CUZ HE WOULDN'T BE ABLE TO DO SOMETHING HEALTHY LIKE WAKE UP WHEN THE BIRDS START CHIRPING.
He'd refuse to remember the saying "The early bird catches the worm."
....
DO VISUAL-KEI PEOPLE PREFER TO LOOK UNHEALTHY?
Do the fans like it too?
!
SHOTARO PRETENDS TO BE THAT WAY TOO.
"VISUAL-KEI PEOPLE"?
What are you...
WASN'T THE STALKER AN ORDINARY GUY?!
Oops...
!
HE WAS ACTU-ALLY...
...A PROFES-SIONAL MUSICIAN?!

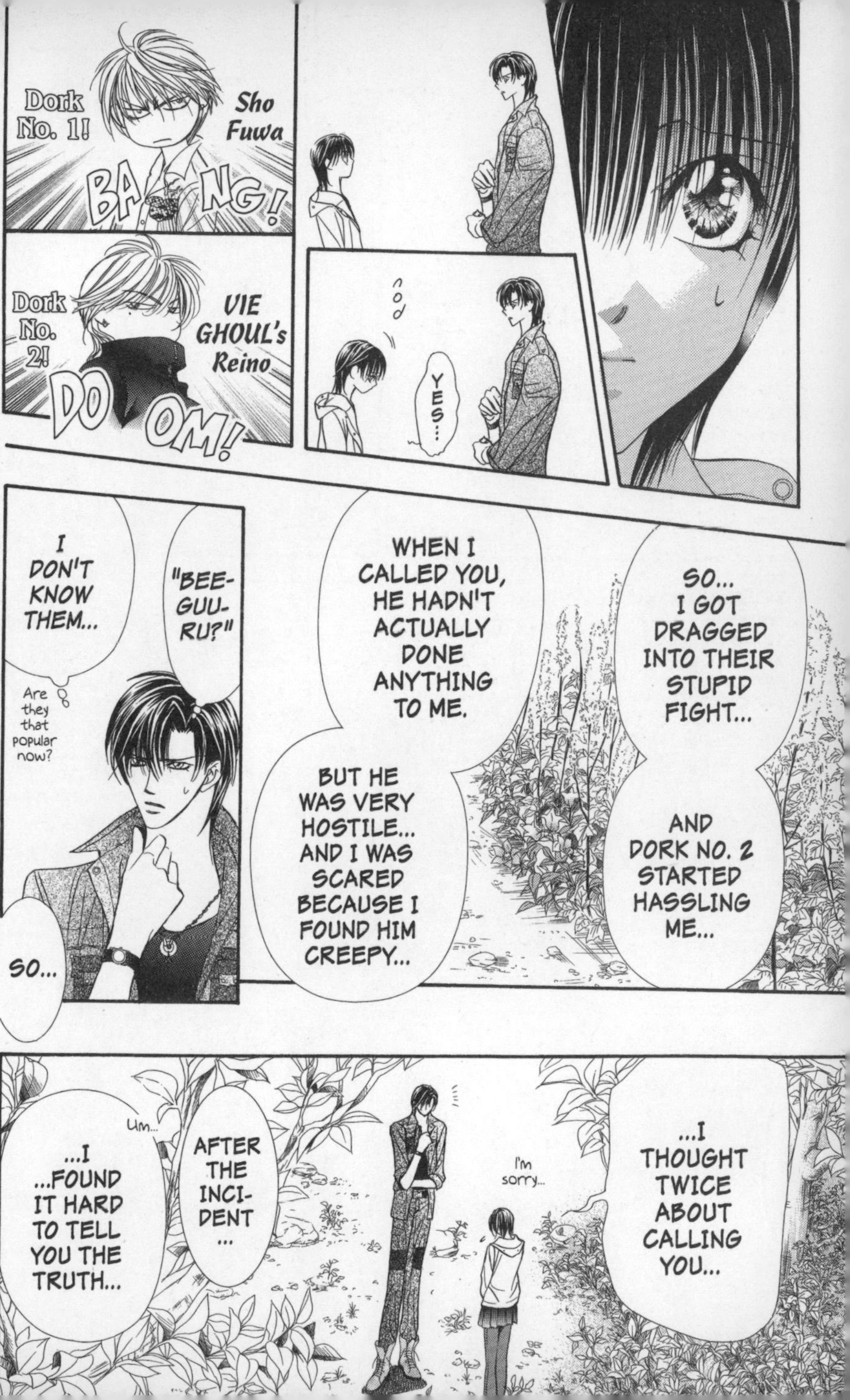
YES...
Dork No. 1!
Sho Fuwa
BANG!
Dork No. 2!
VIE GHOUL's Reino
DOOM!
SO... I GOT DRAGGED INTO THEIR STUPID FIGHT...
AND DORK NO. 2 STARTED HASSLING ME...
WHEN I CALLED YOU, HE HADN'T ACTUALLY DONE ANYTHING TO ME.
BUT HE WAS VERY HOSTILE... AND I WAS SCARED BECAUSE I FOUND HIM CREEPY...
"BEE-GUU-RU?"
I DON'T KNOW THEM...
Are they that popular now?
SO...
...I THOUGHT TWICE ABOUT CALLING YOU...
I'm sorry...
AFTER THE INCI-DENT...
Um...
...I ...FOUND IT HARD TO TELL YOU THE TRUTH...

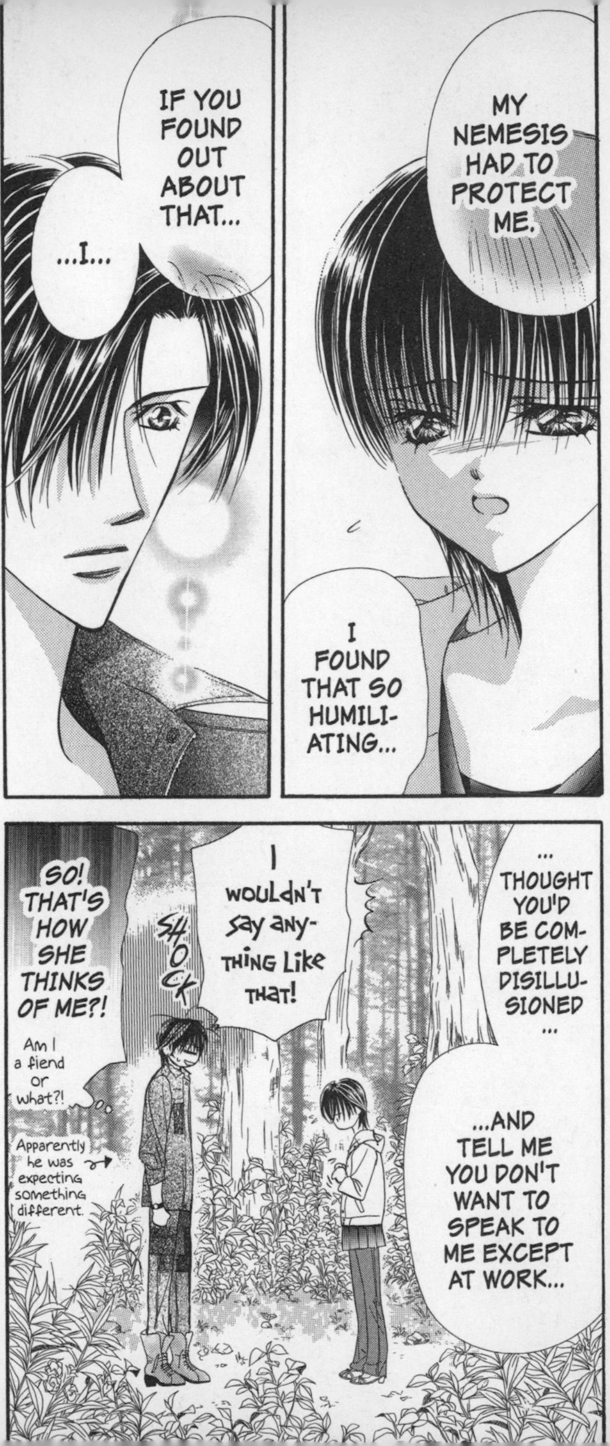
MY NEMESIS HAD TO PROTECT ME.
I FOUND THAT SO HUMILIATING...
IF YOU FOUND OUT ABOUT THAT...
...I...
...THOUGHT YOU'D BE COMPLETELY DISILLUSIONED...
...AND TELL ME YOU DON'T WANT TO SPEAK TO ME EXCEPT AT WORK...
I WOULDN'T SAY ANYTHING LIKE THAT!
SHOCK
SO! THAT'S HOW SHE THINKS OF ME?!
Am I a fiend or what?!
Apparently he was expecting something different.

The Secret of VIE GHOUL

Then why am I revealing the gruesome meanings about the band name here?...if people asked me that... well...the band members gradually became playful (their name is Beagle after all...), so even if the readers found out about the gruesome meanings now, it would cancel each other out... that's what I thought...

...I wrote "Beagle" a few lines back...but "the words that happened to catch my eye" that I wrote in the previous sidebar was a "Beagle" too...no, it was a shining sticker of a corgi puppy... ↖One of my assistants gave me the sticker, and I...had put it on my cell phone, and was looking at it every day, but to me then, it looked like a beagle puppy instead of a corgi puppy and I thought.."Beagle...is there a good word with "Bee" and "Guru" or "Guuru"...that was the beginning of it all...

...So since the band name was derived from "Beagle..." of course Kyoko would call them Beagle... heheh...

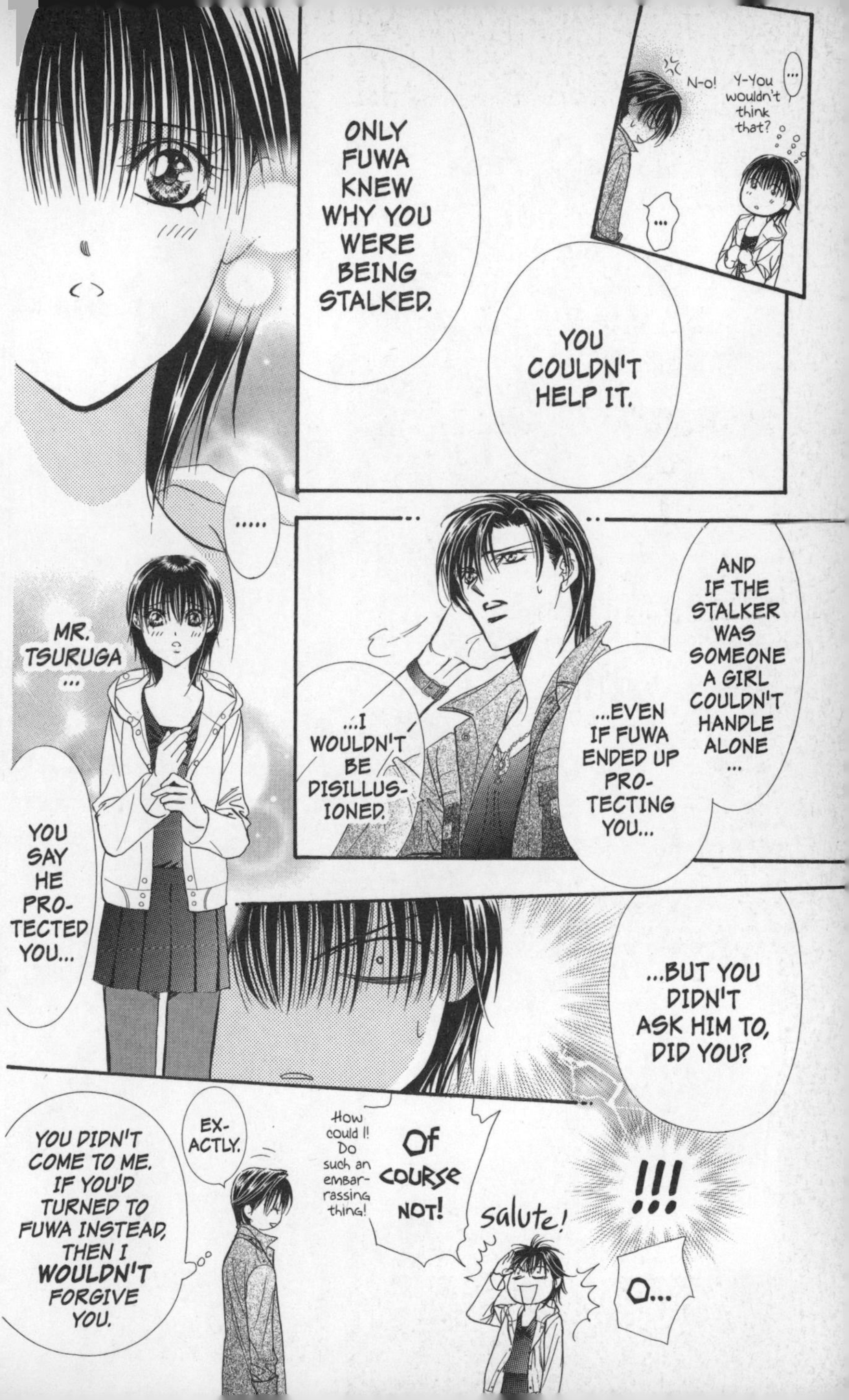
...
Y-You wouldn't think that?
N-o!
...
ONLY FUWA KNEW WHY YOU WERE BEING STALKED.
YOU COULDN'T HELP IT.
AND IF THE STALKER WAS SOMEONE A GIRL COULDN'T HANDLE ALONE...
...EVEN IF FUWA ENDED UP PROTECTING YOU...
...I WOULDN'T BE DISILLUSIONED.
.....
MR. TSURUGA...
YOU SAY HE PROTECTED YOU...
...BUT YOU DIDN'T ASK HIM TO, DID YOU?
!!!
O...
Salute!
OF COURSE NOT!
How could I! Do such an embarrassing thing!
EX-ACTLY.
YOU DIDN'T COME TO ME. IF YOU'D TURNED TO FUWA INSTEAD, THEN I WOULDN'T FORGIVE YOU.

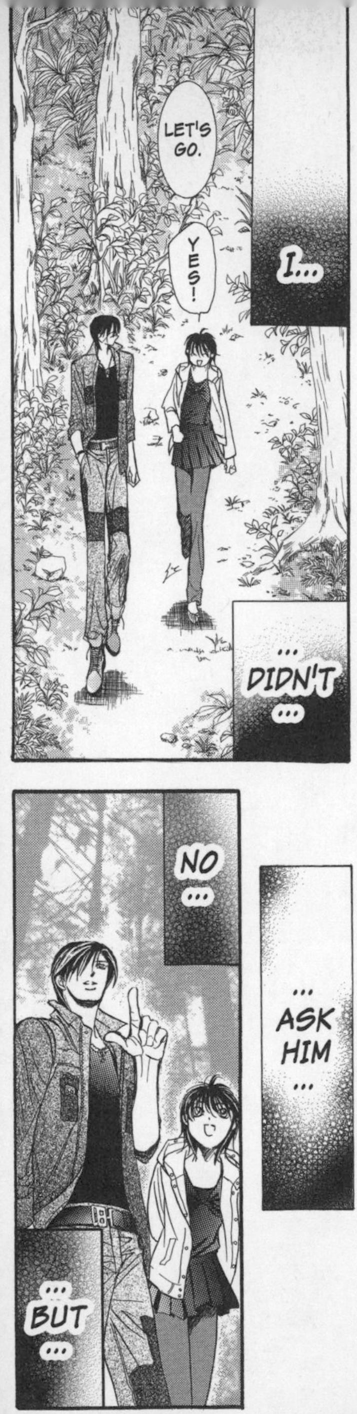
I...
LET'S GO.
YES!
...DIDN'T...
...ASK HIM...
NO...
...BUT...

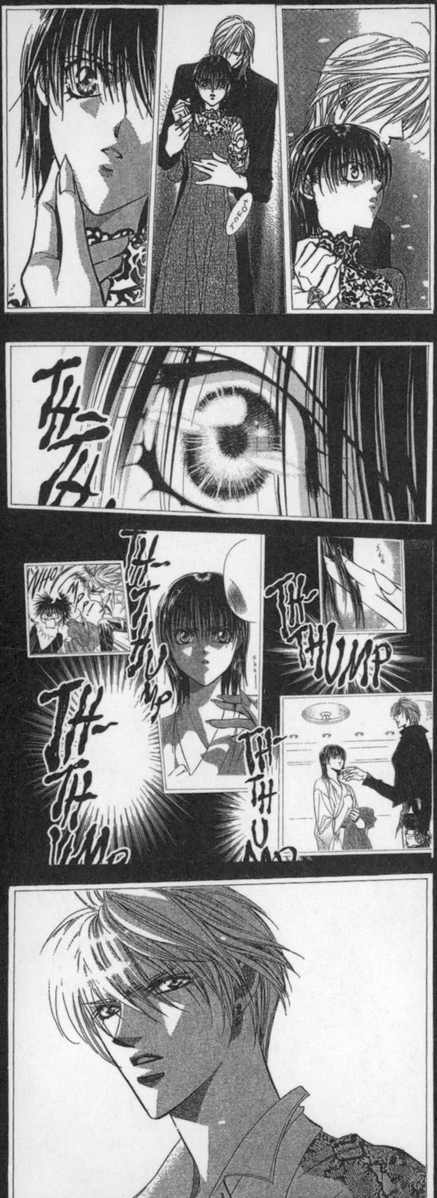
TH-THUMP
TH-THUMP

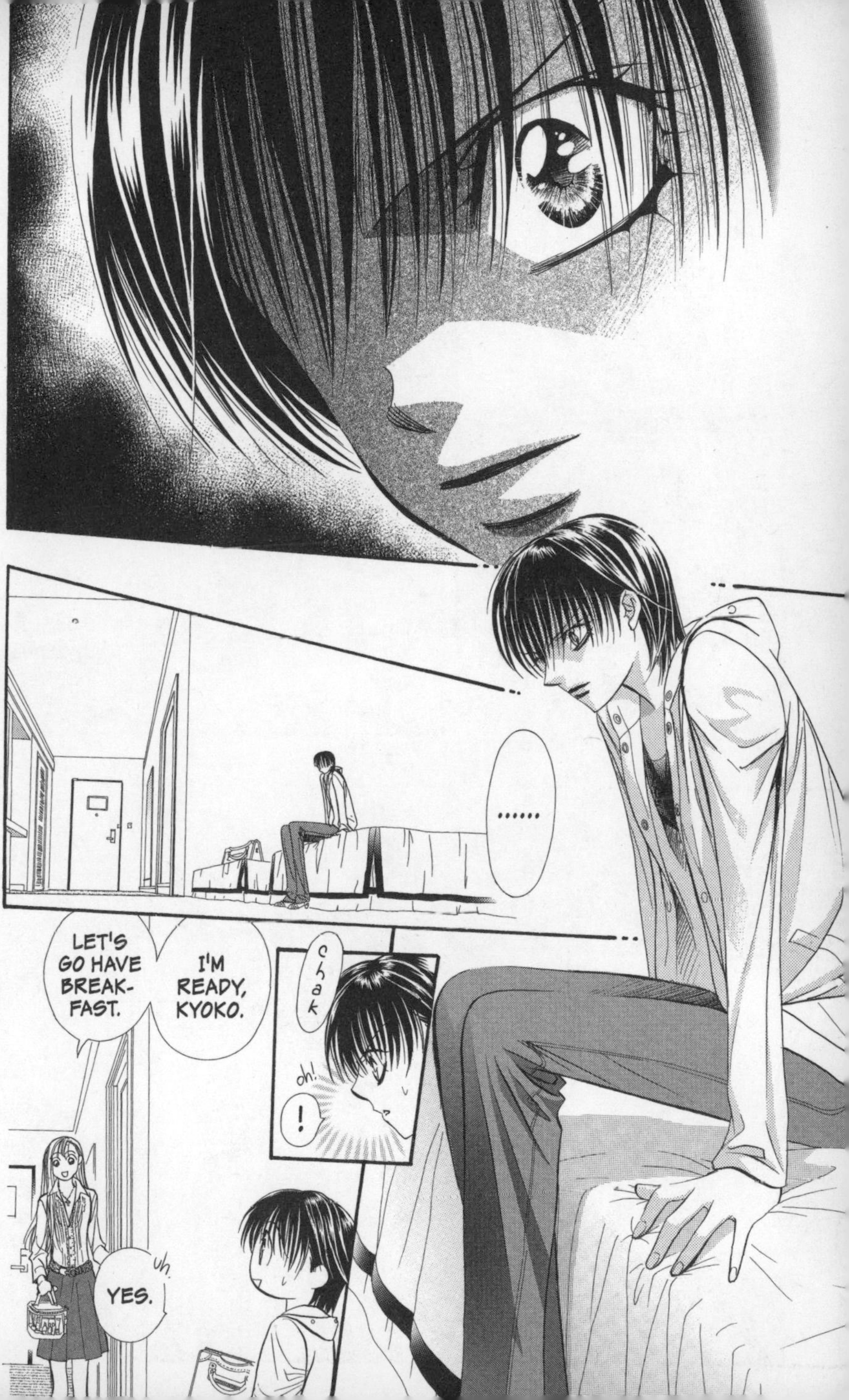
......
chak
oh!
!
I'M READY, KYOKO.
LET'S GO HAVE BREAK-FAST.
uh.
YES.

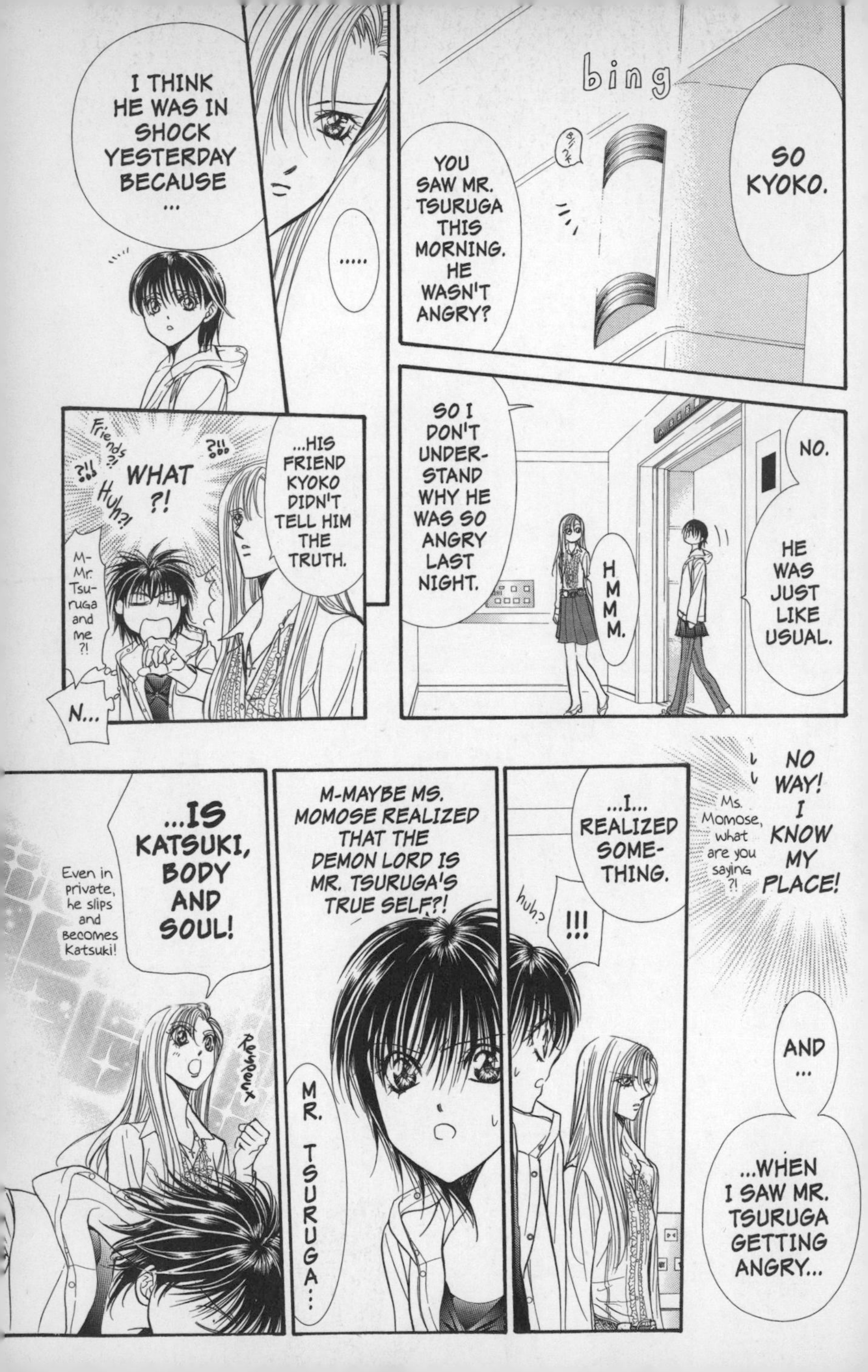
bing
SO KYOKO.
B-blink
YOU SAW MR. TSURUGA THIS MORNING. HE WASN'T ANGRY?
NO.
HE WAS JUST LIKE USUAL.
HMMM.
SO I DON'T UNDERSTAND WHY HE WAS SO ANGRY LAST NIGHT.
I THINK HE WAS IN SHOCK YESTERDAY BECAUSE ...
.....
...HIS FRIEND KYOKO DIDN'T TELL HIM THE TRUTH.
WHAT ?!
?!!
Friends ?!
?!!
Huh?!
M-Mr. Tsuruga and me ?!
N...
NO WAY! I KNOW MY PLACE!
Ms. Momose, what are you saying ?!
AND ...
...WHEN I SAW MR. TSURUGA GETTING ANGRY...
...I... REALIZED SOME-THING.
huh?
!!!
M-MAYBE MS. MOMOSE REALIZED THAT THE DEMON LORD IS MR. TSURUGA'S TRUE SELF?!
MR. TSURUGA...
...IS KATSUKI, BODY AND SOUL!
Even in private, he slips and becomes Katsuki!
Respect

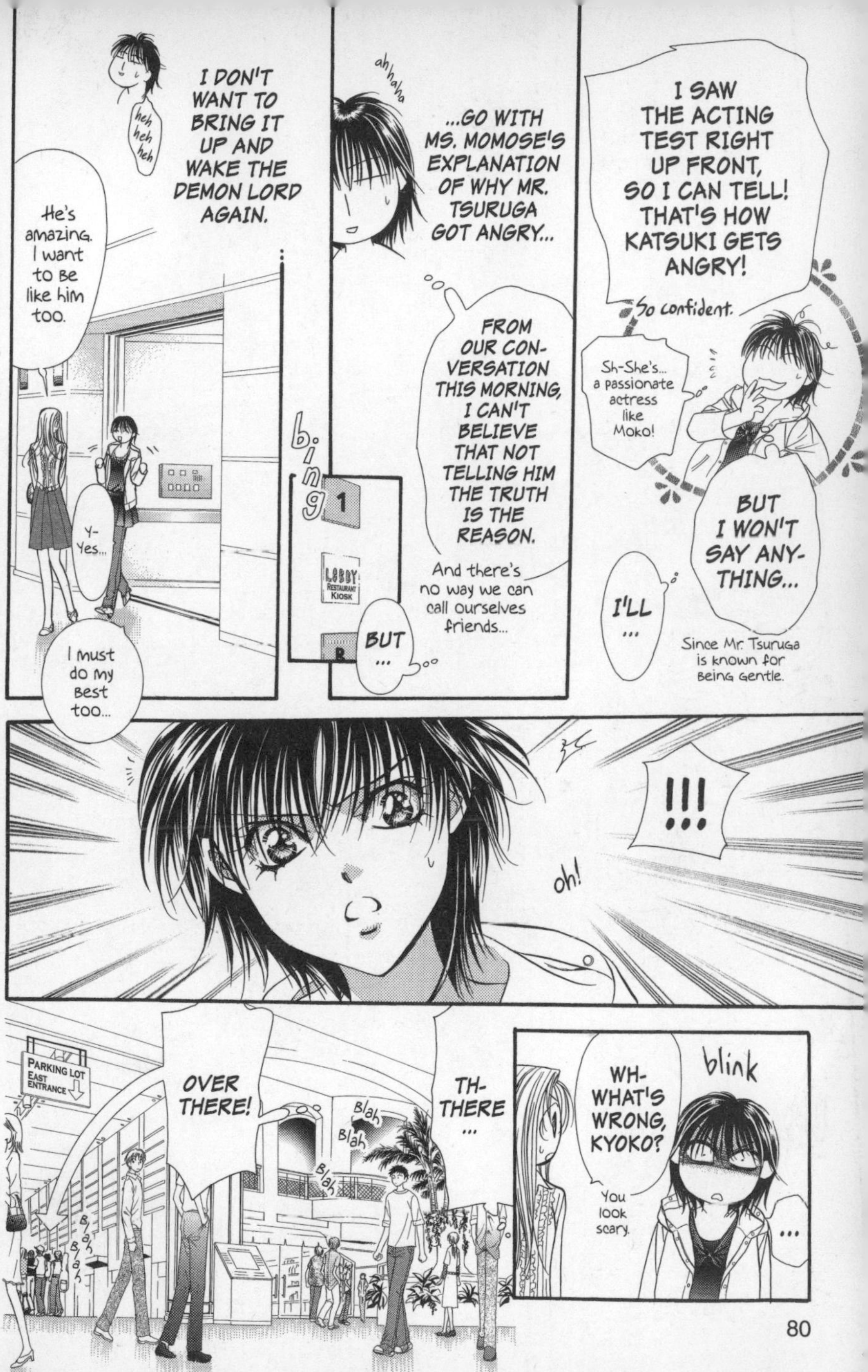
I SAW THE ACTING TEST RIGHT UP FRONT, SO I CAN TELL! THAT'S HOW KATSUKI GETS ANGRY!
So confident.
Sh-She's... a passionate actress like Moko!
BUT I WON'T SAY ANYTHING...
Since Mr. Tsuruga is known for being gentle.
I'LL...
ah haha
...GO WITH MS. MOMOSE'S EXPLANATION OF WHY MR. TSURUGA GOT ANGRY...
FROM OUR CONVERSATION THIS MORNING, I CAN'T BELIEVE THAT NOT TELLING HIM THE TRUTH IS THE REASON.
And there's no way we can call ourselves friends...
bing
1
LOBBY RESTAURANT KIOSK
R
BUT...
I DON'T WANT TO BRING IT UP AND WAKE THE DEMON LORD AGAIN.
heh heh heh
He's amazing. I want to be like him too.
Y-Yes...
I must do my best too...
!!!
oh!
blink
WH-WHAT'S WRONG, KYOKO?
You look scary.
...
TH-THERE...
OVER THERE!
Blah
Blah
Blah
PARKING LOT EAST ENTRANCE
Blah
Blah
Blah

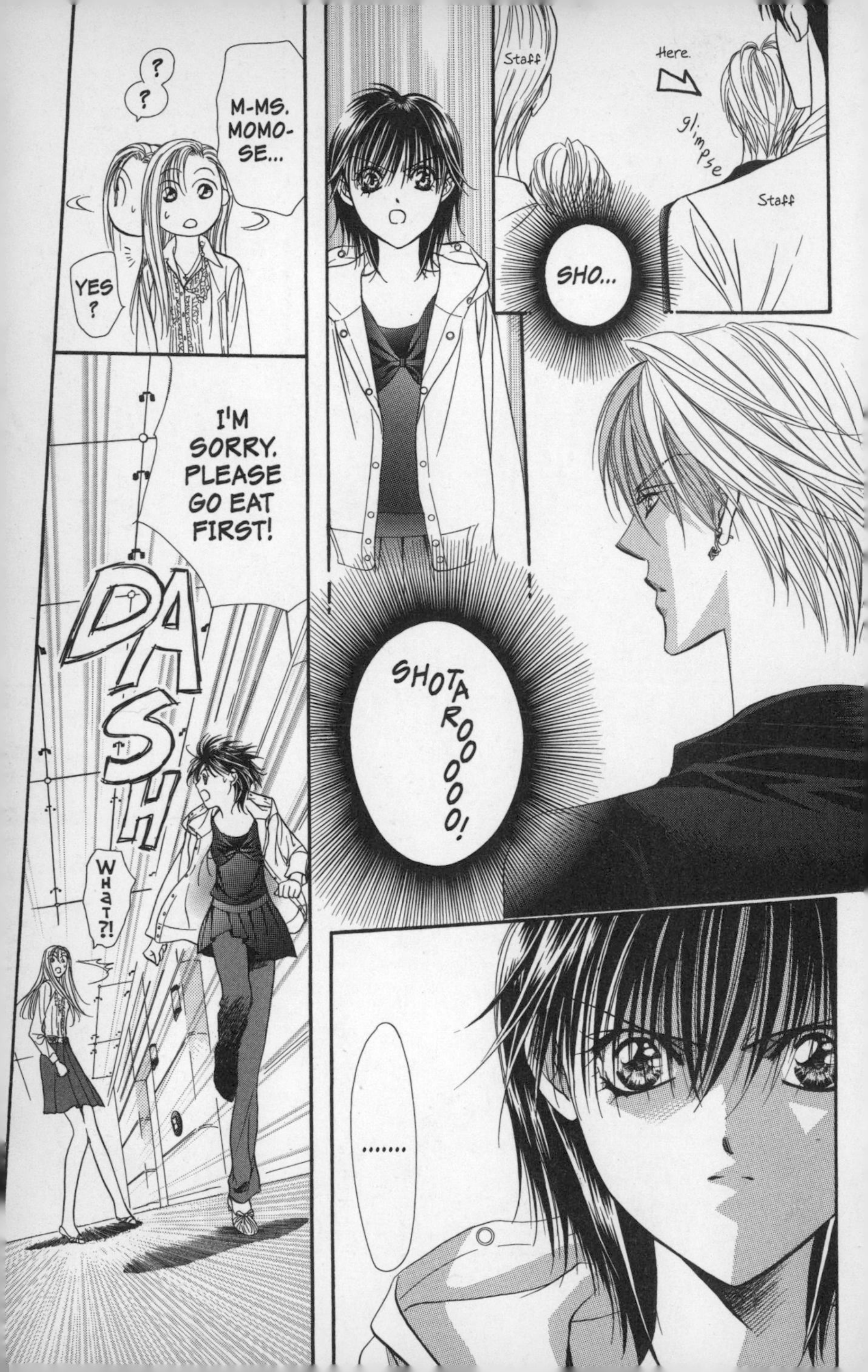
Staff
Here.
glimpse
Staff
SHO...
SHOTAROOOOOOO!
......
?
?
M-MS. MOMOSE...
YES?
I'M SORRY. PLEASE GO EAT FIRST!
DASH
What?!

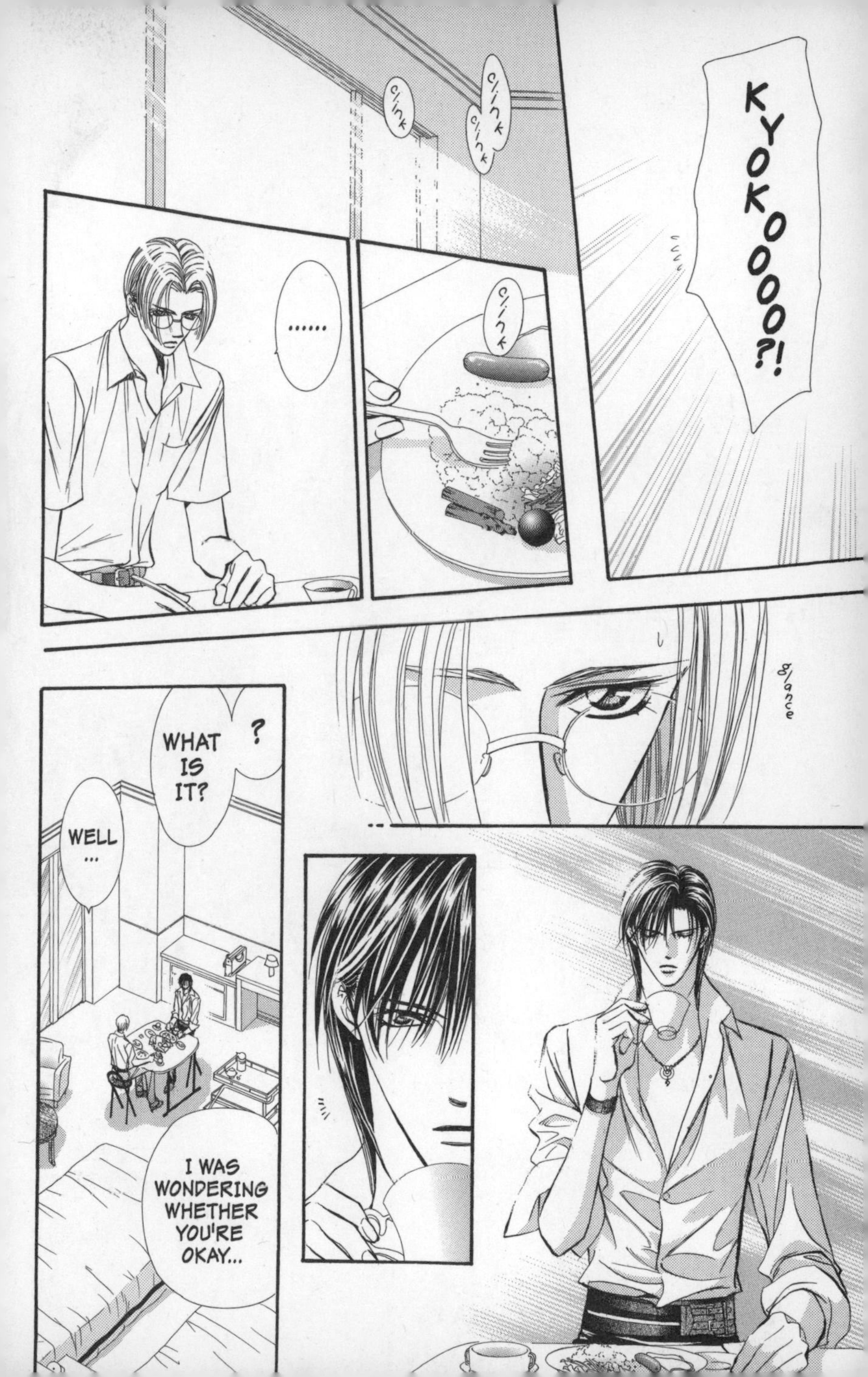
KYOKOOOOO?!
clink
clink
clink
clink
......
glance
?
WHAT IS IT?
WELL...
I WAS WONDERING WHETHER YOU'RE OKAY...

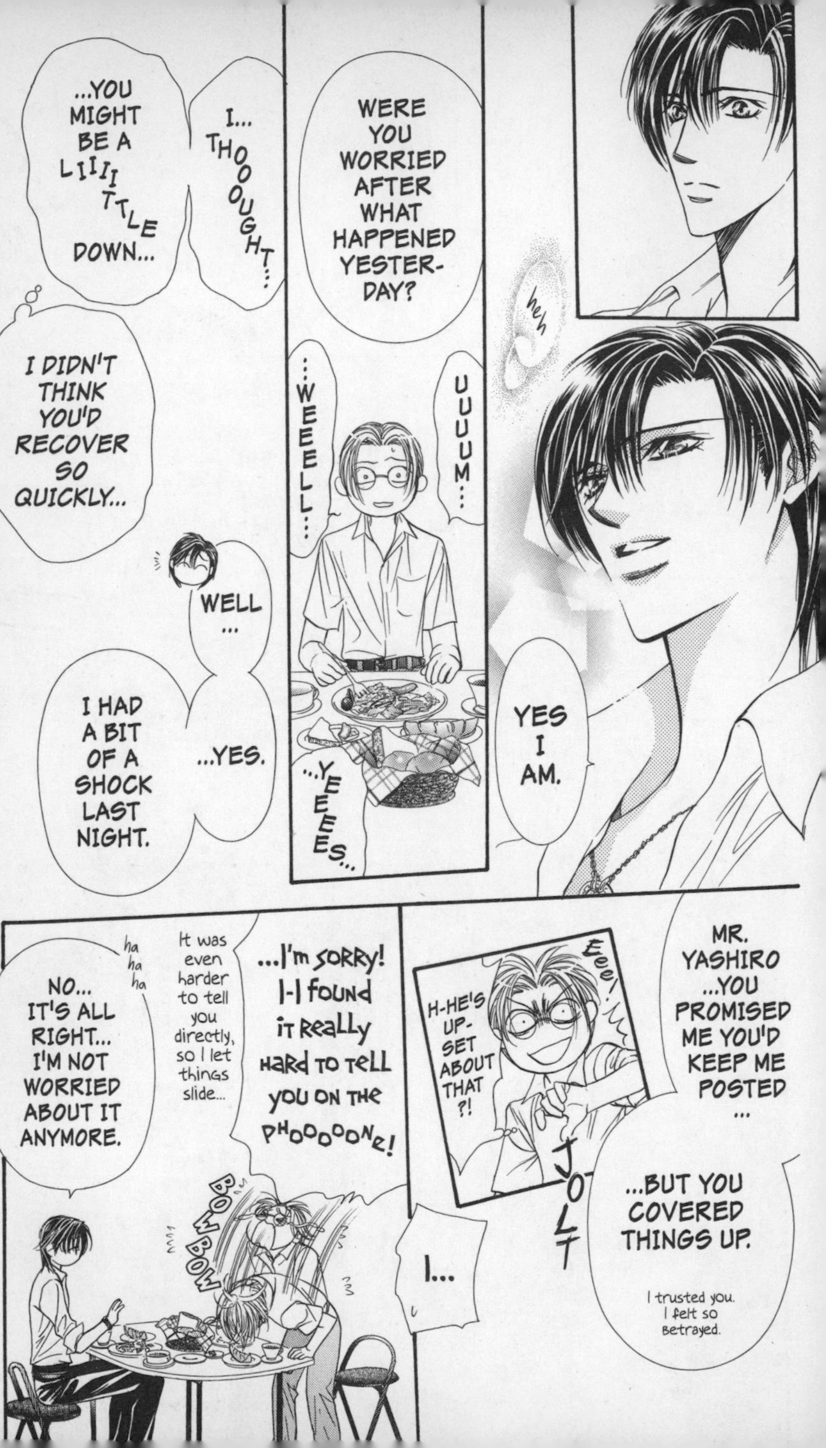
heh
YES I AM.
WERE YOU WORRIED AFTER WHAT HAPPENED YESTER-DAY?
UUUUM...
...WEEELL...
...YEEEES...
I... THOOOUGHT...
...YOU MIGHT BE A LIIIITTLE DOWN...
I DIDN'T THINK YOU'D RECOVER SO QUICKLY...
WELL...
...YES.
I HAD A BIT OF A SHOCK LAST NIGHT.
MR. YASHIRO ...YOU PROMISED ME YOU'D KEEP ME POSTED...
...BUT YOU COVERED THINGS UP.
I trusted you. I felt so betrayed.
Eeee!
H-HE'S UP-SET ABOUT THAT?!
JOLT
I...
...I'm SORRY! I-I found it really hard to tell you on the PHOOOOONE!
It was even harder to tell you directly, so I let things slide...
ha ha ha
NO... IT'S ALL RIGHT... I'M NOT WORRIED ABOUT IT ANYMORE.
BOW BOW

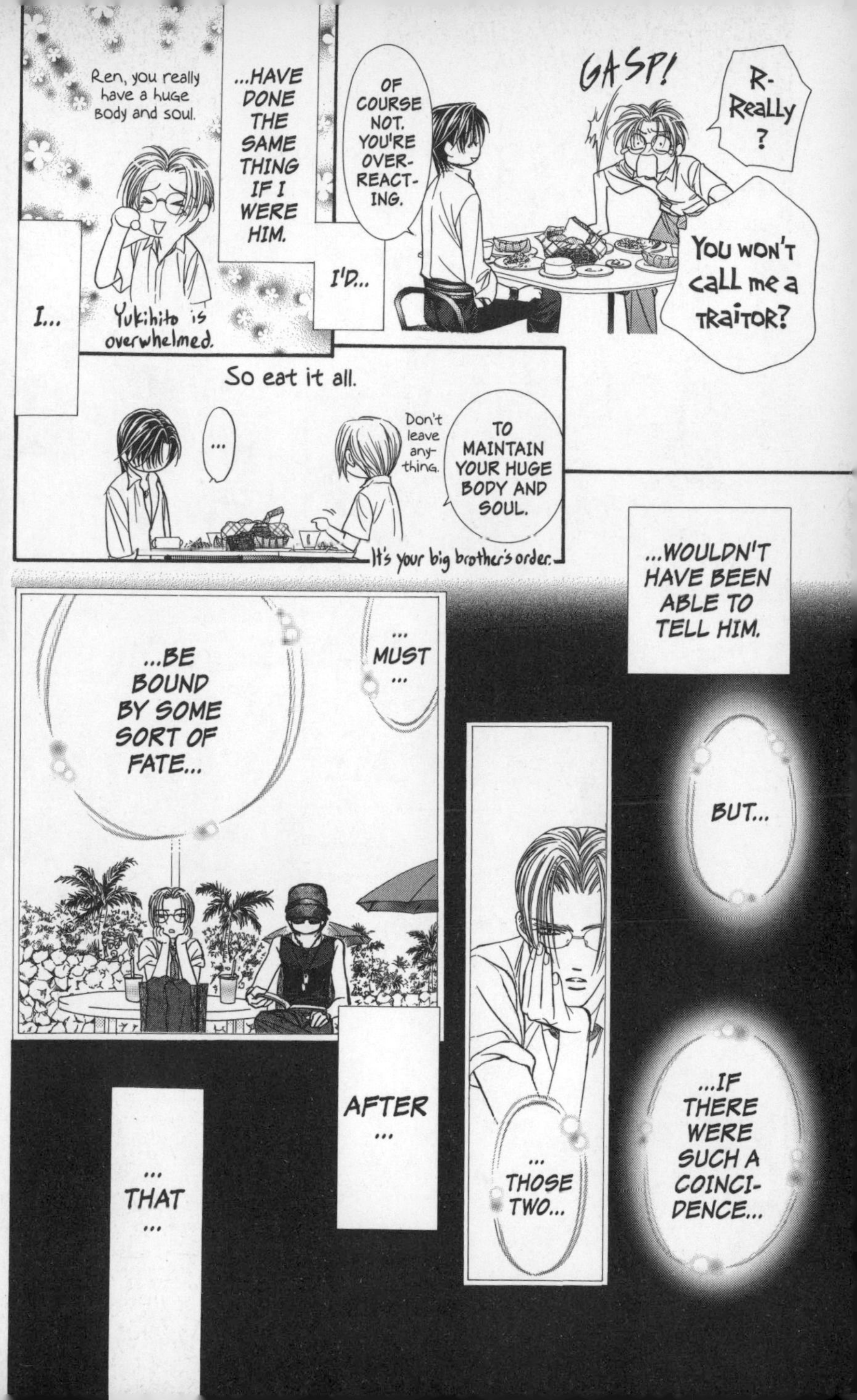
GASP!
R-Really?
You won't call me a traitor?
Of course not. You're over-reacting.
I'd...
...have done the same thing if I were him.
Ren, you really have a huge body and soul.
Yukihito is overwhelmed.
I...
So eat it all.
To maintain your huge body and soul.
Don't leave anything.
...
It's your big brother's order.
...wouldn't have been able to tell him.
But...
...if there were such a coincidence...
...those two...
...must...
...be bound by some sort of fate...
After...
...that...

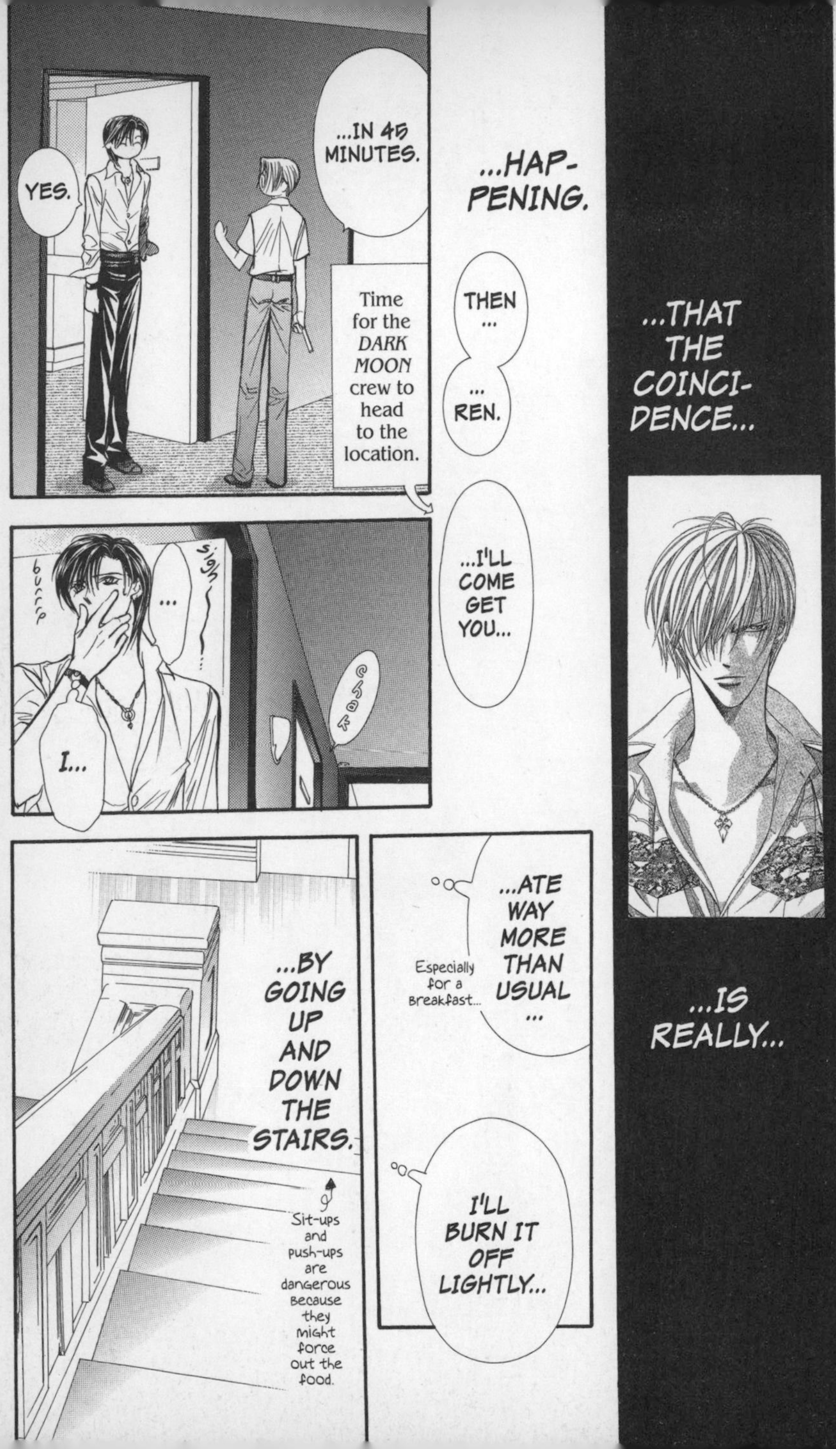
...THAT THE COINCIDENCE...
...IS REALLY...
...HAPPENING.
...IN 45 MINUTES.
YES.
Time for the *DARK MOON* crew to head to the location.
THEN ... ... REN.
...I'LL COME GET YOU...
sigh
...
burrp
chat
I...
...ATE WAY MORE THAN USUAL ...
Especially for a Breakfast...
I'LL BURN IT OFF LIGHTLY...
...BY GOING UP AND DOWN THE STAIRS.
Sit-ups and push-ups are dangerous because they might force out the food.

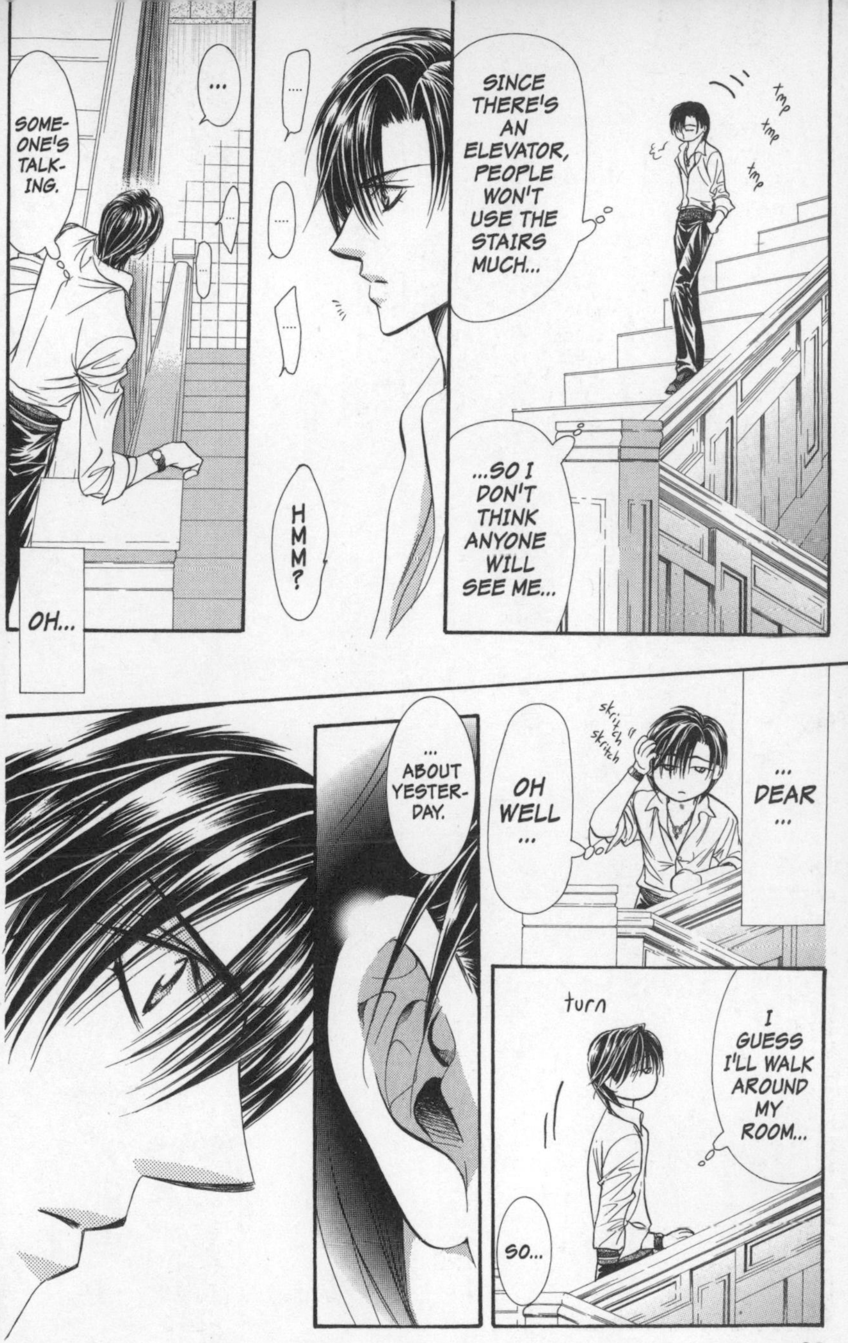
xmp
xmp
xmp
SINCE THERE'S AN ELEVATOR, PEOPLE WON'T USE THE STAIRS MUCH...
...SO I DON'T THINK ANYONE WILL SEE ME...
....
....
....
HMM?
...
...
...
SOME-ONE'S TALKING.
OH...
... DEAR ...
skritch
skritch
OH WELL ...
turn
I GUESS I'LL WALK AROUND MY ROOM...
SO...
... ABOUT YESTER-DAY.

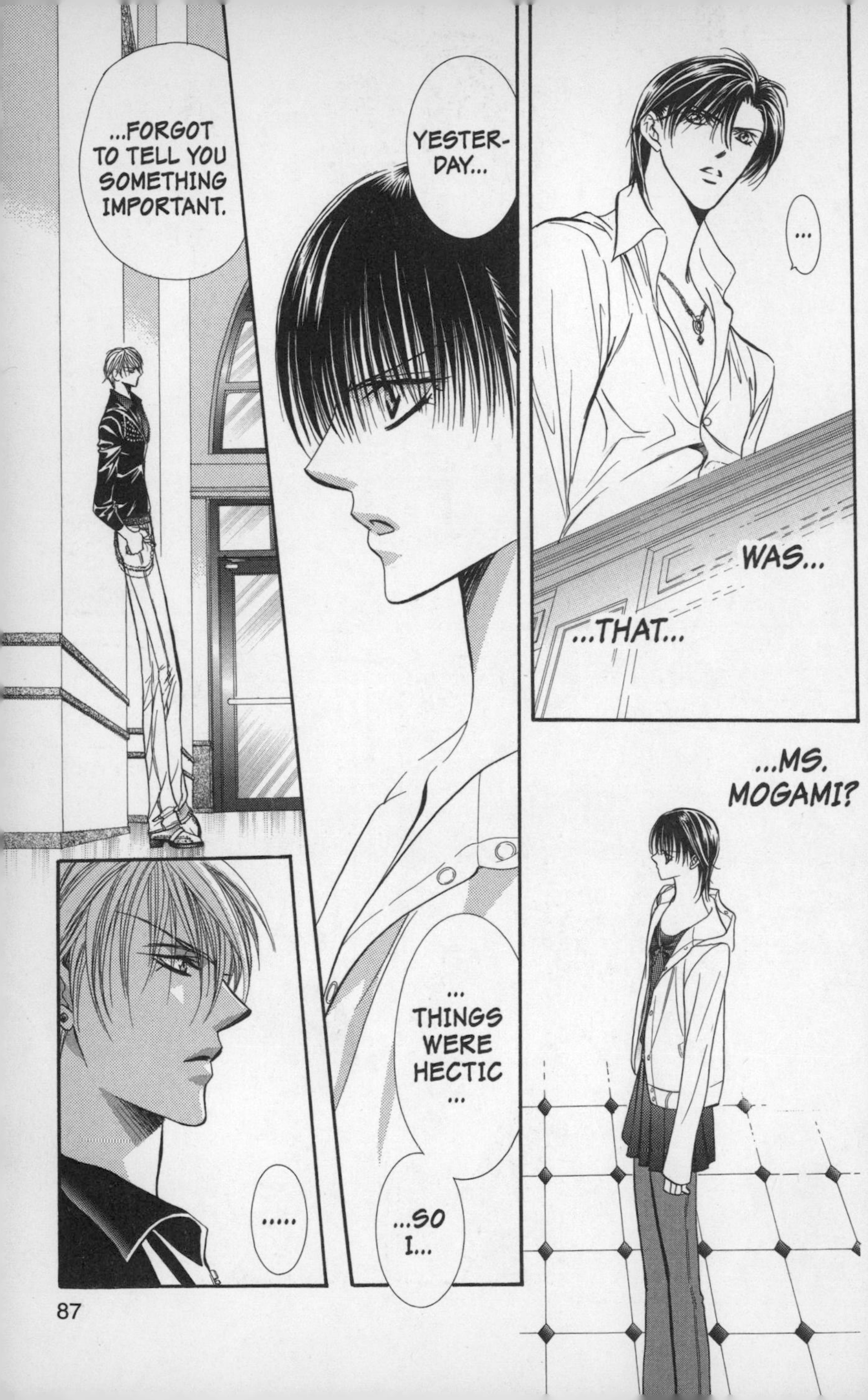
...
WAS...
...THAT...
...MS. MOGAMI?
YESTER-DAY...
...THINGS WERE HECTIC...
...SO I...
...FORGOT TO TELL YOU SOMETHING IMPORTANT.
.....

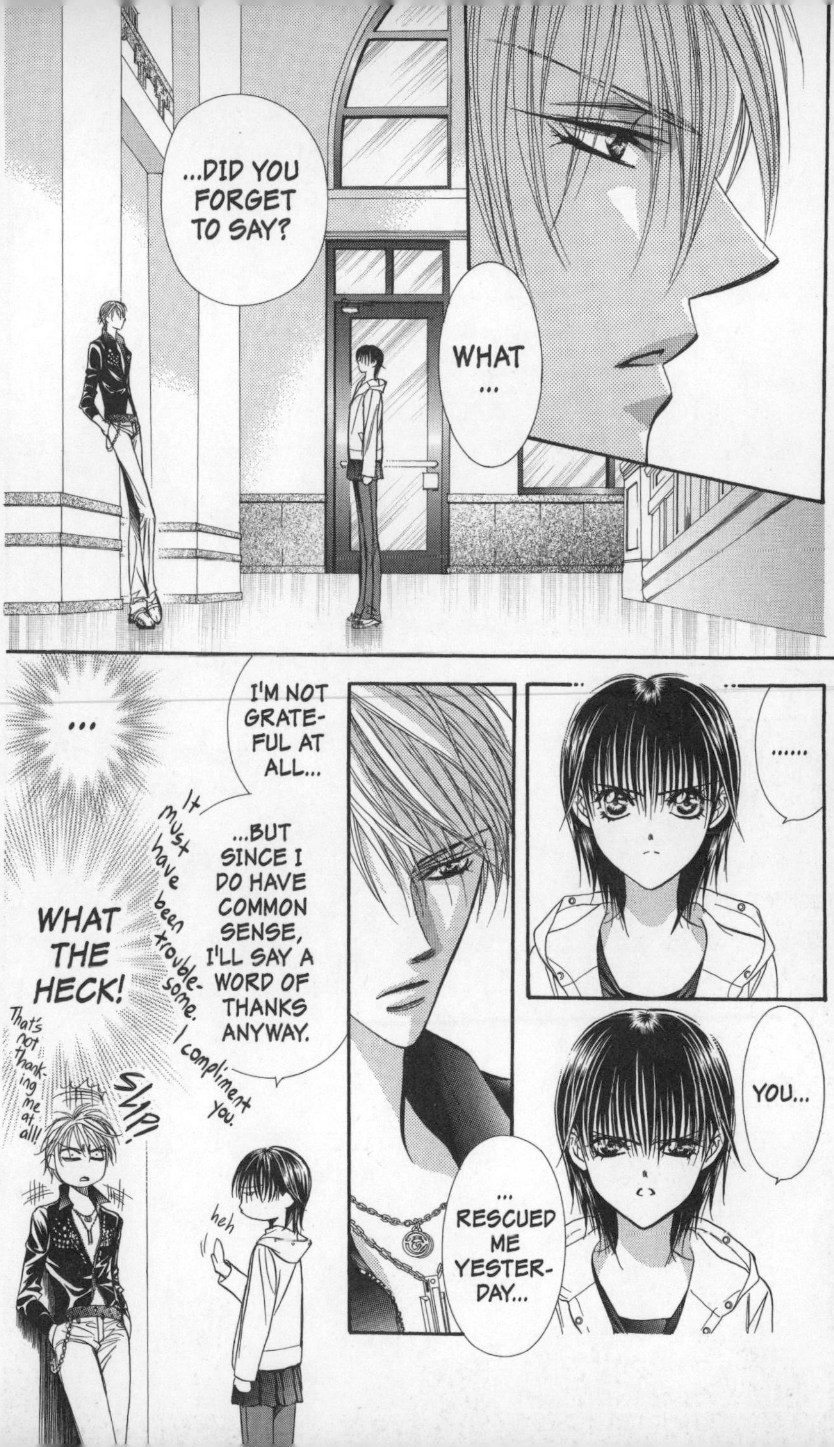
WHAT ...
...DID YOU FORGET TO SAY?
......
YOU...
...RESCUED ME YESTER-DAY...
I'M NOT GRATE-FUL AT ALL...
...BUT SINCE I DO HAVE COMMON SENSE, I'LL SAY A WORD OF THANKS ANYWAY.
It must have been trouble-some. I compliment you.
...
WHAT THE HECK!
That's not thank-ing me at all!
SLIP!
heh

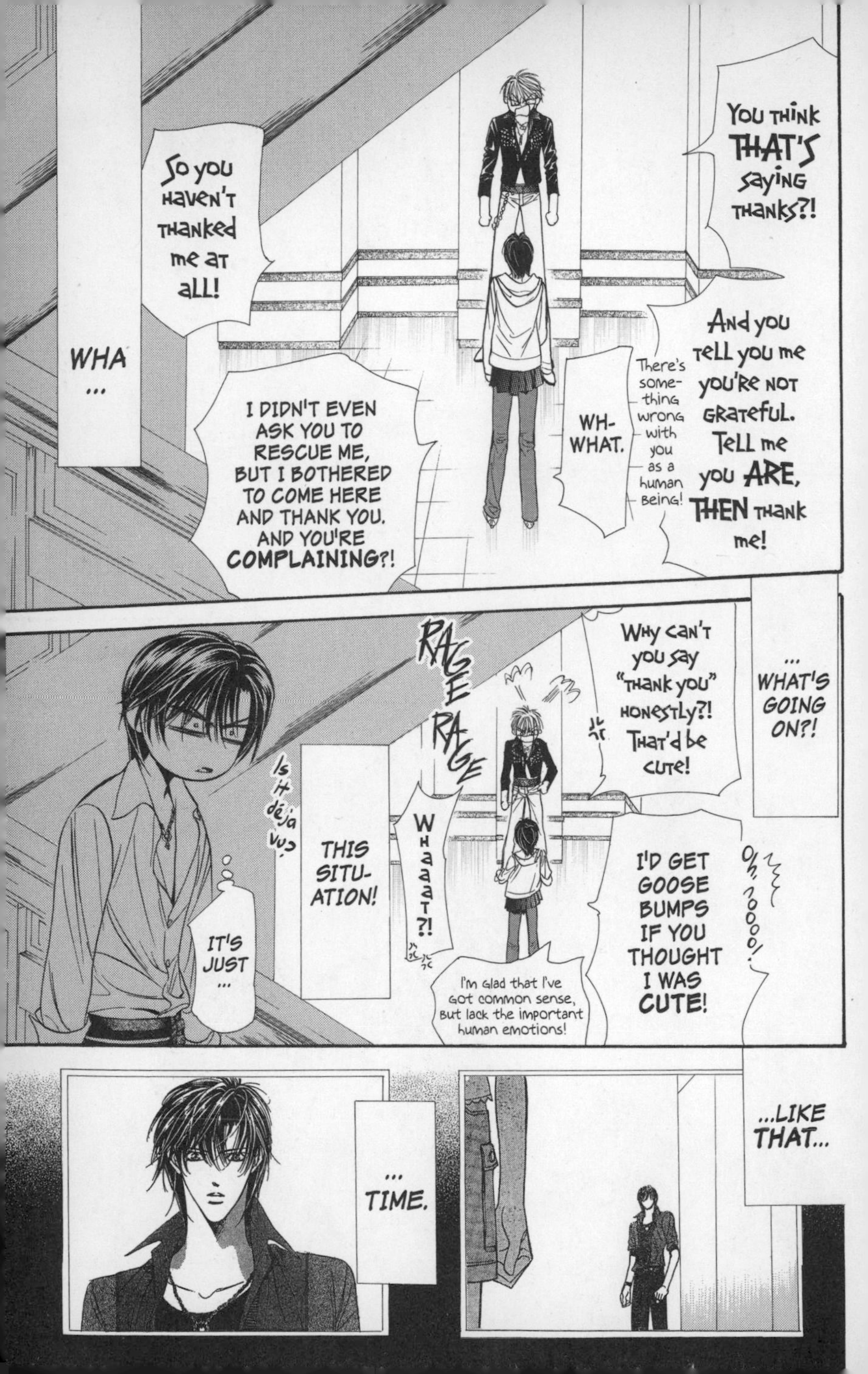
You think THAT'S saying thanks?!
And you tell you me you're not grateful. Tell me you ARE, THEN thank me!
There's some-thing wrong with you as a human being!
WH-WHAT.
I DIDN'T EVEN ASK YOU TO RESCUE ME, BUT I BOTHERED TO COME HERE AND THANK YOU. AND YOU'RE COMPLAINING?!
So you haven't thanked me at all!
WHA ...
... WHAT'S GOING ON?!
Why can't you say "thank you" honestly?! That'd be cute!
RAGE RAGE
I'D GET GOOSE BUMPS IF YOU THOUGHT I WAS CUTE!
Oh, noooo!
I'm glad that I've got common sense, but lack the important human emotions!
Whaaaat?!
THIS SITU-ATION!
Is it déja vu?
IT'S JUST ...
...LIKE THAT...
... TIME.

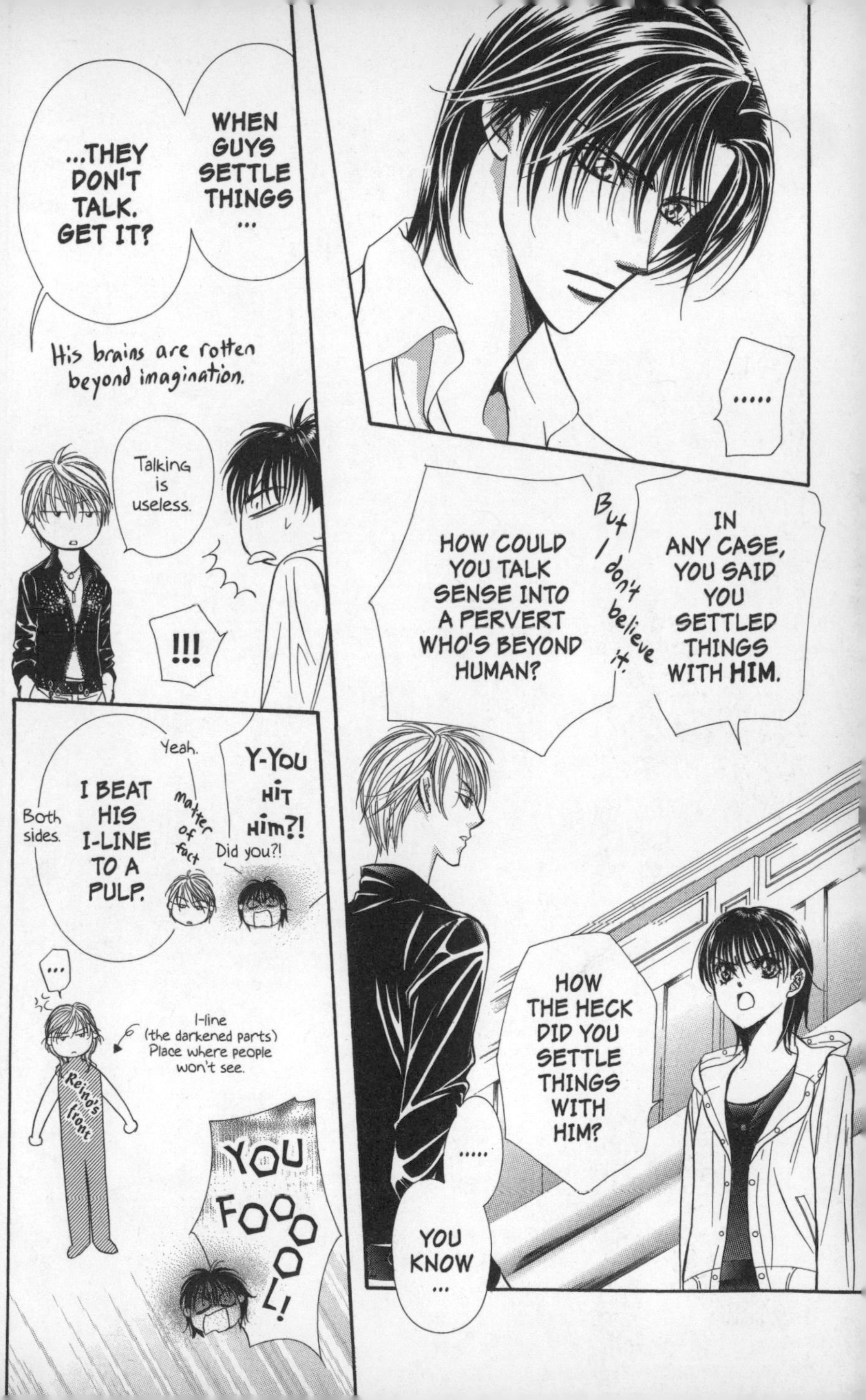

.....
IN ANY CASE, YOU SAID YOU SETTLED THINGS WITH HIM.
But I don't believe it.
HOW COULD YOU TALK SENSE INTO A PERVERT WHO'S BEYOND HUMAN?
HOW THE HECK DID YOU SETTLE THINGS WITH HIM?
.....
YOU KNOW...
WHEN GUYS SETTLE THINGS...
...THEY DON'T TALK. GET IT?
His brains are rotten beyond imagination.
Talking is useless.
!!!
Y-YOU HIT HIM?!
Yeah.
I BEAT HIS I-LINE TO A PULP.
Both sides.
matter of fact
Did you?!
...
I-line (the darkened parts) Place where people won't see.
Reino's front
YOU FOOOOL!

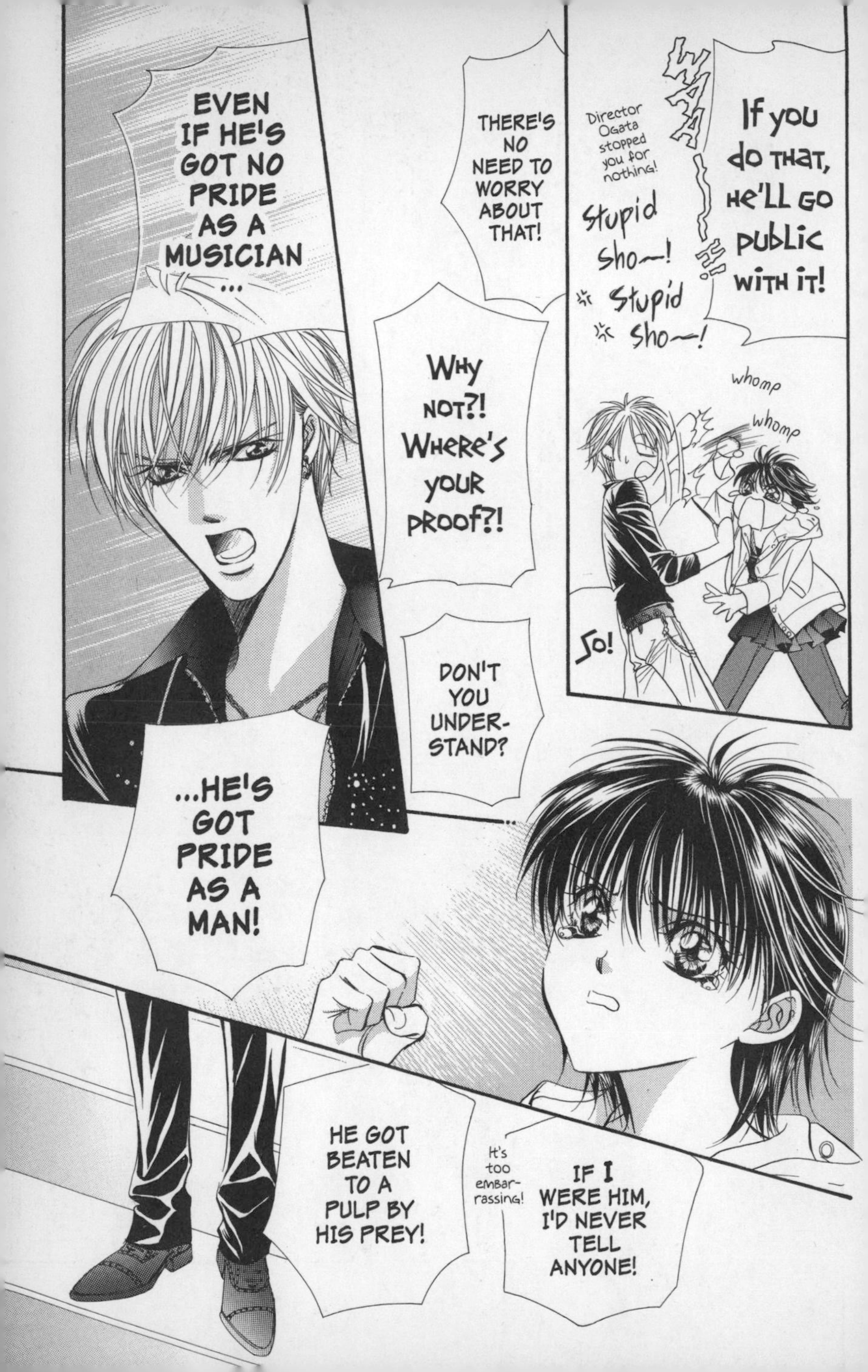
If you do that, he'll go public with it!
WAAA--H!!
Director Ogata stopped you for nothing!
Stupid Sho--!
Stupid Sho--!
whomp
whomp
So!
THERE'S NO NEED TO WORRY ABOUT THAT!
Why not?! Where's your proof?!
EVEN IF HE'S GOT NO PRIDE AS A MUSICIAN...
DON'T YOU UNDERSTAND?
...HE'S GOT PRIDE AS A MAN!
HE GOT BEATEN TO A PULP BY HIS PREY!
IF I WERE HIM, I'D NEVER TELL ANYONE!
It's too embarrassing!

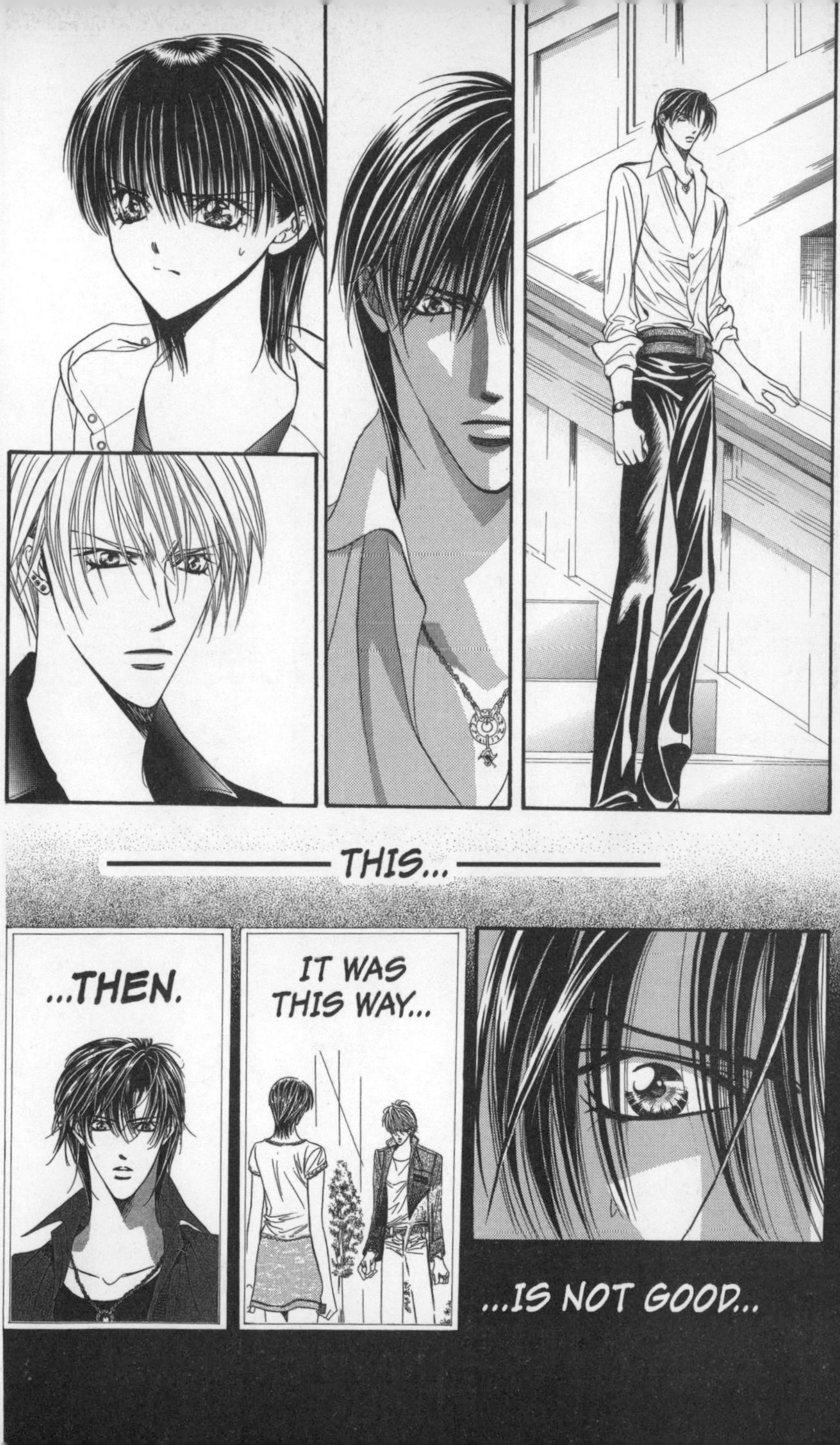
THIS...
...IS NOT GOOD...
IT WAS THIS WAY...
...THEN.

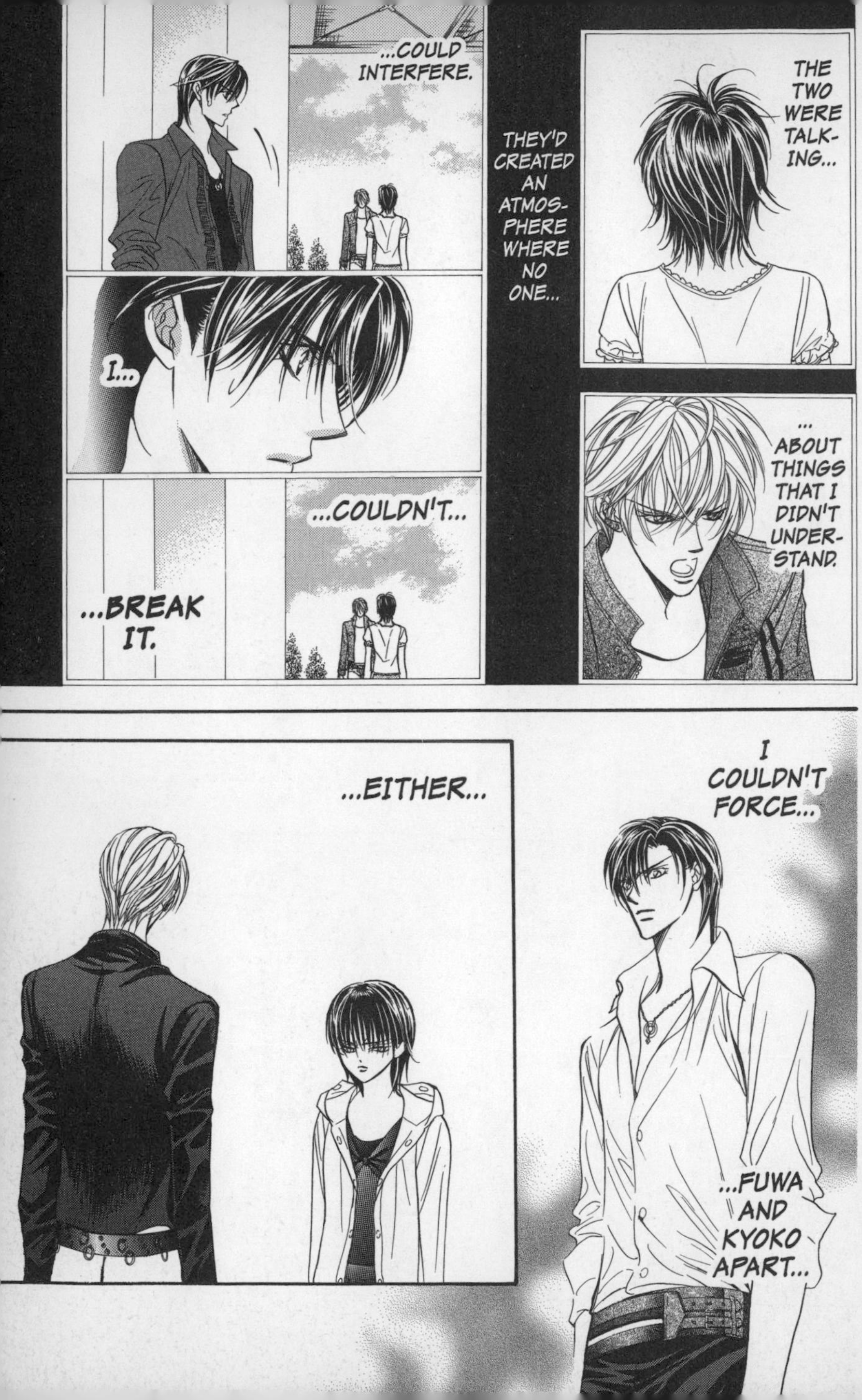
THE TWO WERE TALKING...
...ABOUT THINGS THAT I DIDN'T UNDERSTAND.
THEY'D CREATED AN ATMOSPHERE WHERE NO ONE...
...COULD INTERFERE.
I...
...COULDN'T...
...BREAK IT.
I COULDN'T FORCE...
...FUWA AND KYOKO APART...
...EITHER...

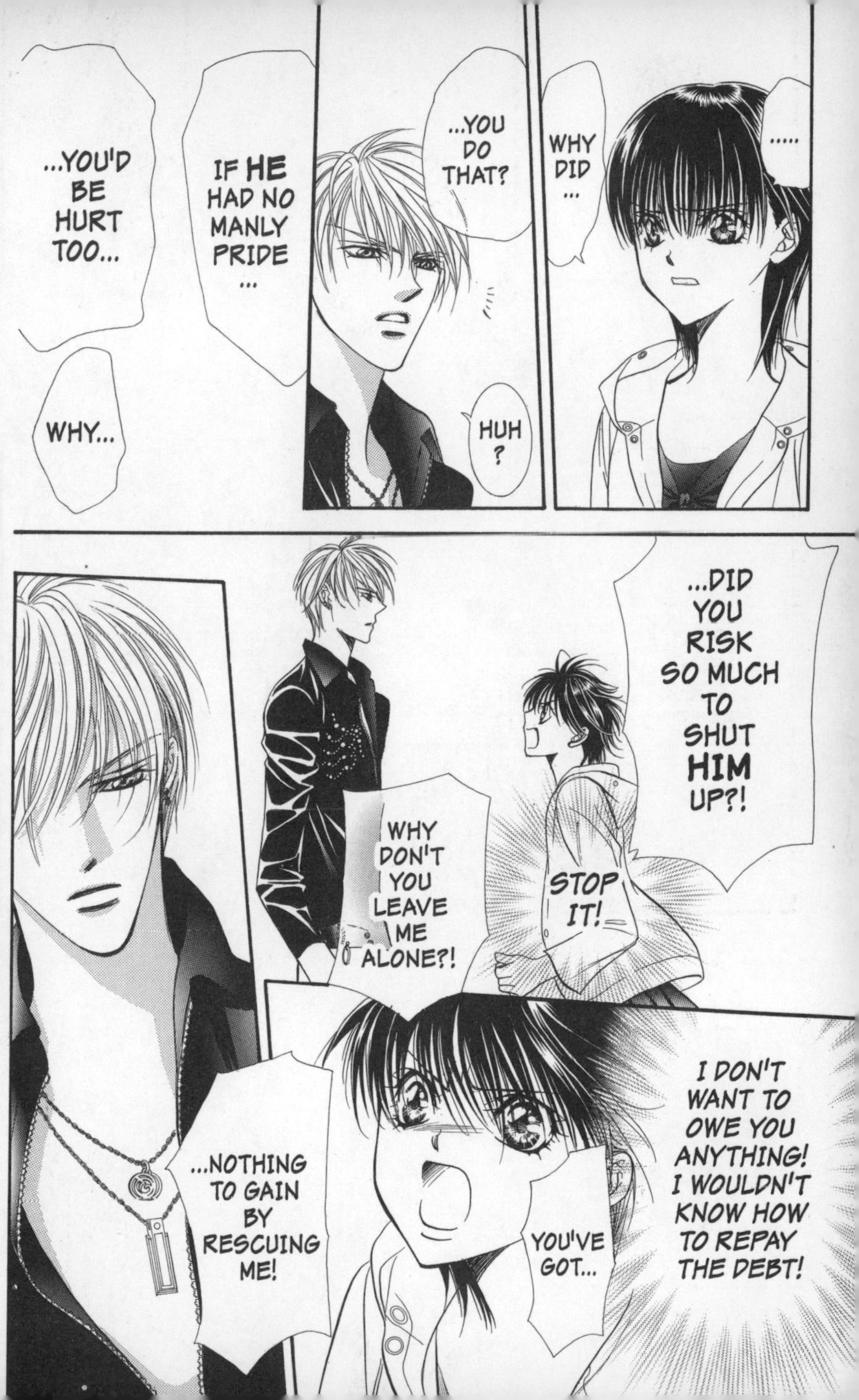
.....
WHY DID ...
...YOU DO THAT?
HUH ?
IF HE HAD NO MANLY PRIDE ...
...YOU'D BE HURT TOO...
WHY...
...DID YOU RISK SO MUCH TO SHUT HIM UP?!
STOP IT!
WHY DON'T YOU LEAVE ME ALONE?!
I DON'T WANT TO OWE YOU ANYTHING! I WOULDN'T KNOW HOW TO REPAY THE DEBT!
YOU'VE GOT...
...NOTHING TO GAIN BY RESCUING ME!

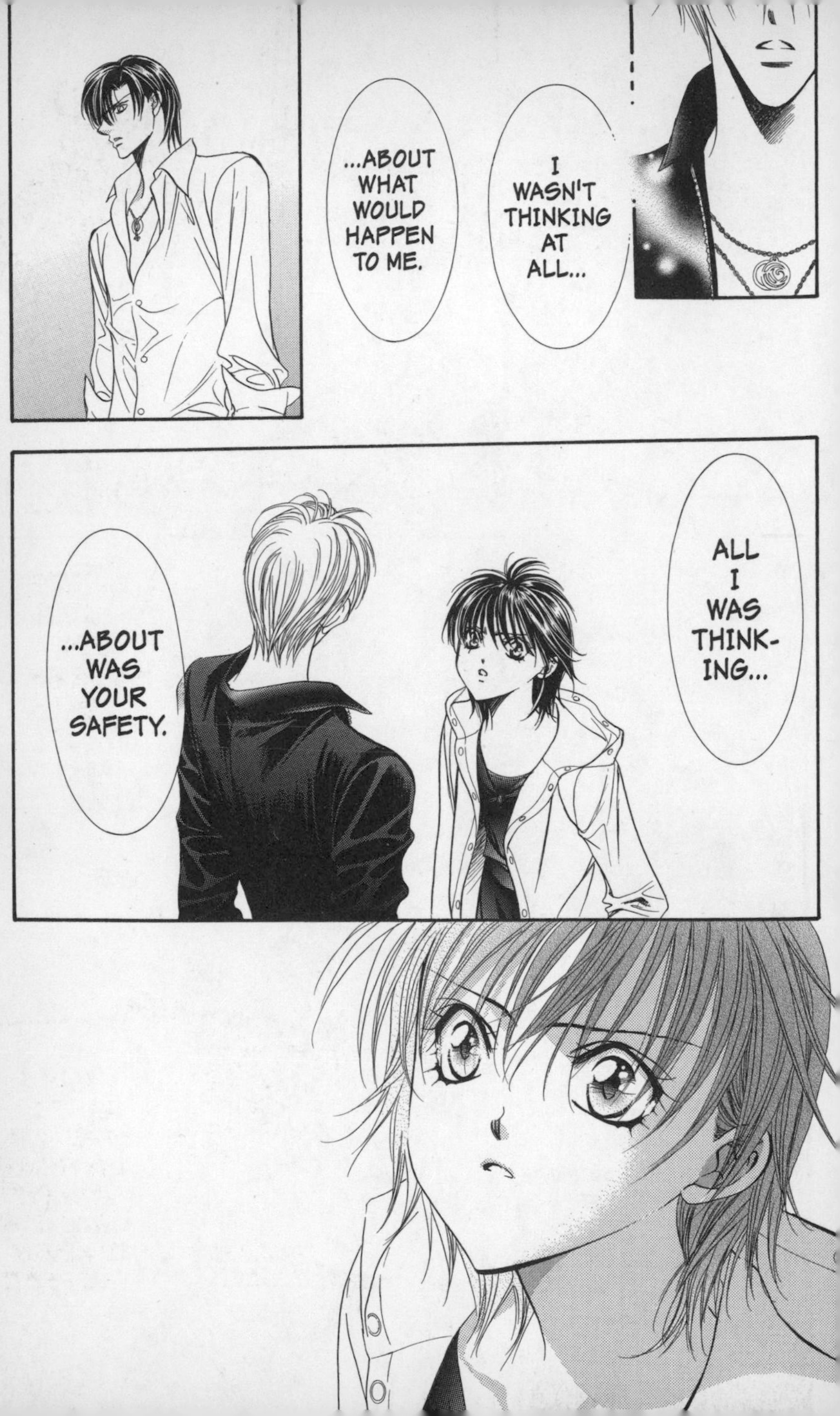
I WASN'T THINKING AT ALL...
...ABOUT WHAT WOULD HAPPEN TO ME.
ALL I WAS THINKING...
...ABOUT WAS YOUR SAFETY.

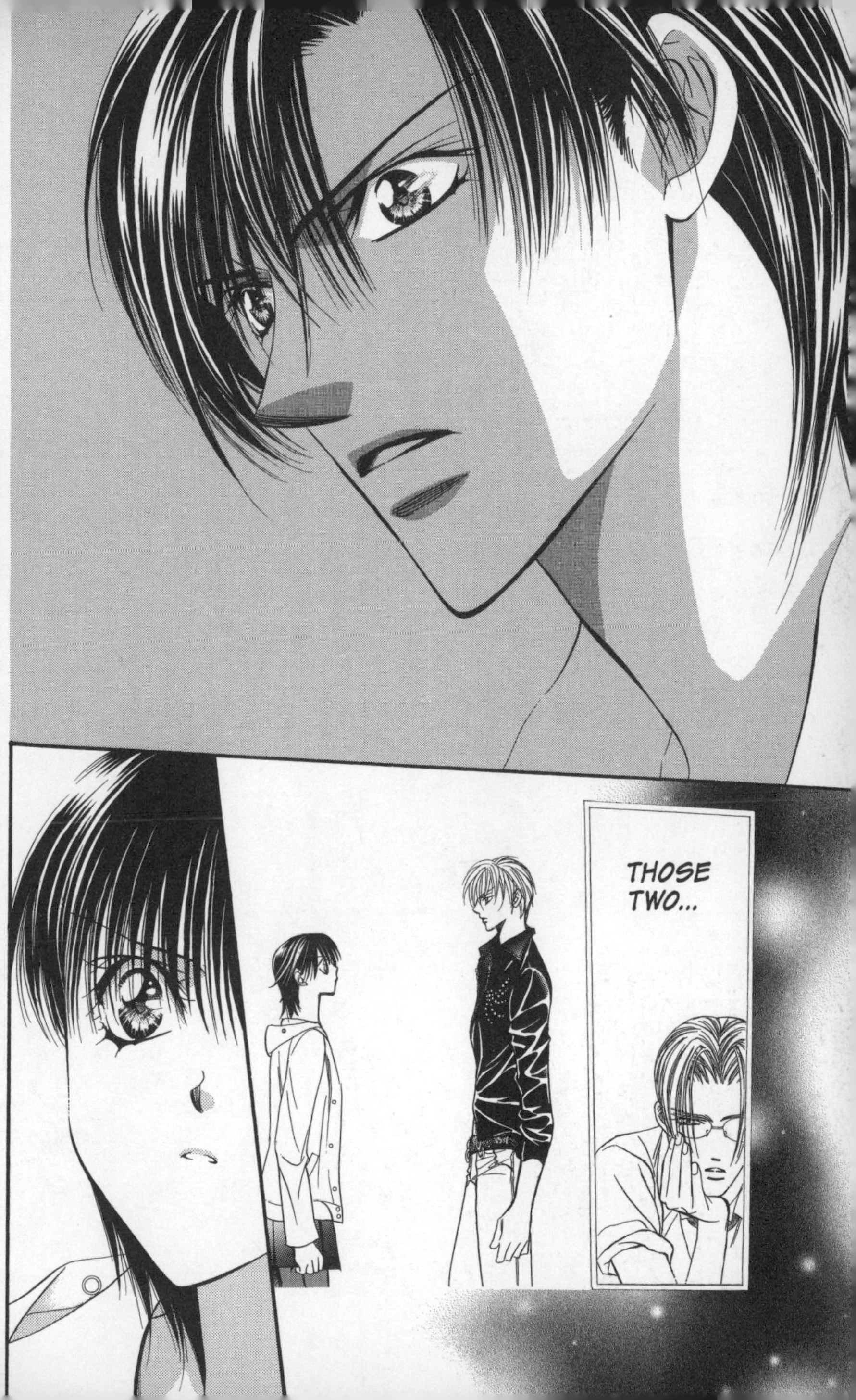
THOSE TWO...

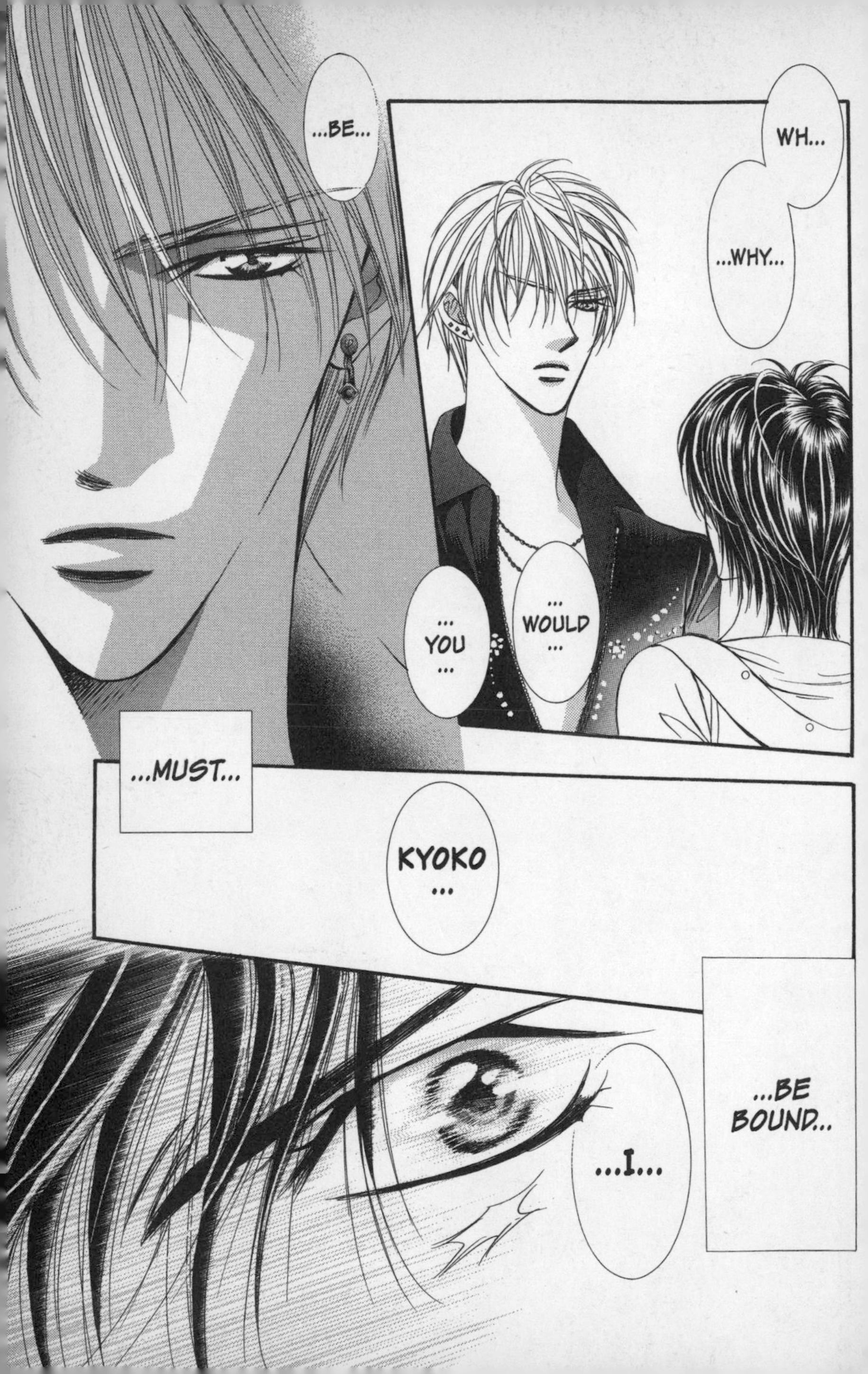
WH...
...WHY...
... WOULD ...
... YOU ...
...BE...
...MUST...
KYOKO ...
...BE BOUND...
...I...

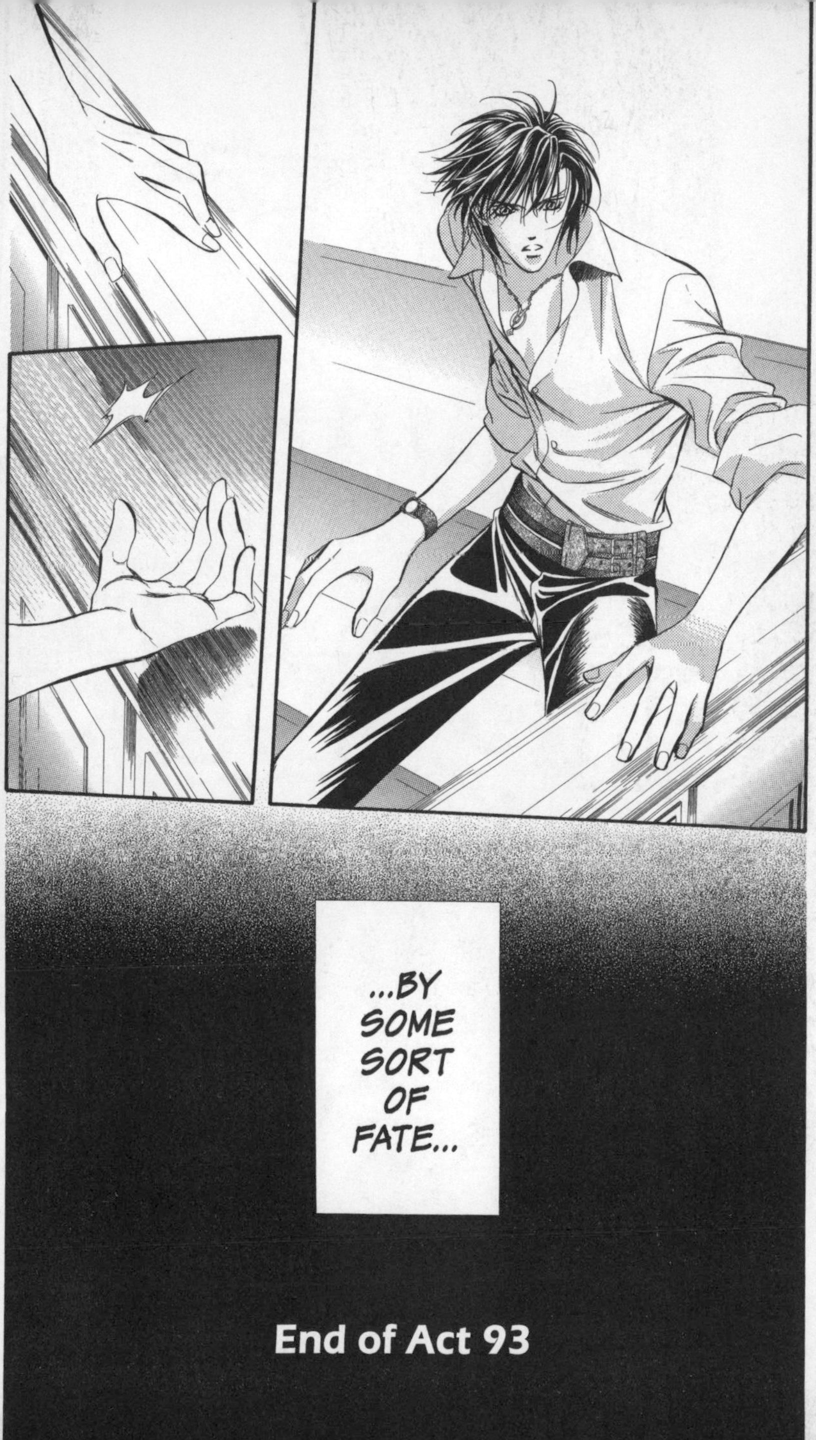
...BY SOME SORT OF FATE...
End of Act 93

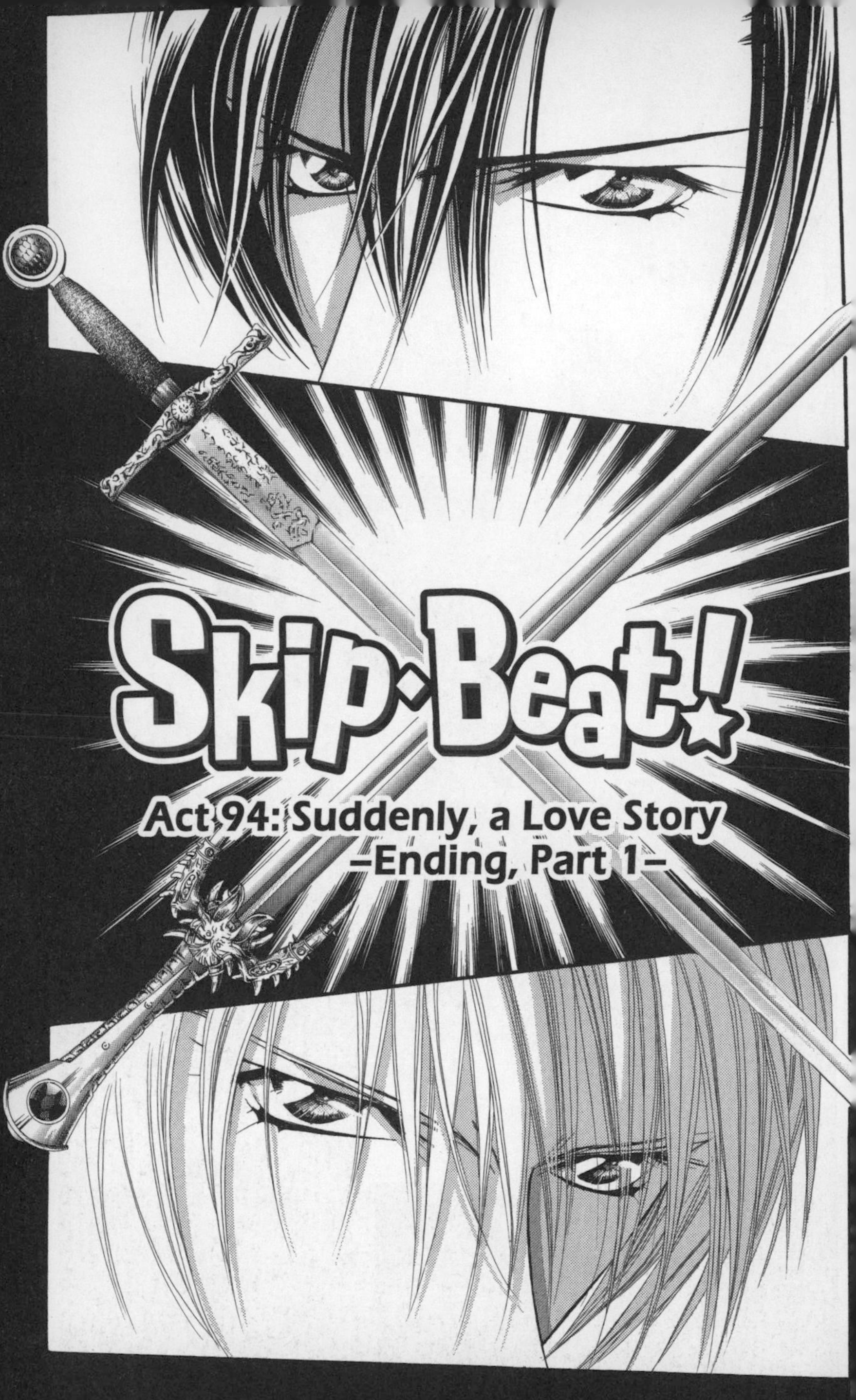
Skip·Beat!
Act 94: Suddenly, a Love Story
–Ending, Part 1–

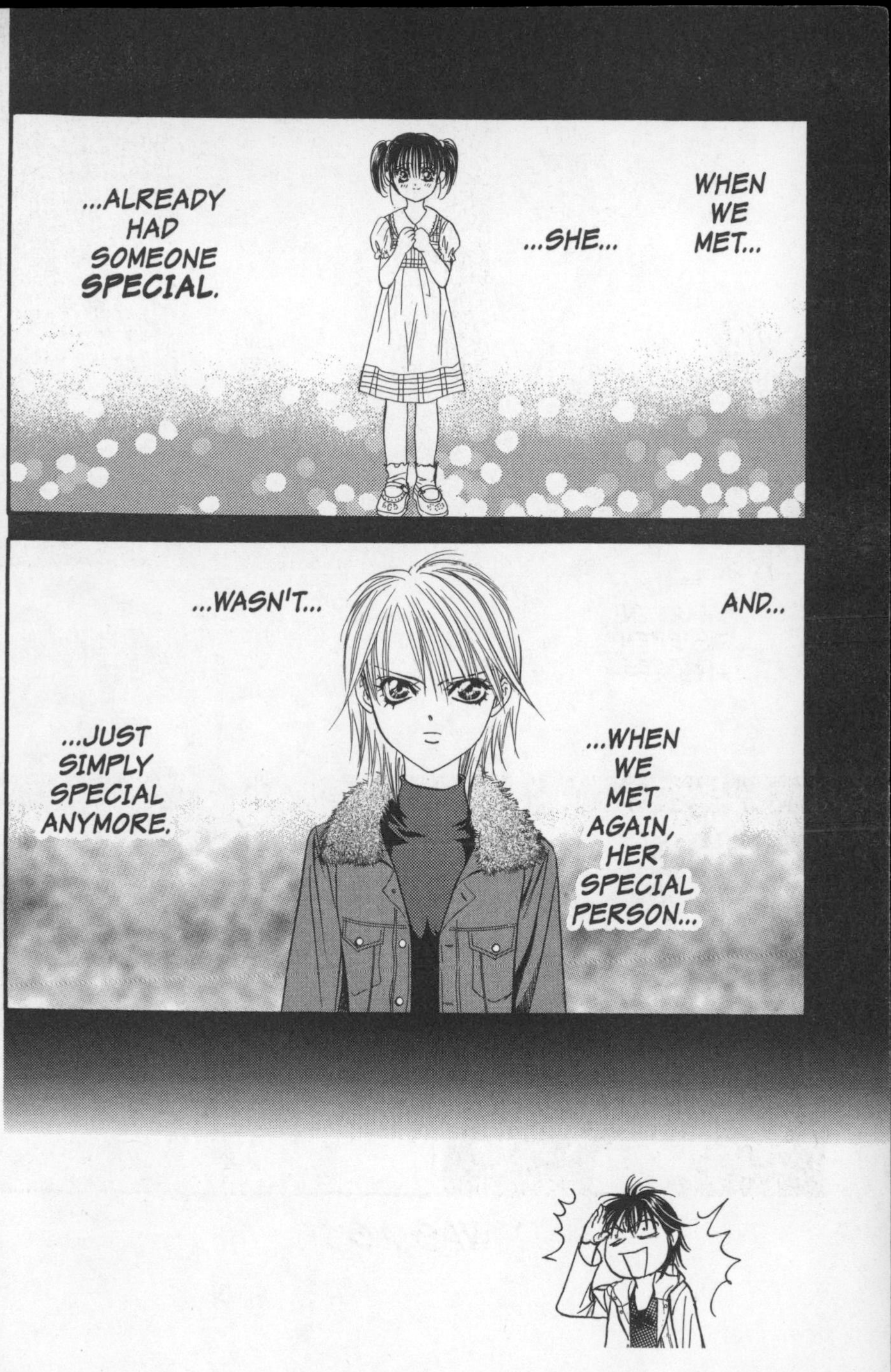
WHEN WE MET...
...SHE...
...ALREADY HAD SOMEONE SPECIAL.
AND...
...WHEN WE MET AGAIN, HER SPECIAL PERSON...
...WASN'T...
...JUST SIMPLY SPECIAL ANYMORE.

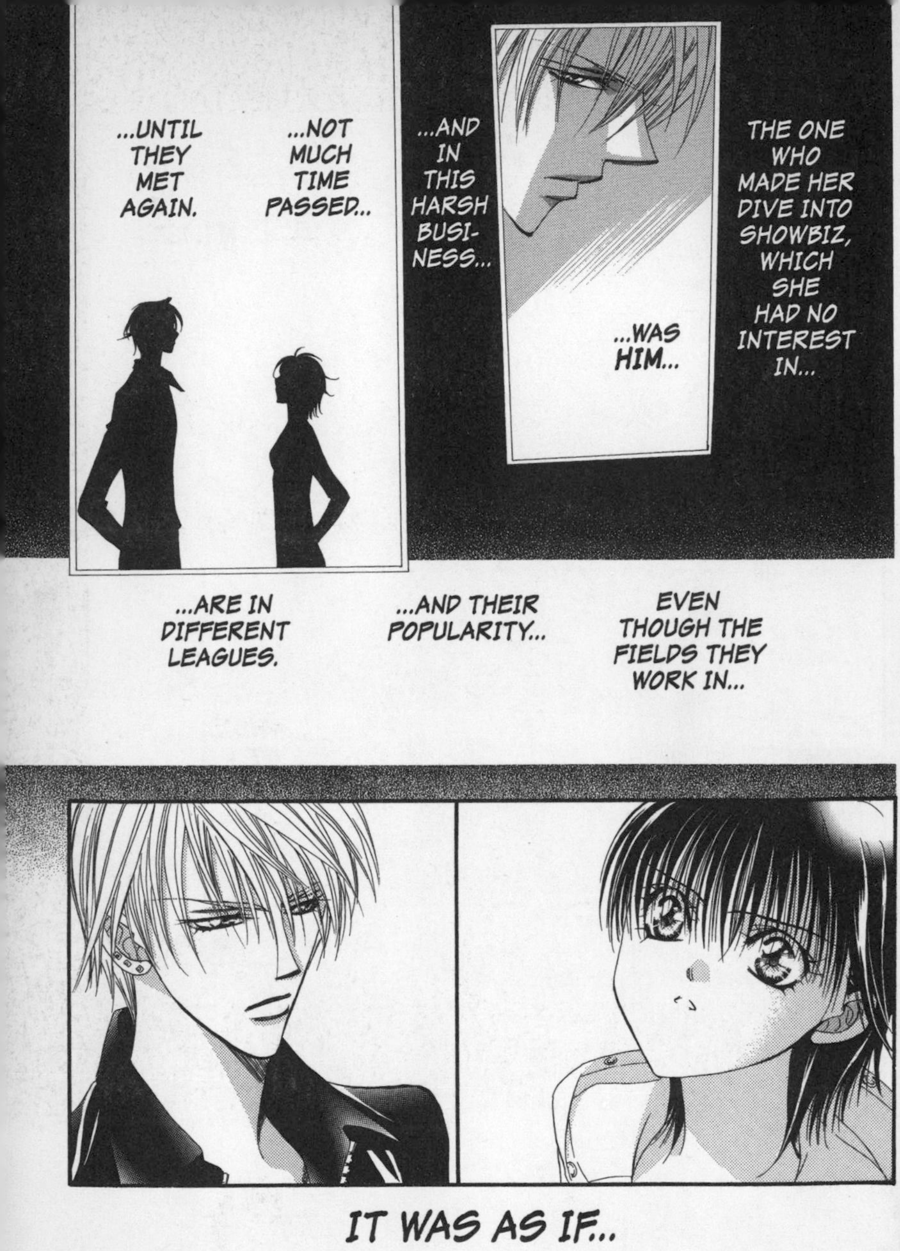
THE ONE WHO MADE HER DIVE INTO SHOWBIZ, WHICH SHE HAD NO INTEREST IN...
...WAS HIM...
...AND IN THIS HARSH BUSI-NESS...
...NOT MUCH TIME PASSED...
...UNTIL THEY MET AGAIN.
EVEN THOUGH THE FIELDS THEY WORK IN...
...AND THEIR POPULARITY...
...ARE IN DIFFERENT LEAGUES.
IT WAS AS IF...

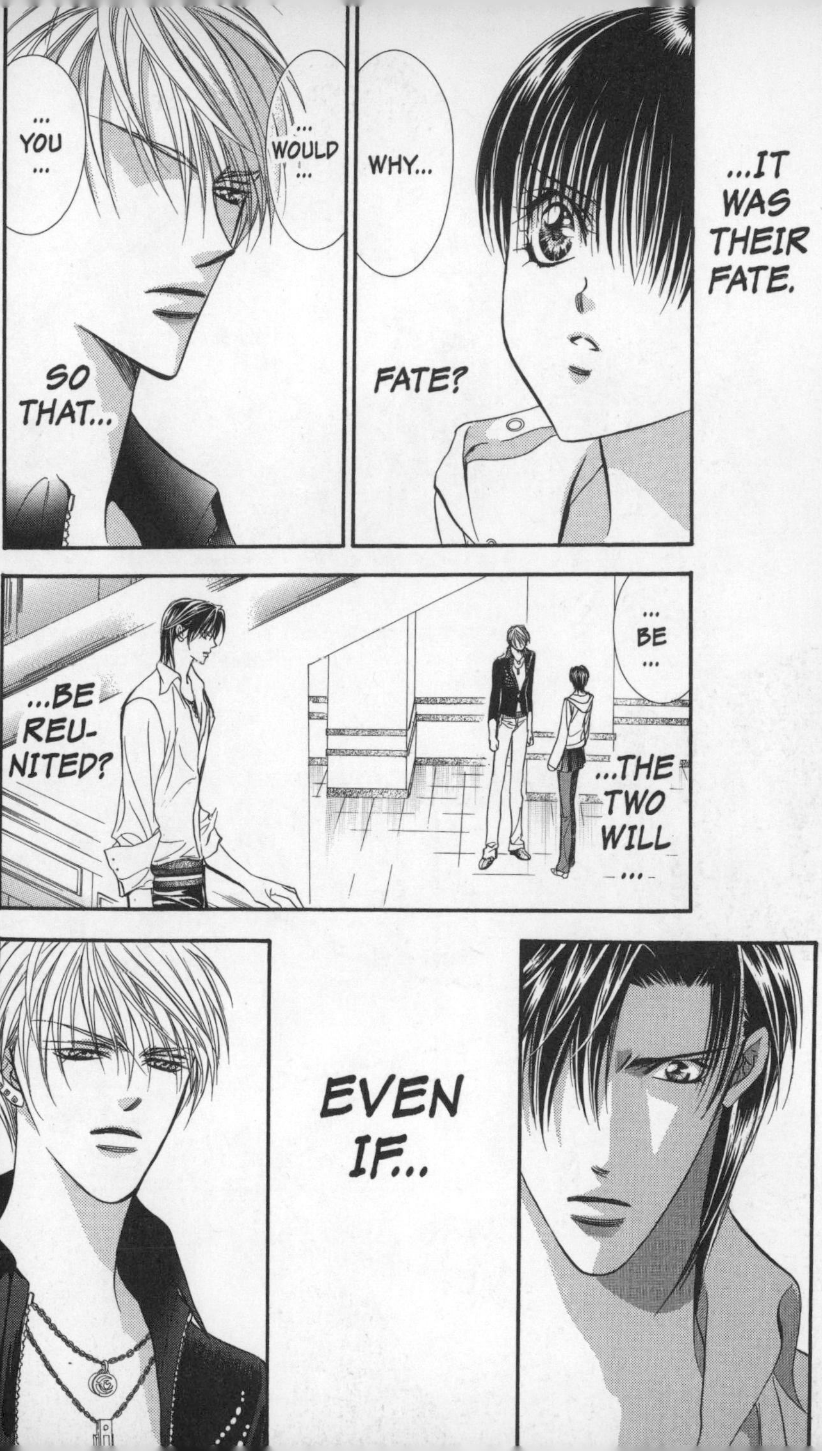
...IT WAS THEIR FATE.
WHY...
FATE?
... WOULD ...
... YOU ...
SO THAT...
... BE ...
...THE TWO WILL ...
...BE REU-NITED?
EVEN IF...

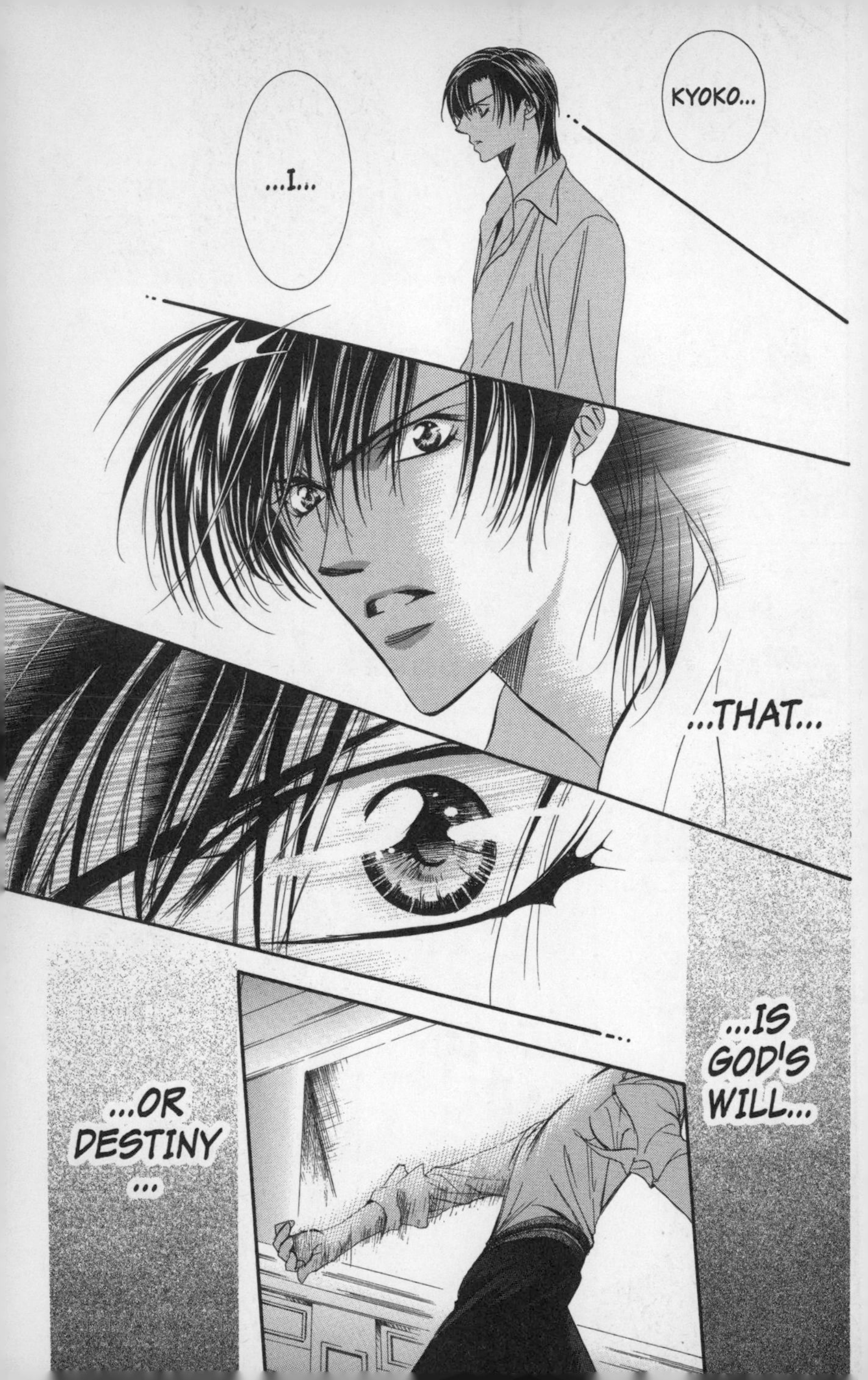
KYOKO...
...I...
...THAT...
...IS GOD'S WILL...
...OR DESTINY ...

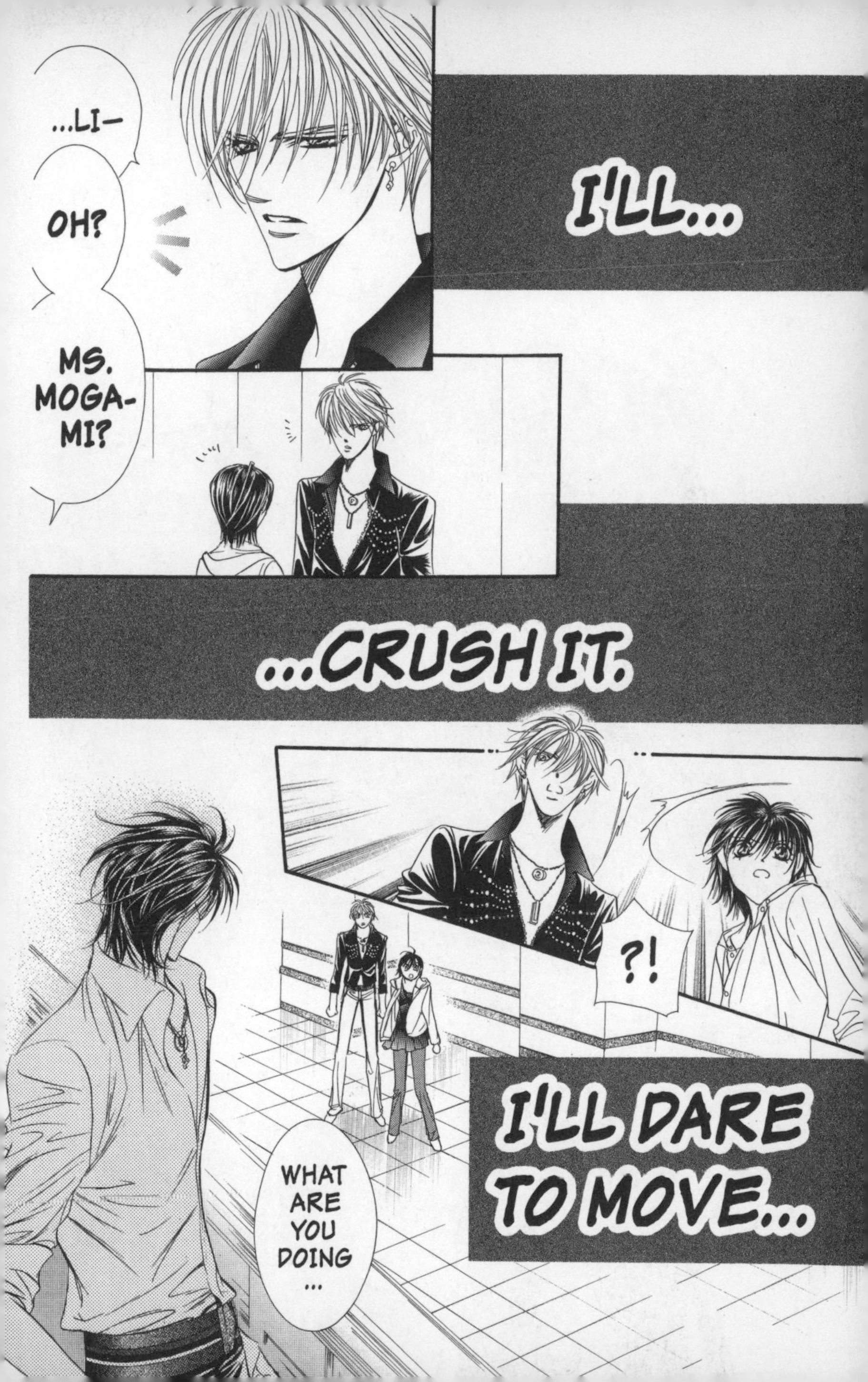
I'LL...
...LI—
OH?
MS. MOGA-MI?
...CRUSH IT.
?!
I'LL DARE TO MOVE...
WHAT ARE YOU DOING ...

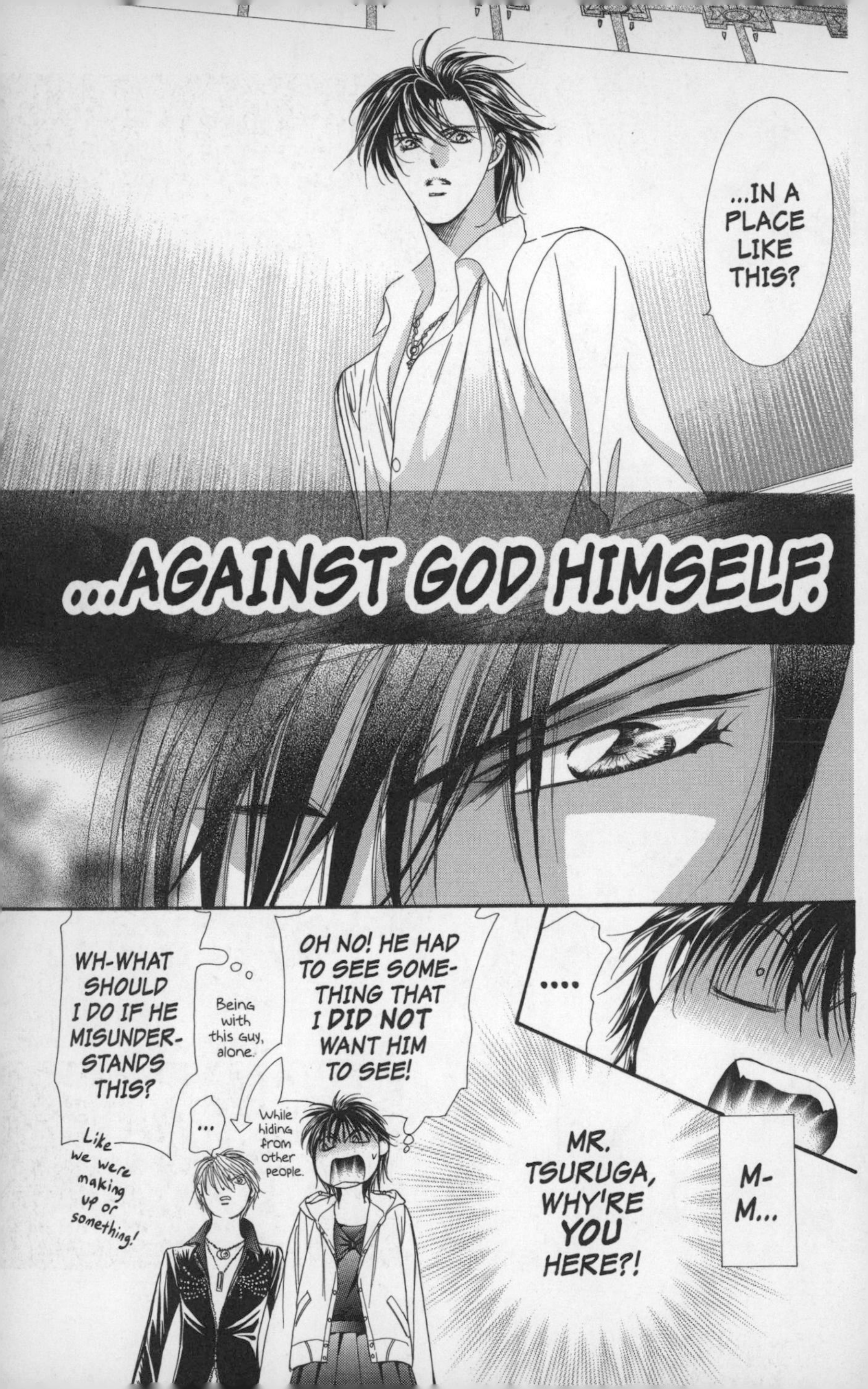
...IN A PLACE LIKE THIS?
...AGAINST GOD HIMSELF.
....
M-M...
MR. TSURUGA, WHY'RE YOU HERE?!
OH NO! HE HAD TO SEE SOME-THING THAT I DID NOT WANT HIM TO SEE!
While hiding from other people.
Being with this guy, alone.
WH-WHAT SHOULD I DO IF HE MISUNDER-STANDS THIS?
...
Like we were making up or something!

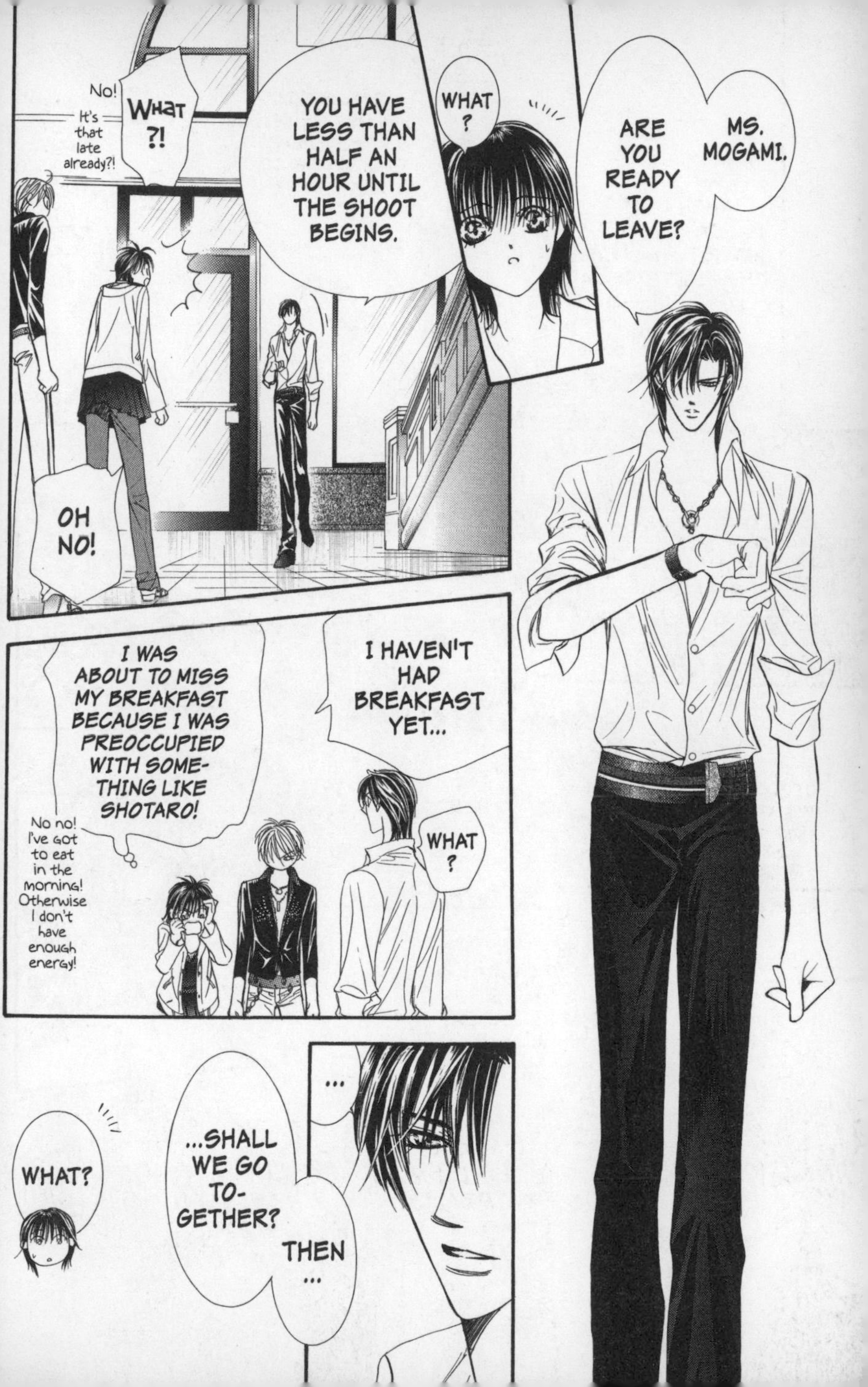
MS. MOGAMI.
ARE YOU READY TO LEAVE?
WHAT ?
YOU HAVE LESS THAN HALF AN HOUR UNTIL THE SHOOT BEGINS.
WHAT ?!
No! It's that late already?!
OH NO!
I HAVEN'T HAD BREAKFAST YET...
WHAT ?
I WAS ABOUT TO MISS MY BREAKFAST BECAUSE I WAS PREOCCUPIED WITH SOME-THING LIKE SHOTARO!
No no! I've got to eat in the morning! Otherwise I don't have enough energy!
...
THEN ...
...SHALL WE GO TO-GETHER?
WHAT?

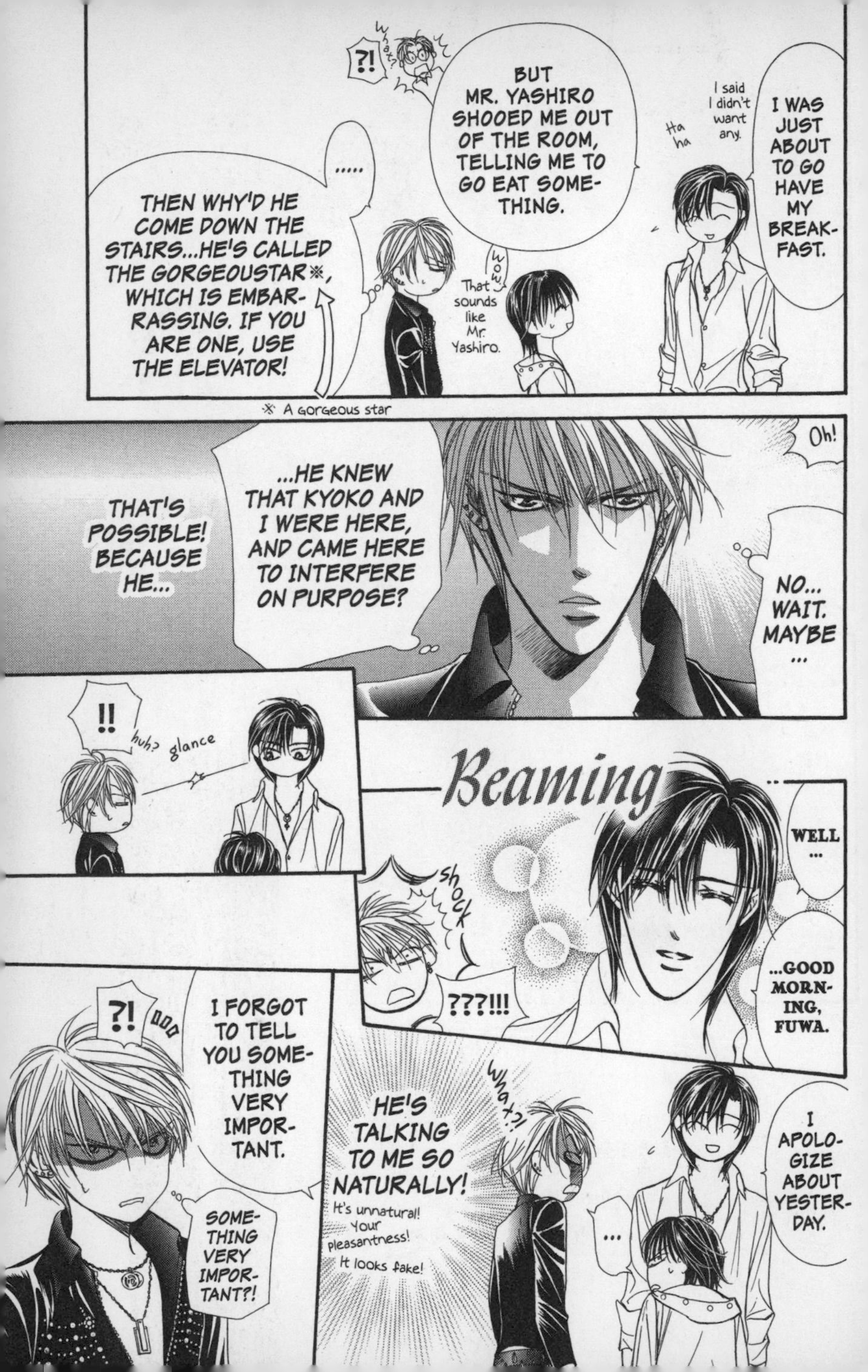
I WAS JUST ABOUT TO GO HAVE MY BREAKFAST.
I said I didn't want any.
Ha ha
BUT MR. YASHIRO SHOOED ME OUT OF THE ROOM, TELLING ME TO GO EAT SOME-THING.
What?
?!
Wow
That sounds like Mr. Yashiro.
.....
THEN WHY'D HE COME DOWN THE STAIRS...HE'S CALLED THE GORGEOUSTAR※, WHICH IS EMBAR-RASSING. IF YOU ARE ONE, USE THE ELEVATOR!
※ A gorgeous star
Oh!
NO... WAIT. MAYBE ...
...HE KNEW THAT KYOKO AND I WERE HERE, AND CAME HERE TO INTERFERE ON PURPOSE?
THAT'S POSSIBLE! BECAUSE HE...
!!
huh?
glance
Beaming
WELL ...
...GOOD MORNING, FUWA.
shock
???!!!
I APOLO-GIZE ABOUT YESTER-DAY.
...
What?!
HE'S TALKING TO ME SO NATURALLY!
It's unnatural! Your pleasantness! It looks fake!
I FORGOT TO TELL YOU SOME-THING VERY IMPOR-TANT.
?!
SOME-THING VERY IMPOR-TANT?!

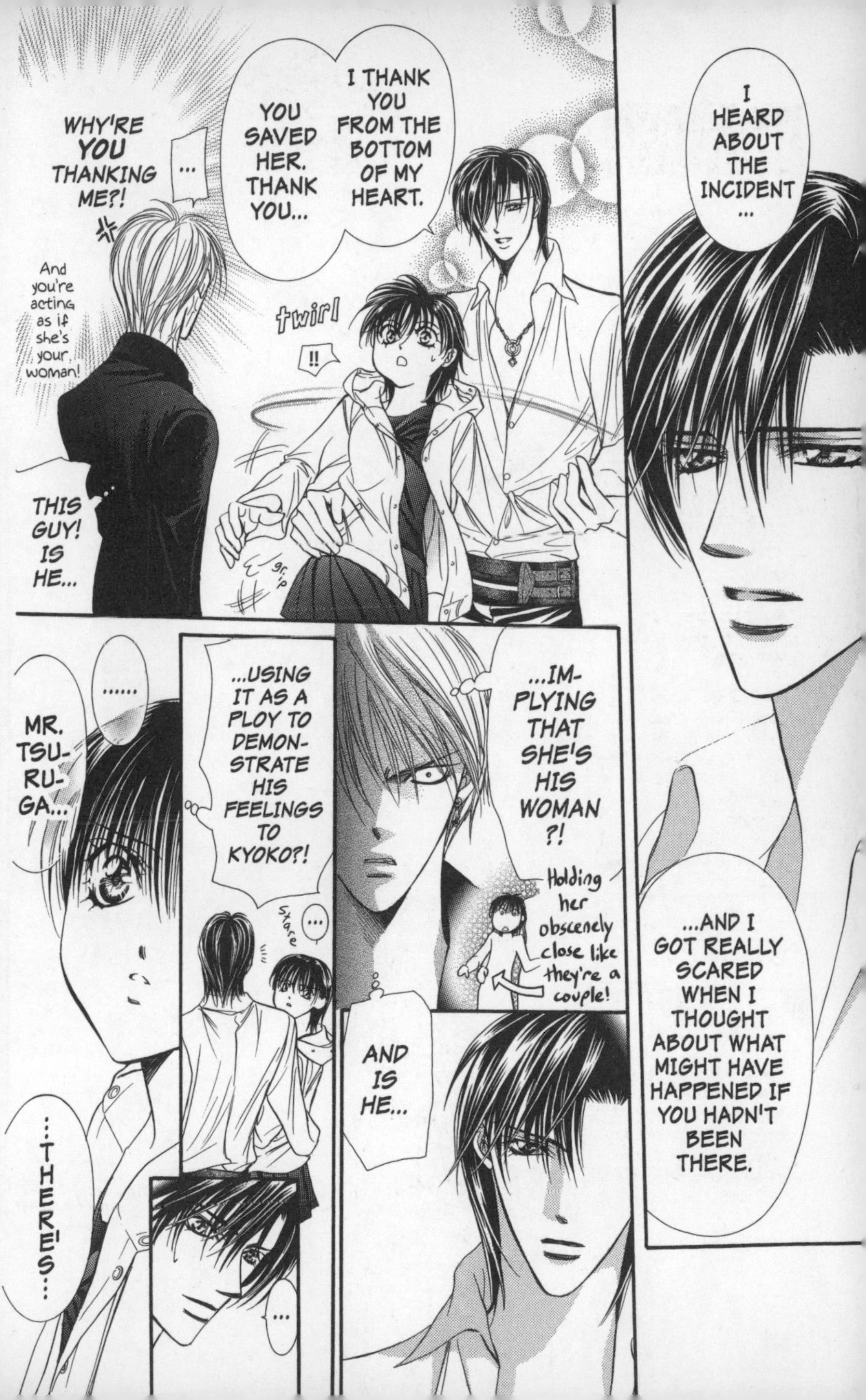
I HEARD ABOUT THE INCIDENT...
...AND I GOT REALLY SCARED WHEN I THOUGHT ABOUT WHAT MIGHT HAVE HAPPENED IF YOU HADN'T BEEN THERE.
I THANK YOU FROM THE BOTTOM OF MY HEART.
YOU SAVED HER. THANK YOU...
twirl
!!
...
WHY'RE YOU THANKING ME?!
And you're acting as if she's your woman!
grip
THIS GUY! IS HE...
...IM-PLYING THAT SHE'S HIS WOMAN?!
Holding her obscenely close like they're a couple!
AND IS HE...
...USING IT AS A PLOY TO DEMON-STRATE HIS FEELINGS TO KYOKO?!
stare
...
...
......
MR. TSU-RU-GA...
...THERE'S...

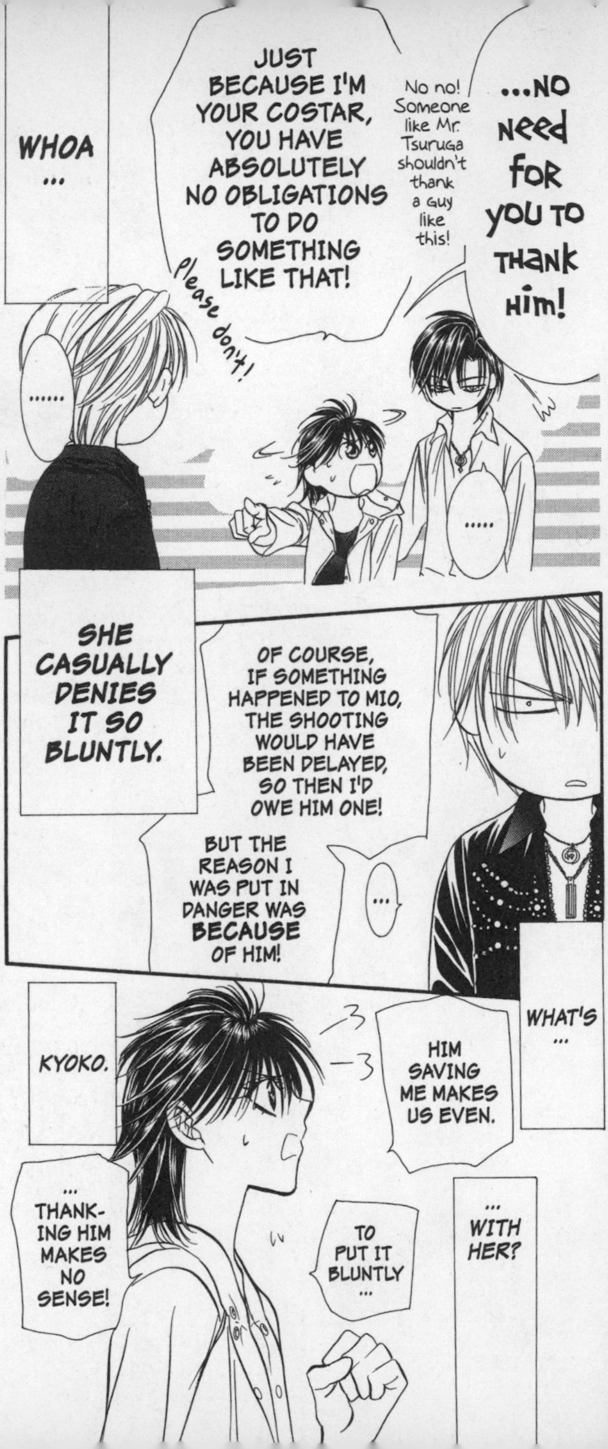
...NO NEED FOR YOU TO THANK HIM!
No no! Someone like Mr. Tsuruga shouldn't thank a guy like this!
JUST BECAUSE I'M YOUR COSTAR, YOU HAVE ABSOLUTELY NO OBLIGATIONS TO DO SOMETHING LIKE THAT!
Please don't!
WHOA ...
......
.....
OF COURSE, IF SOMETHING HAPPENED TO MIO, THE SHOOTING WOULD HAVE BEEN DELAYED, SO THEN I'D OWE HIM ONE!
BUT THE REASON I WAS PUT IN DANGER WAS BECAUSE OF HIM!
...
SHE CASUALLY DENIES IT SO BLUNTLY.
WHAT'S ...
HIM SAVING ME MAKES US EVEN.
KYOKO.
... WITH HER?
TO PUT IT BLUNTLY ...
... THANKING HIM MAKES NO SENSE!

(Vocals) Reino

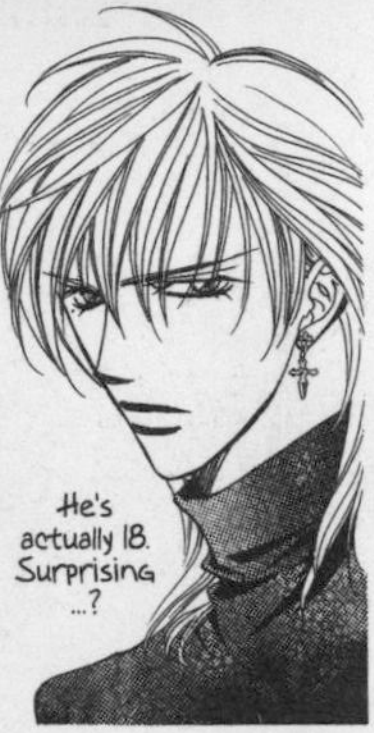
He's actually 18. Surprising ...?

...Do I............like...perverts..........after all...?

(I have a record with my previous work, Tokyo Crazy Paradise's last boss).

To tell the truth... when I was drawing this "Love Story" arc, what I found most fun was drawing Reino when he was using his mysterious powers to sense Kyoko's presence no matter where she was, chasing her until she was torn and tattered, then dropping down like a piercing arrow from the sky (actually, from the top of a bridge)...

...ecstasy...

Apparently the readers accepted my burning heart...there were quite a lot of readers who said they liked that scene, and I'm a bit happy...

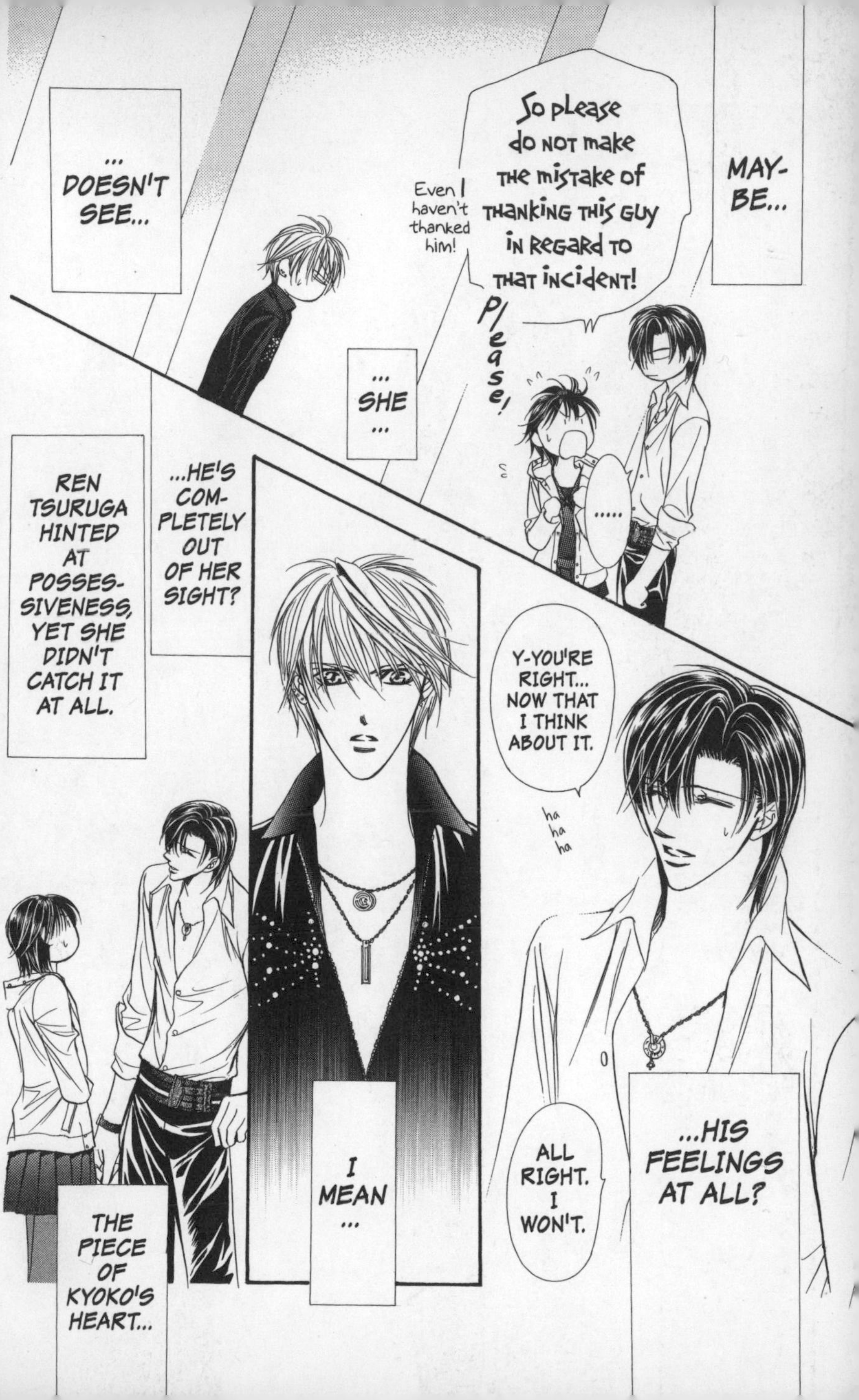
MAY-BE...
So please do not make the mistake of thanking this guy in regard to that incident!
Even I haven't thanked him!
Please!
... DOESN'T SEE...
... SHE ...
.....
...HE'S COMPLETELY OUT OF HER SIGHT?
REN TSURUGA HINTED AT POSSESSIVENESS, YET SHE DIDN'T CATCH IT AT ALL.
Y-YOU'RE RIGHT... NOW THAT I THINK ABOUT IT.
ha ha ha
...HIS FEELINGS AT ALL?
ALL RIGHT. I WON'T.
I MEAN ...
THE PIECE OF KYOKO'S HEART...

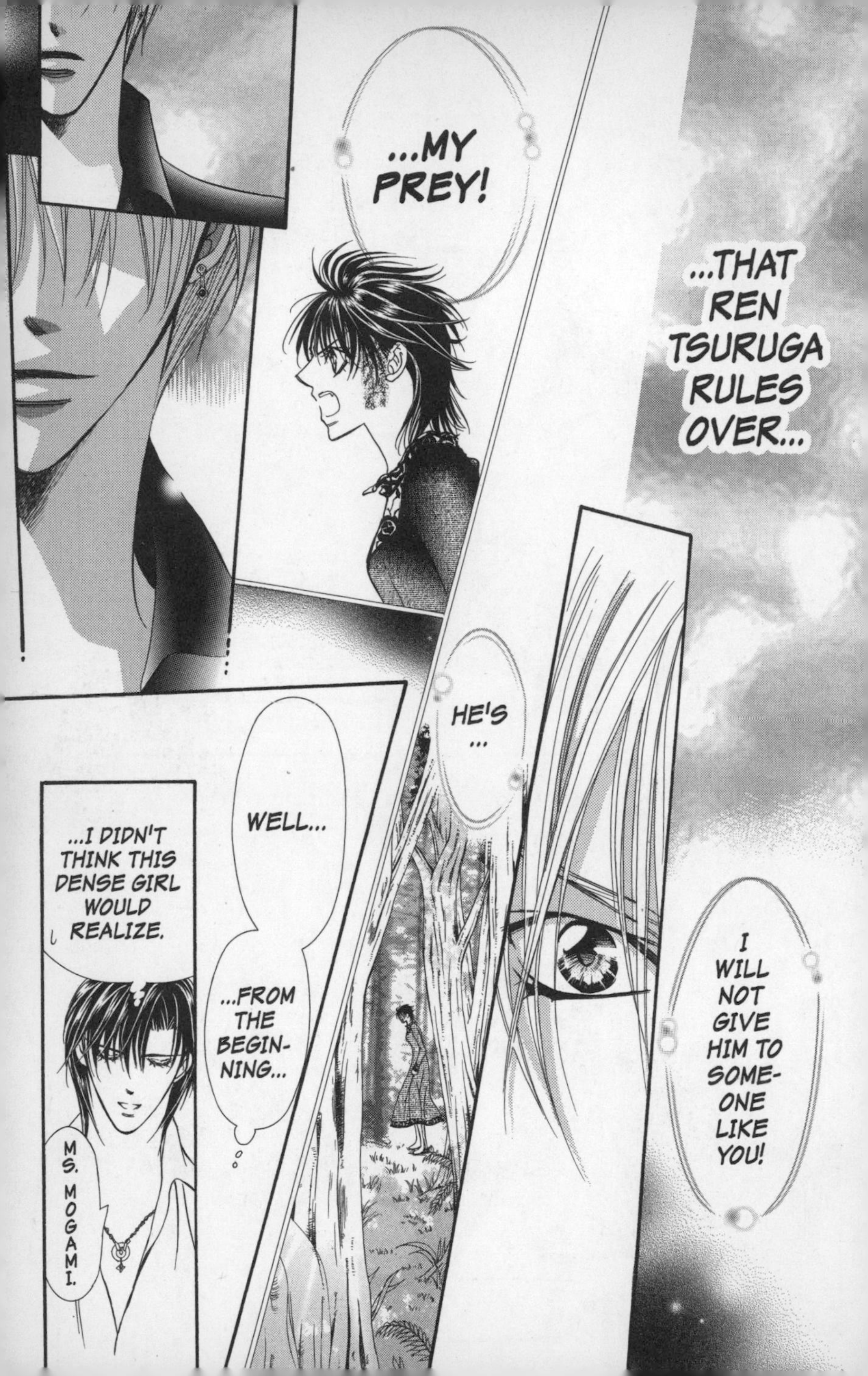
...THAT REN TSURUGA RULES OVER...
...MY PREY!
HE'S ...
I WILL NOT GIVE HIM TO SOMEONE LIKE YOU!
WELL...
...FROM THE BEGINNING...
...I DIDN'T THINK THIS DENSE GIRL WOULD REALIZE.
MS. MOGAMI.

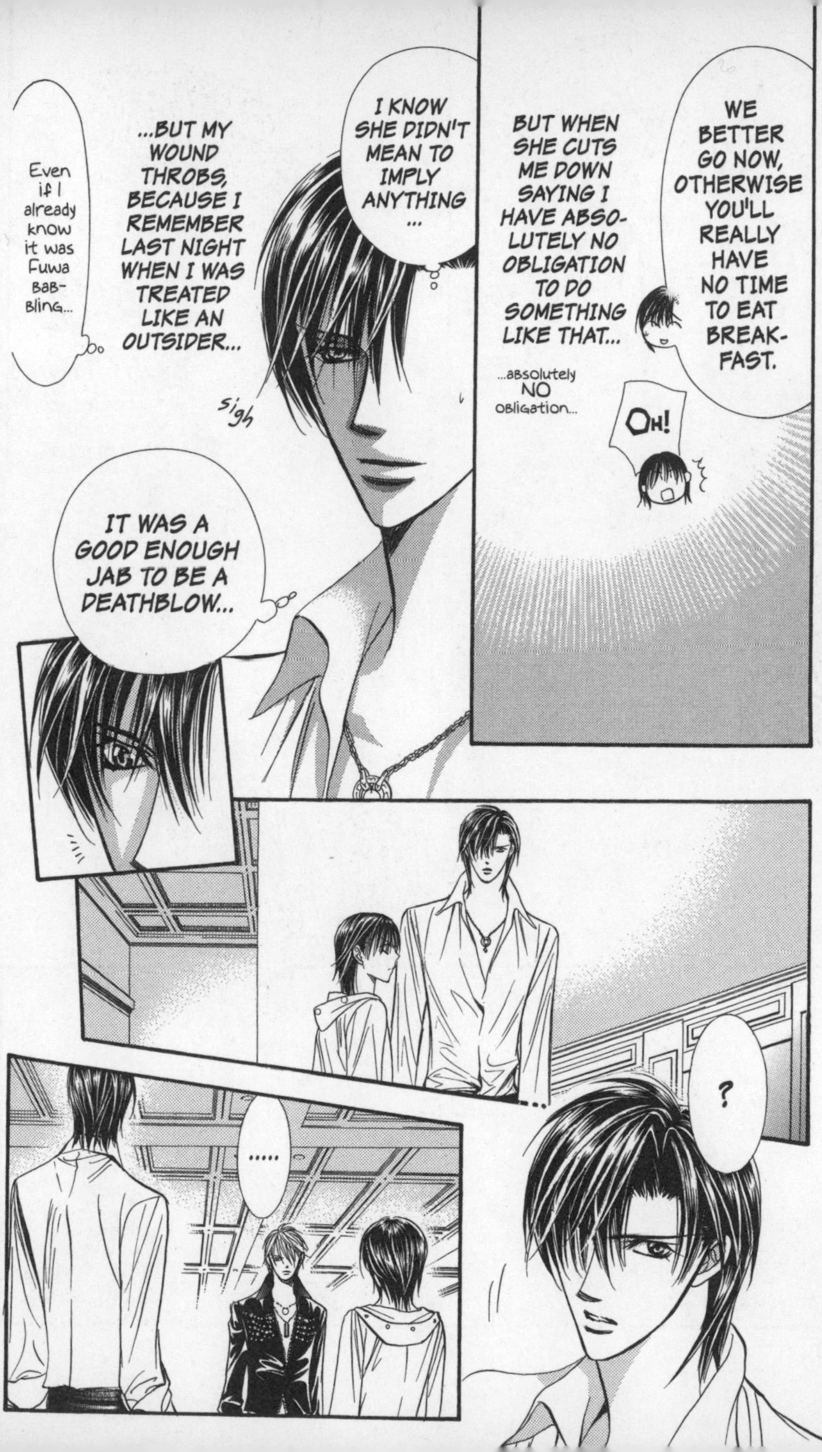
WE BETTER GO NOW, OTHERWISE YOU'LL REALLY HAVE NO TIME TO EAT BREAK-FAST.
OH!
BUT WHEN SHE CUTS ME DOWN SAYING I HAVE ABSO-LUTELY NO OBLIGATION TO DO SOMETHING LIKE THAT...
...absolutely NO obligation...
I KNOW SHE DIDN'T MEAN TO IMPLY ANYTHING ...
...BUT MY WOUND THROBS, BECAUSE I REMEMBER LAST NIGHT WHEN I WAS TREATED LIKE AN OUTSIDER...
Even if I already know it was Fuwa Bab-bling...
sigh
IT WAS A GOOD ENOUGH JAB TO BE A DEATHBLOW...
?
......

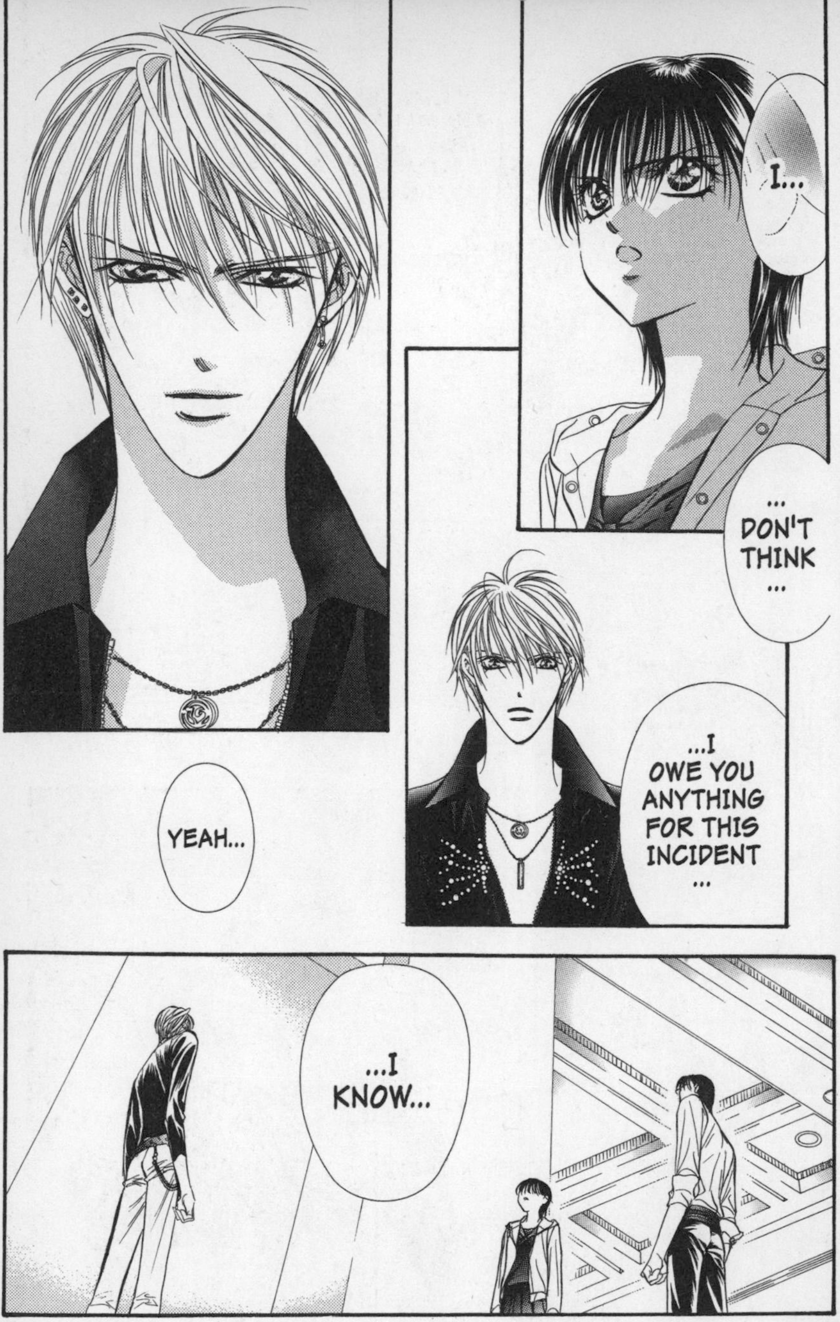
I...
...DON'T THINK...
...I OWE YOU ANYTHING FOR THIS INCIDENT...
YEAH...
...I KNOW...

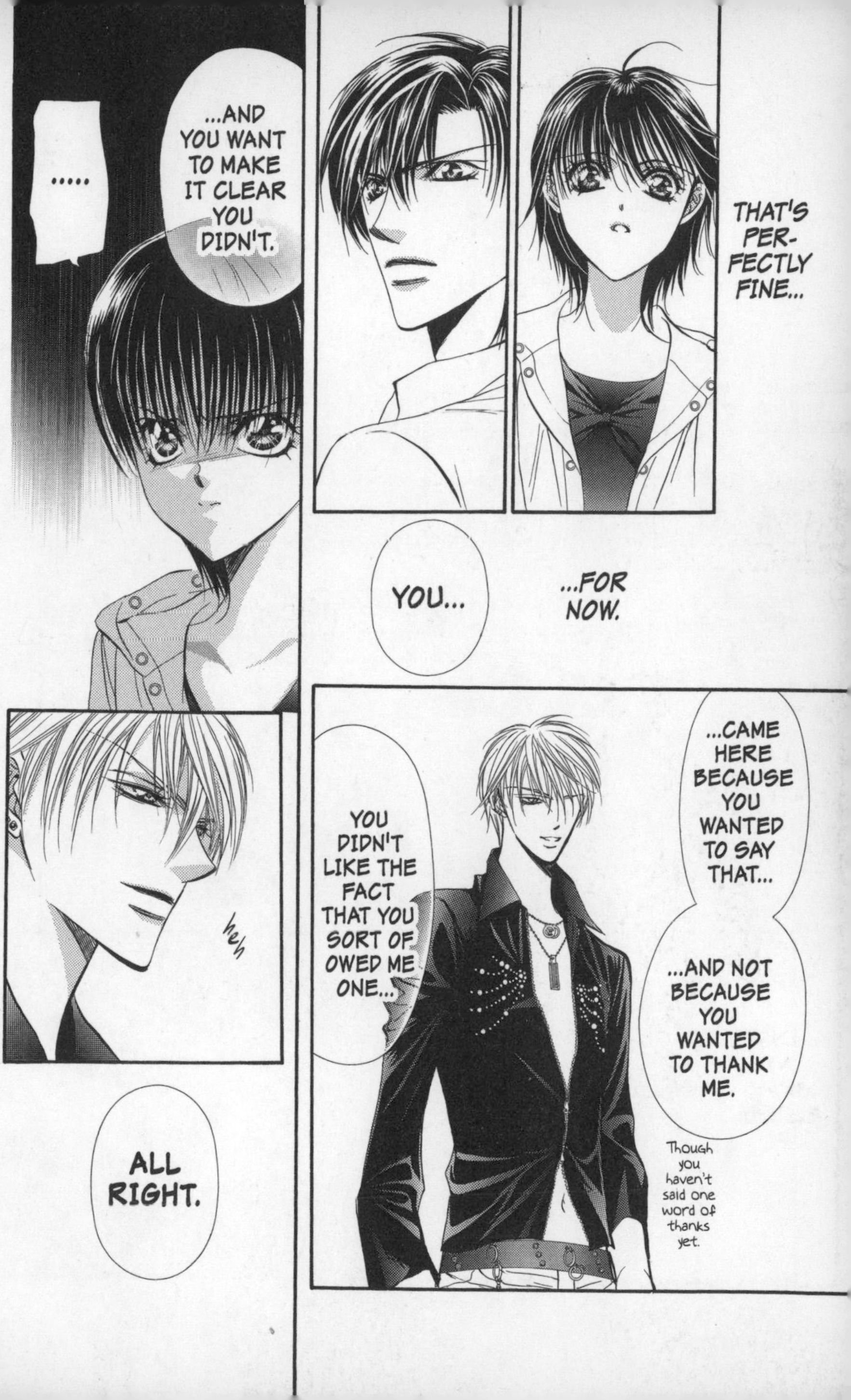
THAT'S PER-FECTLY FINE...
...FOR NOW.
YOU...
...AND YOU WANT TO MAKE IT CLEAR YOU DIDN'T.
.....
...CAME HERE BECAUSE YOU WANTED TO SAY THAT...
...AND NOT BECAUSE YOU WANTED TO THANK ME.
Though you haven't said one word of thanks yet.
YOU DIDN'T LIKE THE FACT THAT YOU SORT OF OWED ME ONE...
heh
ALL RIGHT.

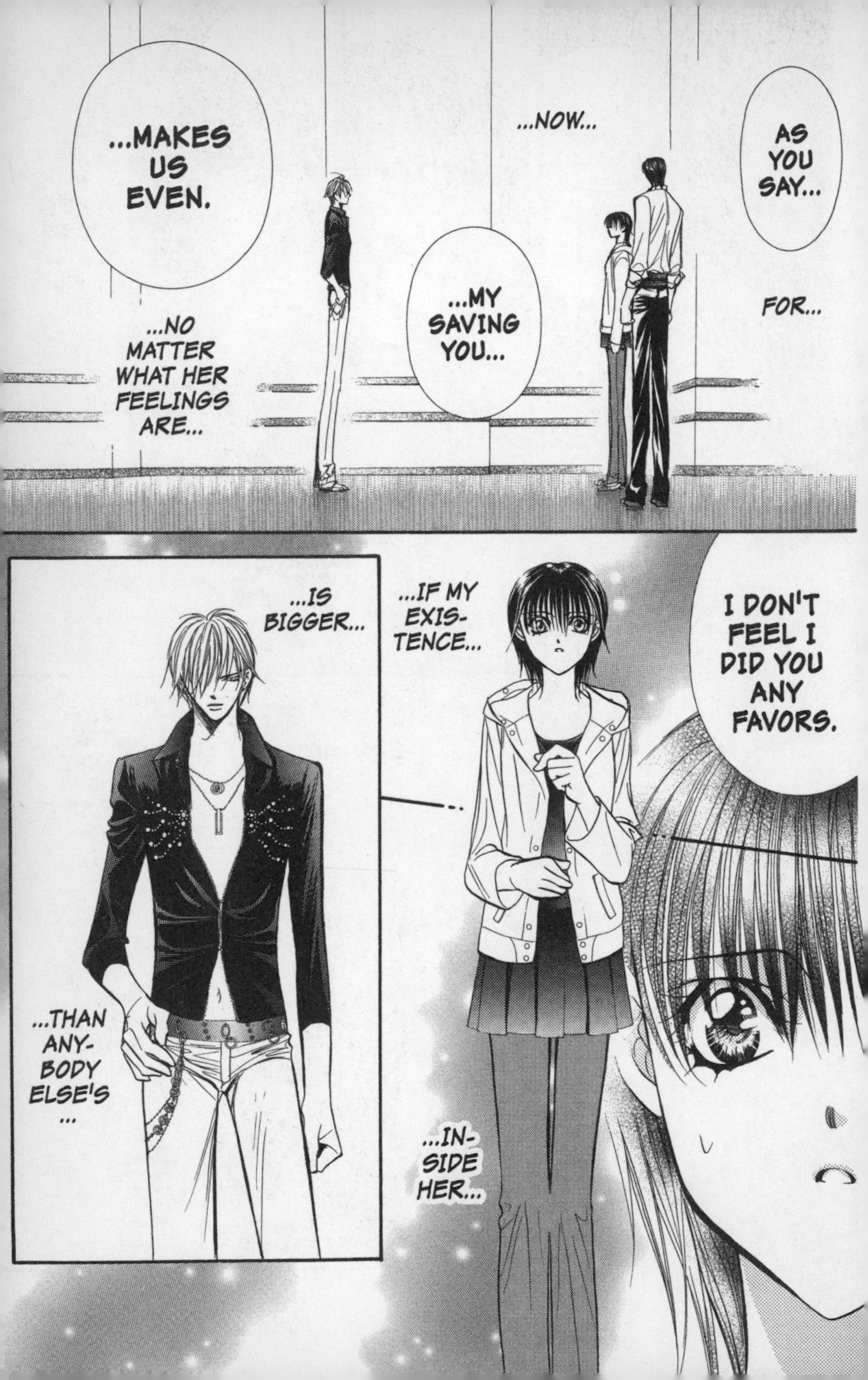
AS YOU SAY...
FOR...
...NOW...
...MY SAVING YOU...
...MAKES US EVEN.
...NO MATTER WHAT HER FEELINGS ARE...
I DON'T FEEL I DID YOU ANY FAVORS.
...IF MY EXIS-TENCE...
...IN-SIDE HER...
...IS BIGGER...
...THAN ANY-BODY ELSE'S ...

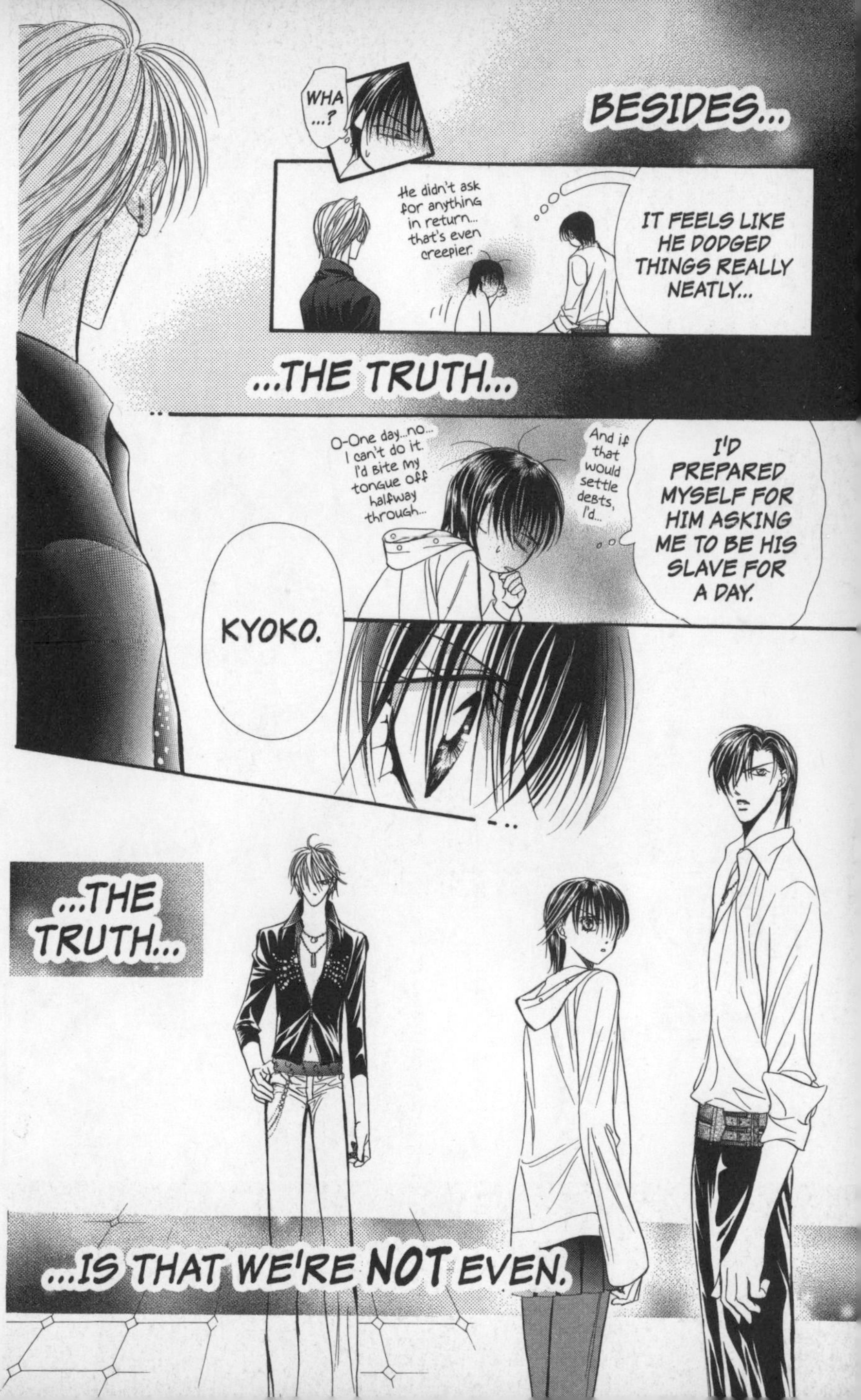
BESIDES...
WHA ...?
IT FEELS LIKE HE DODGED THINGS REALLY NEATLY...
He didn't ask for anything in return... that's even creepier.
...THE TRUTH...
I'D PREPARED MYSELF FOR HIM ASKING ME TO BE HIS SLAVE FOR A DAY.
And if that would settle debts, I'd...
O-One day...no... I can't do it. I'd bite my tongue off halfway through...
KYOKO.
...THE TRUTH...
...IS THAT WE'RE NOT EVEN.

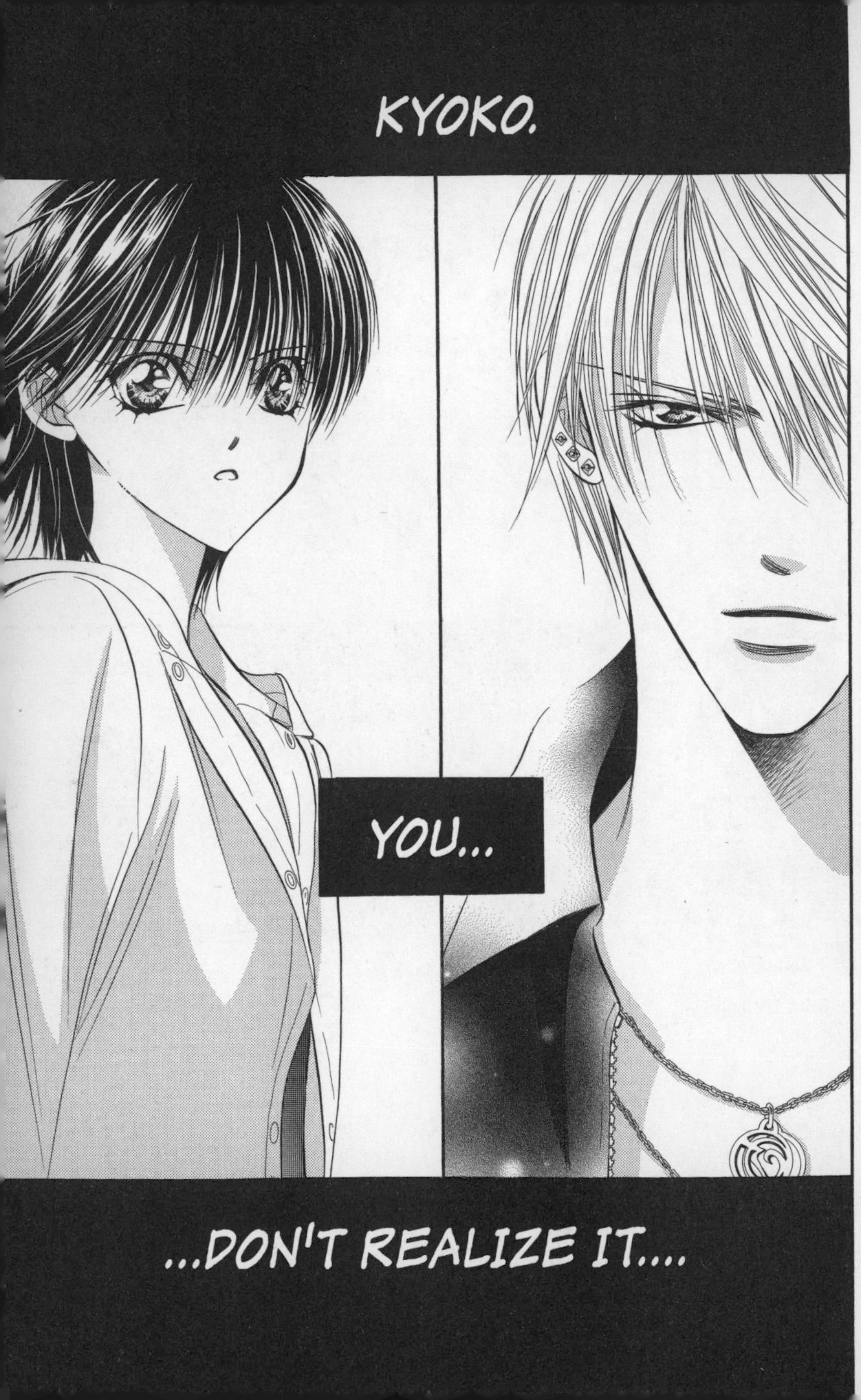
KYOKO.
YOU...
...DON'T REALIZE IT....

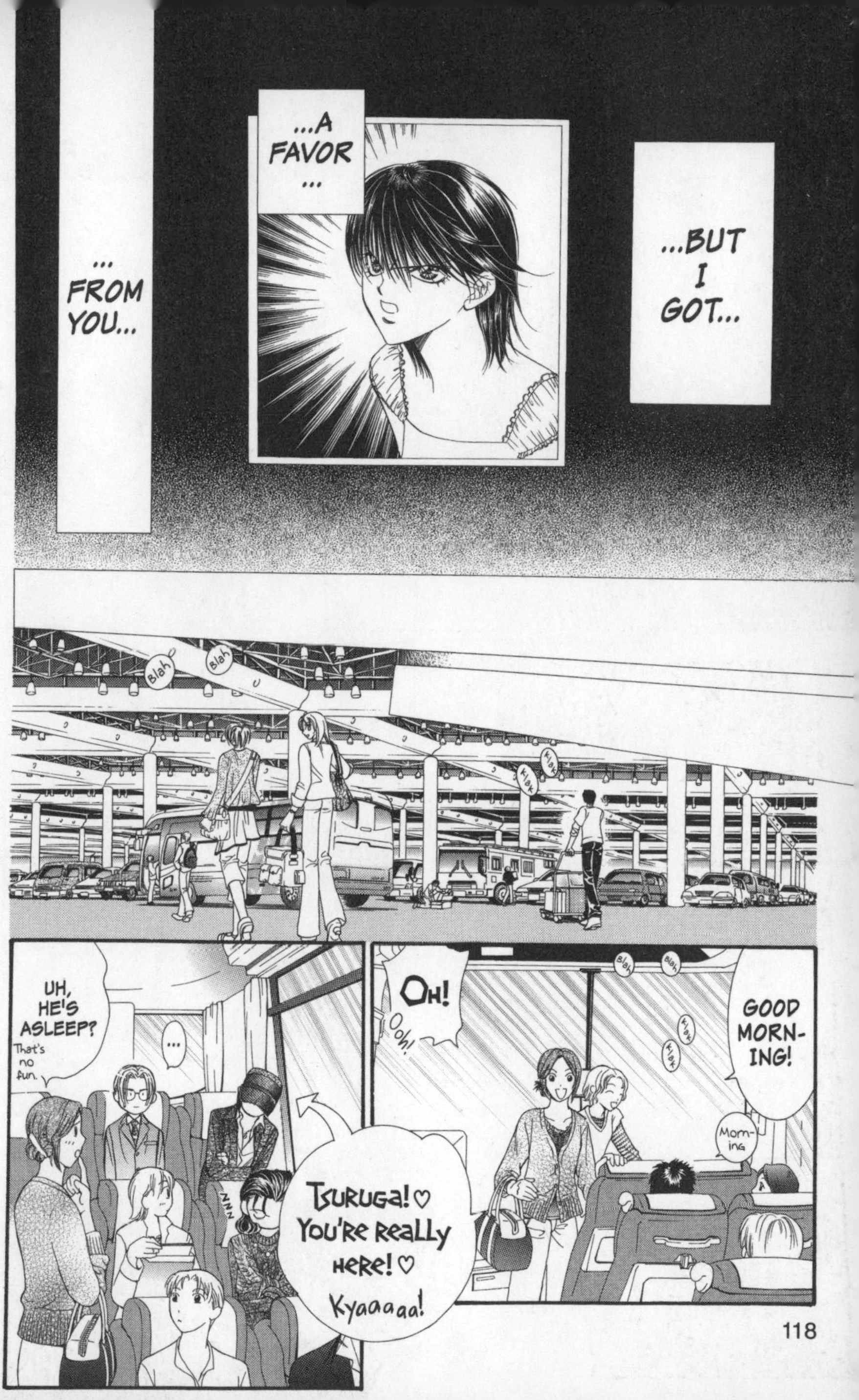
...BUT I GOT...
...A FAVOR...
...FROM YOU...
Blah
Blah
Klak
Klak
GOOD MORNING!
Morning
OH!
Ooh!
Blah
Blah
Klak
Klak
Tsuruga! ♡ You're really here! ♡
Kyaaaaa!
...
ZZZ
UH, HE'S ASLEEP?
That's no fun.

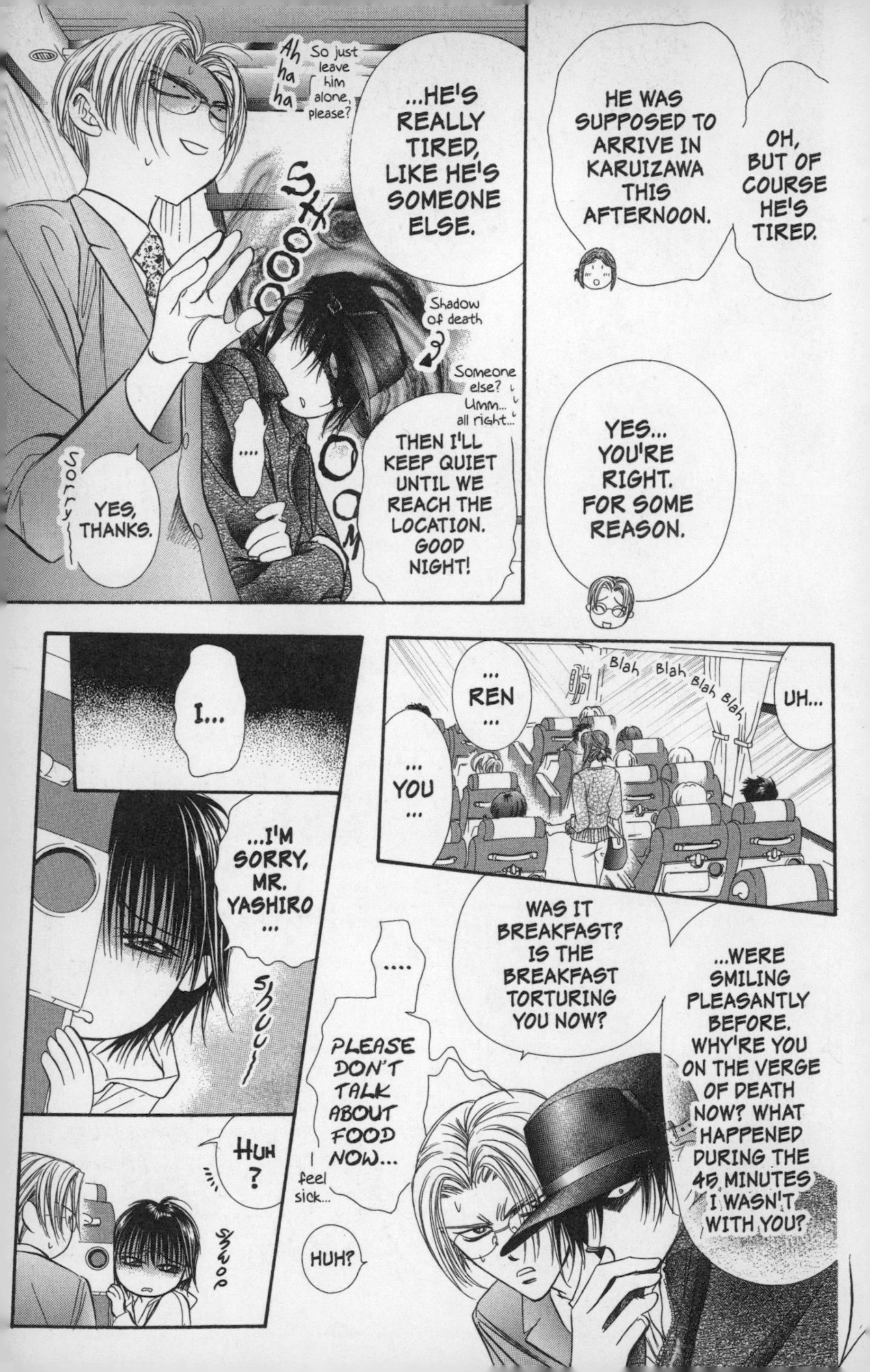
HE WAS SUPPOSED TO ARRIVE IN KARUIZAWA THIS AFTERNOON.
OH, BUT OF COURSE HE'S TIRED.
YES... YOU'RE RIGHT. FOR SOME REASON.
...HE'S REALLY TIRED, LIKE HE'S SOMEONE ELSE.
So just leave him alone, please?
Ah ha ha
SHOOOOOOOM
Shadow of death
Someone else? Umm... all right...
THEN I'LL KEEP QUIET UNTIL WE REACH THE LOCATION. GOOD NIGHT!
....
YES, THANKS.
Sorry—
UH...
Blah Blah Blah Blah
...REN...
...YOU...
...WERE SMILING PLEASANTLY BEFORE. WHY'RE YOU ON THE VERGE OF DEATH NOW? WHAT HAPPENED DURING THE 45 MINUTES I WASN'T WITH YOU?
WAS IT BREAKFAST? IS THE BREAKFAST TORTURING YOU NOW?
....
PLEASE DON'T TALK ABOUT FOOD NOW...
I feel sick...
HUH?
I...
...I'M SORRY, MR. YASHIRO...
SHUUU—
HUH?
SHWOP

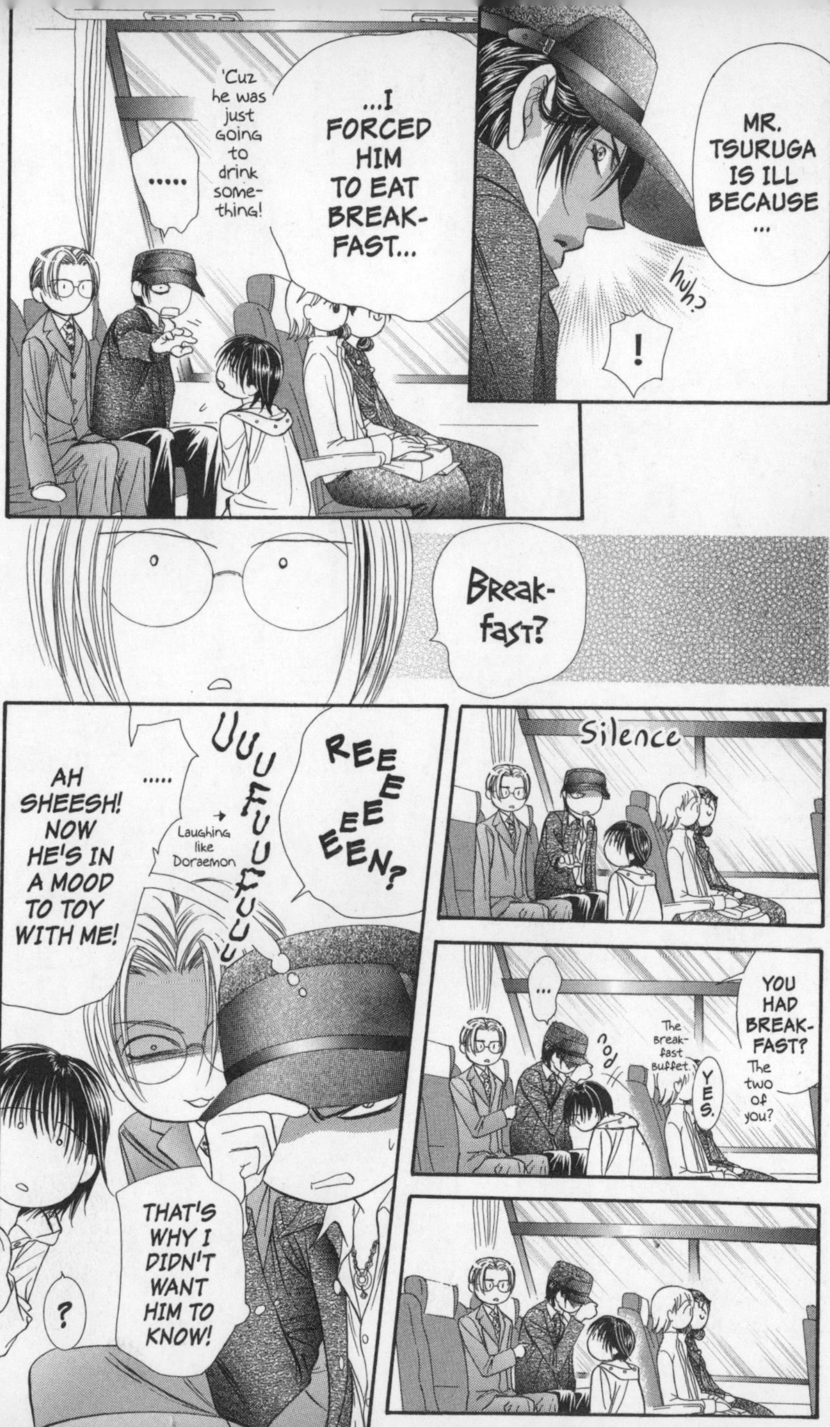
MR. TSURUGA IS ILL BECAUSE...
huh?
!
...I FORCED HIM TO EAT BREAK-FAST...
'Cuz he was just going to drink some-thing!
.....
Break-fast?
Silence
YOU HAD BREAK-FAST? The two of you?
YES.
The Break-fast Buffet.
nod
...
REEEEEEEEEN?
UUUFUUUFUUUU
Laughing like Doraemon
.....
AH SHEESH! NOW HE'S IN A MOOD TO TOY WITH ME!
THAT'S WHY I DIDN'T WANT HIM TO KNOW!
?

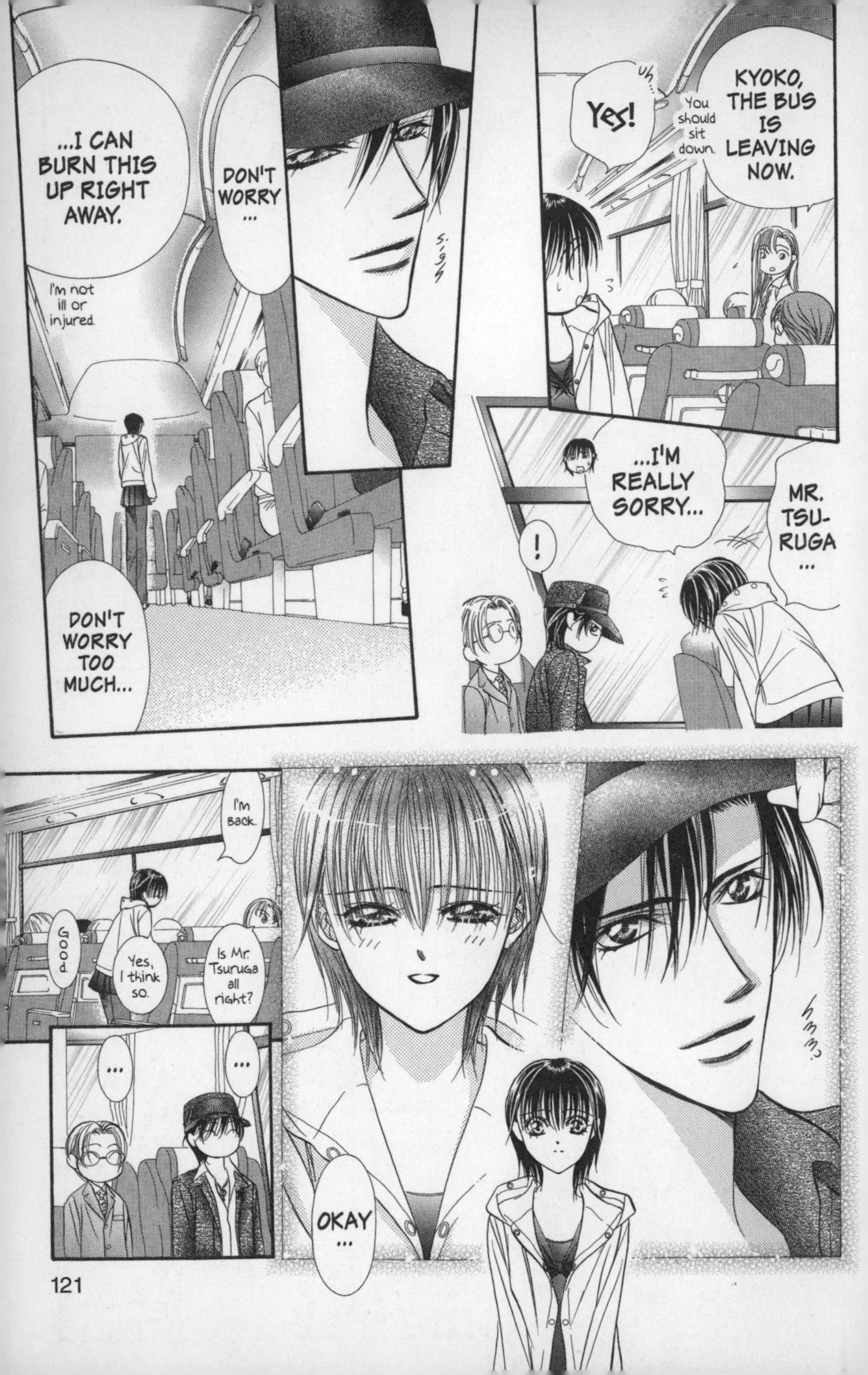

KYOKO, THE BUS IS LEAVING NOW.
You should sit down.
uh...
Yes!
MR. TSURUGA...
...I'M REALLY SORRY...
!
DON'T WORRY...
sigh
...I CAN BURN THIS UP RIGHT AWAY.
I'm not ill or injured.
DON'T WORRY TOO MUCH...
hmm?
OKAY...
I'm back.
Is Mr. Tsuruga all right?
Yes, I think so.
Good.
...
...

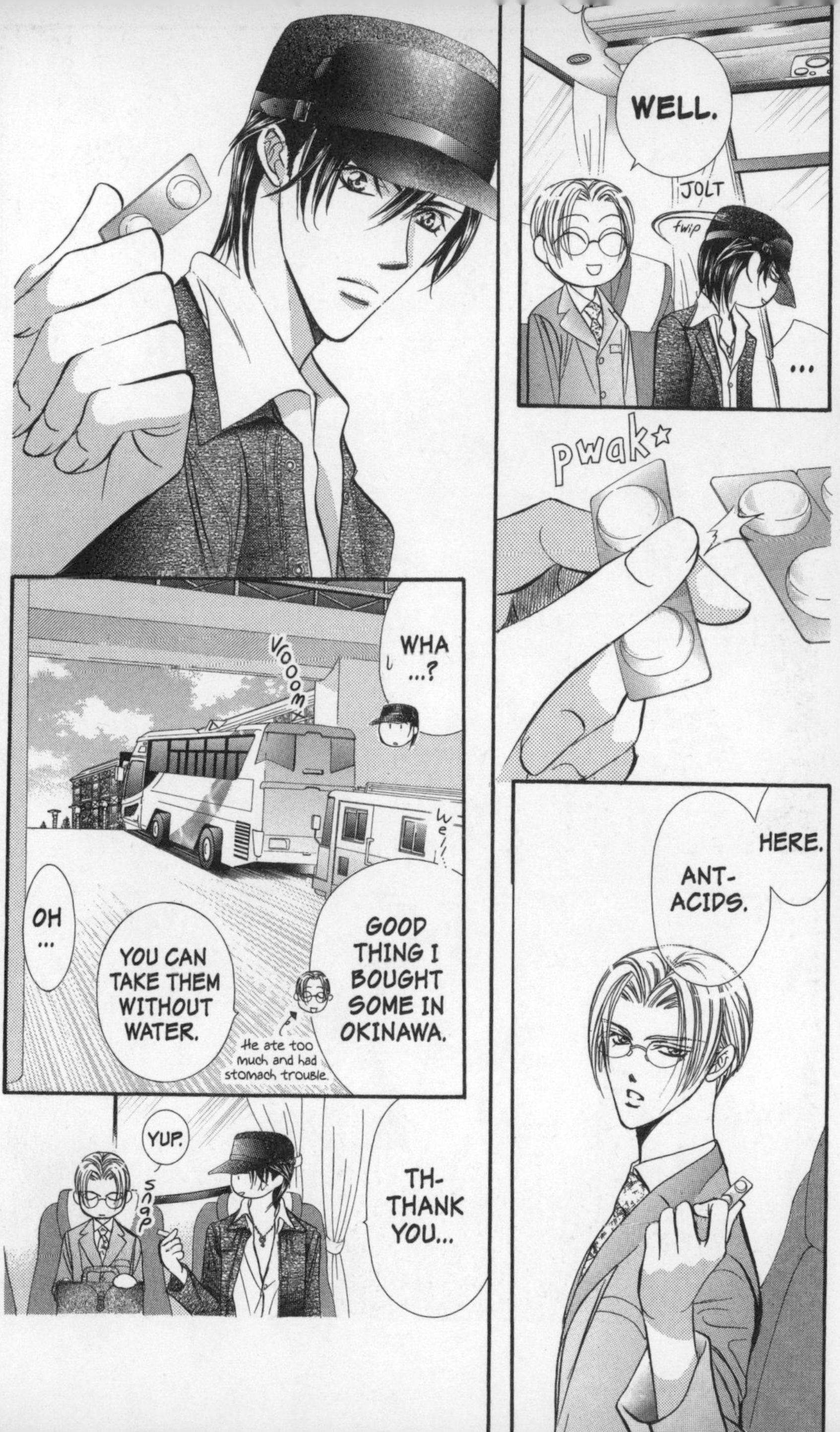
WELL.
JOLT
fwip
...
pwak☆
HERE.
ANT-ACIDS.
WHA ...?
Vrooom
well...
GOOD THING I BOUGHT SOME IN OKINAWA.
He ate too much and had stomach trouble.
YOU CAN TAKE THEM WITHOUT WATER.
OH ...
TH-THANK YOU...
YUP.
snap

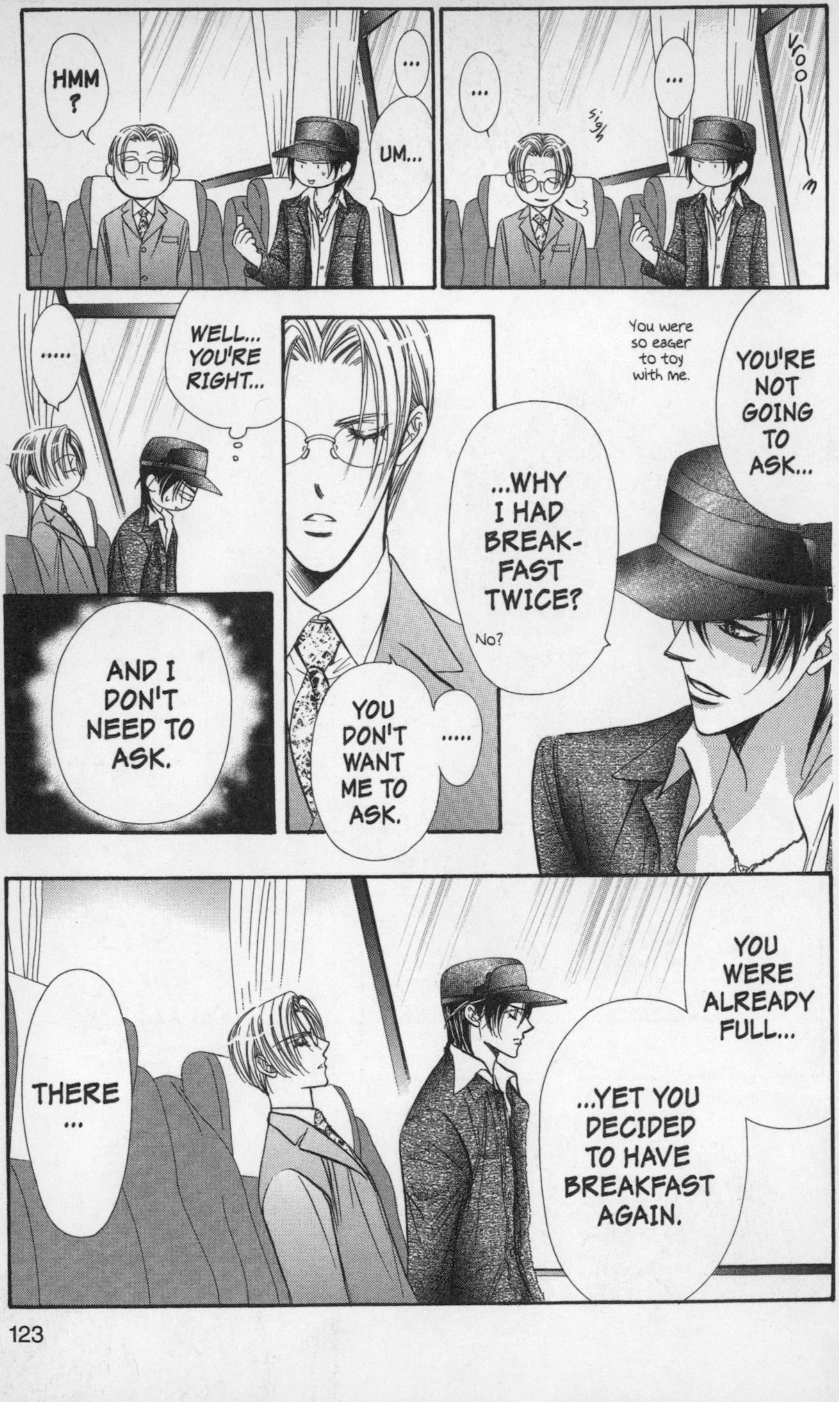
VROOO—M
...
...
sigh
...
UM...
HMM?
YOU'RE NOT GOING TO ASK...
You were so eager to toy with me.
...WHY I HAD BREAK-FAST TWICE?
No?
.....
YOU DON'T WANT ME TO ASK.
.....
WELL... YOU'RE RIGHT...
AND I DON'T NEED TO ASK.
YOU WERE ALREADY FULL...
...YET YOU DECIDED TO HAVE BREAKFAST AGAIN.
THERE...

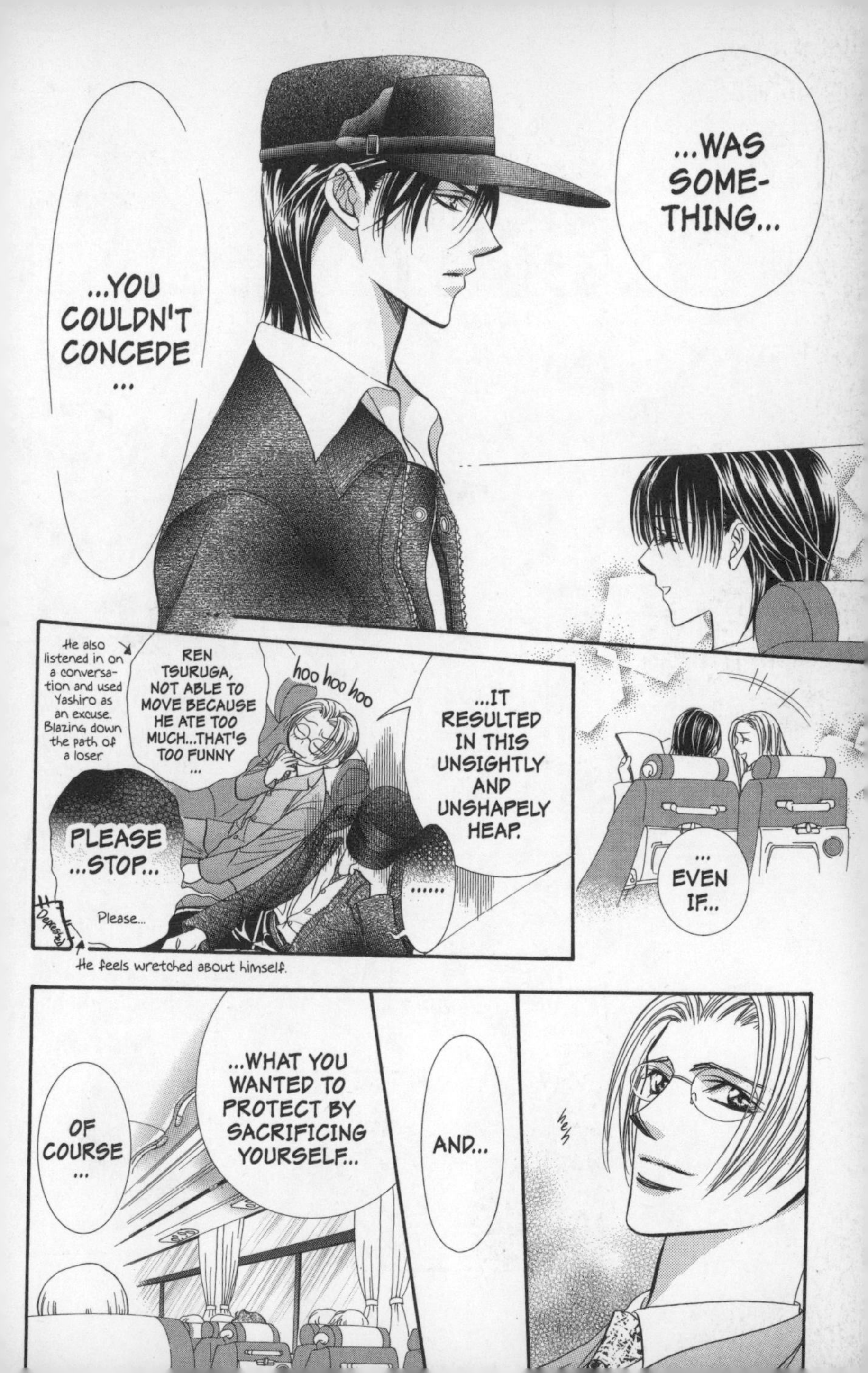
...WAS SOME-THING...
...YOU COULDN'T CONCEDE ...
... EVEN IF...
...IT RESULTED IN THIS UNSIGHTLY AND UNSHAPELY HEAP.
......
hoo hoo hoo
REN TSURUGA, NOT ABLE TO MOVE BECAUSE HE ATE TOO MUCH...THAT'S TOO FUNNY ...
He also listened in on a conversation and used Yashiro as an excuse. Blazing down the path of a loser.
PLEASE ...STOP...
Please...
Depressed
He feels wretched about himself.
heh
AND...
...WHAT YOU WANTED TO PROTECT BY SACRIFICING YOURSELF...
OF COURSE ...

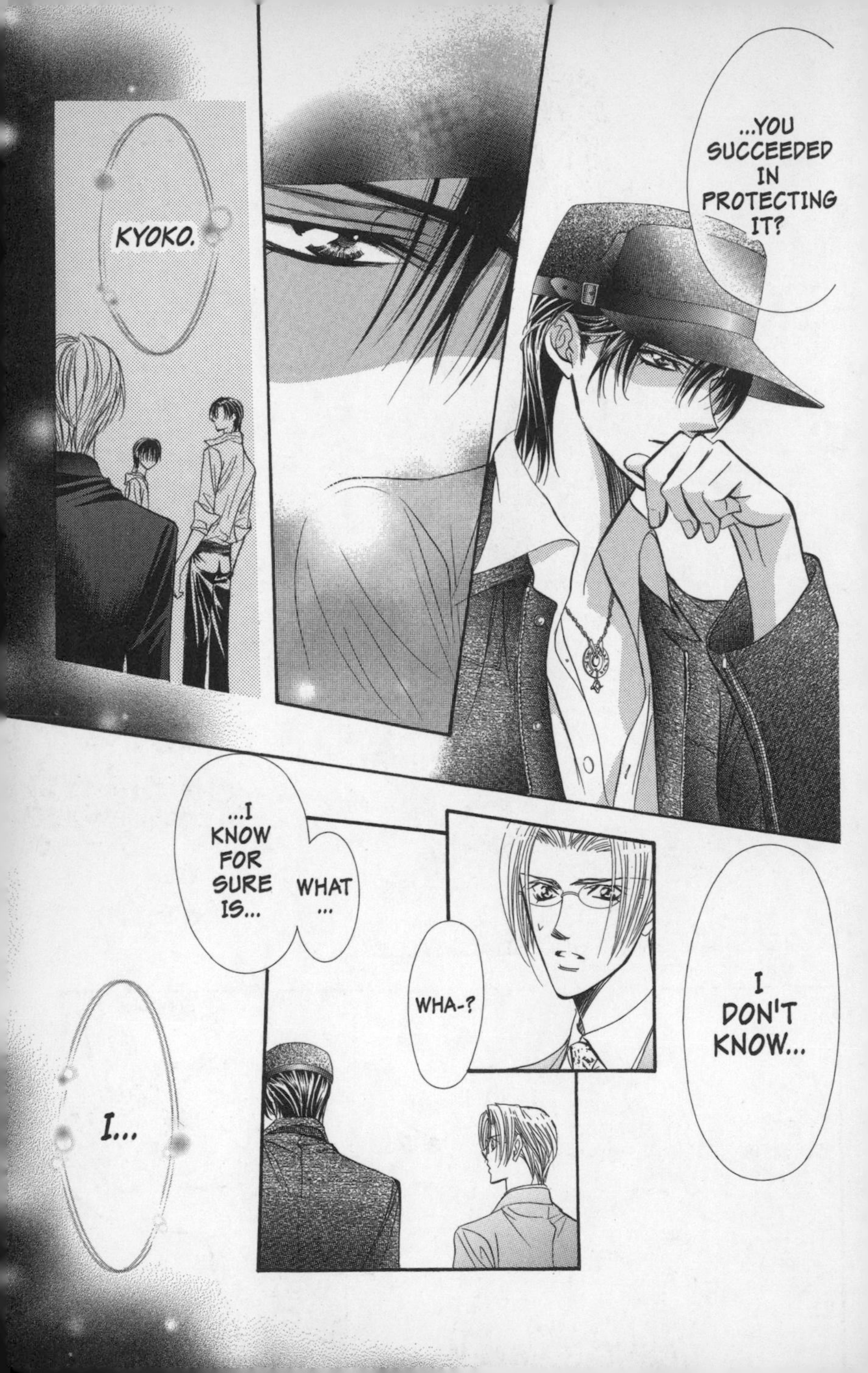
...YOU SUCCEEDED IN PROTECTING IT?
KYOKO.
I DON'T KNOW...
WHA-?
WHAT ...
...I KNOW FOR SURE IS...
I...

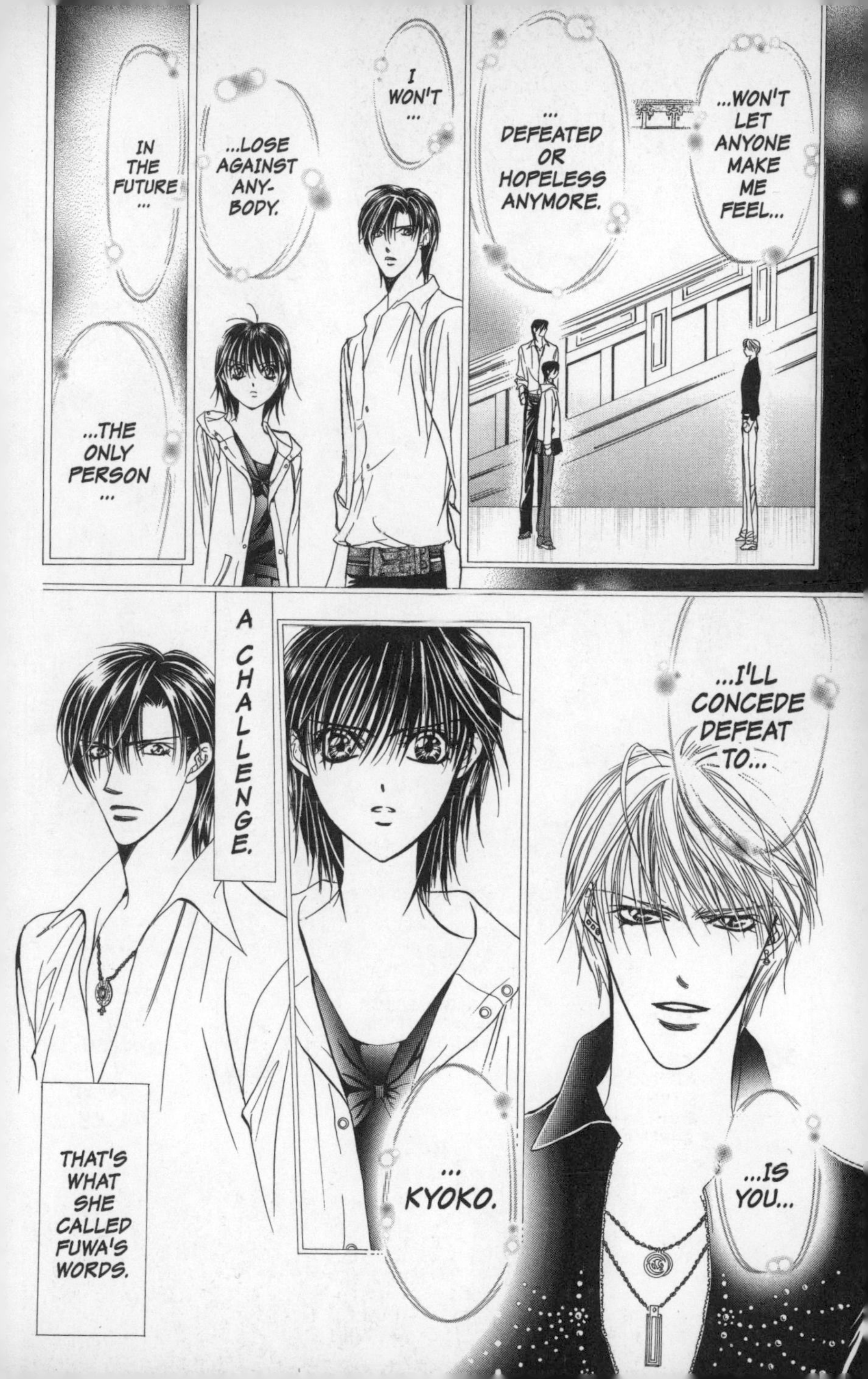
...WON'T LET ANYONE MAKE ME FEEL...
... DEFEATED OR HOPELESS ANYMORE.
I WON'T ...
...LOSE AGAINST ANY-BODY.
IN THE FUTURE ...
...THE ONLY PERSON ...
...I'LL CONCEDE DEFEAT TO...
...IS YOU...
... KYOKO.
A CHALLENGE.
THAT'S WHAT SHE CALLED FUWA'S WORDS.

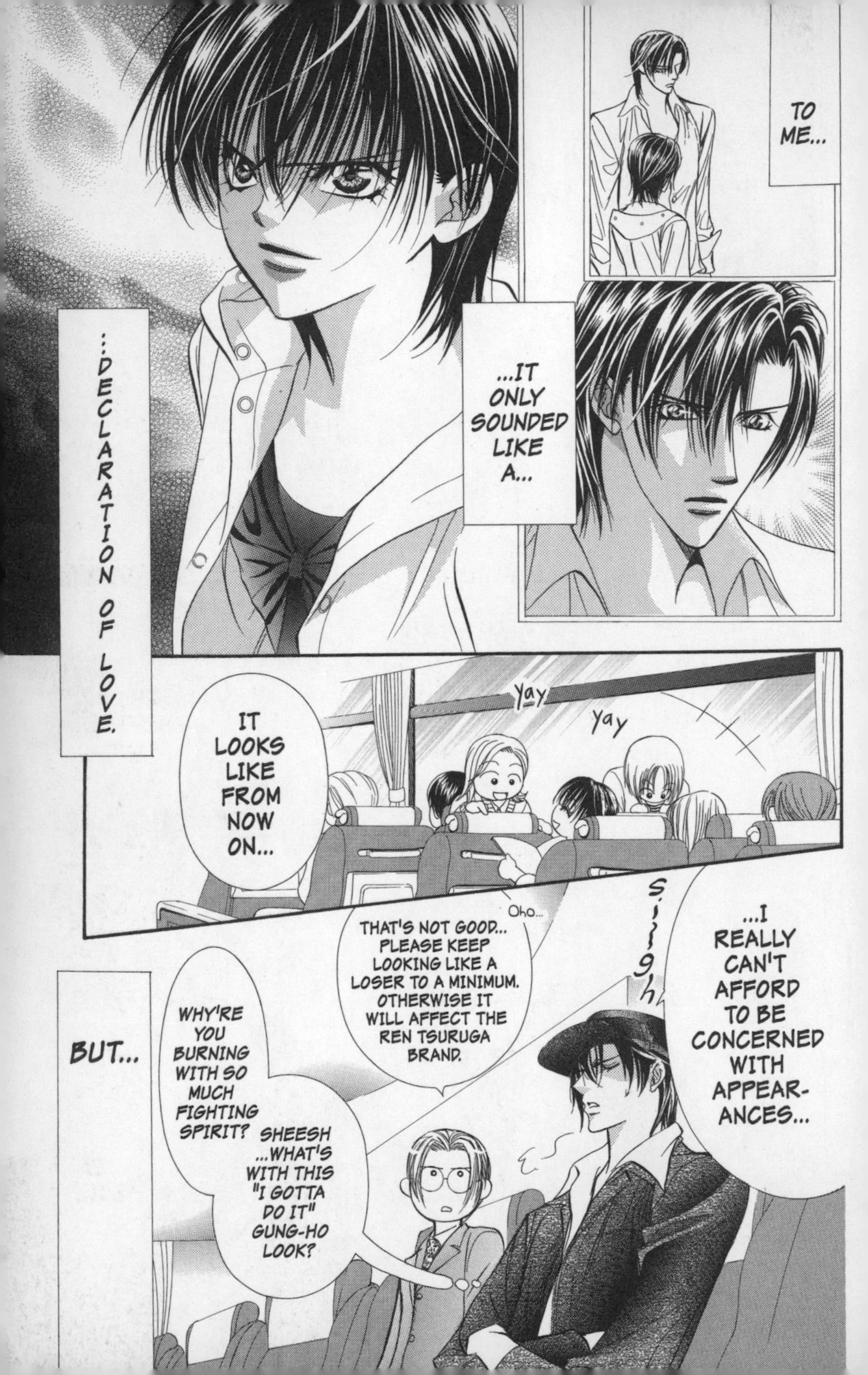
TO ME...
...IT ONLY SOUNDED LIKE A...
...DECLARATION OF LOVE.
yay
yay
IT LOOKS LIKE FROM NOW ON...
...I REALLY CAN'T AFFORD TO BE CONCERNED WITH APPEARANCES...
sigh
Oho...
THAT'S NOT GOOD... PLEASE KEEP LOOKING LIKE A LOSER TO A MINIMUM. OTHERWISE IT WILL AFFECT THE REN TSURUGA BRAND.
WHY'RE YOU BURNING WITH SO MUCH FIGHTING SPIRIT?
SHEESH ...WHAT'S WITH THIS "I GOTTA DO IT" GUNG-HO LOOK?
BUT...

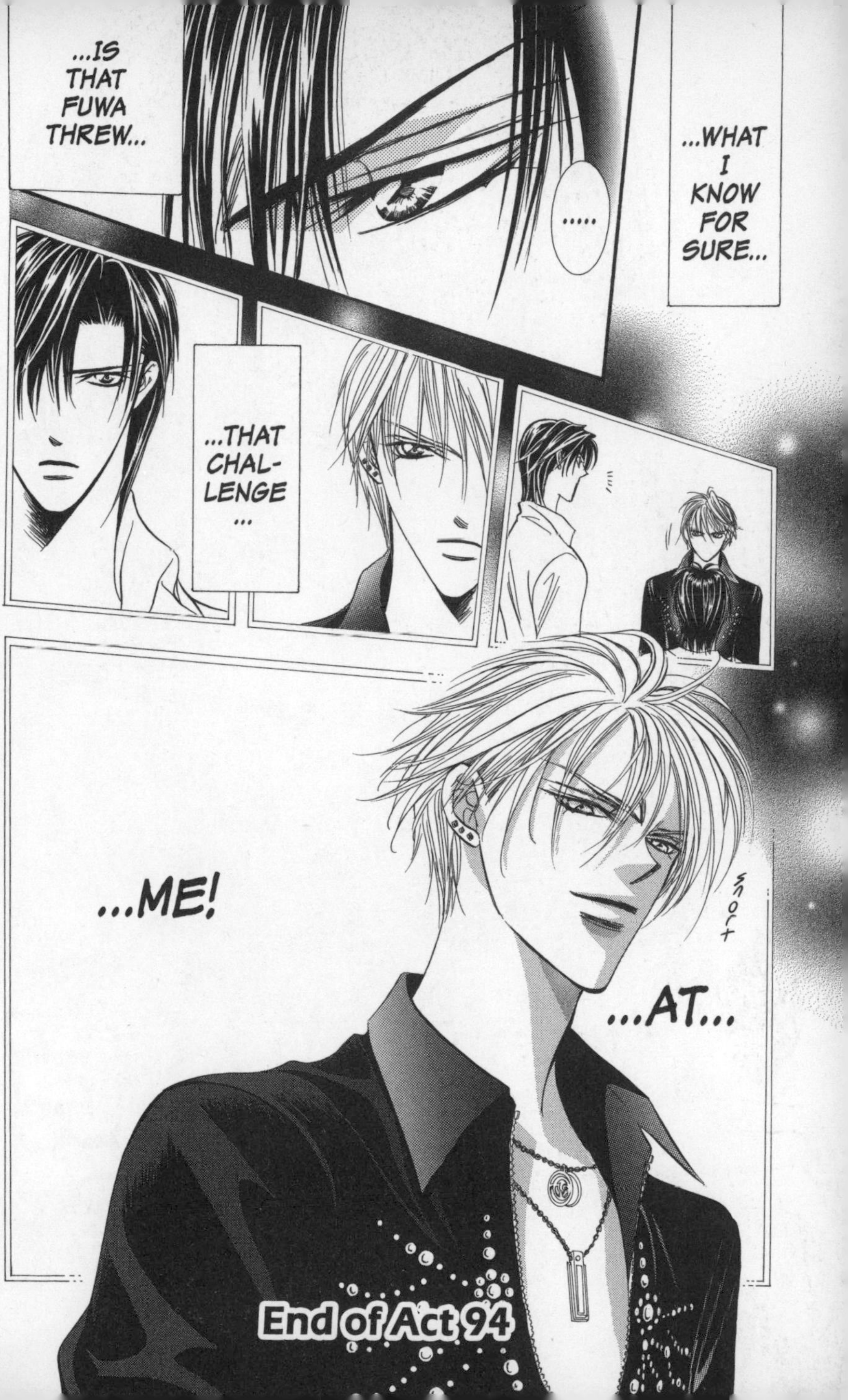
...WHAT I KNOW FOR SURE...
.....
...IS THAT FUWA THREW...
...THAT CHAL-LENGE ...
snort
...AT...
...ME!
End of Act 94

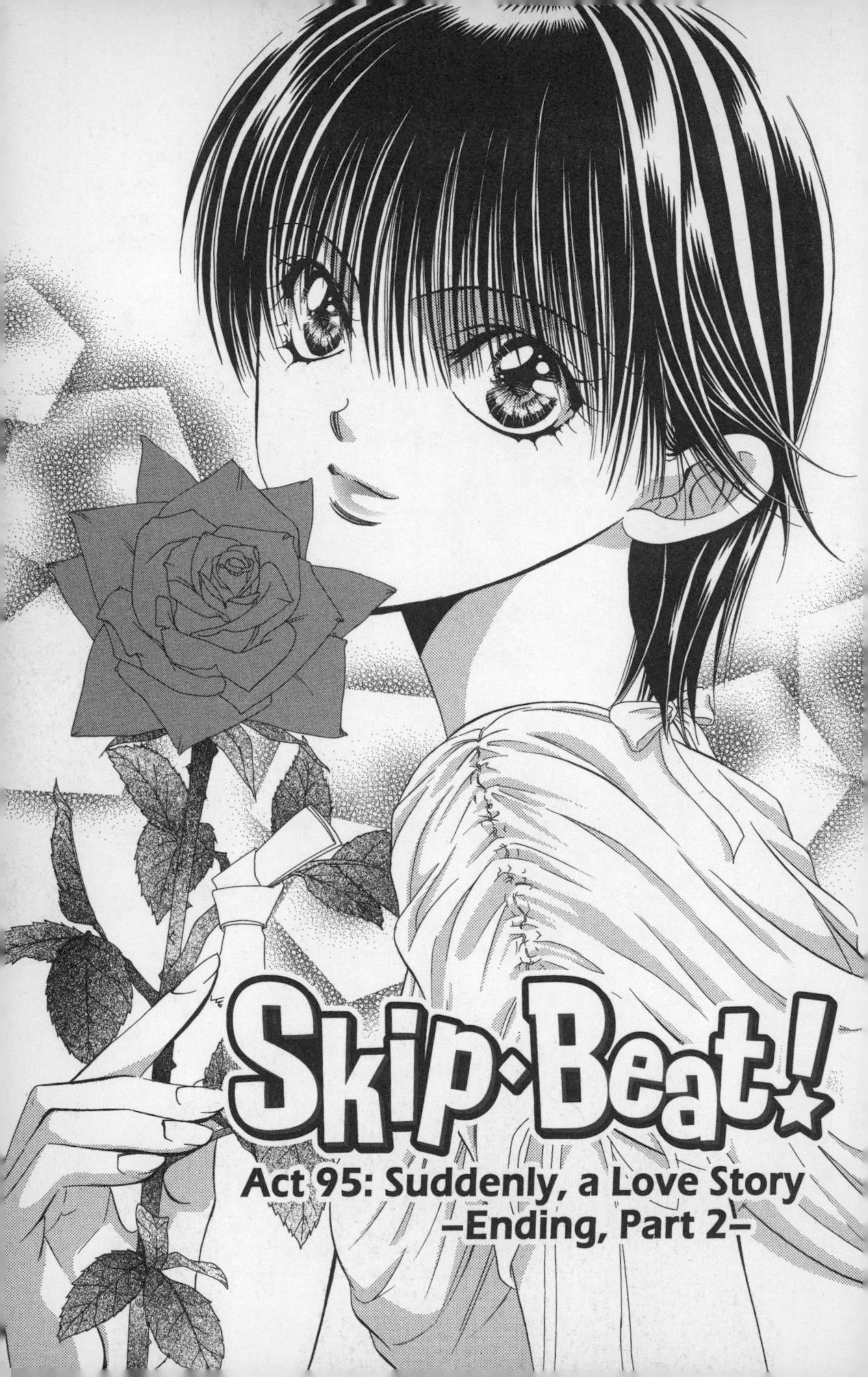
Skip·Beat!
Act 95: Suddenly, a Love Story
-Ending, Part 2-

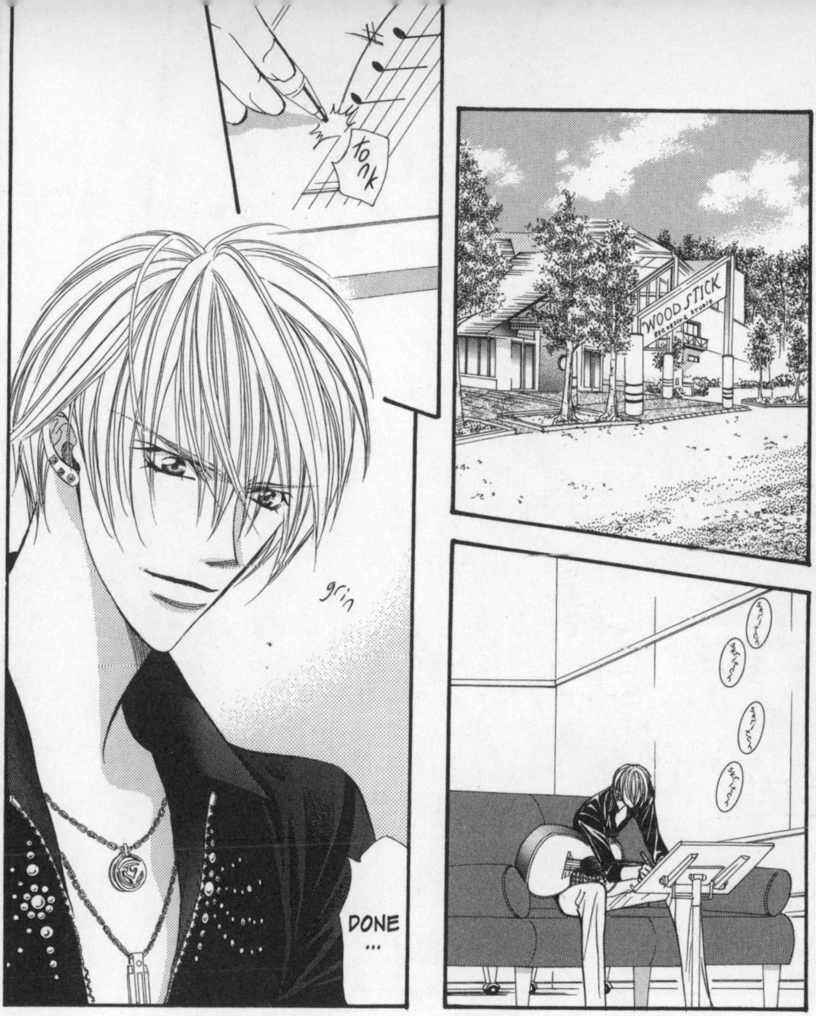
WOOD STICK
RECORDING STUDIO
skritch
skritch
skritch
skritch
tonk
grin
DONE
...
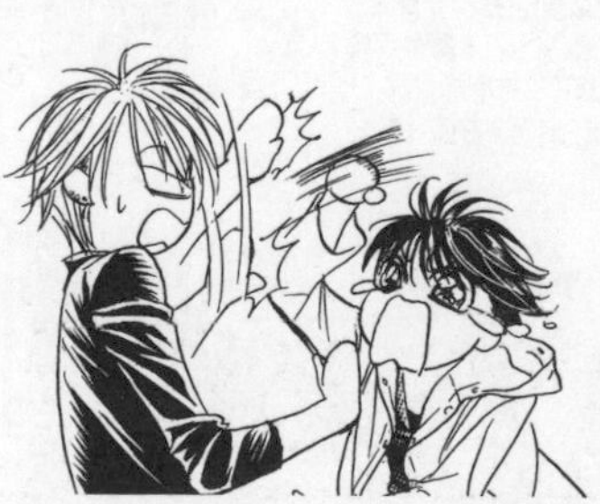

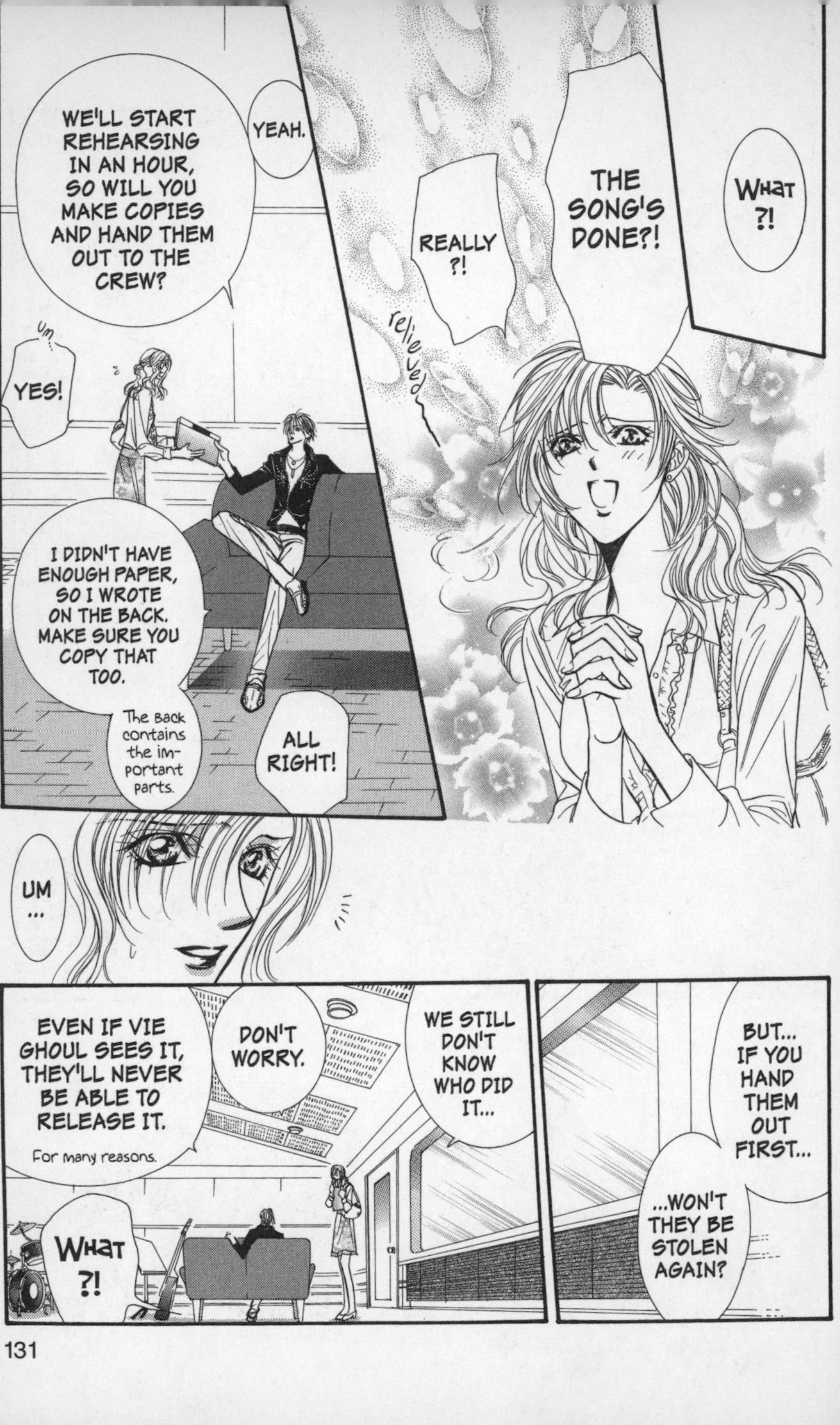
What ?!
THE SONG'S DONE?!
REALLY ?!
relieved
YEAH.
WE'LL START REHEARSING IN AN HOUR, SO WILL YOU MAKE COPIES AND HAND THEM OUT TO THE CREW?
Um
YES!
I DIDN'T HAVE ENOUGH PAPER, SO I WROTE ON THE BACK. MAKE SURE YOU COPY THAT TOO.
ALL RIGHT!
The back contains the important parts.
UM ...
BUT... IF YOU HAND THEM OUT FIRST...
...WON'T THEY BE STOLEN AGAIN?
WE STILL DON'T KNOW WHO DID IT...
DON'T WORRY.
EVEN IF VIE GHOUL SEES IT, THEY'LL NEVER BE ABLE TO RELEASE IT.
For many reasons.
What ?!

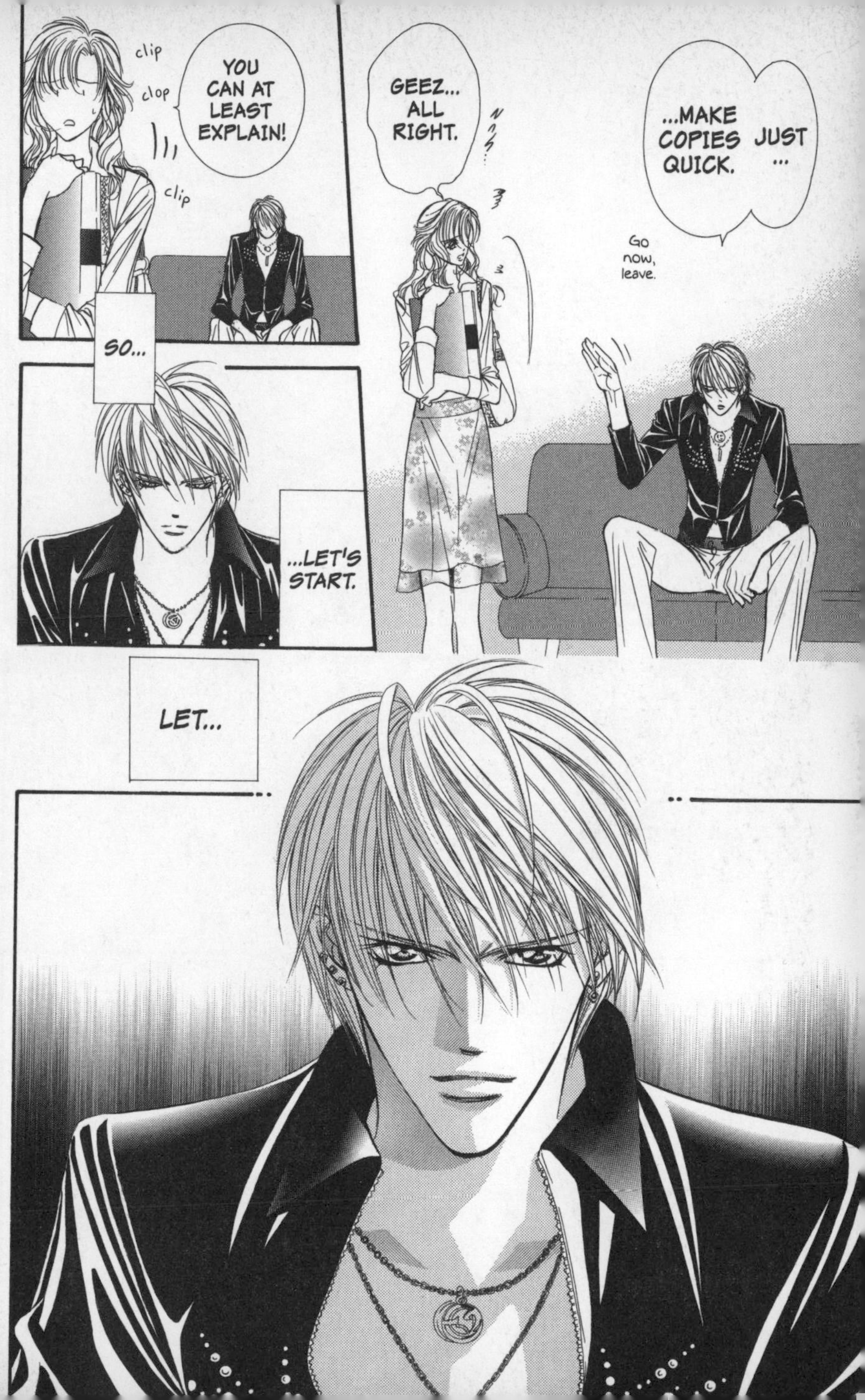
JUST ... ...MAKE COPIES QUICK.
Go now, leave.
GEEZ... ALL RIGHT.
clip
clop
clip
YOU CAN AT LEAST EXPLAIN!
SO...
...LET'S START.
LET...

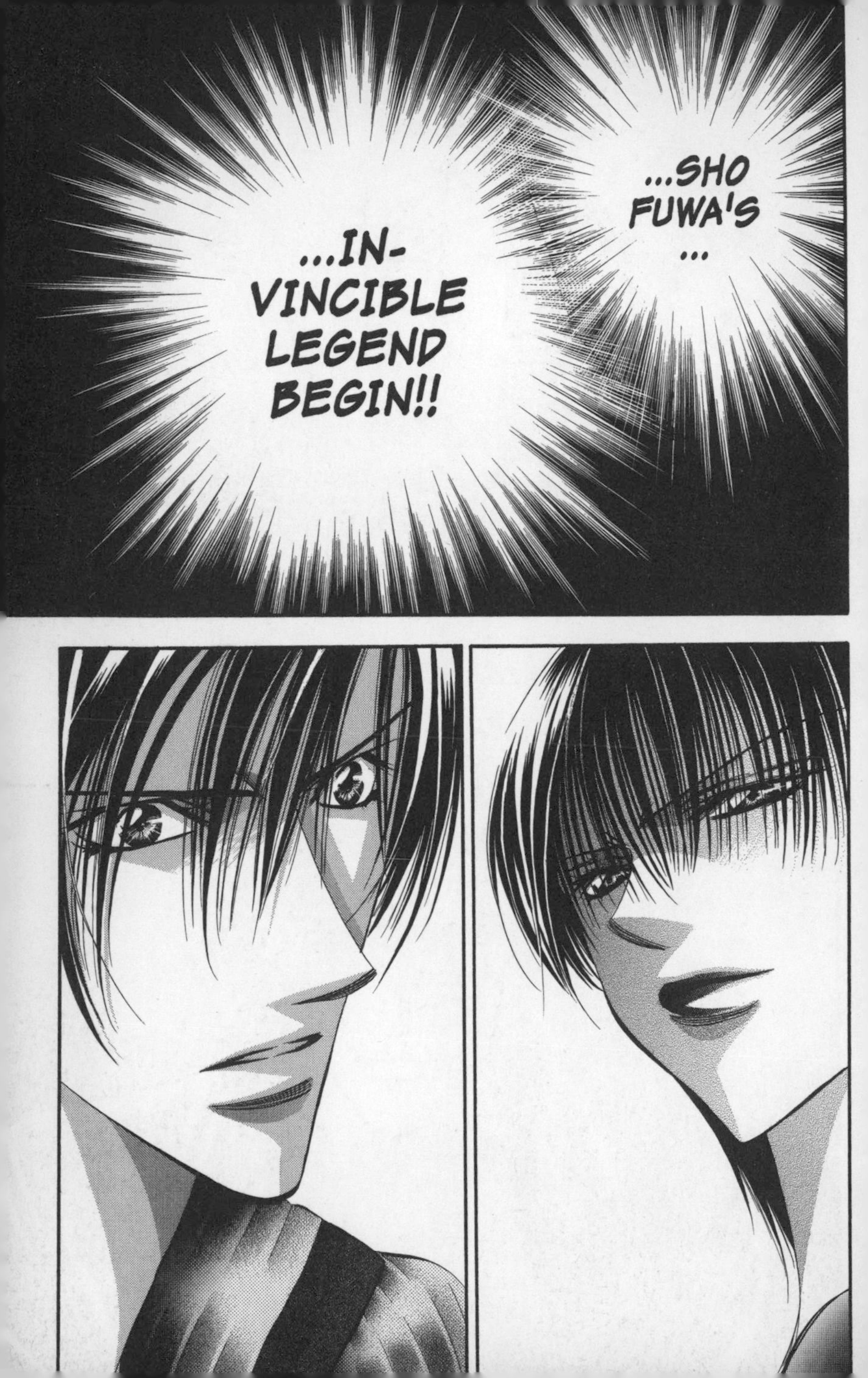
...SHO FUWA'S ...
...IN-VINCIBLE LEGEND BEGIN!!

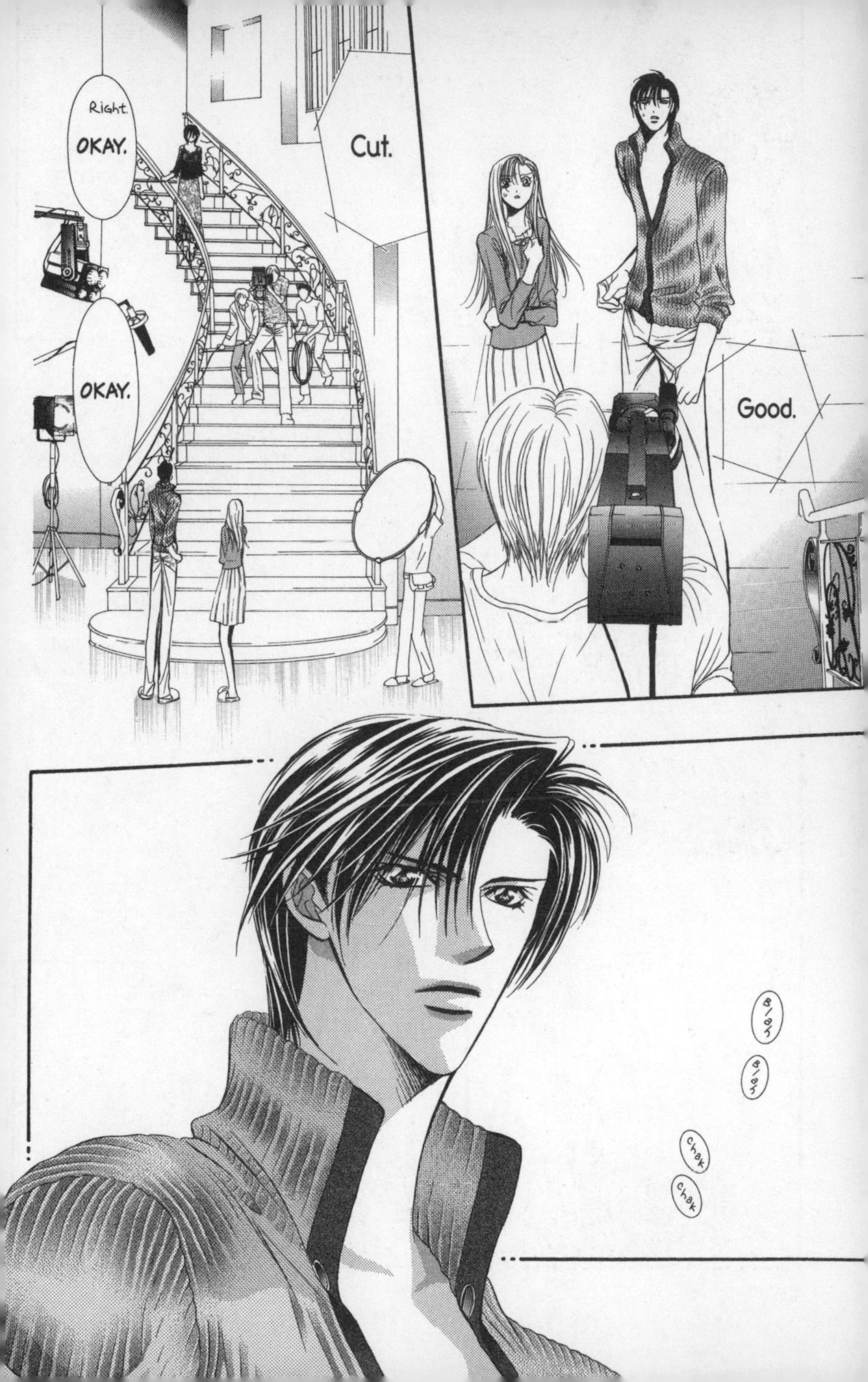
Good.
Cut.
Right.
OKAY.
OKAY.
Blah
Blah
Chak
Chak

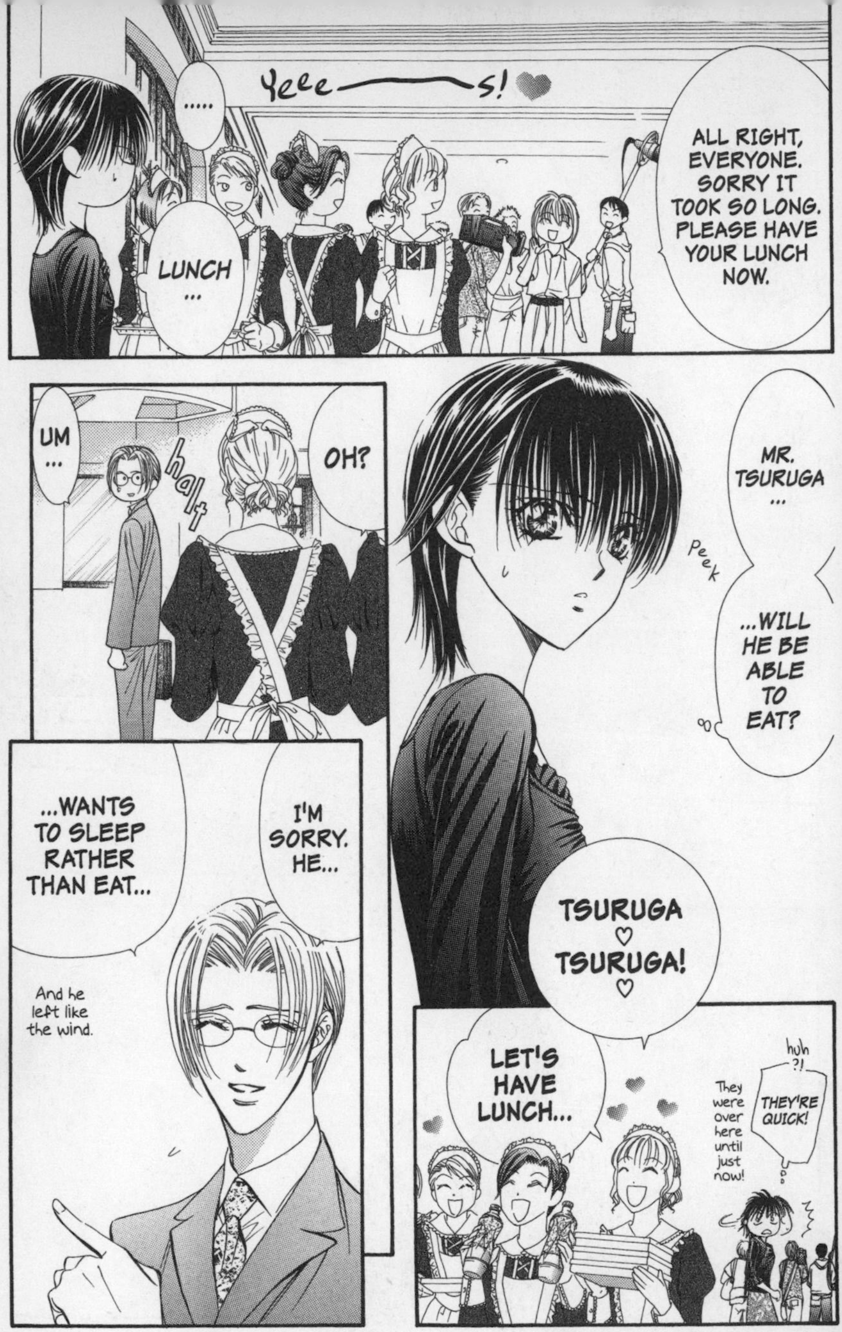
ALL RIGHT, EVERYONE. SORRY IT TOOK SO LONG. PLEASE HAVE YOUR LUNCH NOW.
Yeee——s!
......
LUNCH ...
MR. TSURUGA ...
...WILL HE BE ABLE TO EAT?
Peek
TSURUGA ♡ TSURUGA! ♡
huh ?!
THEY'RE QUICK!
They were over here until just now!
LET'S HAVE LUNCH...
OH?
halt
UM ...
I'M SORRY. HE...
...WANTS TO SLEEP RATHER THAN EAT...
And he left like the wind.

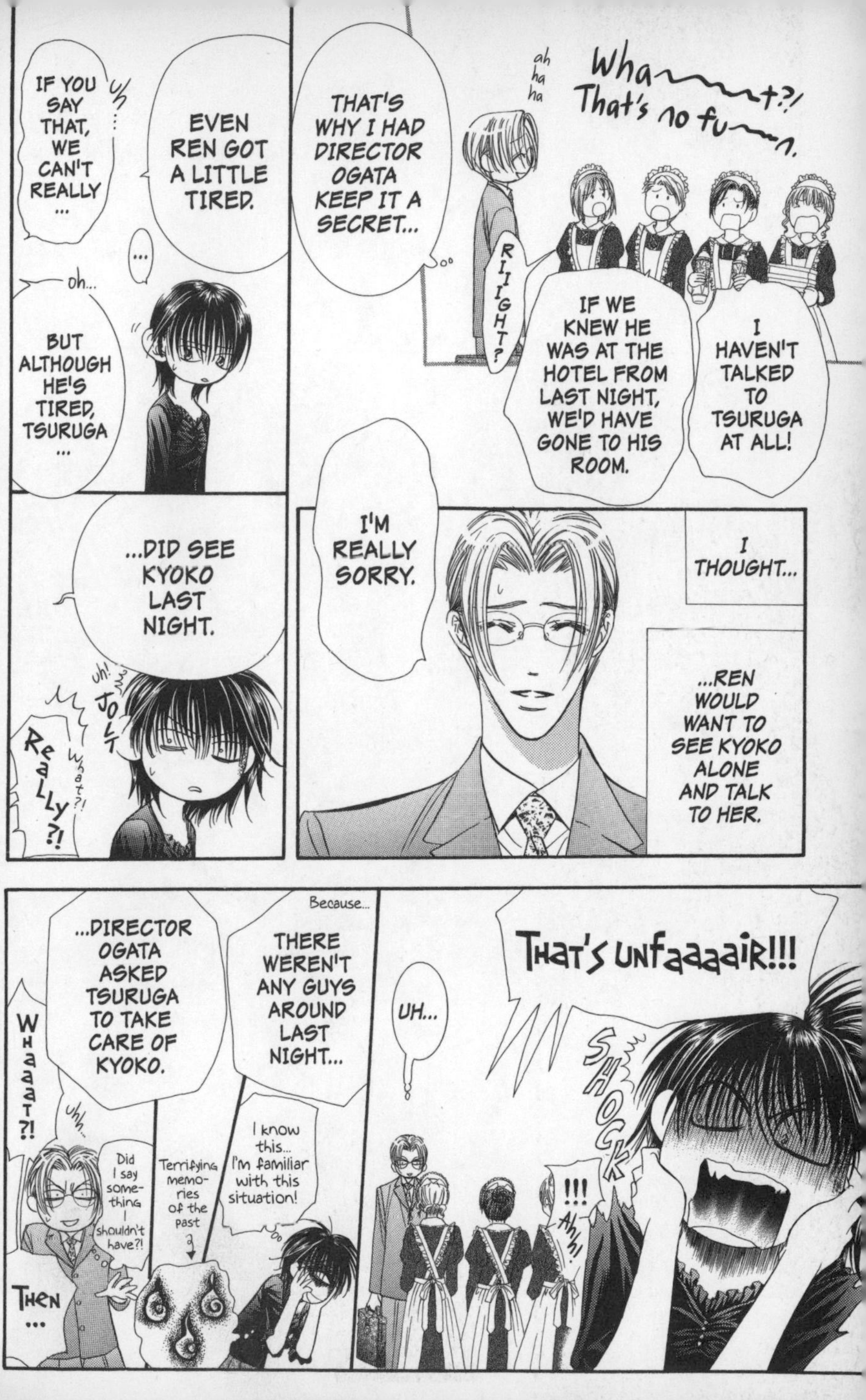
Wha—t?! That's no fu—n.
ah ha ha
THAT'S WHY I HAD DIRECTOR OGATA KEEP IT A SECRET...
RIIIGHT?
I HAVEN'T TALKED TO TSURUGA AT ALL!
IF WE KNEW HE WAS AT THE HOTEL FROM LAST NIGHT, WE'D HAVE GONE TO HIS ROOM.
EVEN REN GOT A LITTLE TIRED.
IF YOU SAY THAT, WE CAN'T REALLY...
uh...
...
oh...
BUT ALTHOUGH HE'S TIRED, TSURUGA...
I THOUGHT...
...REN WOULD WANT TO SEE KYOKO ALONE AND TALK TO HER.
I'M REALLY SORRY.
...DID SEE KYOKO LAST NIGHT.
uh!
JOLT
What?!
Really?!
That's unfaaaair!!!
SHOCK
!!!
Ah!
UH...
Because...
THERE WEREN'T ANY GUYS AROUND LAST NIGHT...
I know this... I'm familiar with this situation!
Terrifying memories of the past
...DIRECTOR OGATA ASKED TSURUGA TO TAKE CARE OF KYOKO.
Whaaat?!
uh...
Did I say something I shouldn't have?!
Then...